Bed and Breakfast
# IRELAND

REVISED AND EXPANDED
5TH EDITION

# Bed and Breakfast
# IRELAND

A trusted guide to over
400 of Ireland's best
bed and breakfasts

ELSIE DILLARD and SUSAN CAUSIN

CHRONICLE BOOKS

SAN FRANCISCO

APPLETREE PRESS

This edition first published in the United States
in 2005 by Chronicle Books LLC.

Text copyright © 2005
by Elsie Dillard and Susan Causin.
Illustrations copyright © 2005
by The Appletree Press Ltd.
Published in association with the K.S. Giniger
Company, Inc., New York, New York 10107, USA

For further up-to-date information, please visit
www.irelandseye.com/breakfast.htm

Library of Congress Cataloging-in-Publication
Data available.

ISBN 0-8118-4740-3

Manufactured in China
Cover design by Ayako Akazawa

Distributed in Canada by Raincoast Books
9050 Shaughnessy Street
Vancouver, British Columbia V6P 6E5

10 9 8 7 6 5 4 3 2 1

Chronicle Books LLC
85 Second Street
San Francisco, California 94105

www.chroniclebooks.com

Contents

# Our Favourite Bed and Breakfasts

Mornington House, Multyfarnham, Co. Westmeath

Carraig Beag, Salthill, Galway, Co. Galway

Abbey Lodge, Killarney, Co. Kerry

Dolmen Lodge, Ballyvaughan, Co. Clare

Abbey House, Thomastown, Co. Kilkenny

Ballinkeele House, Enniscorthy, Co. Wexford

Caldhame Lodge, Crumlin, Co. Antrim

Clone House, Aughrim, Co. Wicklow

Harrington Hall, Dublin, Co. Dublin

Kilbrogan House, Bandon, Co. Cork

Marlagh Lodge Country House, Ballymena, Co. Antrim

O'Leary's Farmhouse, Rosslare Harbour, Co. Wexford

Rosnaree House, Slane, Co. Meath

The Glen Country House, Kilbrittain, Co. Cork

Serenity B&B, Doonierin, Kintogher, Rosses Point, Co. Sligo

Glin Castle Glin, Co. Limerick

Killeen House, Bushy Park, Galway, Co. Galway

Cregg Castle, Corrandulla, Co. Galway

The Shores Country House, Cappatigue, Conor Pass Road, Castlegregory, Co. Kerry

# INTRODUCTION

The Irish people themselves would be reason enough to visit, with their exceptional warmth and hospitality, but add the beauty of the countryside and Ireland becomes the perfect holiday choice.

We have researched over the four seasons, and highly recommend a visit to Ireland in the off-season, when it is easy to get around and there is still plenty to interest the visitor. Each property listed in this guide has been personally visited by us, and there are no charges for inclusion. Our criteria for entry are based upon the warmth of the welcome and cleanliness of the property, with many other factors being taken into consideration. We have covered every county, including areas not normally considered as tourist regions to accommodate business travellers, visiting friends and family gatherings.

The Republic has restrictions on smoking in public buildings, including restaurants, hotels and bars. Most bed and breakfast establishments are completely non-smoking and many others have restrictions on where smoking is allowed—it is best to confirm these details when booking.

Children are welcome unless stated otherwise. Sometimes the location or style of a house makes it unsuitable for children; however, houses which provide facilities for children are noted. Restrictions on pets have also been noted. Parking is always available unless mentioned otherwise.

When booking, it is advisable to verify specifics, such as child reductions, single supplements, access for disabled guests, special break prices, opening times and meals and dietary requirements. Obtaining clear driving directions is also recommended. At the time of publication, price guides were correct, but please be aware of seasonal variations.

Most entries include the owner's name, but it is possible that a change in ownership may have occurred, which could lead to significant changes in the standard of accommodation.

At the time of publication, and to the best of our knowledge, the details in this book were correct. However, changes do occur for which we cannot be responsible. We would like to thank Bord Fáilte and the Northern Ireland Tourist Board for their help in making this book possible.

We would welcome any comments you have on your personal experiences about properties in this book. We would be delighted to receive your recommendations for consideration as future inclusions. Please send your comments and recommendations to Elsie Dillard and Susan Causin,
**48 Nursery Road, Great Cornard, Sudbury, Suffolk, England CO10 3NJ** or in North America to PO Box 54107, Redondo, WA 98054.

Important Note:
*All Bed and Breakfast prices are per person sharing, unless otherwise stated. A "single supplement" refers to the practice of charging a single visitor who stays in a double room the single room rate & additional charge.*

*It is advisable to confirm the rates when booking your room as well as the method of payment. Some establishments may not accept credit cards. The prices listed for accommodation in the Republic of Ireland are given in Euro currency (€). The prices listed for accommodation in Northern Ireland are given in pounds sterling (British pounds) (£).*

## COUNTY DUBLIN

From above Killakee, on the northern slopes of the Dublin Mountains is a wonderful view of both city and county. You can see to the northeast of the majestic sweep of Dublin Bay, the beautiful peninsula of Howth Head, and to the south of the bay, South Killiney Head. The city stretches across the plain, divided by the River Liffey. The large green patch in the northwest, some 116 hectares, is Phoenix Park, one of Europe's finest city parks.

The county north of Howth has long sandy beaches and fishing villages, which in spite of their proximity to the city, retain their character and charm, as well as a wealth of archaeological sites. Howth's castle dates from 1464, but has been altered over the centuries. The gardens, open to the public, are famous for their rhododendrons and eighteenth-century formal garden. Malahide Castle belonged to the Talbot family from 1185 to 1976, when the property was sold to the Dublin County Council. It now houses a large part of the National Portrait Collection.

To the south of the Liffey, Blackrock and Dalkey retain their village identity, and the popular Victorian holiday resort of Dún Laoghaire is one of the main sea-gateways to Ireland.

The city of Dublin is beautifully situated and the people have a friendliness and wit that captivates most visitors. Relatively speaking, it is a small and compact city. The city centre, stretching between Parnell Square and St Stephen's Green north to south, and Dublin Bay and Phoenix Park east to west, can be covered easily by foot. Most points of interest in the city lie between these boundaries. Like most European capitals, there is so much to see in the city that it would take weeks to do it full justice, taking in not only the principal sights of churches, museums and galleries, but taking the time to browse and absorb the atmosphere, the people, shops, theatres and pubs as well. Amongst the sights on top of the list to visit are the National Museum, the National Gallery and the Municipal Gallery. St Patrick's Cathedral dating from 1190; Christchurch Cathedral, restored in the nineteenth century; St Michan's, where intact bodies still lie in vaults; the fine eighteenth-century church of St Anne's; and St Werburgh's Church are amongst the most noteworthy churches to visit.

Dublin Castle, with its beautifully decorated State Apartments, was used by the British for state functions, and since 1938 has been the scene of the inauguration of the Presidents of Ireland. The General Post Office in O'Connell Street is where the Free Republic was proclaimed in 1916. The Custom House is one of the most impressive buildings in Dublin. Parliament House, now the Bank of Ireland, was built in 1785 by James Gandon, Dublin's most famous architect. The Book of Kells is kept in the Library at Trinity College, a restful spot away from the bustle of the city.

## Harrington Hall

70 Harcourt Street, Dublin 2, Co. Dublin
Tel: 02 4753497 Fax: 01 4754544
Email: harringtonhall@eircom.net  Website: www.harringtonhall.com

A family owned and run establishment, Harrington Hall has been magnificently restored and renovated, opening for business in 1998. The splendours of the Georgian architecture and details have been saved, and it offers guests a comfortable, peaceful retreat with every modern amenity in the heart of Dublin. Facilities include private parking, a full bar service, elevator and access to the internet.

St. Stephen's Green is just round the corner, and most of Dublin's famous sites are nearby. All major credit cards accepted.

OWNER Henry King OPEN all year
ROOMS 28 twin/double/family/suite TERMS €86.50–134

## Kilronan House

70 Adelaide Road, Dublin 2, Co. Dublin
Tel: 01 475 5266/1562 Fax: 01 478 2841
Email: info@dublinn.com  Website: www.dublinn.com

Kilronan House is a small Georgian building in a great central location close to St. Stephen's Green and many other attractions. Here you will find welcoming, caring hosts, who go out of their way to make sure their guests have everything they need. The breakfast room is bright and cheerful overlooking the street, and a pleasant sitting area adjoins it; the bedrooms are well-appointed and comfortable. There is private parking for guests. Major credit cards accepted.

OWNER Terry Masterson OPEN all year ROOMS 15 double/twin, all en suite TERMS €45–76; single supplement

## Number 31

31 Leeson Close, Dublin 2
Tel: 01 6765011 Fax: 01 6762929
Email: number31@iol.ie  Website: www.number31.ie

Number 31 is an unusual place to find in the heart of Georgian Dublin off busy Leeson Street. Built by the famous Dublin architect Sam Stephenson as his home it is an oasis of peace and quiet, hidden behind a high creeper-covered wall. The house has many interesting features; the low entrance opens up into a spacious drawing room with a sunken sitting area, featuring a bar, fireplace, high ceilings and tall windows. There are terraces, patios and different levels, and the comfortable en suite bedrooms all have hair-dryer, telephone, TV and tea- and coffee-making facilities. From the back of the house a winding path leads through gardens to the back door of Fitzwilliam Place—a total contrast of architecture and style, it's a beautiful, classical building with ornate ceilings and enormous rooms. Fitzwilliam Place has no public rooms - guests that stay here cross the garden to make use of Number 31's drawing room, and for breakfast, which is quite a feast and is served in either the upstairs dining room or in the enclosed conservatory. Guests at Number 31 experience the very best of Irish charm and welcome from Noel and Deidre Comer. Noel is a never ending font of knowledge of Dublin and all things Irish. Supplied with maps and advice, the visitor cannot go wrong. Off-street, secure parking is available. No pets allowed. American Express, Visa and Mastercard accepted.

OWNER Noel and Deidre Comer OPEN All year
ROOMS 29 twin/ double/ family; all en suite TERMS from €75; single supplement; not suitable for children under 10 years

**Trinity Lodge**
12 South Frederick Street, Dublin 2
Tel: 01 6170900 Fax: 01 6170999
Email: trinitylodge@eircom.net

Trinity Lodge is probably one of the most centrally located guest houses in Dublin, almost next door to Trinity College and surrounded by shops, restaurants, cafes and pubs. A Georgian town house, it has been interestingly renovated and decorated in the original strong, bright, old Irish colours, to match the colours of the paintings by the artist Knuttel (who lives close by). The walls are hung with prints of his work. The house is elegantly furnished and beautifully equipped, each bedroom or suite having a hair-dryer, trouser press, telephone, internet access, TV, air conditioning, safe and tea- and coffee-making facilities. Some rooms are located across the street. No pets. All major credit cards accepted. Although Trinity Lodge does not have its own parking, the staff will make sure parking is available.

MANAGING DIRECTOR Peter Murphy OPEN All year except December 22-26 ROOMS 5 double, 4 deluxe double, 2 single, 5 family; all en suite TERMS from €95; single supplement; child reduction

## DUBLIN 3

**Kincora Lodge**
54 Kincora Court, Clontarf, Dublin 3
Tel: 01 8330220

Caroline and Paul extend a warm welcome to their immaculate red brick townhouse house close to the city, airport and ferry. The spacious, en-suite rooms, have TV, tea makers, hospitality tray, hair-dryer, new modern furnishing, comfortable beds, colourful bed covers and coordinated curtains. Bedrooms are non-smoking areas.

Guests arriving by car would be well advised to leave their car at the house and take the bus to the city centre. Although convenient to most amenities, this is a quiet location, and guests will be comfortable and well taken care of here. Excellent breakfasts are served, and there are several venues for evening meals close by. Golf courses and the beach are within walking distance.

All major credit cards accepted.

OWNER Caroline & Paul Connolly OPEN All year
ROOMS 3 double/twin/family; all en suite TERMS €32.50-45 pps; child reduction; single supplement from €20

**Willowbrook Bed and Breakfast**
14 Strandville Avenue East, Clontarf, Dublin 3
Tel: 01 8333115
Email: willowbrook@ireland.com
Website: willowbrookbandb.com

Joe and Mary Mooney set up in business here ten years ago, to 'semi-retire' from a larger guest house operation. They adapted Willowbrook, which was built twenty years ago, to accommodate bed & breakfast guests. The compact, comfortably furnished bedrooms were made en suite, and they each have tea and coffee-making facilities, water and fruit, and TV. Guests have use of a long sitting room cum breakfast room which overlooks the quite substantial back garden, and the décor and furnishings are in keeping with the style of the house. There is car parking in the front driveway area. Willowbrook is very conveniently located in a quiet residential street in the old part of Clontarf, and is close to Dublin Port and Point Depot–a venue for concerts.

The DART station is three minutes away. No pets.

OWNER Joe & Mary Mooney OPEN All year except Christmas
ROOMS 1 double, 2 twin; all en suite TERMS €40 pps; single supplement

**66 Townhouse**
66 Northumberland Road, Dublin 4
Tel: 01 6600333 Fax: 01 6601051

An elegant refurbished Victorian house, situated in the Diplomatic area, with all the facilities of a first class hotel. The house is furnished in keeping with the period, and the good sized bedrooms have attractive floral bed covers and are immaculately maintained. All have en suite facilities, direct dial phone, TV, tea makers and hair-dryer. There is separate dining room, where a delicious breakfast is served, and a sitting room. Susan and Paul are a great couple, who work as a team to maintain their high standards, and who have thought of everything for guest's needs, including umbrellas for rainy days. This is a popular venue with business people and tourists, early reservations suggested. Non-smokers preferred. A ten minute walk has you in the city centre, and buses run frequently.

OWNER Susan & Paul Keane OPEN All year except for Christmas ROOMS 7 double/twin/single; all en suite TERMS €70–95; child reduction; single supplement negotiable

## Aberdeen Lodge
53 Park Avenue, Ballsbridge, Dublin 4
Tel: 01 2838155 Fax: 01 2837877
Email: aberdeen@iol.ie
Website: www.halpinsprivatehotels.com

Aberdeen Lodge is a substantial, brick-built Edwardian house in an elegant residential area, easily accessible both to the centre of Dublin and Dun Laoghaire. Considerable renovation work has been done here over the years and a lot of the original features have been saved, such as the ceiling work and fireplaces. The décor is elegant and tasteful and it is nicely furnished. All bedrooms have hair-dryer, telephone, trouser press and TV.

The drawing room and dining room are comfortable, pleasant rooms, and a 'drawing room' menu is available offering light snacks and wines to residents in the afternoons and evenings. Other amenities include air conditioning and internet access. The house has a large peaceful garden, beyond which is the cricket ground. There is off-street car parking in front of the house. No pets. Major credit cards accepted. Central Dublin can be reached in a few minutes on the DART railway.

OWNER Pat Halpin OPEN All year ROOMS 6 twin, 3 triple, 2 family, 7 double; all en suite TERMS from €65; single supplement; child reduction MEALS light drawing room menu is offered during the day

## Anglesea Town House
63 Anglesea Road, Ballsbridge, Dublin 4
Tel: 01 668 3877 Fax: 01 668 3461

Built in 1800, Anglesea House, is a modest looking brick built house set back from the road. Helen Kirrane has been in business for many years, and built up a great word of mouth clientele, and has a reputation for serving great breakfasts. It has been furnished in a formal style with lots of ornaments, photographs, pictures and knick knacks. The bedrooms are very comfortable with luxurious bathrooms. Anglesea House is in the Ballsbridge part of town and within easy access of all Dublin has to offer. No pets. All major credit cards accepted.

OWNER Helen Kirrane OPEN all year ROOMS 5 double/twin, 2 single; all en suite TERMS €65

## Glenogra Guesthouse
64 Merrion Road, Dublin 4
Tel: 01 668 3661 Fax: 01 668 3698
Email: glenogra@indigo.ie

Glenogra is a beautifully appointed Georgian residence in an excellent location, close to the city centre, DART and all amenities. The house has been furnished to a high standard of comfort in pleasing fabrics and colours. The good sized bedrooms all have TV, telephone, hair-dryer and tea- and coffee-making facilities. The dining room, where breakfast only is served, is quite ornate with pillars, a decorative ceiling and a fireplace. Seamus and Cherry McNamee offer all the facilities of a hotel, combined with the warmth and personal service of a private residence. No pets and no smoking. Visa, Mastercard and American Express accepted. Glenogra is opposite the Four Seasons Hotel in Ballsbridge. Off-street parking in front of the house.

OWNER Seamus & Cherry McNamee OPEN January 20–December 20 ROOMS 10 double, 2 twin; all en suite
TERMS €50; single supplement €25 child reduction

## Glenveagh
31 Northumberland Road, Ballsbridge, Dublin 4
Tel: 01 668 4612 Fax: 01 668 4559

Glenveagh is an impressive Victorian house retaining many original features, including beautiful cornices and a ceiling rose. There are antique furnishings, including a grandfather clock in the hallway. The well-appointed bedrooms are decorated and furnished to a high standard, providing all the comforts of a first-class hotel in an inviting atmosphere. Improvements are ongoing - the kitchen has now been moved upstairs, and two additional bedrooms have been added.

Glenveagh is spacious, beautifully maintained, extremely comfortable, and retains the warmth and friendliness of a private house. Joe and Bernadette are a gracious couple who enjoy welcoming people to Dublin and are happy to offer advice on what to see. Freshly-prepared breakfasts are presented on fine china at separate tables in the elegant dining room, which has a fireplace, soft, restful wallpapers and matching curtains. The lounge has soft furnishings and a fireplace. A quiet spot in which to relax after a busy day. Glenveagh is delightful in every way, a good choice for visitors wanting first-class accommodation in a convenient location. There is an excellent bus service to town, and the house is minutes from the DART station. There are several venues for evening meals within walking distance. Visa and Access accepted.

OWNER Joe & Bernadette Cunningham OPEN All year
ROOMS 5 double, 3 twin, 3 family; all en suite
TERMS €89 per room; child reduction; single supplement (seasonal)

### Merrion Hall
54 Merrion Road, Ballsbridge, Dublin 4
Tel: 01 6681426 Fax: 01 6684280
Email: merrionhall@iol.ie Website: www.halpinsprivatehotels.com

This substantial Victorian brick-built house is set back off the main road, opposite the Royal Dublin Showground (RDS) in the heart of Ballsbridge, an elegant Dublin suburb. Expansion into the adjoining building and further renovation work has turned this establishment into one offering top quality, comfortable accommodation. The building has been elegantly furnished: amenities include air conditioning, an elevator and internet access. Comfortable bedrooms all have TV, hair-dryer, telephone and trouser press. The centre of Dublin is easily reached by DART railway, or regular bus service. No pets. Major credit cards accepted. Off street parking available infront of house.

OWNER Pat Halpin OPEN All year ROOMS 9 double, 6 twin, 3 family, 4 triple; all en suite TERMS from €65; single supplement; child reduction MEALS light drawing room menu daily €11–25

Merrion Hall

**Raglan Lodge**

10 Raglan Road, Ballsbridge, Dublin 4

Tel: 01 660 6697 or 086 3288010 Fax: 01 660 6781

In a quiet residential road within walking distance of the centre, Raglan Lodge is a welcoming, peaceful place, with a friendly, charming owner. Dating from 1861 it is an impressive Victorian house, which, in its more recent past was turned into flats and allowed to deteriorate. It has now been restored back to its original character of well proportioned rooms and high ceilings. The bedrooms all have TV and telephone. The poet Patrick Kavanagh lived on Raglan Road in the 1940s, and one of his poems is entitled 'On Raglan Road'. Off street parking on the premises. Major credit cards are accepted.

OWNER Helen Moran OPEN All year except for Christmas
ROOMS 5 double, 2 single; all en suite
TERMS from €70; single supplement

**Waterloo House**

8-10 Waterloo Road, Ballsbridge, Dublin 4

Tel: 01 660 1888 Fax 068 607 1955

Email waterloohouse@eircom. Website: www.waterloohouse.ie

Waterloo House is situated on a tree lined avenue. It combines two refurbished Georgian houses, in the prestigious Ballsbridge district. It is tastefully furnished in keeping with the character of the house, and decorated to a very high standard. An elegant lounge and conservatory overlook the garden. The large, comfortable bedrooms are well appointed, each have a hair-dryer, trouser press and telephone. Most have a bath and shower combination. There is an extensive breakfast menu, served in the dining room overlooking the conservatory and gardens.

Evelyn Corcoran is very welcoming and helpful, and the house is immaculately kept. An added bonus is the lift, and there is safe parking. Credit cards taken.

OWNER Evelyn Corcoran OPEN All year except for Christmas
ROOMS 17 family/double/twin; all en suite TERMS from €59–99 pps; single supplement; child reduction

## DUBLIN 9

**Egan's House**

7-9 Iona Park, Glasnevin, Dublin 9

Tel: 01 830 3611 Fax: 01 830 3612 Email: eganshouse@tinet.ie

Egan's House is an attractive red brick turn-of-the-century house which started out as two separate houses, tastefully converted to provide comfortable accommodation. Extensive renovations have been undertaken by the new owners. The elegant dining room has Victorian and Edwardian furniture, and the living room retains its original cornices and marble fireplace. There are over 100 videos for guests to select. A drink can be obtained from reception.

The bedrooms have good-sized modern bathrooms, quality furnishings and are individually decorated in soft shades and rich colours of blue, grey, green and wine. There are 12 ground floor bedrooms. The house is impeccably maintained and retains many original features, including covings and fireplaces. Two lounges provide comfortable areas in which to relax, and are furnished in keeping with the character of the house, with rich green velvet curtains. The house is situated in a quiet residential area, 1.6 km from the city centre. The bus stop is just a few minutes' walk; guests who have a car would be well advised to leave it behind and take the bus. All major credit cards accepted.

OWNER Patrick and Monica Fina OPEN All year except December 20-27
ROOMS 32 double/ twin/family; all en suite TERMS from €45-70 pps; child reduction; single supplement (seasonal)

## Iona House
5 Iona Road, Dublin 9, Co Dublin
Tel: 01 830 6217 Fax: 01 830 67632
Email: conrad.shouldice1@btinternet.com

This attractive red brick residence was built at the turn of the century and is situated in one of Dublin's Victorian quarters. Jack and Karen Shouldice bought the property in 1963, which they have refurbished to provide comfortable accommodation with a taste of luxury. Décor and furnishings are rich and tasteful, and several original features remain, such as attractive coving, a ceiling rose and a marble fireplace. Fine prints adorn the walls, and the spacious lounge, with predominantly green décor, is available to guests, as is a furnished patio.

Bedrooms are of a good size, well-appointed and colour-coordinated. Breakfasts are served in the dining room, which has booth-style tables, and there are several venues for evening meals within walking distance. The house is well situated for the airport and convenient to the city centre.

OWNER Jack & Karen Shouldice OPEN All year
ROOMS 4 double, 4 twin, 2 single; all en suite
TERMS €44.50; child reduction; single supplement (seasonal)

## Joyville

24 St Alphonsus Road, Drumcondra, Dublin 9
Tel: 01 830 3221

Roma Gibbons is a delightful, kindly lady who extends a warm welcome to her immaculate red brick Victorian house, situated opposite
St Alphonsus Convent and Church 2 km from the city centre. There
is a good local bus service; guests would be well advised to take
local transport to avoid the parking and traffic problems.

The bedrooms are average in size with orthopaedic beds. There are
no en suite rooms, but there are two shower rooms and two WCs
exclusively for guests' use. The family lounge has a marble fireplace,
which guests are welcome to share. Roma Gibbons enjoys meeting
people and would be happy to recommend pubs and restaurants for
evening meals. Joyville is good value accommodation and a popular
B&B. Visitors to Dublin should reserve in advance.

OWNER Roma and John Gibbons OPEN All year except Christmas
ROOMS 1 double, 3 twin TERMS €30 pps; child reduction; single supplement

## Moyne House

17 Botanic Road, Dublin 9
Tel: 01 830 9337

Mrs Susan Forde has been in business for 24 years offering good
value accommodation. Many of her visitors return; advance reservations are advised. Susan is interested in crafts: one of her tapestries
hangs in the lounge, and her embroidered cushions reflect a Celtic
design. The house is immaculate and the bedrooms have country
diary bedspreads. Substantial breakfasts are served; guests help
themselves to starters, followed by a traditional cooked breakfast.
Vegetarians can be catered for if pre-arranged. Botanic House is
across the road, the city centre bus stop is a two-minute walk, and
the airport is 9 km away. Plenty of establishments within walking distance serve evening meals. Parking available.

OWNER Mrs Susan Forde OPEN All year
ROOMS 2 double, 1 twin, 1 triple; 3 en suite TERMS €28 pps

## Parknasilla

15 Iona Drive, Drumcondra, Dublin 9
Tel: 01 8305724

Teresa Ryan runs a clean and bright house, with easy reach of the
city centre and the airport. The rooms are of a good size in this
detached, large red brick Edwardian House. Families are welcome
and baby-sitting services are available. It is well maintained and spot-

lessly clean: good value accommodation, and a non-smoking house. A fresh cooked breakfast is well-presented, and Teresa is happy to assist visitors in any way she can. If arriving by car, guests would be advised to take the bus to the city centre.

OWNER Mrs Teresa Ryan OPEN January 1–December 21
ROOMS 4 double/twin/family; 2 en suite
TERMS €30-32.50; child reduction; single supplement from €8

## DUBLIN 15

### Ashbrook House
River Road, Ashtown, Castleknock, Dublin 15
Tel: 01 838 5660 Fax: 01 838 5660
Email: evemitchell@hotmail.com

Set in peaceful countryside, Ashbrook is a quiet oasis, yet very close to Phoenix Park and the city centre. Given its proximity to urban life it comes as a delightful surprise. Imagine arriving at night by taxi to a city address, and waking up in the morning to birds singing, surrounded by fields and gardens, and not a building in sight! Ashbrook is a beautifully maintained Georgian house, on a more manageable, smaller scale than some, decorated in bright welcoming colours and with comfortable furniture. The spacious bedrooms have telephones. The two sitting rooms have rounded ends, as does one of the bedrooms, and the dining room, where breakfast is served, easily seats twelve people. The grounds include a grass tennis court and walled garden. Ashbrook is popular with business people, and Eve Mitchell, who is a delightful hostess, runs a busy establishment. No pets. Visa and Mastercard accepted. To reach Ashbrook exit the N3 at the roundabout with the Halfway House Pub, cross the railway line, and turn on to River Road. It might be advisable to request directions.

OWNER Stan & Eve Mitchell OPEN January 2– December 20
ROOMS 1 double, 1 twin, 2 family; all en suite
TERMS €45; single supplement; child reduction

## DUBLIN 17

### Belcamp Hutchinson
Carr's Lane, Malahide Road, Balgriffin, Dublin 17
Tel: 01 846 0843 Fax: 01 848 5703
Email: belcamphutchinson@eircom.net
Website: www.belcamphutchinson.com

This superb, ivy-clad Georgian house, hidden away down a narrow lane off the main Malahide road, is named after Francis Hely-Hutchinson, third Earl of Donoughmore. Renovated with the utmost care, the house has preserved its features and elegance, whilst intro-

Belcamp Hutchinson

ducing the best of modern comforts. It stands in seven hectares of fields and gardens, including a walled garden and a maze.

The house is superbly furnished and extremely comfortable, and has an easygoing, relaxed atmosphere. Each spacious bedroom has been decorated with a different colour scheme and has a hair-dryer, TV, telephone and tea- and coffee-making facilities. Copious breakfasts are served at the enormous table in the elegant dining room, and the large, long drawing room has an honesty bar. The attractive little seaside village of Malahide is close by, Dublin can easily be reached by bus, and it is only a few minutes' drive to the airport.

Belcamp Hutchinson is a peaceful and relaxing place to stay, on arrival or departure from Ireland, or as a base for visiting Dublin. Dogs are welcome. Visa, Access, Mastercard accepted.

OWNER Doreen Gleeson & Karl Waldburg
OPEN February 1– December 20
ROOMS 8 double/twin; all en suite
TERMS €70; not suitable for children under 10 years

## DÚN LAOGHAIRE

### Lynden Town House
2 Mulgrave Terrace, Dún Laoghaire, Co. Dublin
Tel: 01 280 6404  Fax: 01 230 2258
Email: lynden@iol.ie

You feel welcome the minute you step through the door of this 160 year old terraced house on a quiet residential street very close to the centre of town. Maria Gavin is a bubbly, cheerful host who has owned and run, together with husband Stephen, this B&B for the last 24 years.

The bedrooms are simple and comfortable and there is a lounge and breakfast room. Early breakfasts can be arranged, and there is off-street parking in front of the house. Both the DART station and ferry port and a few minutes walk away. Pets welcome by arrangement. American Express, Visa and Mastercard are accepted.

OWNER Stephen & Maria Gavin OPEN all year
ROOMS 4 double/ twin; 2 en suite
TERMS €32–34; single supplement; child reduction

## The Cumberland Lodge

54 York Road, Dún Laoghaire, Co. Dublin
Tel: 01 280 9665 Fax: 01 284 3227
Email: cumberlandlodge@tinet.ie

David and Mariea Jameson have done a fine job of putting back
together this attractive Georgian house. They have chosen strong,
rich colours, and have interesting pictures and furniture. The breakfast area is at one end of the comfortable drawing room, and a quiet
back garden is also available for guests' use. The bedrooms have TV,
tea- and coffee-making facilities and telephones. A warm welcome,
and delicious breakfast await the visitor here. It is just up the hill
from the ferry terminal and a few minutes walk to the DART station. No pets, no smoking in bedrooms. All major credit cards
accepted. Secure parking.

OWNER David & Mariea Jameson OPEN All year
ROOMS 6 double/twin/family; all en suite
TERMS €38; single supplement €12.50

## King Sitric

East Pier, Howth, Co. Dublin
Tel: 01 832 5235 Fax: 01 839 2442
Email: info@kingsitric.ie
Website: www.kingsitric.com

At the extreme eastern end of Howth stands the King Sitric
Restaurant, a gaily painted, modest building with nothing to obstruct
90 degree views from its windows to the harbour, the southern cliffs
and out across the Irish sea. Originally the old Harbour Master's
house, the MacManus' have owned King Sitric since 1971 and built
up a reputation as a first class fish restaurant. Just six years ago they
virtually rebuilt the whole premises, creating 8 very comfortable
bedrooms, all with telephone, hair-dryer, TV and tea- and coffee-making facilities. Each one has a sea view and they are named after light-
houses. The cleverly designed first floor restaurant ensures that
every table can enjoy the view, and an atmospheric bar on the
ground floor incorporates the cellar, which is stocked with a superb
selection of wines, of which Aidan and Joan are justifiably proud.

   Apart from its proximity to the centre of Dublin and the airport,
Howth is a delightful place to visit, with its fishing harbour, marina,
cliff walks and golf courses. Major credit cards accepted.

OWNER Aidan & Joan MacManus OPEN All year except for
Christmas  ROOMS 8 double/ twin; all en suite TERMS from €69;
MEALS dinner

**Druid Lodge**
Killiney Hill Road, Killiney, Co. Dublin
Tel: 01 285 1632 Fax: 01 284 8504
Email: dlodge@indigo.ie Website: www.druidlodge.com

Built in 1832, this delightful family home stands in an old fashioned
garden, complete with "folly" tower, and has beautiful views over
Killiney Bay. The main rooms have lovely carved pine door surrounds, painstakingly stripped by the owners, as was the staircase.
The McClenaghans have lived here 25 years and brought up six children. The two front bedrooms are enormous, with two or three
beds apiece, and they have cleverly hidden, small en suite bathrooms
which in no way detract from the original shape of the rooms.
Smaller rooms on the ground floor do not have sea views, but are
comfortable, and all rooms have TV. Guests eat breakfast at one
large table in the dining room, and there is a lovely, comfortable
drawing room. No pets. Killiney Hill Road is above the centre of
Killiney and Druid Lodge is located between Druid's Chair Pub and
Killiney Avenue. It is a 10 minute walk from the DART station, with
trains running every 15 minutes into central Dublin. Visa and
Mastercard accepted.

OWNER Ken & Cynthia McClenaghan OPEN All year except for
Christmas ROOMS 2 double, 2 family; all en suite
TERMS from €45; child reduction

**South Lodge**
Portmarnock, Co. Dublin
Tel: 01 8461356 Fax: 01 8461365
Email: southlodgebb@eircom.net
Website: www.southlodgebb.com

This very attractive compact brick building stands just inside an
impressive gateway right next to the golf course, beyond which is
the sea. It has been the family home of Pat and Colin Burton for the
last thirty years, and just five years ago they started a bed & breakfast business. To offer the best accommodation possible they cleverly
redesigned the house, creating a small wing for themselves and
rebuilding the first floor, which now provides four charming bedrooms. They are spacious, furnished and decorated with simplicity,
and have beamed pitched, attic-like ceilings. Some of the rooms

overlook the golf course, and three are en suite. They have TV, hair-dryer, tea and coffee, books and packs of cards. There is a sitting area in the breakfast room which has views of the golf course beyond the small attractive garden. The patio in front of the house is a nice place to enjoy fine weather. South Lodge, built in 1873, was a gate lodge to the James family home, of distiller fame, now the Portmarnock Links Hotel. This fabulous location for the golf lover has great access to Dublin (bus stop just outside) and the airport, and the lovely sandy beach of Portmarnock is a few minutes away. Pets OK in cars. Visa, Mastercard and American Express accepted.

OWNER Pat & Colin Burton OPEN All year except for Christmas ROOMS 4 double/twin; 3 en suite TERMS €38; single supplement; child reduction

## ST MARGARET'S

**Newtown House**
St Margaret's, Co. Dublin
Tel: 01 834 1081

This delightful old Georgian farmhouse is surrounded by a golf course, driving range and various other enterprises. In spite of all the activity, the house is completely private and has a peaceful outlook overlooking the golf course. It is beautifully furnished in a very tradi-tional manor, and guests have use of a drawing room and TV sitting room. Only minutes from Dublin Airport, Newtown House makes a great start- or end-point for visitors. Sheila Wilson-Wright only takes guests who have pre-booked. Not suitable for children. The gates from the road to the golf course and house are closed at mid-night. No pets.

OWNER Mrs Sheila Wilson-Wright OPEN All year except for Christmas ROOMS 2 twins/ 2 public bathrooms (one with shower, one with bath) TERMS €51; single supplement

## COUNTIES LOUTH AND MEATH

The Boyne Valley cuts right through the centre of this area—one of the most historic and evocative places in Irish history, and for thou-sands of years the centre of political power. Innumerable remains from every century lie scattered across this fertile, green valley. Dominating the town of Trim are the ruins of King John's Castle, the largest Anglo-Norman castle in Ireland, dating from 1172. The Duke of Wellington's family came from here, as did the family of Bernardo O'Higgins, a prominent figure in Chilean history.

Apart from a few earthworks, there is not much left to see at the Hill of Tara, seat of Ireland's kings since prehistoric times. Imagination is needed to conjure up the sight of great buildings and a mass of warriors and nobles who inhabited this place in days gone by.

At the attractive village of Slane, the old castle overlooks the river, and a little farther along the valley is Brugh na Boinne (the Palace of the Boyne), an enormous cemetery with graves dating back to the Neolithic era, the main sites of which are at Newgrange, Knowth and Dowth.

The pretty village of Kells in the Blackwater Valley was the site of the settlement of the Columban monks, who moved here from Iona in 807. St Columba's house still stands, and the church holds a copy of the famous Book of Kells.

Monasterboice and Mellifont are the sites of the two ancient ecclesiastical centres, and at Drogheda, in the Church of St Peter, one can see the preserved head of St Oliver Plunkett, former Archbishop of Armagh. The Cooley Peninsula is an attractive and unspoilt area with lovely views, and the old town of Carlingford has lots of historical sites, including King John's Castle.

## COUNTY LOUTH

### CARLINGFORD

**Viewpoint**
Carlingford, Co. Louth
Tel: 042 9373149 Fax: 042 9373149
Email: paulwoodsviewpoint@hotmail.com
Website: www.viewpointcarlingford.com

Enjoying spectacular views of the town and harbour and across to the Mourne Mountains, Viewpoint is a modern house standing above the road on the edge of Carlingford. The bedrooms are motel-style, with their own entrances and en suite shower rooms, and most have a view. They are comfortably furnished with modern fittings. The large breakfast room with separate tables takes full advantage of the view, and visitors are invited to use the owners' sitting room. No pets. Visa and Mastercard accepted. The house is signposted off N1.

OWNER Paul & Maria Woods OPEN All year except for Christmas
ROOMS 4 double, 2 twin, 2 family; all en suite TERMS from €35 pps

### DROGHEDA

**Harbour Villa**
Mornington Road, Drogheda, Co. Louth
Tel: 041 9837441

Harbour Villa is an attractive, vine-covered old country house on the banks of the River Boyne, just three kilometres south of town, yet-close to the beach, with golf and possibilities for horse riding nearby. Eileen Valla offers her guests a warm welcome. The gardens are most attractive, and there is a garden house containing a sun lounge where guests can relax. The bedrooms are small, clean and simply furnished,: the comfortable lounge has the original marble fireplace.. No pets. Smoking permitted in the TV lounge.

OWNER Eileen Valla OPEN All year ROOMS 1 twin, 2 double, 1 single; 2 en suite, 1 public bathroom TERMS €30pps; child reduction

### Highfield House
Termonfeckin, Drogheda, Co. Louth
Tel: 041 9822172

Highfield House can be found in the middle of the village of Termonfeckin by its signs for meats and delis (as well as the Bord Failte sign). The main house, built in 1725, stands just off the road, and behind are attractive white-washed farm buildings, where Kitty McEvoy's son has his butcher's shop and deli. He rears his own pigs, hens and beef to supply the shop. Kitty herself is a chatty, friendly lady. The bedrooms are very spacious and comfortably furnished, and the large dining room has a decorative bar in one corner. Guests also have use of a sitting room. The sea is only five minutes away. Visa and Mastercard accepted. No pets.

OWNER Kitty McEvoy OPEN March 1–October 31 ROOMS 3 double/twin; 2 en suite, 1 private bathroom TERMS €30; child reduction

## DUNDALK

### Blackrock House
Main Street, Blackrock, Dundalk, Co. Louth
Tel: 04293 21829
Email: blackrockhsedundalk@eircom.net
Website: www.blackrockhouse.net

Blackrock is a small seaside community a short distance south of Dundalk, and Blackrock House is right on the seafront, in the middle of the village. When Gerry and Brenda Rogers built the house 25 years ago they had a hardware shop on the ground floor and lived upstairs. The shop has been converted into guest bedrooms, save one end, which is the Post Office. Bedrooms are small and simple: none have sea views. The view has been saved for the guests' sitting room on the first floor which has a large patio, right above the water. Brenda is a friendly, efficient host, and husband Gerry is Postmaster. Blackrock House is conveniently located for Dundalk Golf Club: there are of pubs and eating establishments within easy walking distance.

No pets or credit cards.

OWNER Gerry & Brenda Rogers OPEN closed for Christmas
ROOMS 6 double/twin/triple, all en suite
TERMS €30–35; single supplement

RIVERSTOWN
**Cooley Lodge**
Mountbagnal, near Carlingford, Riverstown, Dundalk, Co. Louth
Tel: 042 9376201

Cooley Lodge itself is one of a disparate collection of converted old
stone farm buildings whichwhich make up the bed & breakfast range
of buildings,including a row of self-catering cottages and the owner's
house. The property lies at the foot of the Cooley Mountains in
lovely countryside and is only a short distance to the medieval town
of Carlingford, a mecca of good restaurants and pubs. The bed and
breakfast building was originally a cow shed.

  The bedrooms are all very spacious, individually decorated in various motifs, such as Edwardian, Victorian, etc. and are equipped with
telephone, TV and hair-dryer, and many have lovely mountain views.
There is a sitting area at one end and a conservatory at the other,
and outside a tennis court for guests' use. Breakfast is served in the
galleried dining room., Cooley Lodge can be found just off the R173
9 miles or so from Dundalk. No pets. Visa and Mastercard accepted.

OWNER Geraldine Lynn OPEN May 1–October 31
ROOMS 2 twin, 4 double; all en suite TERMS €45 pps; single supplement

## COUNTY MEATH
ATHBOY
**Woodtown House**
Woodtown West, Athboy, Co. Meath
Tel: 046 9435022 Fax: 046 9435022
Email: woodtown@iol.ie
Website: www.iol.ie/~woodtown

Way out in the countryside at the end of a long no-through road is
this delightfully restored Georgian house, surrounded by mature gardens. It has a friendly, family lived in atmosphere and the house is full
of knick knacks, particularly in the lower level's cosy vaulted breakfast room, and where the old bells of the house can still be seen.
Woodtown is a beautifully proportioned building with a bow fronted
dining room. Of the three bedrooms, the double is a smaller room
and its private bathroom has the original decorated loo and old-

fashioned bath tub, the remaining two bedrooms are extremely spacious, each en suite, and one has two old sinks and a fireplace.

There are five acres of grounds, including a traditional walled garden—currently derelict, but ripe for restoration! Fishing can be organised. Pets in cars only. Visa and Mastercard accepted. Woodtown is five miles south west of Athboy - directions are advisable.

OWNER Anne & Colin Finnegan OPEN April 1–September 30
ROOMS 1 double, 1 twin, 2 family; en suite or with private bath
TERMS €28.50; child reduction

## DOWTH

### Glebe House
Dowth, nr. Drogheda, Co. Meath
Tel: 041 9836101 Fax: 041 9843469

This attractive, whitewashed, small country house is covered in wisteria, clematis and roses. Set in a pretty garden, and with lovely views over the tennis court to distant hills, Glebe House is at the heart of the Boyne valley, between Newgrange and Drogheda.

Mrs Addison is a delightful welcoming person, who apart from her bed & breakfast business, specialises in small functions and private dinner parties. The reception rooms are welcoming and warm, with fireplaces in both the large formal drawing room and the small, cosy study/sitting room and mauve carpets cover the entire ground floor. The bedrooms are pretty and comfortable. Cream teas are served to public. No pets. No credit cards. For those who wish to improve their art skills, there are art workshops. Glebe House is signposted at Dowth.

OWNER Elizabeth Addison OPEN Closed for Christmas
ROOMS 2 double, 2 twin; all en suite TERMS €55–60; child reduction

## DULEEK

### Annesbrook
Duleek, Co. Meath
Tel: 041 982 3293 Fax: 041 982 3293

An impressive gate and a long wooded drive lead to the interesting house of Annesbrook, the core of which is seventeenth century with additions of different periods. The pedimented portico of the house and the ballroom were added on to impress George IV who visited in 1821, and the front entrance hall is beautifully proportioned with a lovely winding staircase. Another distinguished visitor was William Thackeray. The formal hospitality of those days has been replaced by a relaxed and welcoming family atmosphere. All of the bedrooms are spacious and comfortable, with folders detailing events of local interest and suggested walks and drives to local attractions.

Each bedroom has tea- and coffee-making facilities and hair-dryer. The reception rooms have big log fires. The décor of the purple and gold dining room is a little unusual, the ceiling almost matching the carpet. No pets. The house can be found south of Duleek on the R152.

OWNER Kate Sweetman OPEN Mid-April–end September
ROOMS 5 double/twin/family; all en suite
TERMS €50–56; single supplement; child reduction

## KELLS

**Lennoxbrook**
Carnaross, Kells, Co. Meath
Tel: 046 92 45902 Fax: 046 92 45902
Email: lennoxbrook@unison.ie

Lennoxbrook is an old farmhouse standing just off the main road. The back part of the house is over 200 years old, and the surrounding farmland is let out. It is an Old World family home with plain, but comfortable bedrooms and dinner available if booked in advance. There are also self-catering facilities. Guests may use laundry room. Pets outside only. Mastercard, Visa and Laser accepted. Lennoxbrook is three miles north of Kells on the N3.

OWNER Pauline Mullan OPEN All year ROOMS 2 double, 1 twin, 1 triple; 2 en suite, 2 public bathroom TERMS €35 pps; single supplement; child reduction MEALS dinner €25

## NAVAN

**Gainstown House**
Navan, Co. Meath
Tel: 046 90 21448

This small country house dating from the early nineteenth century stands in peaceful lawned gardens surrounded by 80 hectares of farmland. The house is simply furnished and decorated. The drawing room with open fireplace leads off the large entrance hall. Breakfast is served in the dining room. A patio at the rear of the house overlooks the garden. No pets. No smoking. Gainstown House is signposted in the N3 Navan to Dublin road at Old Bridge Inn.

OWNER Mrs Mary Reilly OPEN July 1–August 1
ROOMS 2 family, 2 twin; 1 en suite, 2 public bathrooms
TERMS €26.50; single supplement €6.50; child reduction

## Lios Na Greine

Athlumney, Navan, Co. Meath
Tel: 046 9028092 Fax: 046 9028092
Email: www.liosnagreine@eircom.net

Lios Na Greine, meaning 'enclosure of the sun', is a modern house in a sunny location. Set back off the road one and a half kilometres from the town centre on the Duleek to Ashbourne airport road, the house is immaculate and decorated with matching wallpapers, fabrics and cosy duvets.

One room is on the ground floor and there is a comfortable TV lounge where tea is served in the evening. Breakfast is served in the bright and cheerful dining room, and evening meals are available by arrangement.

The pleasant garden is a nice spot to sit after exploring Newgrange and the Boyne Valley, which are within easy reach. No smoking. Pets are accepted in the car or garage.

OWNER Mary Callanan OPEN All year ROOMS 2 family en suite, 1 family with private bathroom TERMS €33 pps; single supplement; child reduction MEALS dinner €19

## Village B&B

Kilmessan Village, Navan, Co. Meath
Tel: 046 9025250
Website: www.meathvillagebandb.com

Right in the centre of the village this brightly coloured, neatly kept, old house is easy to find. The wing that accommodates guests was originally a shop. Teresa and Gerard Brennan rebuilt the interior to provide 6 rooms, two of which are suitable for disabled guests. There are wooden floors throughout, pine furniture, and simple, clean décor. The cosy breakfast room is in the original part of the house. Pets are accepted.

OWNER Teresa & Gerard Brennan OPEN all year ROOMS 2 doubles, 4 twin/double; all en suite TERMS from €35; single supplement; child reduction

## Knockbrack

Oldcastle, Co. Meath
Tel: 049 8541771
Email: kittybevan@eircom.net

Set in 60 acres of park and farmland Knockbrack is in a delightful, peaceful position. Dating from 1821 it has an attractive garden, and views to the Loughcrew Hills and to Mullaghmeen Forest. There are spacious, comfortable public rooms for guests' use. An enormous drawing room, is part of a later addition including a large bedroom with an enormously long bathroom.

Kitty Bevan is a welcoming, chatty host, and an innovative cook, using vegetables and herbs from the garden, and local produce. Loughcrew Cairns and Loughcrew Gardens are close by. Pets allowed. Visa and Mastercard accepted.

OWNER Mrs. Kitty Bevan OPEN January 15–December 15
ROOMS 2 double with private bathroom, 1 twin en suite
TERMS €50 single supplement MEALS dinner €30

## Loughcrew House
Oldcastle, Co. Meath
Tel: 049 8541356 Fax: 049 8541921
Email: info@loughcrew.com
Website: www.loughcrew.com

The Loughcrew estate has been in the Naper family for over 400 years, and Charles and Emily's home is a conversion of what used to be an elegant conservatory designed by Cockrell. It stands next to part of the ruins of the old house, and the estate comprises a lake, tennis court, the family church of St. Oliver Plunkett and Loughcrew Gardens, which are open to the public.

Emily Naper is an amazing woman, a friendly person with boundless energy—she is one of Ireland's leading gilders, and has a studio adjoining the house where she restores gilt furniture and frames and designs hand-finished decorative furniture. She also runs a school for gilding and specialist paint finishes and courses in botanical watercolour painting and ceramic sculpture. This is all in addition to running the house, garden and tending to the needs of her children. Charles is the cook, producing fine meals from local produce and home-grown herbs.

Loughcrew is a lived in family home, an eccentric and unusual place, with whimsical décor, some frescoes and interesting pieces. Guests have use of a long room for breakfast combined with a sitting room, as well as a small cosy sitting room with wood burning stove. Visitors here enjoy the atmosphere and countryside. Visa, Mastercard and Laser accepted.

Loughcrew can be found off the N3 thirteen miles north west of Kells—directions to the house will be given when booking.

OWNER Charles & Emily Naper OPEN January 5–December 18
ROOMS 1 double, 2 twin, 1 single; private bathroom
TERMS €60; single supplement; child reduction MEALS dinner €30

**Rosnaree House**
Slane, Co. Meath
Tel: 041 982 0975 Fax: 041 982 4162
Email: rosnaree@eircom.net

Robert and Aisling Law moved back from several years in Africa four
years ago to take over their family home. Set in 200 acres of garden,
woodlands and farmland the property stretches down to and along
the Boyne. From the house, built in 1700, there are views of the
River Boyne and to Newgrange. It was from here that the High Kings
from Tara would wait before crossing to Newgrange.

   A splendid old house with a distinctly family home atmosphere,
much of it has been renovated since Robert and Aisling took over.
The furniture and furnishings are an interesting mixture of old family
pieces, furniture and artifacts from Africa, and sculptures and artwork
created by Aisling and her side of the family. The bedrooms vary in
shape, size and décor—one has an all encompassing mural partly painted by Aisling. The old library is used as a film club, is where Aisling
sometimes teaches yoga, and is a comfortable place to relax. Dinner
is available for four or more people, if booked in advance, and there
is fishing on the Boyne. Weddings and private functions can also be
booked. Child and pet friendly.

   To reach Rosnaree from the N2 turn east at the brown sign for
Newgrange south of Slane. The driveway is through white gates on a
sharp bend on the left of the road.

OWNER Robert & Aisling Law OPEN All year except for Christmas
ROOMS 2 double, 1 twin, 1 family, en suite or with private bathroom
TERMS €70 pps; single supplement; child reduction MEALS dinner €45

**Crannmór**
Dunderry Road, Trim, Co. Meath
Tel: 046 94 31635 Fax: 046 94 38087
Email: crannmor@eircom.net
Website: www.crannmor.com

This old country house is in a peaceful setting surrounded by pleasant gardens and 2.5 hectares of fields. The O'Regans took over the
house at the beginning of 2000 and have done a lot of refurbishment. Three of the bright, cheerful guest rooms are on the ground
level in what was once the stable block, and one is particularly suited for disabled guests. The fourth room is on the first floor in the
main part of the house. The breakfast/sitting room is very charming
with antique furniture and an open fire. Anne O'Regan is a cheerful,
capable woman, who has been in the guest house business for many

years, and Crannmór is a friendly and comfortable place to stay. Historic Trim, which boasts the largest Norman castle in Ireland is only one kilometre away. One of Trim's attractions is the annual Trim Fair, 'The Power and the Glory'—a multimedia exhibition explaining the background of Trim's medieval ruins. Pets in car only. Visa and Mastercard accepted. To reach Crannmór from Trim, leave Super Valu on the right, take the next right, stay right at next junction and the house is 400 yards on the right.

OWNER Anne O'Regan OPEN All year except for Christmas ROOMS 1 double, 1 twin, 3 family; all en suite TERMS €32–33; single supplement; child reduction

## COUNTY WICKLOW

Lying just to the south of Dublin, this is an area of hills and mountains, lakes and streams—a pleasant, peaceful place of escape after the bustle of the city. From Dublin one comes first to Bray, a large seaside resort, and then to Enniskerry. Here one can visit the gardens of Powerscourt Estate. The house, which had been one of the most beautiful in Ireland, was destroyed in the 1950s, leaving only the shell still standing. Glendalough is a beautiful, scenic place in the mountains, set between two small lakes near the ruins of St Kevin's Kitchen, the church and the cathedral founded by St Kevin in 520. Just beyond is the small twelfth-century priory of St Saviour. The county town, Wicklow, is on the coast, and farther south is Arklow, a popular resort and fishing centre. At Blessington is Russborough House, a beautiful Palladian-style house, containing a marvellous art collection, and the Poulaphouca Reservoir, which has been formed by damming the River Liffey.

### ARKLOW

**Ballykilty House**
Coolgreany, Arklow, Co. Wicklow
Tel: 0402 37111 Fax: 0402 37272
Email: ballykiltyfarmhouse@eircom.net

This 200-year-old house stands in a lovely garden with a tennis court in peaceful countryside. It is part of an 80-hectare dairy farm with 100 milking cows. Annie Nuzum is a friendly lady and the house has a warm and welcoming atmosphere. There are two cosy sitting rooms with open fires each side of the front door, and one has a TV. The dining room was the original kitchen and still has the old beams and cooking pots, and a big open fireplace. The bedrooms have hairdryers, and there are tea- and coffee-making facilities in the rooms.

This is a good base for exploring Powerscourt and Mount Usher gardens, Avondale House and Forest Park, Russborough House, Castleruddery Transport Museum, and the Vale of Avoca. No pets. Visa and Mastercard accepted. Ballykilty is on the road between Coolgreany and Arklow, five kilometres from Arklow.

OWNER Mrs Annie Nuzum OPEN March 1–November 1
ROOMS 2 double, 2 twin, 1 triple; all en suite
TERMS €35; single supplement; child reduction

## Fairy Lawn
Wexford Road, Arklow, Co. Wicklow
Tel: 0402 32790

This brick and plaster house, set back off the main road, is located one kilometre from Arklow on the N11 road to Gorey. The comfortable bedrooms are regularly redecorated and are simply furnished. There is a comfortable guest lounge with TV, and breakfast only is served in the dining room. Mr Kelly is a keen gardener, maintaining the well landscaped gardens and colourful window boxes. No pets. Visa, Mastercard and Eurocard accepted.

OWNER Rita Kelly OPEN All year except for Christmas
ROOMS 4 double/twin/family; 3 en suite, 1 public bathroom
TERMS €30-32.50 pps; single supplement; child reduction

## Moneylands Farm
Arklow, Co. Wicklow
Tel: 0402 32259 Fax: 0402 32438
Email: mland@eircom.net
Website: www.moneylands.com

This neat, small, whitewashed farmhouse is located down a quiet country lane on the outskirts of Arklow and has pleasant views. The ground floor family room has a small sitting area and French doors that open on to the garden. All bedrooms have hair-dryers, and tea and coffee facilities are on hand in the conservatory. The comfortable lounge leads through to the large conservatory, where breakfast is served. Mr and Mrs Byrne, who are a kindly couple, have made many additions to the farm. They include an indoor heated swimming pool, gym, sauna and tennis court, which are available both to bed & breakfast guests, as well as to those staying in the self-catering courtyard of renovated stone built coach houses. Pets in car only. Visa, Mastercard and American Express accepted. Moneylands Farm is one kilometre south of Arklow off the N11.
OWNER Michael & Lillie Byrne OPEN February 1–November 1
ROOMS 3 double, 2 twin, 1 family; 5 en suite, 1 private bathroom

TERMS €35; single supplement; child reduction

## Plattenstown House
Coolgreaney Road, Arklow, Co. Wicklow
Tel: 0402 37822 Fax: 0402 37822
Email: mcdpr@indigo.ie
www. plattenstownhouse.com

This old farmhouse was built in 1853 for Lady Jane O'Grady. It is set
in 20 hectares of farmland, supporting cows and goats, and has a
lovely, peaceful, mature front garden. The attractive, whitewashed
farm buildings are at the back of the house. There is a comfortable
drawing room, a small TV sitting room with fireplace, and a conservatory. Guests have use of bicycles—beaches can be found within 5-7
kilometres—and there are pleasant forest walks. Pets outside only.
Visa, Mastercard and Access accepted. Plattenstown House is five
kilometres from Arklow on the Coolgreaney road.

OWNER Mrs Margaret McDowell OPEN Closed for Christmas
ROOMS 2 double, 1 twin; all en suite TERMS €35–40; single supplement; child reduction MEALS dinner €27

## AUGHRIM

## Clone House
Aughrim, Co. Wicklow
Tel: 0402 36121 Fax: 0402 36029
Email: stay@clonehouse.com
Website: www.clonehouse.com

A historically interesting house dating back to the 1600s, it was
burnt to the ground in 1798, rebuilt in 1805, and has a priest's hiding
place and underground passage extending some 500 metres. Old features still intact include the fine molding in the drawing room, which
dates pre-1840. For the past 50 years of its life it has been a guest
house, acquired by the Watsons a few years ago when they moved
to Ireland from the United States. They have done wonders to the
house and grounds—major refurbishment of the house and the creation of a lovely garden. Every bedroom is a different shape and size,
and each one individually decorated. Gourmet five course dinners
are served in the formal dining room, and for less formal occasions
the small dining room is used. The music room is a cosy place with a
roaring fire, two pianos and a flagstone floor.
  Carla (Uruguayan-Italian) is a gregarious, conservatively-flamboyant
lady, and a passionate cook. She uses all natural foods, including produce from the kitchen garden, and Jeff (American) is an avid gardener, who is responsible for the landscaping project.
  Clone House is set in the heart of the countryside with views of

the Wicklow Mountains. Luckily there are plenty of signs to the house from Aughrim and Woodenbridge. Visa and Mastercard accepted.

OWNER Carla Watson OPEN All year
ROOMS 7 double/twin; all en suite TERMS €60–90;
single supplement MEALS Dinner €45-55

## AVOCA

### Keppel's Farmhouse
Ballanagh, Avoca, Co. Wicklow
Tel: 0402 35168 Fax: 0402 30950
Email: keppelsfarmhouse@eircom.net
Website: www.keppelsfarmhouse.com

Built around 1880, Keppel's Farmhouse is set in quiet countryside with beautiful views over the Vale of Avoca. A recently added wing contains a large dining room (where breakfast including home-made bread and preserves is served), a lounge, and two first floor bedrooms. The bedrooms are clean and bright and full of fresh country air; all have hair-dryers, TV and tea- and coffee-making facilities. An ironing board and trouser press are available.

Guests are welcome to walk around the farm, watch the cows being milked and observe the famous Avoca handweavers nearby.

A woodland path is now in use giving visitors the option of taking a pleasant 20-minute stroll to Avoca. No pets. Visa, Mastercard and Eurocard accepted. To reach Keppel's turn right in front of 'Fitzgerald's Bar' having crossed the bridge into the village. There are signs from the village.

OWNER Charles & Joy Keppel OPEN April 1–October 31
ROOMS 2 twin, 2 double, 1 triple; all en suite
TERMS €32 pps; single supplement

Keppel's Farmhouse

**Rathsallagh House**
Dunlavin, Co. Wicklow
Tel: 045 403112 Fax: 045 403343
Email: info@rathsallagh.com
Website: www.rathsallagh.com

Set in 214 hectares of beautiful, mature parkland, the house is reached up a majestic, long, sweeping driveway across the Rathsallagh Championship Golf Course which, were it not for the odd sign to stop and watch for golfers, one would hardly be aware of. The original house was built in the early 1700s and was burnt down in the rebellion of 1798. Unable to afford to rebuild the house, the family moved into the Queen Anne stables, which now form Rathsallagh House. Its long rooms and comparatively lower ceilings give it a relaxed, country house feel, in comparison to the more formal, high ceilinged ornate Georgian houses. It is built around a courtyard, the bedrooms arranged off one side of the long narrow corridors. Some rooms are very spacious with lovely parkland outlooks and are comfortably and unfussily furnished. They have every amenity including hair-dryer, iron and ironing board, telephone, TV/DVD, computer connection, and tea- and coffee-making facilities. The food at Rathsallagh is an experience: beautifully presented dishes are served in the light panelled dining room, and there is an extensive breakfast buffet, and excellent menus in the evening using organically produced food, fresh fish and game when in season. There are any number of activities within the estate for guests to enjoy, including golf, tennis, croquet, snooker, swimming in the indoor pool, sauna and massage. Arrangements can be made for riding, shooting, deer stalking and archery. Major credit cards accepted. Pets by arrangement. Rathsallagh is signposted in Dunlavin village.

OWNER O'Flynn family OPEN All year ROOMS 31 double/twin; all en suite TERMS €130–150; single supplement; not suitable for children MEALS lunch €3.50–15 tea €13.50, dinner €60

**Tynte House**
Dunlavin, Co. Wicklow
Tel: 045 401561 Fax: 045 401586
Email: stay@tyntehouse.com
Website: www.tyntehouse.com

Built in the early 1800s, Tynte House is a tall, whitewashed building standing right in the middle of town. In its later days it was a pub until 1930. John Lawler's father bought the house and there was still a lot of work to be done on it when John and Caroline took it over. It has been furnished and decorated appealingly in keeping with its style and age. The bedrooms, some of which are on the second floor, have telephone, TV, hair-dryer and tea- and coffee-making facilities, and are unfussily furnished and decorated. There is a cosy snug room, and the dining room is in two different areas—separate tables in a darker, inner room, and one big table in a large, bright room with a sitting area at one end. There is also a games room. Caroline is friendly and welcoming, and also offers eight self-catering mews cottages in the courtyard, which were originally stables and lofts. There is a hard tennis court, a children's playground and golf courses and riding nearby. Pets by arrangement. Mastercard accepted.

OWNER John & Caroline Lawler OPEN All year except for Christmas ROOMS 5 double/twin, 1 family; all en suite TERMS €35; single supplement; child reduction MEALS packed lunch €5, dinner €25

## ENNISKERRY

**Ferndale**
Enniskerry, Co. Wicklow
Tel: 01 2863518 Fax: 01 2863518
Email: ferndale@eircom.net
Website: www.ferndalehouse.com

This attractive, 160 year old house stands right in the centre of Enniskerry and has been in Noel Corcoran's family for a good part of its life. He and his wife, Josie, took it over a few years ago and did up the whole house, almost to the extent of rebuilding it. There is a relaxing drawing room, and elegant bedrooms with brass and old iron beds, all of which have TV, hair-dryers and tea- and coffee-making facilities. The dining room, with one large table covered with a white linen tablecloth, is in the basement and leads into the conservatory, which in turn has doors out to the pretty terraced rear garden with a gazebo, which eventually ends in the car park. Pets outside only. Dublin is only 12 miles away, served by a regular bus service, and Ferndale is close to Powerscourt.

OWNER Noel & Josie Corcoran
OPEN April 1–October 31
ROOMS 2 twin, 2 double; all en suite
TERMS €40 pps; child reduction

## GLENDALOUGH

**Carmel's Bed & Breakfast**
Annamoe, Glendalough, Co. Wicklow
Tel: 0404 45297 Fax: 0404 45297
Email: carmelsbandb@eircom.net

The house was built by the Hawkins in 1970, and has been added on to a few times, most recently to enlarge the lounge/ dining area and bedrooms. Carmel's is a warm and welcoming house, set back off the main road in 0.5 hectare of immaculately kept garden, where everyone is treated as a family friend and plied with cups of tea or coffee on arrival. All bedrooms are on the ground floor, have hairdryers, and two bedrooms have two toilets. Mr and Mrs Hawkins are local people, willing to assist with sightseeing and local events. Glendalough Fun Park is close by: hiking and walking can also be enjoyed. No pets. Carmel's is on R755 from Glendalough to Dublin.

OWNER Carmel Hawkins OPEN March–November
ROOMS 1 double, 1 twin, 2 family; all en suite
TERMS €33; single supplement; child reduction

### Doire Coille House
Glendalough, Cullentragh, Rathdrum, Co. Wicklow
Tel: 0404 45131

Just off the R755 road in the Avonmore Valley, Doire Coille is a pleasant farmhouse, surrounded by a large, colourful garden, with nice views of the wooded valley. Behind are the farm buildings and land, used for sheep rearing, stretching up the hill. Mary Byrne is a welcoming, down to earth lady who runs a clean and efficient house. The rooms are small, and simply furnished in pine, and have good firm beds. A large ground floor room, which has doors out to the garden doubles as breakfast room and sitting area. No pets. Mastercard and Visa accepted.

OWNER Mary Byrne OPEN 1 April–30 November ROOMS 7 double/ twin, all en suite TERMS €35; single supplement; child reduction

## GLENEALY

### Ballyknocken House & Cookery School
Ashford, Glenealy, Co. Wicklow
Tel: 0404 44627 Fax: 0404 44696
Email: info@ballyknocken.com
Website: www.ballyknocken.com

Ballyknocken House, built in the 1850s, is set in a pretty wooded valley below Carrick Mountain. The Byrne family acquired the house in the 1940s and today Catherine Byrne Fulvio is the third generation of the family to own Ballyknocken. She and her Italian husband, Claudio, have carried out renovation work, including transforming the old kitchen with its original inglenook fireplace into an additional dining room, and decorating and finishing the bedrooms in keeping with the period of the house. The rooms are fresh and bright, and some have brass beds, and the bathrooms claw foot baths. However, the main feature of Ballyknocken is the warmth of an unhurried welcome and its casual informality. Catherine exudes an infectious special warmth and enthusiasm and makes her guests feel immediately at home. She and Claudio are experts in food and wine, and guests enjoy wonderful culinary experiences at dinner and breakfast.

Ballyknocken Cookery School opened recently and offers a selection of courses, including an introduction to Irish bread and baking. Guests are welcome to use the tennis court and wander around the gardens and the adjoining forest. Mastercard and Visa accepted. No pets. To find Ballyknocken from the N11 in Ashford turn right (from the Dublin direction) after the Texaco station and continue for three miles. The house is on the right.

OWNER Catherine & Claudio Fulvio
OPEN January 29–December 3
ROOMS 1 family, 4 double, 2 twin; all en suite
TERMS from €55; single supplement; child reduction
MEALS dinner €34

## KILTEGAN

### Barraderry House
Kiltegan, Co. Wicklow
Tel: 059 6473209 Fax: 059 6473209
Email: jo.hobson@oceanfree.net
Website: www.barraderrycountryhouse.com

On the western edge of the Wicklow Mountains, Barraderry is an attractive Georgian house, surrounded by its own farmland with lovely mountain views, and is set in a peaceful location. It has been the Hobson family home since 1950 and was farmed by John until recently Now, one of their daughters has a few sheep and horses, and the rest of the land is leased.
With the children gone, Olive started a B&B business just nine years ago, and offers a warm and friendly welcome. The four large bedrooms are comfortable and have TV, hair-dryer and tea- and coffee-making facilities. Guests have use of a sizeable drawing room, with breakfast served in the dining room. A feature of the grounds is an unusual 250-year old twin grafted beech tree.

Barraderry is approached up a long driveway through a park-like setting off the Baltinglass to Kiltegan road. Golf and racing are well catered for, with 6 golf courses within 30 minutes; Punchestown, Naas and The Curragh racecourses are nearby. Pets in car only. Children welcome. Visa and Mastercard accepted.

OWNER Olive & John Hobson OPEN mid-January–mid-December
ROOMS 1 twin, 1 single, 2 double; all en suite
TERMS €40–45; single supplement; child reduction

## Humewood Castle

Kiltegan, Co. Wicklow
Tel: 059 6473215 Fax: 059 6473382
Email: humewood@iol.ie
Website: www.humewood.com

This imposing, magic-like castle was the last of its kind to be built in Ireland. Dating from the 1860s it is a masterpiece of Victorian architecture, said to be the "finest and most important 19th-century castellated mansion in Ireland". Right on the edge of the village of Kiltegan, it is approached up a long avenue. Its 500-acre walled estate, which includes two small lakes, is considered one of the best duck shoots in Ireland. Additional acreage on nearby properties offers pheasant shooting as well.

Humewood is a luxurious family home and can be booked for individuals on a nightly basis, and also caters for conferences and corporate entertainment. Each bedroom is a different shape and size and decorated and furnished in a unique style. The castle tower, reached by a narrow winding staircase, contains one of the honeymoon suites.

The interior is majestic and palatial with enormous rooms and painted, beamed ceilings. The public rooms include a ballroom, dining room, drawing room and cosy sitting room attached to the bar. The bathroom on the lower level is the same size as the bedroom above, and with windows all around affords a 360-degree view of farmlands and the Wicklow Mountains.

A wealth of activities can be arranged for the visitor, including clay pigeon shooting, horse riding, fishing, deer stalking, polo, golf, hunting, hill walking, falconry and tennis. No smoking in bedrooms. Major credit cards accepted. Humewood Castle offers a unique experience—enjoy a night being treated like royalty!
OWNER Renata Coleman OPEN April–January
ROOMS 12 deluxe double, 2 twin, 1 single; all en suite
TERMS €300–480 per room (depending on room & time of year)
MEALS lunch and dinner

## RATHNEW

### Hunter's Hotel

Newrath Bridge, Rathnew, Co. Wicklow
Tel: 0404 40106 Fax: 0404 40338
Email: reception@hunters.ie
Website: www.hunters.ie

This attractive, long, low building, covered with climbing plants, was originally an old coaching inn. Built in 1720, Rathnew stands on what used to be the main road, though now it is one kilometre off the new Dublin road, five kilometres outside Wicklow.

Owned and run by the Gelletlie family, it has been in the same ownership since 1840. It is comfortable and old-fashioned, combining a lot of Old World charm with modern comforts. Several rooms overlook the beautiful, colourful garden, and others on the ground floor are suitable for disabled guests. Tables and chairs are dotted around the garden, which lies along the banks of the River Vartry, a delightful place for afternoon tea or a pre-lunch or dinner drink.

The garden room is available for small conferences or private parties. Smoking in public lounges only. All major credit cards accepted. Mount Usher Gardens are nearby.

OWNER The Gelletlie family OPEN All year except for Christmas
ROOMS 16 double/twin; all en suite
TERMS €95–115
MEALS lunch from €22, dinner from €42, tea from €6.50

## Tinakilly Country House
Rathnew, Co. Wicklow
Tel: 0404 69274 Fax: 0404 67806
Email: wpower@tinakilly.ie
Website: www.tinakilly.ie

Built in 1883, Tinakilly, meaning "house of the wood", was constructed for Captain Robert Halpin, who as Commander of *The Great Eastern*, was responsible for laying most of the world's transoceanic telegraph cables. A fine print of *The Great Eastern* hangs in the house, together with a collection of sea-faring pictures in ornate frames.

The British Government footed the considerable bill for the mansion's construction, and the best architects, materials and craftsmen were used in the creation of this splendid Victorian building. William and Bee Power acquired the house in 1982, adding more wings to it in 1991 and 1997, and today Tinakilly belongs to their son and daughter-in-law, Raymond and Josephine, who continue the tradition of maintaining the atmospheric Victorian character of the building, and the high standard of food and service.

The house is surrounded by gardens and parkland and has magnificent views over the Irish Sea. There is a tennis court, croquet lawn and heliport, and nearby are excellent golf courses, as well as riding and walking in the Wicklow Mountains. All major credit cards accepted. The entrance to Tinakilly is on the R750 on the Wicklow side of Rathnew.

OWNER Raymond & Josephine Power OPEN All year
ROOMS 51 double/twin/junior suites; all en suite
TERMS €128–163; single supplement
MEALS dinner €50–55

## Saraville
Redcross, Co. Wicklow
Tel: 0404 41745 Fax: 0404 41745

Right in the middle of the little village of Redcross, Saraville is a small, modernised house with some farm buildings at the back. The Flemings farm in a small way and keep horses. The house is immaculately clean, the cooking fresh and wholesome, with freshly-squeezed orange juice for breakfast and homemade food using local produce available by request for dinner and lunch. The bedrooms have TV and there is a living room with TV. Pets outside only. Children are very welcome, the hostess is charming, and the atmosphere is friendly and relaxing.

OWNER Henry & Sarah Fleming OPEN May 1–September 30
ROOMS 3 double; 2 en suite, 1 public bathroom TERMS €35; single supplement; child reduction MEALS dinner €18, packed lunch, light tea

## Kilpatrick House
Redcross, Co. Wicklow
Tel: 0404 47137 Fax: 0404 47866
Email: info@kilpatrickhouse.com
Website: www.kilpatrickhouse.com

Between the N11 and Redcross, Kilpatrick House is a most attractive Georgian country house set in nicely landscaped gardens, enjoying pleasant farmland views, and is part of a beef rearing farm. The bedrooms are spacious and guests have use of a formal sitting room. Pets accepted. Mastercard and Visa taken. The house is signposted off the N11 at Jack White's Cross.

OWNER Shirley Kingston OPEN April 1–November 5
ROOMS 1 double, 1 twin, 1 family en suite
TERMS €30-35; single supplement; child reduction

## Park Lodge
Clonegal, Shillelagh, Co. Wicklow
Tel: 055 29140
Email: parklodge@hotmail.com

This charming, whitewashed Georgian farmhouse is in a peaceful, rural setting enjoying lovely views of the Wicklow Mountains. It is surrounded by its 200 acre mixed farm, and sheep, geese and guinea fowl roam close to the house. Guests here enjoy genuine Irish farmhouse hospitality with home baking, fresh farm produce, and a cheerful, friendly atmosphere. The house offers old fashioned comfort with large rooms and pretty, quilted bedcovers. Local amenities include horse riding, fishing, golf and walking. Park Lodge stands just above the very minor road from Shillelagh to Clonegal. Pets outside only. Major credit cards accepted.

OWNER Mrs Bridie Osborne OPEN Easter–end October
ROOMS 3 double/twin en suite TERMS €35; single supplement

## WICKLOW

### Lissadell House
Ashtown Lane, Wicklow, Co. Wicklow
Tel: 0404 67458
Email: lissadellhse@eircom.net

Built in the Georgian style, Lissadell is a modern house surrounded by its own grounds on the outskirts of Wicklow, and is part of a mixed farm. The Klaues, who built the house themselves, are a most friendly couple, and the house has a welcoming, warm atmosphere. The rooms are plainly decorated and furnished, and there is a pleasant sitting room and dining room. Both rooms have French windows that open onto the lawn and garden. Pets outside only. To reach Lissadell House turn off the N11 Wicklow to Wexford road at the Beehive Pub on to the R751. Signposted at the first turning to left.

OWNER Patricia Klaue OPEN April 1–November 1
ROOMS 3 double/twin, 1 family; 2 en suite, 2 public bathrooms
TERMS €30–34; single supplement; child reduction

### Silver Sands
Dunbur Road, Wicklow, Co. Wicklow
Tel: 0404 68243
Email: lyladoyle@eircom.net

This modern, friendly bungalow is on the coast road just outside the town centre. It has a reputation for its warm welcome and has lovely sea views. The bedrooms are on the small side, immaculately clean and simply furnished. They have hair-dryers and tea- and coffee-making facilities, and three are on the ground floor. Guests share the family lounge and breakfast is served in the bright dining room overlooking the sea. Lyla Doyle is down to earth and friendly, always willing to help plan outings to local events and places of interest. Pets outside.

OWNER Mrs Lyla Doyle OPEN All year except for Christmas
ROOMS 2 double, 2 twin, 1 family; en suite or private bathrooms
TERMS €35; single supplement; child reduction

# COUNTY CORK

Ireland's largest county has a spectacular coastline which alternates between long, sandy beaches and wild, rugged cliffs, high, rocky mountains, corn-covered farmland and subtropical gardens. Cork city is a bustling, cosmopolitan, friendly place founded by St Finbar in the sixth century on some dry land in the Great Marsh of Munster—Cork meaning 'a marsh.' The appearance of much of the city is nineteenth-century, with elegant, wide streets.

The famous Blarney stone-kissing—it gives you the gift of the gab—is at the castle, one of the largest and finest tower houses in Ireland. Nineteenth-century Cóbh, with its Gothic cathedral, is Cork's harbour, some 24 km from the city. Beyond, westward along the coast, is Kinsale, an attractive old town, popular with yachtsmen, and packed with people enjoying its many restaurants and old buildings. There are marvellous cliffs at the Old Head of Kinsale and the remains of a fifteenth-century castle, plus a lovely sandy beach at Garretstown.

Youghal is a most attractive seaside town, with many interesting things to see, including the Clock Gate and St Mary's Collegiate Church. Sir Walter Raleigh is said to have planted the first potato in his garden during the time he was mayor of the town. Nearby is Shanagarry with its pottery, where William Penn lived, and Ballycotton, a small fishing village.

The coastal scenery west of Skibbereen is particularly beautiful, and the view from Gabriel Mountain, which can be easily climbed, is spectacular. Garnish Island has a wonderful garden, which can be visited most days. Bantry House is a most interesting house with a superb view. Castle Hyde, a Georgian house close to Fermoy and former home of Douglas Hyde, first President of the Irish Republic, is one of the most beautiful houses in Ireland. Macroom is set in glorious countryside—the road across the pass of Keimaneigh and through the forest of Gougance Barra is particularly beautiful.

## BALLYLICKEY

**Ballylickey Manor House**
Ballylickey, Co. Cork
Tel: 027 50071 Fax: 027 50124
Email: ballymh@eircom.net
Website: www.ballylickeymanorhouse.com

On the boundary of Cork and Kerry, amidst sheltered lawns, flower gardens and parkland and bordered by sea, river and mountains, stands Ballylickey House. Commanding a magnificent view over Bantry Bay, Ballylickey was built some 300 years ago by Lord Kenmare as a shooting lodge. It has been the home of the Graves family for over four generations. Robert Graves, the poet, was an

Ballylickey Manor House

uncle of the present owner. The house was burnt down in recent years, but was rebuilt, incorporating the best of the old features with a new standard of comfort. This elegant residence is exquisitely decorated with many pieces of antique furniture. One of the main features of a stay at Ballylickey is the food, which is superbly prepared and presented, and served with great elegance in the attractive dining room. The bedrooms are luxurious and all have TV, telephone, hair-dryers and trouser press. The suites include bedroom, sitting room and bathroom. Some of the rooms are in the manor house, and others are delightful garden cottages around the swimming pool and gardens. A restaurant by the pool is open for lunch. The four hectares of grounds include a croquet lawn. There are two golf courses nearby, miles of mountainous coastline, fishing, and two of the finest botanical gardens to visit. No pets. Visa and American Express accepted. The house is between Bantry and Glengarriff on the N71.

OWNER Mr & Mrs Graves OPEN April–November
ROOMS 7 suites, 7 double; all en suite TERMS €80–170
MEALS dinner from €47

## BANDON

### Glebe Country House
Ballinadee, Bandon, Co. Cork
Tel: 021 4778294 Fax: 021 4778456
Email: glebehse@indigo.ie
Website: indigo.ie/~glebehse

Set next to the church in the centre of Ballinadee, Glebe Country House is a very pretty Georgian rectory, which was carefully renovated and subsequently redecorated after extensive damage during the 1997 Christmas storm. The bedrooms are spacious and attractively decorated and furnished, some with views of the river. All have hair-dryers, telephone, irons and tea- and coffee-making facilities. Guests have the run of the house, which includes a large drawing room with television and open fire, and the dining room where good home-cooked dinners are served featuring organically home-grown salads and herbs.

Guests should bring their own wine. Gill Good is a bright, cheerful person, and the atmosphere is friendly and informal. The attractive garden contains a croquet lawn and 'fun' grass tennis court. Three self-catering units are available. Ballinadee is a 15 minute drive from Kinsale. There are several nearby golf courses, and river fishing and sea angling can be arranged. Dogs by arrangement. Visa and Mastercard accepted.

OWNER Gill Good OPEN All year except Christmas and New Year ROOMS 2 double, 2 twin; all en suite TERMS €45–50 pps; single supplement; child reduction MEALS dinner €30

## Kilbrogan House
Kilbrogan Hill, Bandon, Co. Cork
Tel: 023 44935/086 3689939 Fax: 023 44935
Email: fitz@kilbrogan.com
Website: www.kilbrogan.com

Kilbrogan House is a real labour of love for Catherine FitzMaurice—a twelve year project to restore this lovely Georgian townhouse, which Catherine did while still working in London. Doors, ornate ceilings and wooden and tile floors have all been meticulously pre-served, as has the old conservatory, which is halfway up the stairs between the ground and first floors and overlooks the extensive, nicely landscaped back garden. The gracious reception rooms encom-pass a dining room, downstairs sitting room, computer room and original first floor drawing room. Bedrooms are comfortable, spa-cious and all have bathrooms with bath and shower. Dinner is avail-able, if arranged in advance. Kilbrogan House is an ideal base for exploring south and west Cork. No pets. Most major credit cards.

OWNER Catherine FitzMaurice OPEN March 1–October 31 ROOMS 4 double, 1 twin; all en suite TERMS €45 pps; single supplement MEALS dinner €25

## St Anne's
Clonakilty Road, Bandon, Co. Cork
Tel: 023 44239 Fax: 023 44239
Email: stannesbandon@eircom.net

This attractive Georgian house was in need of work when Anne Buckley bought it. She did a great job renovating it, and now the house offers bright and attractively furnished bedrooms, equipped with TV and tea- and coffee-making facilities. Both the dining room, where breakfast only is served, and the sitting room have their origi-

St Anne's

nal fireplaces, and guests can enjoy the pretty garden at the back of the property. Anne is an ex-school teacher, very charming and attentive to the needs of her guests. No pets. No smoking in the bedrooms. St Anne's is 1 km from Bandon on the N71 to Clonakilty.

OWNER Anne Buckley OPEN All year except for Christmas ROOMS 1 double, 1 twin, 1 single, 2 family; all en suite TERMS €30 pps; single supplement; child reduction

## BANTRY

### Bantry House
Bantry, Co. Cork
Tel: 027 50047 Fax: 027 50795
Website: www.hidden-ireland.com/bantry

Bantry House, overlooking Bantry Bay, is one of the finest stately mansions in Ireland. Purchased by the White family in 1739, it is furnished with the most wonderful collection of pictures, furniture and works of art. The White family were also responsible for laying out the formal gardens. Both the east and west wings of Bantry House provide newly refurbished en suite accommodation, all with telephone, hair-dryers and tea- and coffee-making facilities. Residents have use of a sitting room, bar, library and a balcony TV room overlooking the Italian garden with its fountain, parterres and 'stairway to the sky'. There is a wine license, and guests are welcome to help themselves to drinks from the bar. Bantry House is open to the public and overnight guests are admitted at no extra charge. There is a tennis court, tea room and craft shop on the premises. Evening meals are sometimes available, but must be booked by noon. No pets. Smoking permitted in bar and lounge. Visa, Mastercard and American Express accepted.

OWNER Egerton Shelswell-White OPEN March 1–October 31 ROOMS 5 double, 2 twin, 1 family; all en suite TERMS €108–150 pps; MEALS dinner €31.50

## Dunauley

Seskin, Bantry, Co. Cork
Tel: 027 50290 Fax: 027 50290
Email: rosemarymcauley@eircom.net
Website: www.dunauley.com

Dunauley stands in a spectacular position with magnificent views of
Bantry Bay and the Caha Mountains. It is located above Bantry town
in its own garden. Rosemary McAuley is a warm and welcoming host
and serves a wonderful breakfast, including freshly-squeezed orange
juice and drop scones, in the spacious lounge-cum-dining room,
which takes full advantage of the view. Three of the bedrooms are
on the ground floor, and they are furnished simply and comfortably
and have hair-dryers and tea- and coffee-making facilities. There is a
self-catering unit available.

   Dunauley is an ideal base for hill walking, cycling and for exploring
the gardens and west Cork bays. Pets in car only. Arriving in Bantry,
follow signs for hospital until Dunauley is signposted.

OWNER Rosemary McAuley OPEN May 1–September 30
ROOMS 2 double, 2 twin; all en suite TERMS €35–40;
single supplement; not suitable for children

## Hillcrest House

Ahakista, Bantry, Co. Cork  Tel: 027 67045
Email: agneshegarty@oceanfree.net
Website: www.ahakista.com

Hillcrest is an attractive, old stone dairy farm that was renovated a
few years ago, and stands in a lovely position on top of a hill overlooking Dunmanus Bay on the 'Sheep's Head' peninsula. An extension
was built onto the house, linking it with the old barn which now
houses the games room, where guests can play table tennis and
darts. There are flagstone floors, peat fires and simply furnished and
decorated bedrooms, which have hair-dryers and tea- and coffee-
making facilities.

   Fresh farm produce is used for evening meals and breakfast, as is
home baking. Hillcrest is a five minute walk to a sandy beach ; there
is good sea fishing and mountain walking behind the house, and the
Sheep's Head Way walking path runs by the property. Pets outside
or in car only. The house is signposted from Durrus.

OWNER Mrs Agnes Hegarty OPEN All year
ROOMS 2 double, 2 twin, 2 family; en suite or with private bathrooms
TERMS €35; single supplement; child reduction
MEALS dinner, high tea

## The Mill

New Town, Glengarriff Road, Bantry, Co. Cork
Tel: 027 50278 Fax: 027 50278
Email: bbthemill@eircom.net
Website: www.the-mill.net

Tosca and Kees Kramer fell in love with Bantry while on an Irish
holiday from their native Holland, so they stayed and made Ireland
their home. The Mill is a chalet-style house, set back from the road
in colourful gardens. Most of the bedrooms are on the ground floor
and have hair-dryers and TV. Kees Kramer is not only a craftsman,
making all the wardrobes, cabinets and dining room tables, but also
an artist. A selection of his work can be found around the house.

A conservatory in front is furnished with cane pieces, is a warm,
sunny spot for visitors to sit and relax. The Mill offers a laundry
service, there is a kitchen area for guests to make drinks, and there
are bicycles for hire. The house is on the main Bantry to Glengarriff
road and the town centre is only a five minute walk away. There are
plenty of excellent pubs and restaurants in the area, and close by are
possibilities for golf, fishing and horseback riding. No pets.

OWNER Tosca Kramer OPEN Easter–October 31 ROOMS 6 double,
4 twin, 1 family; all en suite TERMS €35; single supplement; child
reduction

## BLARNEY

## Ashlee Lodge

Tower, Blarney, Co. Cork
Tel: 021 4385346 Fax: 021 4385726
Email: ashlee@iol.ie
Website: www.welcome.to/ashleelodge

Ashlee Lodge is a modern, whitewashed bungalow with a porticoed
front porch standing in the village of Tower, three kilometres from
Blarney. John and Anne, who used to be in the hotel business, constantly strive to offer their guests top quality accommodation.

The latest refurbishment has resulted in spacious rooms equipped
with every possible need, including air conditioning, whirlpool baths,

Ashlee Lodge

wide screen TV, hi-fi unit, safe and internet access. One room is suitable for the disabled. Ashlee Lodge is professionally run and immaculately clean, and has a pleasant open plan sitting/dining room with cathedral ceilings and fireplace.

Aromatherapy, Reiki, Reflexology and Massage can be arranged, and there is an outdoor hot tub and courtesy mini bus. There is a pet friendly room. Mastercard, Diners, Visa and American Express cards are accepted. The house can be found on the R617 Blarney to Killarney road.

OWNER Anne & John O'Leary OPEN All year ROOMS 3 double, 3 twin, 4 suites; all en suite TERMS €70–100 pps; single supplement; child reduction MEALS Snack menu

## The Gables
Stoneview, Blarney, Co. Cork
Tel: 021 4385330
Website: www.gablesblarney.com

Surrounded by lovely gardens, and right on the edge of the golf course The gables is well outside the hustle and bustle of Blarney. A Victorian bulding, it was until 1971 the rectory for Blarney. Anne Lynch is a quietly, friendly lady and her husband is interested in geneaology and history, and is a great source of knowledge for visitors. The house has a lot of character and is comfortably furnished. A tiny sun room at the top of the stairs is a great spot to sit and look out over the garden. There are views of Blarney Castle from parts of the house, The Gables is two kilometres outside Blarney.

OWNER Anne Lynch OPEN 1 March–30 November ROOMS 1 triple, 2 double/twin, all en suite TERMS €30 single supplement

## Traveller's Joy
Tower, Blarney, Co. Cork
Tel: 021 4385541

Traveller's Joy is an unassuming little bungalow set in a pretty garden, but what makes it special is the friendly welcome from warm-hearted Gertie O'Shea and the atmosphere of a home away from home. The rooms are basic and spotlessly clean and there is a cosy guest lounge with TV, off which is the small breakfast room where breakfasts 'to last you the day' are served. A recent extension to the front of the house has enlarged the lounge area and one of the bedrooms.

The O'Sheas are happy to offer advice on local sightseeing and where to find the best traditional entertainment. Pets outside only, and smoking is permitted in the lounge. Visa and Mastercard are accepted. Traveller's Joy is in the village of Tower, 3km from Blarney.

OWNER Sean & Gertie O'Shea OPEN January 10– December 20
ROOMS 1 twin, 2 family; all en suite TERMS €30–32; child reduction

BUTLERSTOWN

**Sea Court**
Butlerstown, Co. Cork
Tel: 023 40151 & 023 40218 or 513 961 2527 (U.S.A.)
Fax: 513 721 5109 (U.S.A.)
Email: seacourt_inn@yahoo.com

Set in four hectares of wooded parkland, Sea Court is a handsome
Georgian country house, built in 1760 by the Longfield family. David
Elder, an American, acquired it on a visit to Ireland some 25 years
ago–a daunting project as he spends the greater part of the year
practising law in Kentucky, and the house was in serious need of
repair. Restoration took place, gradually but meticulously, and eventually it was opened up to overnight visitors during the summer, and
for self-catering parties at other times of the year. It has been furnished simply with antiques and has comfortable bedrooms, one of
which used to be the Edwardian ballroom wing, and four have sea
views. Breakfasts are quite a feast and include scones made from the
owner's own recipe. Gourmet dinners are available if booked in
advance - guests are welcome to bring their own wine. Pets in car,
or outbuilding. Sea Court lies between Courtmacsherry Bay and
Dunworley Bay and is within walking distance of the Coolim Cliffs,
said to be the second highest in Ireland, Timoleague with its monastic ruins is 7 kilometres away, Kinsale and the Old Head Golf
Course is a 40 minute drive and Clonakilty within easy reach. The
house can be found a couple of hundred yards from the centre of
Butlerstown.

OWNER David A. Elder & Monica Bohlen OPEN June 1–August 20
ROOMS 4 double, 1 twin, 1 family; 5 en suite, 1 private bath
TERMS €60–70; child reduction MEALS dinner €40

CASTLELYONS

**Ballyvolane House**
Castlelyons, nr. Fermoy, Co. Cork
Tel: 025 36349 Fax: 025 36781
Email: ballyvol@iol.ie
Website: www.ballyvolanehouse.ie

In a magnificent parkland setting, Ballyvolane is a gracious, beautifully
restored country house. It is surrounded by its own farmland, wooded grounds (quite spectacular in bluebell time), formal terraced gardens and three restored lakes stocked with trout. It was built in
1728 on the site of an older house and later altered to the Italianate

style. Guests experience here a blend of elegance, informality and charming hosts. Justin and Jenny Green recently took over the house from Justin's parents, Merrie and Jeremy - so the tradition of great hospitality continues.

Ballyvolane House

The Greens have done a superb job, gradually furnishing and restoring the house, which offers nine very comfortable and spacious bedrooms, all with hair-dryer and TV, and one of the bathrooms has a wonderful old bathtub, encased in wood and raised on two steps. The lovely pillared hall has a baby grand piano and plenty of comfortable chairs in front of the open fire. Beautifully presented delicious food is served in the elegant dining room at the long dining room table, the open fire is lit both in the evening and at breakfast time. Guests serve themselves drinks from the honesty bar by the sitting room. Salmon fishing is available by arrangement on Ballyvolane's own stretch of the River Blackwater; there is trout fishing in the lakes and a croquet lawn. Pets in car or outhouse only. Visa, Mastercard, Diners and American Express accepted. There are signs for the house on the N8 at River Bride and the R628 just before Rathcormac coming from Cork.

OWNER Justin Green OPEN All year except for Christmas ROOMS 6 double, 3 twin; all en suite TERMS €90; single supplement; child reduction MEALS dinner €40

## CASTLETOWNSHEND

### Bow Hall
Castletownshend, Co. Cork
Tel: 028 36114

Dating from the late seventeenth century, Bow Hall is right in the centre of the picturesque village of Castletownshend, whose one steep street leads to the harbour and sea. The Vickerys are a delightful retired couple from New York state who have lived here in excess of 20 years and have created a charming home. The bedrooms are light and spacious, with some American furniture.

Breakfast is a grand affair, with home-made sausages and pancakes a particular treat. Good home-cooked dinners are served in the dining room and the large drawing room-cum-library has floor to ceiling bookshelves at one end with a fireplace at the other; all kinds of ornaments and knick-knacks are found throughout the house. The slate-faced frontage overlooks a very large, immaculately kept walled garden. No smoking. No pets.

OWNER Dick & Barbara Vickery OPEN All year except for Christmas ROOMS 3 double; 1 en suite TERMS from €35; single supplement MEALS dinner from €25

## CLONAKILTY

### An Garran Coir
Rathbarry, Clonakilty, Co. Cork
Tel: 023 48236 Fax: 023 48236
Email: angarrancoir@eircom.net
Website: www.angarrancoir.com

The original family farmhouse is close to the old farm buildings, some 200 metres up the lane. An Garran Coir was built by the Calnans and then extended to accommodate bed & breakfast guests. It offers clean and comfortable rooms equipped with TV, tea- and coffee-making facilities and hair-dryers. Facilities include a jacuzzi, a smartly decorated lounge with plush red chairs, and a dining room with a piano and a reception with an Irish Coffee Bar. Evening meals using fruit and herbs from the herb garden are available by arrangement, and you can pick your own free-range eggs for breakfast. Children are well catered for with their own play area, and they can go for rides with a leading rein on the farm pony. Adults can use the tennis court, play croquet or take a lovely walk to the award winning village of Rathbarry. Pets outside. Smoking outside. The farm is signposted off Skibbereen to Clonakilty road.

OWNER Michael & Jo Calnan OPEN All year ROOMS 2 double, 2 twin, 1 family; all en suite TERMS €33–35; single supplement; child reduction MEALS dinner €15–25

### Ard Na Greine
Ballinascarthy, Clonakilty, Co. Cork
Tel: 023 39104 Fax: 023 39397
Email: normawalsh1@eircom.net
Website: www.ardnagreine.com

Ard Na Greine is a working dairy farm set in pleasant farming countryside and enjoying lovely views. The atmosphere is friendly and informal, and guests immediately feel at home, many returning year after year. Pets by arrangement. Norma Walsh is hospitable, warm-hearted and offers simple farmhouse comfort, as well as copious amounts of good home-cooked food. The bedrooms are comfortable and have hair-dryers, and there is a cosy TV lounge and dining room with separate tables where both breakfast and dinner or lighter meals are served. There is no license, but guests are welcome to provide their own wine. Ard Na Greine is well placed for Kinsale and visiting the attractive south and west Cork coastlines, and some guests like to watch the cows being milked. Visa accepted. Farm is signposted on N71 near Ballinascarthy, 8 miles from Bandon, 4 miles from Clonakilty

.

OWNER Norma Walsh OPEN All year ROOMS 1 double, 2 twin, 2 family en suite, 1 single; 1 public bathroom TERMS €35–40; single supplement; child reduction MEALS dinner €25–35

## Duvane Farm
Ballyduvane, Clonakilty, Co. Cork
Tel: 023 33129 Fax: 023 33129

This Georgian farmhouse was built around 1870 and has been in the McCarthy family for quite a while; before that it belonged to a bishop. It is beautifully furnished and has some brass and half tester beds, and all the bedrooms have hair-dryers. The farm supports cattle, the attractive farm buildings lying behind the house, there is woodland, and a lovely garden where guests can sit and relax. Breakfast includes honey from the farm's own bees. Pets can be accommodated in the stables. Duvane Farm can be found on the N71, two kilometres west of Clonakilty.

OWNER Noreen McCarthy OPEN March 15–November 15 ROOMS 4 double/twin/family; 3 en suite, 1 private bathroom TERMS €33–35; single supplement; child reduction MEALS dinner €20–21, high tea €14

**CORK**

## Garnish House
Western Road, Cork, Co. Cork
Tel: 021 4275111 Fax: 021 4273872
Email: garnish@iol.ie
Website: www.garnish.ie

Conveniently located on the western edge of town opposite University College Cork, Garnish House is a double-fronted Victorian town house, set back from the main road by its parking area. It is a comfortable house, efficiently run in a businesslike fashion by pleasant, helpful staff and offering such facilities as a night porter and a 24-hour service for arrivals and departures. The bedrooms vary in size, some being quite spacious, and quite a few have jacuzzi baths. They all have hair-dryers, trouser press, telephone, TV and tea- and coffee-making facilities, as well as fresh fruit and flowers. Guests have use of a small TV lounge, and breakfast with its extensive menu is served in the dining room 6 a.m. until 11 a.m. or midday. No pets. All major credit cards accepted.

OWNER Johanna Lucey OPEN All year ROOMS 3 twin, 1 single, 8 double, 3 family; all en suite TERMS €50–70; single supplement; child reduction

### River View
Douglas East, Cork, Co. Cork
Tel: 021 4893762 Fax: 021 4893762
Email: edwardsc@eircom.net

River View, which is a Georgian style house built in the Victorian era, can be found right in the centre of Douglas village. Mr and Mrs Edwards are a charming couple who offer their guests a personal service, and the atmosphere is warm and welcoming. The lounge/dining room has the original fireplace and is interestingly furnished, and the bedrooms are a good size with comfortable beds, TV, hair-dryers and tea- and coffee-making facilities. No pets and no smoking. The house is 100 metres from Barry's Pub, next to the Garda Station, and about one and a half kilometres from the centre of Cork, which can be reached by bus.

OWNER Catherine Edwards OPEN All year except for Christmas ROOMS 1 double, 2 twin; all en suite TERMS €35 pps; single supplement €9.50; child reduction

## DONERAILE

### Creagh House
Main Street, Doneraile, Co. Cork
Tel: 022 24433 Fax: 022 24715
Email: creaghhouse@eircom.net
Website: www.creaghhouse.ie

Michael O'Sullivan and Laura O'Mahony, both environmental engineers, were looking for a small house in Co. Cork. They ended up with 10,000 square feet of Creagh House–room for themselves and guests! Renovation was a mammoth task, but the results are quite spectacular. Built in the early 1800s, Creagh House, is considered to be one of the finest and largest Georgian townhouses outside Dublin. The magnificent ceiling cornices have been painstakingly restored, and the sheer size of the rooms is almost overpowering.

The hallway, broken down into two halves by double doors, the drawing and dining room are each 600 square feet in size. The house has many literary associations, including Thackeray (whose wife was a Creagh), Elizabeth Bowen, Canon Sheehan and Daniel O'Connell. For anyone with an interest in history or literature Michael is an enthusiastic expert.

Off street parking. Major credit cards accepted. Supper must be booked by noon, and is served from 8-10 p.m. Creagh House is adjacent to the Golf Club and Doneraile Court.

OWNER Michael O'Sullivan & Laura O'Mahony
OPEN March–October ROOMS 3 double en suite
TERMS €70–90; single supplement MEALS supper €25

## FARRAN

**Farran House**
Farran, Co. Cork
Tel: 021 733 1215 Fax: 021 733 1450
Email: info@farranhouse.com
Website: www.farranhouse.com

When Patricia Wiese and John Kehely bought Farran House it was a bigger undertaking than they had imagined. Restoration work took five years, and they opened for business in 1997. It is a gracious Georgian residence, built in 1750 and remodelled in 1806, standing in lovely grounds with wonderful views of the hills of the Lee Valley and overlooking the medieval castle and abbey of Kilcrea. In later years the house was divided into seven flats, and Patricia and John were lucky enough to have the drawings of the 1806 house, which they've restored back to the layout of that era. They have sympathetically left large rooms intact and converted whole rooms into bathrooms. The result is four exceptionally large bedrooms, one of which is a four-poster, each one having windows on two sides affording a lot of light and different aspects of the surrounding countryside. The rooms have TV, phone and hair-dryers, and all have very large bathrooms, one with a claw foot bath and fireplace. Downstairs there is a drawing room, billiard room and dining room with patio off for fine weather breakfasts.

The house retains its wooden floors, and the furniture and decor is simple, tasteful and unfussy. Tea and coffee are available in the dining room, and a kitchen adjacent to the dining room can be used if the whole house is let to one group. The coach house, which used to be the old kitchen with servants' quarters above, is now a delightful self-catering unit with one enormous open room downstairs and three bedrooms above. No pets. Major credit cards accepted. Farran House can be found off the N22, 15 kilometres west of Cork.

OWNER Patricia Wiese & John Kehely OPEN April 1–October 31
ROOMS 4 double/ twin; all en suite TERMS €70–100; single supplement €15; child reduction; MEALS dinner €31.50

**Glanworth Mill**
Glanworth, Co. Cork
Tel: 025 38555 Fax: 025 38560
Email: glanworth@iol.ie
Website: www.iol.ie/glanworth

This late eighteenth century mill below the ruins of medieval
Glanworth Castle and beside the narrow fifteenth-century bridge is
in an idyllic setting. Lynne Glasscoe and Emelyn Heaps have done
wonders renovating the old building, which they acquired in
September 1997 and opened for business 22 weeks later. The restaurants are open to the public, as is the new craft shop.

The Mill Tea Rooms, an attractive flag stoned room where the old
mill wheel turns, offers light meals, and the charming restaurant,
plainly furnished and decorated in fresh, bright colours is where dinner is served. A small cosy drawing room/library leads into the tea
rooms, beyond which are the attractively laid out courtyard
gardens–a popular place to eat when the weather is fine enough, and
the site of the new leisure gardens.

Each bedroom has its own theme and decor based on the literary
figures associated with the area and with its name inscribed on a
piece of slate on the door. One room–the Seamus Murphy
room–has the exposed stone of the hillside into which it is built.
Major credit cards accepted.

OWNER Lynne Glasscoe & Emelyn Heaps OPEN All year except for
Christmas ROOMS 10 double; all en suite TERMS €57–64; single supplement €12.50 MEALS à la carte meals all day

**Ardnagashel Lodge**
Glengarriff, Co. Cork
Tel: 027 51687
Email: ardnagashel@eircom.net

Neither the original Lodge, or the big house still stand. Built by the
Ronaynes in the early 1990s with bed & breakfast guests in mind,
this replacement Lodge is a neat, attractive, small whitewashed
house. Ardnagashel Lodge stands in pretty gardens just inside a massive stone archway off the main road between Bantry and
Glengarriff. The bedrooms are bright and simply decorated, there's
an attractive small sitting room and breakfast is served in the con-

servatory like room overlooking the gardens. TV and tea and coffee can be put in the rooms by request. Golf, fishing and good restaurants and pubs are nearby.

No smoking, no pets. Not suitable for children. There is a 3% charge if a credit card is used for payment.

OWNER Eleanor Ronayne OPEN May–September
ROOMS 2 twin, 1 double; all en suite
TERMS €30–35; single supplement €10

## Cois Coille
Glengarriff, Co. Cork
Tel: 027 63202
Email: coiscoille@eircom.net

This modern house is approached up a very steep driveway and stands in a commanding position overlooking Bantry Bay and Garnish Island, and is set in a lovely hillside garden. It is a peaceful spot by the woodlands of Glengarriff and within walking distance of the village.

The house has been taken over from Rita Barry-Murphy by her daughter, Niamh, who continues the high standards of welcome and comfort set by her mother. The attractive bedrooms are all en suite, and have hair-dryers and tea- and coffee-making facilities, and there is an extensive breakfast menu. Pets to be kept in the car. Cois Coille is off the Bantry road on the edge of the village.

OWNER Niamh Barry-Murphy OPEN April–October
ROOMS 3 double, 2 twin, 1 family; all en suite
TERMS €34; single supplement; child reduction

## GOLEEN

### Fortview House
Gurtyowen, Toormore, Goleen, Co. Cork
Tel: 028 35324
Email: fortviewhousegoleen@eircom.net

Although built only a few years ago by the Connells, Fortview House has an air of rustic charm. A small, stone built farmhouse on a working dairy farm, it is an excellent location for exploring the Mizen Head, Sheep's Head and the Beara Peninsula. The interior of the house is very attractive: fresh and bright and quite simply but comfortably furnished with pine floors, antique country pine furniture, brass and iron beds. Drinks are available by donation in the sitting room. The bedrooms all have hair-dryers and mineral water. The dining room has a tiled floor, wood-burning stove; excellent breakfasts are served which include freshly-squeezed orange juice and pancakes. Evening meals are available by arrangement and are served in the conservatory. There is also a self-catering cottage. No pets. Fortview House is located 10 km from both Schull and Goleen on the R591, signposted at Toormore.

OWNER Violet Connell OPEN March 1–November 1
ROOMS 5 double/twin/family; all en suite TERMS from €38; single supplement MEALS dinner from €25

### The Heron's Cove
The Harbour, Goleen. Co. Cork
Tel: 028 35225 Fax: 028 35422
Email: suehill@eircom.net
Website: www.heronscove.com

Right on the edge of the water, The Heron's Cove, is in an idyllic spot overlooking a small picturesque cove on the edge of the little village of Goleen. Four of the five bedrooms have this view, which is better still from their balconies. Downstairs a large room with wooden floors and simple pine furniture and the same lovely out-look serves as bar, cosy sitting area and restaurant. A small outside patio is a wonderful place on a sunny day. The restaurant is known for its organic fare and fresh fish, but duck, lamb and vegetarian choices are also on the menu. Goleen is ten kilometres from Mizen Head, Ireland's spectacular most south westerly point, with the Fastnet Rock lighthouse. The Heron's Cove is a great place for beaches and hill walking along majestic cliffs. No pets. Most major credit cards accepted.

OWNER Sue Hill OPEN closed for Christmas ROOMS 1 twin, 3 double, 1 family; all en suite TERMS €25–35; single supplement; child reduction MEALS dinner

## KANTURK

### Glenlohane
Kanturk, Co. Cork
Tel: 029 50014 Fax: 029 51100
Email: info@glenlohane.com
Website: www.glenlohane.com

Glenlohane is a superb Georgian country house set in beautiful parkland grounds with some wonderful old trees and views to the distant mountains. The present owners are direct descendants of the family who built it in 1741. Desmond lived and worked in the United States and Melanie is American, and between them they have combined the very best of modern comforts with the character and atmosphere of the past. Glenlohane is an informal house with good food and log fires to relax in front of. The large comfortable drawing room features a square bay window, a superb full-length mirror, baby grand piano, grey marble fireplace and interesting pictures and furniture. There is also a small study filled with books, a dining room and a country kitchen. A traditional stable yard is attached to the house, where visitors' horses can be housed by arrangement. There are plenty of animals around, and the farm includes sheep and cattle. Guests are welcome to watch the daily farm activities, to play croquet, or just relax in the old walled garden. With notice, riding, or hunting with the Duhallow Hunt, the oldest pack of hounds in Ireland, can be arranged. Fishing is available only one kilometre away on the River Blackwater, and there are a variety of golf courses and lovely walks nearby. To reach Glenlohane from Kanturk take the Glenlohane

R576 towards Mallow, bear left on the R580 towards Buttevant, then take the first right towards Ballyclough. Look for the first residential entrance on the left after 2.2 kilometres - there is no sign. Pets by arrangement. Visa, Mastercard and American Express accepted.

OWNER Desmond & Melanie Sharp Bolster OPEN All year
ROOMS 3 double, 2 twin; all en suite TERMS €100;
single supplement; not suitable for children under 12
MEALS dinner €40

KILBRITTAIN

**The Glen Country House**
Kilbrittain, Co. Cork
Tel: 023 49862
Email: dianaandguy@eircom.net
Website: www.glencountryhouse.ie

This Victorian farmhouse set in 300 acres of its own farmland with views of Courtmacsherry Bay offers guests a wonderfully relaxing stay. The tenth generation of the family to have lived on the property, Guy and Diana Scott completely renovated the house in 2003, both for their own family, and with guests in mind.

Bedrooms are spacious and beautifully furnished, some having views of the bay, and the family suite's two rooms has a bathroom in between, which is ideal for families. Produce from the walled kitchen garden, free-range eggs, and local organic food provide the breakfast ingredients. A baby-sitting service can be provided and dogs can be accommodated  in an outside building. Kinsale, with its many restaurants, is a 20-minute drive away, and within ten minutes are many other restaurants to choose from. There are beautiful sandy beaches, golf courses, sea and river fishing, riding and endless walking opportunities nearby.

All major credit cards accepted except American Express.

OWNER Diana & Guy Scott OPEN Easter–October 31
ROOMS 4 double/twin, 1 family; all en suite TERMS €60

## KILLEAGH

**Ballymakeigh House**
Killeagh, Co. Cork
Tel: 024 95184 Fax: 024 95370
Email: ballymakeigh@eircom.net
Website: www.ballmakeighhouse.com

The friendliest of welcomes, superb food and comfortable rooms make Ballymakeigh House a delightful place to stay. The 250 year old farmhouse is located in the rich farmlands of east Cork and guests are welcome to walk around the intensive dairy farm and watch the cows being milked. For the energetic there are bicycles available, a full-size hard tennis court and horseback riding with a variety of courses on offer at the new Equestrian Centre, run by the Browne's daughter. The conservatory offers lots of sunny sitting space, and the bedrooms are constantly being upgraded and are equipped with every comfort, including hair-dryers. Margaret has won countless awards over the years, including Housewife of the Year, Guesthouse of the Year, AA Landlady of the Year, and has written a book containing some of her favourite recipes - 'Through my Kitchen Window'. Copies are available for sale at the house. Dinner is now available at the newly opened restaurant - Brownes - which is two miles away on the main road to Youghal, and transport is provided for those who don't want to drive. Margaret is a superb cook, and a stay at Ballymakeigh would not be complete without a meal at Brownes. This is a marvellous spot in peaceful and tranquil surroundings, convenient to beaches, Fota Wildlife Park, Trabolgan Leisure Centre and Blarney Castle. No pets. Visa and Mastercard accepted. Ballymakeigh is signposted at the Old Thatch pub in the village of Killeagh on N25.

OWNER Margaret Browne OPEN March–November
ROOMS 3 double, 2 twin, 1 single; all en suite TERMS €50–55;
single supplement; child reduction MEALS dinner €39

**Chart House**
6 Denis Quay, Kinsale, Co. Cork
Tel: 021 4774568 Fax: 021 4777907
Email: charthouse@eircom.net
Website: www.charthouse-kinsale.com

Down a side street off the harbour, Chart House is a delightful Georgian townhouse, which has been completely renovated by Billy and Mary O'Connor. It has a calm and peaceful atmosphere and has been beautifully furnished with antiques. The bedrooms, save the single, are spacious, and some have big bathrooms. Each room has its own colour theme and they all have antique beds (but the best quality mattresses!). Afternoon tea or coffee is offered on arrival in the attractive reception/sitting area. A good menu is available for breakfast, which is served at the William IV table in the dining room. All Kinsale's amenities are within easy walking distance. No pets. Major credit cards accepted.

OWNER The O'Connor family OPEN All year except Christmas
ROOMS 2 double/twin, 1 double, 1 single; all en suite
TERMS €55–85 pps; single supplement

**Desmond House**
42 Cork Street, Kinsale, Co. Cork
Tel: 021 4773575 Fax: 021 4773575
Email: DesmondHouse@compuserve.com

In a quiet spot, in the very centre of Kinsale, Desmond House is a nineteenth-century town house, once the parish priest's home. It has four exceptionally large en suite bedrooms and is comfortably furnished. The rooms have TV, hair-dryers and tea- and coffee-making facilities. The Scallys pride themselves on their breakfast (including home baking and home-made preserves), served in the ground floor breakfast room. Some off street parking is available. No smoking.

OWNER Liam Scally OPEN All year except Christmas
ROOMS 4 twin/ double; all en suite TERMS €60–70; single supplement €15–20

**Old Bank House**
11 Pearse Street, Kinsale, Co. Cork
Tel: 021 4774075 Fax: 0214774296
Email: oldbank@indigo.ie
Website: www.oldbankhousekinsale.com

As its name implies it was originally a bank, dating back some 250 years. When Michael and Marie Riese bought the house fifteen years ago they didn't realise what a massive project they were taking on. The whole building was virtualy gutted and is now transformed into a luxury place to stay with plenty of charm and character. The bedrooms are beautifully furnished and equipped, and a little on the small side, each one having the ability of being either a double or twin.

Breakfast is an occasion, cooked by Michael, a well-known restaurateur in his previous life, and served in the atmospheric long dining room with the original exposed brickwork. The elevator is a big asset to those with bedrooms on the third floor. The Old Bank House is in the very middle of Kinsale, with its harbour, marina, wine bars, pubs and restaurants. All major credit cards, except Diners, accepted.

OWNER Michael & Marie Riese OPEN closed 1–28 December
ROOMS 17 double/twin TERMS from €85; single supplement

## Perryville House
Kinsale, Co. Cork
Tel: 021 4772731 Fax: 021 4772298
Email: sales@perryville.iol.ie
Website: www.perryvillehouse.com

This spectacular house stands right in the centre of Kinsale on the quay overlooking the marina and the colourful streets of the medieval fishing port. Laura Corcoran, who previously owned Albany House in Dublin, bought Perryville House in a very run-down state and transformed it into a place of elegance and comfort, opening for business in 1997. The house is run with a quiet air of friendly professionalism. It has lovely furniture and tasteful décor, the hessian covered floors offsetting colourful rugs.

The bedrooms, which are luxuriously appointed, vary in shape and size, some overlooking the harbour, some in a new wing, but even the smallest room is a good size. They all have TV, hair-dryers, telephone, trouser press and mineral water, and the majority have separate baths and showers in the en suite bathrooms.

The drawing room, where morning coffee and afternoon tea are served daily, is comfortable and elegant, and the large, open reception area is another place to sit and relax. Substantial buffet-style breakfasts are available in the dining room, including home-baked breads and preserves, local cheeses and fresh fruit. No pets, no smoking and no children under 13 years. Visa, Access and Mastercard accepted.

OWNER Laura Corcoran OPEN April 8– end October
ROOMS 22 double/twin/ 4 junior suites; all en suite
TERMS €100–190 MEALS Irish breakfast €12

**Raheen House**
Ballinspittle, Kinsale, Co. Cork
Tel: 021 4778173 Fax: 021 4778173
Email: info@raheenhouse.com
Website: www.raheenhouse.com

Raheen House belonged to Maria Sweetnam's grandparents. Maria, a bright, cheerful mother of teenage children, and her builder husband, have added to and improved the house over the years. Guests now enjoy very comfortable accommodation, with three en suite rooms upstairs and a perfect family suite of two bedrooms and bathroom on the ground floor. All rooms have TV, tea- and coffee-making facilities and hair-dryers. There is a sitting room and dining room, both facing the sweeping views over rolling farmland to the sea and Old Head of Kinsale. Breakfast includes home baking, and there is a conveniently placed restaurant at Ballinspittle for evening meals. The land surrounding the house is used for keeping and breeding show horses, which is an activity the Sweetnams are involved in. The house is signposted between Ballinspittle and Ballinadee, and is approximately ten kilometres from Kinsale. Pets outside, or in stables only. Horseriding, fishing, sailing and golf are available locally, as are lovely beaches, historic forts and museums. Visa and Mastercard accepted.

OWNER Mrs Maria Sweetnam OPEN April 1–end October ROOMS 3 double, 1 family; all en suite TERMS €33–35 pps

**The Lighthouse**
The Rock, Kinsale, Co. Cork
Tel: 021 4772734 Fax: 021 4773282
Email: info@lighthouse-kinsale.com
Website: www.lighthouse-kinsale.com

A stay at The Lighthouse is an experience, from the Tudor style architecture and unusal furnishings, to the charmingly hospitable and eccentric host. Carmel Kelly-O'Gorman. Carmel has an amazing collection of ornaments and knick knacks collected on many trips abroad, and a whole array of family silver in the dining room. The bedrooms tend to be small and dark, but have plenty of atmosphere with four poster and canopy beds, and one has a conservatory sitting room. The Lighthouse is also known for its champagne breakfasts, served at separate tables with silver cutlery. A piano, open fireplace, beamed ceiling, plants, statues and exotic chair coverings can be found in the sitting room. The Lighthouse is a short uphill walk from the centre of town. No pets. Major credit cards accepted.

OWNER Carmel Kelly-O'Gorman OPEN closed Christmas until mid-February ROOMS 5 double/twin, 4 double, all en suite

TERMS €35–55; single supplement;not suitable for children

## MACROOM

**An Cuasan**
Coolavokig, Macroom, Co. Cork
Tel: 026 40018
Email: cuasan@eircom.net
Website: www.welcome.to/cuasan

This small, modern, country house stands above the N22 in an attractive garden. It is comfortable and clean, and has a relaxed atmosphere, and traditional music for guests is played by family musicians. Two en suite rooms are on the ground floor, and all rooms have hair-dryers. The large conservatory is used both as a lounge and to accommodate the overflow from the dining room. The patio is a nice spot on sunny days, and a shed for the tackle and refrigeration of bait is available for the angler. An Cuasan is a good spot for visiting Kerry and western Cork, and for riding, fishing and walking. No pets. Smoking in lounge only. The house can be found 9 kilometres west of Macroom on N22. Visa, Access, Mastercard and Eurocard accepted.

OWNER Sean & Margaret Moynihan OPEN April–October
ROOMS 2 double, 3 twin, 1 family; 5 en suite, 1 public bathroom
TERMS €25.50-30; single supplement €8.50; child reduction

## MALLOW

**Dromagh Castle Farm**
Mallow, Co. Cork
Tel: 029 78013

The property's name is an apt description–a 1930 farmhouse beside a ruined late 16th century castle. Ronnie's father bought the farm, which included the castle, in the 1920s. At that time he lived in a house in the castle courtyard, later building the present-day farmhouse. The castle is an impressive square ruin with four towers. The enormous courtyard was used in later years as the farmyard. The house is clean and bright and pleasantly furnished, and has a subdued atmosphere. Of the two double front facing rooms, one is known as the 'twins room'. Here, in the 1930s, twins were born weighing only 1 1/2 lb each, and miraculously both survived. The twin bedded room is popular as it has views of the castle. Some of the pictures have interesting connections to the history of the property, and there is a floor to ceiling press on the upstairs landing which was built at the same time as the house. Most credit cards accepted, as are pets. Dromagh Castle is reached up a long driveway through farmland off N72, about half way between Mallow and Killarney.

OWNER Anne O'Leary OPEN all year ROOMS 1 twin, 1 double,
1 family; all en suite TERMS €25–30, single supplement; child reduction

## Longueville House
Mallow, Co. Cork
Tel: 022 47156 Fax: 022 47459
Email: info@longuevillehouse.ie
Website: www.longuevillehouse.ie

This impressive, listed Georgian manor house is set in beautiful park
like grounds with lovely views overlooking the Blackwater River valley, surrounded by 200 hectares of woods, farmland, a vineyard and
gardens which include 1.2 hectares of kitchen gardens. Visitors flock
to Longueville House primarily for its food, which mostly comes
from the river, garden and farm and is under the direction of William
O'Callaghan. The lovely peaceful setting, the salmon fishing on the
Blackwater, which runs through the estate; and its position as a good
touring base for exploring both the south and south west coasts
also contribute to its popularity.

   Bedrooms are supremely comfortable, ranging in shape and size,
and seven have mini suites which include sitting areas and luxury
bathrooms. All have hair-dryers, telephone in both bedroom and
bathroom, TV and bath robes. In spite of the grandeur, the atmosphere is warm and welcoming: guests have use of the drawing room,
and games room with full size billiard table. The old conservatory
has been restored and is now used as part of the dining room. As
well as breakfast and dinner, lunch is available all week. Other amenities include bicycle hire, clay pigeon shooting and walkup shooting.
All major credit cards accepted. Three miles west of Mallow on N72.

OWNER William & Aisling O'Callaghan OPEN All year except for
Christmas ROOMS 10 double, 5 twin, 2 single, 3 family; all en suite
TERMS from €90; single supplement; child reduction
MEALS lunch €5.50 dinner €50–65

### MIDLETON

## Barnabrow Country House
Cloyne, Midleton, Co. Cork
Tel: 021 4652534 Fax: 021 4652534
Email: barnabrow@eircom.net
Website: www.barnabrowhouse.com

The cathedral at Cloyne was the seat of George Berkeley, the well-
known philosopher after whom the Californian university was
named. Built in 1639, with two wings added later, Barnabrow—meaning a fairy fort—stands on a hill surrounded by its own 14 hectares
and enjoys pleasant country views. The house was gutted and has

been most interestingly restored with the four large second floor bedrooms having high raftered ceilings. Apart from one bedroom on the first floor, the remainder are in two ranges of converted farm buildings at the back of the house, one of which also houses the bar and restaurant above it. The rooms all have hair-dryers, telephone and bottled water. The house has been unusually decorated and plainly and simply furnished with a mixture of old and new, and strong, vibrant and bright colours are used on the walls, reflecting the colours of Guatemala. A lot of the interestingly shaped furniture and the flooring are made from imported teak from Botswana. The restaurant's chef spent some time at the Ballymaloe cookery school which, together with Ballymaloe House, is just down the road. Organically grown vegetables from the walled garden are a part of the delicious food on offer, and the outside terrace is used for bar-becuing. There is now an African furniture and crafts shop open daily, and the enlarged restaurant can cater for weddings, conferences and large parties. Self-catering cottages will be open for the 2005 season. Pets are accepted in the courtyard rooms. Visa, Laser and Mastercard taken. Barnabrow is one and a half miles from Cloyne on the Ballycotton road.

OWNER Geraldine O'Brien OPEN All year except for Christmas ROOMS 2 family, 7 twin, 10 double; all en suite TERMS €60–85; single supplement; child reduction MEALS lunch €27, dinner €50

### Glenview House
Ballinaclasha, Midleton, Co. Cork
Tel: 021 4631680 Fax: 021 4634680
Email: info@glenviewmidleton.com
Website: www.glenviewmidleton.com

Dating from 1780, this Georgian house stands in 8 hectares of grounds and gardens in a lovely rural setting. When the Sherrards bought the house some 30 years ago, it was derelict, with ivy grow-ing through the floor. They added the bow-shaped end of the draw-ing room that faces south, and in the course of renovation and fur-

Glenview House

nishing, bought the contents of 16 houses, using what they needed and auctioning off the remainder. One of these acquisitions is the old bath with a brass surround.

Evening meals are served in the attractive dining room, and there is a wide hall with a fireplace at one end. Visitors to Glenview find it a relaxing and peaceful place, the ideal setting in which to paint or write. The ground floor double bedroom has outside access and is suitable for disabled guests, and all the rooms have hair-dryers and tea and coffee facilities.

There are doors leading from the bar out onto the patio, which is a nice sunny spot to sit on fine days. Guests have use of the grass tennis court and croquet lawn, and there are also two coach house apartments, one of which is designed for wheelchair users. No pets. American Express, Visa and Mastercard accepted. Glenview is signposted off L35 Midleton to Fermoy road.

OWNER Ken & Beth Sherrard OPEN All year
ROOMS 6 double, 1 twin; all en suite TERMS €65–70;
single supplement; child reduction MEALS dinner €40

## MILLSTREET

### Ballinatona Farm
Ballinatona, Millstreet, Co. Cork
Tel: 029 70213 Fax: 029 70940

Not your typical farm, this is a most unusual and wonderful place, set in beautiful countryside, with outstanding views of mountains, moors and farmland. What makes it such a special place is cheerful, welcoming Jytte Storm, who immediately makes her guests feel at home. Jytte's Danish origins have a big influence on the décor and the house, which she and her husband originally built 20 years ago, and then added on to. Ballinatona was meant to be for their retirement, which is a pretty active one, what with running a 40-hectare dairy farm and a six bedroom guesthouse.

It seems every room in the house was built to take advantage of the best views. The sitting room, conservatory and dining room are all bright with large windows, as is the honeymoon suite reached up a very narrow spiral staircase. Décor and furnishings are simple, clean cut and very bright, and the bedrooms all have hair-dryer, TV and tea- and coffee-making facilities.

Ballinatona Farm is a walker's dream - from the doorstep there are wonderful hikes, including this most remote and beautiful part of the Blackwater Way, which is part of the coast to coast walk and runs the other side of Clara Mountain, one of the viewpoints from the house. Snacks are available. Visa and Mastercard accepted. Ballinatona Farm is three kilometres from Millstreet on the R582.

OWNER Jytte Storm OPEN All year
ROOMS 6 double/twin/family; all en suite
TERMS from €30; single supplement; child reduction
MEALS snacks

## Rock Cottage

Barnatonicane, Schull, Co. Cork
Tel: 028 35538 Fax: 028 35538
Email: rockcottage@eircom.net
Website: www.rockcottage.ie

Barbara (from Germany) was formerly the head chef at Blairs Cove
Restaurant, just a few miles away. She bought Rock Cottage (named
for a small rock outcrop at the back of the house) and opened for
business ten years ago. Decidedly a Georgian house, it is by the
1800s standards a cottage, and was in fact built as a hunting lodge. It
offers delightful, simple, bright accommodation - pine has been used
quite extensively - and rooms have TV and hair-dryers. There is an
attractive sitting room, and superb meals are served at separate
tables in the dining room. Apart from three bedrooms in the house,
there are self-catering units in the grounds, built from renovated
attractive stone farm buildings. The house is beautifully positioned,
on the Mizen Head peninsula, within a short distance of the sea on
either side, and stands in lovely park-like grounds, with sheep, horses, donkeys, geese and a pet pig. Dinner served from 7–8 p.m.: bookings should be made the previous day. Major credit cards accepted.
No pets. Unsuitable for children. Rock Cottage is on R591 between
Durrus and Toormore.

OWNER Barbara Klotzer OPEN All year ROOMS 2 triple en suite,
1 double with private bathroom. TERMS €55–65; single supplement
MEALS three-course dinner €40

## Stanley House

Colla Road, Schull, Co. Cork
Tel: 028 28425 Fax: 028 27887
Email: stanleyhouse@eircom.net
Website: www.stanley-house.net

Although it has a modern look, Stanley House is actually a renovated
old farmhouse about one kilometre from Schull. The house is surrounded by 3 hectares of fields with deer and colourful gardens, in a
wonderful position overlooking Schull harbour, Roaring Water Bay
with its many islands, and Mount Gabriel. Nancy Brosnan has been
doing bed & breakfast for more than 20 years and has a far-flung cir-

cle of guests who return again and again to this home away from home. Maeve Binchy is among her regular visitors and she has written "This is my fifth visit to the gleaming place where all the guests stare in wonder at the sparkling surfaces and shining windows and wonder do folk from another world come and do the housework at night." TV and tea- and coffee-making facilities are in all the bedrooms, and the small dining room has separate tables where breakfast is served. The comfortable TV lounge has a sun porch beyond which is the terrace - a great place to sit and take in the views.

The Brosnans have quite a presence in Schull: Nancy's husband runs the Spar supermarket and her son manages the restaurant and bar. They also have four houses for self-catering, including a thatched cottage.

It is a lovely walk into the village, which runs the length of one main street; there are ferries to the islands two or three times a day in summer; bicycles can be hired, or the energetic can climb to the top of 412-metre Mount Gabriel—well worth it for the wonderful view. Visa and Mastercard accepted. Pets in cars only.

OWNER Nancy Brosnan OPEN March 1—October 31
ROOMS 2 double, 1 twin, 1 family; all en suite TERMS €32; single supplement; child reduction

## SHANAGARRY

### Ballymaloe House
Shanagarry, Co. Cork
Tel: 021 4652531 Fax: 021 4652021
Email: res@ballymaloe.ie
Website: www.ballymaloe.ie

Famous as one of Ireland's top restaurants and training ground (at Ballymaloe Cookery School) for many of Ireland's best chefs, food undoubtedly lures many visitors to this lovely old family home. Set in 160 hectares of its own farmland, Ballymaloe is built around an old Geraldine castle, the fourteenth-century keep still intact.

The bedrooms, which vary in size and character are in the main house; around the old coachyard, with four on the ground floor designed to take wheelchairs, and in the gatehouse, where there are five newer rooms. Bedrooms all have hair-dryers, and on request TV, iron and ironing boards. Three small dining rooms open off the main room, with an interesting collection of modern Irish paintings, including works by Jack B. Yeats, brother of poet William Butler Yeats.

In addition to Ballymaloe House, Cookery School and farm, the Allens run a craft shop on the premises, and Crawford Art Gallery restaurant in Cork. Estate facillities include a heated outdoor swimming pool (summer), tennis court, small golf course, children's play equipment and a craft shop. Kennel accommodation for pets. All major credit cards accepted. Ballymaloe is 3 km outside Cloyne on Ballycotton road.

OWNER Mrs Myrtle Allen OPEN All year except for Christmas
ROOMS 3 single, 16 double, 15 twin; all en suite TERMS €145; single supplement MEALS lunch €30, dinner €58, children's menu

## SKIBBEREEN

### Bunalun House
Skibbereen, Co. Cork
Tel: 028 21502

Mrs. Crowley offers the best of Irish farmhouse hospitality and welcome at Bunalun, a pristinely kept, attractive 200 year old house. Colourful flowers surround the front of the building, which lies in pleasant farmland, supporting dairy cows and beef cattle, just off the main Skibbereen to Bantry road. The entrance hall has the original tiled floor, and there are wooden floors in the attractive small sitting room and dining room where breakfast is served at separate tables. No pets. Most major credit cards accepted.

OWNER Mrs. T. Crowley OPEN May 1–November 1
ROOMS 1 family en suite, 1 twin with private bathroom, 2 double
TERMS €30–34; single supplement; child reduction

### Grove House
Skibbereen, Co. Cork
Tel: 028 22957 Fax: 028 22958
Email: relax@grovehouse.net

One kilometre from Skibbereen, Grove House stands in two acres of wild gardens and fields, a kilometre off N71 on R593 in Bantry direction. The Warburtons bought the house in the early 1990s, spending a couple of years on renovation before opening for business. There is a pretty drawing and dining room where delicious home-cooked candlelit dinners are served.

Bedrooms in the house, which vary in size, are simply furnished and have TV. Behind the house the pretty, old stables and barn buildings provide three very attractive, cleverly converted bedroom suites. There are self-catering cottages nearby. Three course dinners including wine, are available if booked in advance. Pets allowed in the courtyard cottages only. Visa and Mastercard accepted.

OWNER Anna Warburton OPEN All year
ROOMS 4 double,
1 twin; all en suite
TERMS €49–59; single supplement; child reduction
MEALS dinner €24

## Lis-Ardagh Lodge

Union Hall, Co. Cork
Tel: 028 34951
Email info@lis-ardaghlodge.com
Website: www.lis-ardaghlodge.com

Lis-Ardagh Lodge is a striking stone built house, constructed by the
Kearneys four years ago, and has nice views over farmland. The beautiful gardens surrounding the house were created by Jim, who is a
landscape gardener, and beyond are fields with sheep.

The interior of the house has wooden floors and pine furniture,
and the rooms are spacious, clean and bright. Guests have use of a
large sitting room, and breakfast is served at separate tables in the
pleasant dining room. There are also two self catering units. No pets.
There is a sign for the house on the N71.

OWNER Jim & Carol Kearney OPEN all year
ROOMS 2 family, 1 double, all en suite
TERMS from €30; single supplement; child reduction

## Aherne's

163 North Main Street, Youghal, Co. Cork
Tel: 024 92424 Fax: 024 93633
Email: ahernes@eircom.net
Website: www.ahernes.com

The Fitzgibbon family have owned Aherne's for three generations.
The inn started life as the family's pub and small grocery store that
made sandwiches. It is the present generation of the family that
made the transformation from sandwiches to a restaurant, and later
built on an entire wing for accommodation.

At the heart of the historic walled port of Youghal, Aherne's is a
renowned seafood restaurant serving freshly-caught local fish, including lobster, prawns, crab, salmon, oysters and sole. Decorated in
warm, glowing colours, there are two small, cosy bars with prints
and pictures. Bedrooms are exceptionally large, restfully decorated
with very big beds. Each have TV, trouser press, telephone and hair-
dryer. The drawing room has an open fireplace, books and antique
furniture. Residents are served breakfast in the new wing's bright
dining room. A recent addition is a small conference room. River and
deep-sea fishing, horseback riding, hill walking and visiting magnificent
beaches are activities that can easily be undertaken from Youghal, not
to mention the seven nearby golf courses. Pets in cars only. The
restaurant is open from 6.30 to 9.30 daily and bar food is available
at lunchtime. Access, Visa, American Express and Diners accepted.

OWNER The Fitzgibbon Family OPEN All year except for Christmas
ROOMS 8 double, 5 twin, 10 single, 3 family; all en suite
TERMS from €77; single supplement MEALS dinner, bar food

## Glenally House

Copperalley, Youghal, Co. Cork
Tel: 024 91623 Fax: 024 91623
Email: enquiries@glenally.com
Website: www.glenally.com

On the edge of Youghal and reached down a narrow lane, Glenally
House was built in 1826, in seven acres of gardens and fields. It is a
plain, and somewhat austere looking building, greatly improved by
Fred and Herta Rigney, who moved here seven years ago. The house
is simply furnished using a mixture of old and modern pieces and
bright colours. Many of the rooms have the original wooden floors,
some of which have been painted. The bedrooms have TV and tea-
and coffee-making facilities. Breakfast, and dinner by arrangement, is
served in the dining room, and for a larger number of people the
morning room is also used for meals. Fred and Herta enjoy guests,
and make sure their stay is enjoyable. Pets outside only. Visa and
Mastercard accepted.

OWNER Herta & Fred Rigney OPEN March 1–December 15
ROOMS 3 double en suite, 1 twin with private bathroom
TERMS €50–60; single supplement MEALS dinner €40

## COUNTY KERRY

Every tourist wants to visit Kerry to see the beauty of the landscape. There is an inconsistency in the weather—wind and rain from
the Atlantic, misty drizzle or bright light and sunshine—making each
day or part of a day different from the next and projecting a constantly changing pattern over the mountains, lakes and streams. Each
type of weather brings its own peculiar beauty to the landscape.

Killarney town caters to large numbers of tourists and is full of
hotels, yet the lakes, mountains and woods of the surrounding countryside remain unspoiled. Close by is the ruined fourteenth-century
Ross Castle. From here one can hire a boat to Inisfallen Island and
visit the ruins of the twelfth-century Augustinian Inisfallen Abbey.
Muckross House is now a folk museum and has the most beautiful
garden. From the Gap of Dunloe there is a marvellous view of the
Black Valley where huge torrents of water poured through the Gap
at the end of the Ice Age.

The Ring of Kerry is a famous scenic drive around the Iveragh

Peninsula. Killorglin is known for its annual horse and cattle fair, Puck Fair, held for two days in August, a great event with pagan origins, when a wild mountain goat is captured and enthroned in the centre of the town. Waterville is the principal resort on the Ring of Kerry, and at Cahirsiveen one can see the magnificent police barracks, which were meant to have been built in the north-west frontier of India, but the plans got mixed up. At Ballinskelligs, which is an Irish-speaking area, there are the ruins of a monastery and a fine beach with wonderful views. The Skelligs are rocky islands off the Ring of Kerry, which can be visited to see wild birds, notably kittiwakes, guillemots, petrel, shearwater and fulmar. One can also see the ruins of the old monastery that stands 183 m above the landing place and is approached by long flights of stone steps. There are also beehive huts, stone crosses, the Holy Well, oratories and cemeteries. This is a beautiful, peaceful spot in fine weather, but terrifying in a storm.

The Dingle Peninsula is made up of beautiful mountains, cliffs, glacial valleys, lakes and beaches. Some 2,000 prehistoric and early Christian remains have been discovered, and a little old Gaelic culture can be observed at the tip of the peninsula. The little village of Ventry was the scene of a legendary battle, and at Fahan lies the greatest collection of antiquities in Ireland: stone beehive huts, cave dwellings, standing and inscribed stones and crosses, souterrains, forts, cahers and a church. The spectacular views around Slea Head, formed the backdrop for the film *Ryan's Daughter*. Beyond Ballyferriter is Gallarus, the most perfect example of early Irish building and dry-rubble masonry. The principal town of Kerry is Tralee, a trading and industrial centre. At Ardfert, the cathedral, which was built in 1250 and has the ruins of its Franciscan Friary, is the most striking building.

## ANASCAUL

### Four Winds
Anascaul, Co. Kerry
Tel: 066 915 7168 Fax: 066 9157174
Kathleen O'Connor has been running her B&B for about 17 years; she enjoys meeting people and sharing her house and is an accommodating host. There are views of the Anascaul Mountains and Dingle Bay and Ross Beigh from the house. The simply furnished rooms are fresh and bright. There is a unique chaise longue in the hallway. Anascaul is the birthplace of the Antarctic explorer Tom Crean and the well-known sculptor Jerome Connor. Tasty freshly-prepared breakfasts are served in the cosy dining room and there is also a comfortable TV lounge. There are plenty of activities for the visitor, including walks, fishing, sandy beaches, mountain climbing and archaeological sites. The house is situated on the Dingle/Tralee Way Walk. Drying facilities available.

OWNER Kathleen & P. J. O'Connor OPEN All year ROOMS 1 double, 2 twin, 1 family; 3 en suite TERMS €29 pps; child reduction; single supplement

### The 19th Lodge
Golf Links Road, Ballybunion, Co. Kerry
Tel: 068 27592 Fax: 068 27830
Email: the19thlodge@eircom.net
Website: www.the19thlodgeballybunion.com

A luxurious four star guest house in a superb location overlooking Ballybunion Golf Course—a two-minute walk to the first tee, and a good seven iron to the club house: a golfer's paradise. The property has recently been upgraded, inside and out. The bedrooms are furnished with rich wood, pretty pastel fabrics and lace curtains. The sitting room is pleasantly furnished and there is a conservatory for guests' use. The guest lounge overlooks the golf course, with a mini bar available. Breakfast is plentiful and is available as early as 6 a.m. for the golfer. Owners Mr and Mrs Beasley are a most accommodating couple, who go out of their way to ensure their guests have everything they need. Tea or coffee is offered upon arrival, and golf storage and a drying room are made available.

Guaranteed tee times on Ballybunion Old Course are available for residents. The house is not suitable for children. Breakfast only is served, but there is no shortage of restaurants and pubs for other meals in Ballybunion. Five minutes from sandy beaches, salmon fishing, cliff walks and seaweed baths on the beach. All major credit cards accepted.

OWNER Mr and Mrs Beasley OPEN All year except for Christmas ROOMS 2 double, 1 twin, 1 family, 1 single, 1 triple; 5 en suite TERMS €50–85 pps; single supplement

### The Country Haven
Car Ferry Road, Ballybunion, Co. Kerry
Tel: 068 27103
Email: countryhaven@eircom.net

This superb Georgian-style house is ideally situated—just three kilometres from the golf course and a 10-minute drive from the Tarbert car ferry. The driving range with 12 all-weather indoor bays will enable you to practice your golf and enjoy panoramic views of the Atlantic Ocean at the same time. Mrs Eileen Walsh is a friendly lady with a good sense of humour, who takes excellent care of her guests. The house sits on a 65-hectare farm, and there are 7.5

hectares of young forest and a 6.5km designated walk. The spacious bedrooms are of a very high standard, tastefully decorated with every comfort. There is a ground floor room with a small conservatory. A honeymoon suite is also available. The house has antique furniture throughout and most bedrooms have sea views. Full Irish breakfast is offered with home-made scones, breads and marmalade; early breakfast prepared for golfers. All guests may use the putting green, tennis court and driving range. Guests will be extremely comfortable here, and have easy access to two golf courses and the scenic countryside. Visa accepted.

OWNER Mrs Eileen Walsh OPEN April 1–November 31
ROOMS 6 twin/double/family/single; all en suite
TERMS €35 pps; child reduction; single supplement

## CAHERDANIEL

### Moran's Seaside Farmhouse
Bunavalla, Caherdaniel, Co. Kerry
Tel: 066 9475208
Email: nancymoran@eircom.net

Moran's is a modern bungalow with the most spectacular views, overlooking Derrynane and the Atlantic, and just a five-minute walk to the sea. There are two clean sandy beaches where guests can swim, hike, boat or just relax and enjoy the beautiful scenery. The house is well-maintained and has a pleasant, welcoming atmosphere. All bedrooms are on the ground floor. Moran Farm is a working farm of sheep and cows. Home-cooked wholesome evening meals are available by arrangement.

Nancy Moran is happy to assist visitors in every way to ensure they have a comfortable stay, and to give advice on what to see and do in the area. Daniel O'Connell's House and Gardens and wonderful walks are close by. Six miles from Waterville on main ring of Kerry. Farm is signposted.

OWNER Nancy Moran OPEN April 1–November 1
ROOMS 4 double/twin; all en suite TERMS €32pps ; child reduction (40% when sharing); single supplement MEALS dinner

## CAHIRSIVEEN

### Cul Draiochta
Points Cross, Cahirsiveen, Co. Kerry
Tel: 066 947 3141 Fax: 066 947 3141
Email: inugent@esatclear.ie

Cul Draiochta means 'Magic Nook' in Irish, and this is a magical area of the Ring of Kerry. Situated at the foot of the Bentee Mountains overlooking Valentia Harbour, the house was designed as a bed & breakfast and was built to ensure that guests have every comfort. The well-appointed good-sized bedrooms are light and airy. They have cherrywood furniture, pink candystriped duvets, and are attractively decorated with coordinated fabrics; all have orthopaedic beds and overlook the view. All bedrooms have TV, clock radio and hairdryer. Owners Ian and Ann Nugent are from a farming family in North Kerry and are very hospitable. They have been in business for nearly a decade, and have built up a fine reputation for offering very good value accommodation. Tea or coffee is offered upon arrival and other times on request. Excellent breakfasts and table d'hôte dinners are served in the conservatory-style dining room overlooking the view, and packed lunches can be provided upon request. Vegetarian meals are also available with advance notice. The lounge is very comfortable and has multi-channel TV. Smoking in conservatory only. Routes for walkers are provided. An ideal spot for nature lovers.

OWNER Ian & Anne Nugent OPEN All year
ROOMS 5 double/ twin/family; all en suite
TERMS €26; child reduction; single supplement MEALS dinner

## The Final Furlong
Cahirsiveen, Co. Kerry
Tel: 066 947 3300 Fax: 066 947 2810
Email: finalfurlong@eircom.net

This immaculate, warm bungalow sits in a tranquil location on the banks of the River Fertha estuary, and enjoys lovely views. It is part of a 40-hectare farm with a suckler cow herd and a Sport Horse Enterprise. Approved riding stables offer beach gallops and horseback riding in secluded areas of the Ring of Kerry. Guests can also view the ruins of the old Union Workhouse, and a detailed history is available. The rooms are immaculately maintained and attractively decorated.

Breakfasts and prearranged four-course dinners are served on a large refectory table in the dining room. Kathleen O'Sullivan is an excellent cook (seafood is a speciality) who enjoys chatting with guests and provides information on the area. Smoking is permitted in the lounge only.

Kathleen O'Sullivan's motto is, "You may come as a stranger, but we hope you will leave as a friend". Group rates are available with special offers during May, June, September and October. Deep-sea angling packages as well as trips to Skellig Rock from a nearby pier are offered. Visa, Mastercard, Access, and American Express accepted.

OWNER Kathleen O'Sullivan OPEN March 1–November 1
ROOMS 1 double, 1 twin, triple family, double/single; all en suite

TERMS €25.50; child reduction 20%; single supplement €8.50
MEALS dinner from €21.50

## CARAGH LAKE

**Glendalough House**
Caragh Lake, Co. Kerry
Tel: 066 976 9156 Fax: 066 976 9156
Email: IrelandJournal@eircom.net
Website: www.kerryweb.ie

Glendalough House is a charming Victorian residence just a short distance from the shores of Caragh Lake. It is a warm country house with mature gardens and views of the lake and Ireland's highest mountain range, the McGillycuddy Reeks. It is furnished with antiques and there are several old paintings. An ideal spot for those looking for peace and tranquillity, the house is approached by a long private gravel drive, bordered with trees, shrubs and wildflowers. There is a garden inhabited by a colourful peacock and peahen. Peace is also maintained by the lack of television.

Candlelit dinners featuring Caragh salmon and succulent mountain lamb are served in the elegant dining room. There is a conservatory and also a mews that comprises two double en suite bedrooms with a private living room and south-facing terrace. Smoking is permitted in the conservatory and on the terrace.

Glendalough House is truly a house for all seasons and all tastes: there are several championship golf courses where tee times can be arranged, there is trout and salmon fishing, wonderful walks, and it is an excellent base from which to tour the Ring of Kerry and the Dingle Peninsula. The house is not suitable for children. Visa, Mastercard and American Express credit cards are accepted.

OWNER Josephine Roder-Bradshaw OPEN March 1–October 31
ROOMS 4 double, 4 twin; 7 en suite, 1 private bath
TERMS €70; single supplement €19 MEALS dinner

## CASTLEGREGORY

**The Shores Country House**
Cappatigue, Conor Pass Road, Castlegregory, Co. Kerry
Tel: 066 7139196 Fax: 066 7139195
Website: www.theshorescountryhouse.com

If you are looking for that special place, Shores Country House, will more than satisfy the most discerning traveller. It stands in lovely grounds, on the Conor Pass Road, overlooking Brandon Bay. This luxurious, Five Diamond property, offers superb accommodation, yet has an informal, friendly ambience. Annette extends the warmest of welcomes, and has deservedly been the recipient of several awards.

Everything is first class, the spacious, individually decorated bedrooms, i.e. The Gothic Room, the Laura Ashley Room, and the Balcony Room, have elegant furniture, exquisite fabrics, power showers, and TV. Many rooms have views of the bay. Annette, is a gourmet cook, and evening meals alone, are reason enough to book in here. A sample menu could be, baked blue brie cheese in filo pasty, and a choice of seven entrées, featuring such delights as Baked Wild Atlantic Salmon, and, Roast Rack of Kerry Lamb. Mouth-watering home-made desserts could include crepes and ice cream, with a butterscotch sauce and toasted almonds.

The food is beautifully presented and served in the dining room overlooking the bay. Dinners must be pre-booked and special diets are catered with advance notice.

There are miles of sandy beaches, mountain climbing and scenic walks close by. Ten miles from Dingle. There is an apartment, and a water's edge cottage, available for rent. Credit cards taken.

OWNER Mrs Annette O'Mahoney OPEN February 15–November 15
ROOMS 6 en suite TERMS €37.50; single supplement

## CASTLEISLAND

### The Gables B&B
Dooneen, Limerick Road, Castleisland, County Kerry
Tel: 066 7 I 4060 Fax: 066 7 I 4060
Email: gablesdillon@eircom.net
Website: www.homepage.eircom.net/-gablesbnb

The Gables stands in its own grounds, in an attractive landscaped garden with panoramic views of the new Castleisland Golf Course. Course fees are modest: your host, Lilian Dillon can arrange tee times, and tours of the area. There are four spotlessly clean ground floor bedrooms, all have TV, tea makers and a hair-dryer. Three are en suite, the fourth has private bathroom.

Excellent freshly-prepared breakfasts are served in the dining room/sitting room, which feature fresh fruit, pancakes as well as a cooked variety. There is a small, snug sunroom, for guests to relax in and enjoy the views. Lilian is a very hospitable host, and the ambience is homely and friendly. On chilly nights, a hot water bottle may be found in your bed. Castleisland, two miles away, has several venues for evening meals. Situated on N21 Limerick Road.

OWNER Lilian Dillon OPEN All year, except for Christmas
ROOMS 4 double/twin/family; 3 en suite
TERMS €90 pps; single supplement; child reduction

## Ard na Greine

Spa Road, Dingle, Co. Kerry
Tel: 066 915 1113 Fax: 066 915 1898
Email: mayhoul@indigo.ie

This warm and inviting bungalow in a quiet location is just a five-minute stroll to the town centre. Mary Houlihan wanted to ensure that her guests had everything they could need, and she has certainly accomplished her goal. All the bedrooms, which are on the ground floor, are equipped with satellite TV, tea makers, electric blankets, hair-dryers, irons and ironing boards, direct dial phones, and bath/shower combinations; the latest additions are refrigerators. The orthopaedic beds have Dorma-designed duvets, and the rooms are bright and attractive.

There is a breakfast menu featuring smoked herring, salmon, home-baked breads, Irish cooked breakfast, etc. you certainly won't need lunch. An added bonus is the delightful owner, Mary Houlihan. The house is extremely good value and there is a home-away-from-home atmosphere. The beautiful shamrock/harp tapestry displayed in the dining room was hand-made by Mary's sister. Mastercard and Visa accepted. Third house past the Highgrove Hotel.

OWNER Mary Houlihan OPEN March–October ROOMS 6 double/twin; all en suite TERMS €35; child reduction; single supplement

## Cill Bhreac

Milltown, Dingle, County Kerry
Tel: 066 9151358
Email: info@cillbhreachouse.com
Website: www.cillbhreachouse.com

An attractive spacious residence in a tranquil location, overlooking Dingle Bay and Mount Brandon. The house is immaculate, tastefully decorated and well-maintained. Rooms are of a good size, and are comfortably furnished. The bedrooms are well equipped, with tea/coffee-makers, TV, clock radio and hair-dryer. All bedrooms have orthopaedic beds and electric blankets. Children are welcome and cots are provided. No smoking in the bedrooms. There is an extensive breakfast menu (special diets can be catered for) prepared fresh daily, juices, cereals, cooked choices, and brown bread; you won't need lunch.

The conservatory also overlooks the bay and is a perfect spot in which to relax after a busy day of sightseeing. Guests may also have use of the garden. The ambience is friendly and Angela McCarthy is very helpful, providing lots of assistance with what to see and in the area. Close by are facilities for angling, golf, horse riding, sailing, and sandy beaches. Several pubs in the area serve food and have traditional Irish music. Irish is spoken.

Credit cards accepted. Coming into Dingle on the N86, turn left at first roundabout and left and 2nd roundabout crossing the bridge. Cill Bhreac is the third house on the right.

OWNER Mrs Angela McCarthy OPEN February 15–November 30 ROOMS 6 double/twin/family; all en suite TERMS up to €33 pps; child reduction; single supplement

### Devane's Farmhouse
Lispole, Dingle, Co. Kerry
Tel: 066 915 1418

A warm welcome awaits you at this family-run farmhouse, a working dairy farm of 16 hectares nestled at the foot of the mountain with beautiful views all around. The Farmhouse is very popular with walkers and tourists, as it is situated on the Dingle Way Walk. The bedrooms are clean, if a little small, but the owners are so hospitable, offering tea and home-baked bread and cake to guests, that room size seems unimportant. There is an extra cot available.

The sitting room leads out to the conservatory with stunning views of the bay and mountains. Smoking is permitted in conservatory only. Tea and coffee facilities in the dining room, and hair-dryers, irons and a trouser press are available on request. Dinner is by advance arrangement only, but there are several establishments for evening meals in Dingle, which is just 5 km away.

Guests return here year after year, and visitors new to the property sometimes book in for a night and end up staying for a week or more. Guests may use the garden, and are welcome to enjoy the daily farm activities, watch the sheep grazing or walk in this beautiful area. The farmhouse is located on a small side road, but don't give up; just when you think you have passed it, the farm comes into view. Visa and Mastercard accepted.

OWNER Mary Devane OPEN April 1–November 1 ROOMS 3 double/ twin, 1 family; 3 en suite TERMS €23; child reduction 25% if sharing (under age 4 free); single supplement €6.50 MEALS dinner

### Duinin House
Conor Pass Road, Dingle, Co. Kerry
Tel: 066 915 1335 Fax: 066 915 1335
Email: pandaneligan@eircom.net
Website: homepage.tinet.ie/~pandaneligan

Duinin, meaning 'little fort', is a friendly ranch-style bungalow with beautiful views of the sea and mountains. There is a large front garden with a manicured lawn and lots of pretty flowers and shrubs. Guests enjoy tea outside on warm days, or in the conservatory that overlooks Dingle Harbour and Valley. The comfortable lounge has a VCR that guests may use, plus an additional lounge for reading or just relaxing after a busy day. This is a non-smoking house. All of the bedrooms are on the ground floor, with modern furnishings, large, fitted wardrobes and chairs. The front bedrooms have lovely views. The extensive breakfast menu, with fresh baked breads, is served in the sunny dining room overlooking the harbour. Golf, fishing, boat trips, beaches, hill walking and excellent pubs and restaurants nearby. Visa, Mastercard, American Express accepted.

OWNER Anne Neligan OPEN February 1–November 30
ROOMS 5 double/twin; all en suite TERMS €28–33; child reduction; single supplement

## Greenmount House
Gortonora, Dingle, Co. Kerry
Tel: 066 915 1414 Fax: 066 915 1974
Email: mary@greenmount-house.com
Website: www.greenmount-house.com

Greenmount House, also known as Curran's Bed and Breakfast, stands in an elevated site over-looking Dingle town and the harbour. A special feature are the wonderful breakfast feasts: guests help themselves from an enormous buffet choice of fruits, cereals, home-baked bread, muffins, fresh juices, puddings and other delights, fol-lowed by tasty omelettes or a traditional Irish breakfast. An added bonus is that it is served in a lovely conservatory/dining room that overlooks the bay. Little wonder the establishment was awarded the Certification of Merit Award.

  Most of the rooms have been upgraded, and are tastefully decorat-ed with warm autumn colours in Laura Ashley designs. Rooms have refrigerators and direct dial telephone. There are seven superior suites and five charming bedrooms. Each suite has a full bathroom, large sitting area, many more extras, and sea views. There are two lounges for guests' use. The house is beautifully maintained by John and Mary Curran, who have been in business for over 25 years. The owners are from local, long established families, and will provide guests with an unlimited amount of knowledge on the area. Plenty of written information is provided. Local amenities include golf, fishing, horse riding and trips to see Fungi the Dolphin, whom you might even see from your bedroom window. Visa and Mastercard accepted.

OWNER John & Mary Curran OPEN All year
ROOMS 12 double/twin/family; all en suite
TERMS €40–62 pps; child reduction (from age 8 if sharing)

## The Lighthouse

High Road, Ballinaboula, Dingle, Co. Kerry
Tel: 066 915 1829  Email: info@lighthousedingle.com
Website: www.lighthousedingle.com

This pleasant two-storey spacious house stands in its own grounds overlooking Dingle Harbour. A galleried landing and a pine staircase lead to the spacious bedrooms, all of which have a bath/shower combination; one is on the ground floor. Bedrooms are bright and fresh; they are furnished with pine and have bright colourful duvets. The lounge and dining room overlook the view.

Breakfast only is served at The Lighthouse, but there are several choices for evening meals in Dingle, within walking distance.

The Lighthouse offers a high standard of accommodation. Mary Murphy is very helpful indeed, with information for visitors on attractions in this scenic area. Credit cards accepted. To locate drive up main street to town outskirts: house is on the right.

OWNER Mary & Denis Murphy OPEN February 1–November 30
ROOMS 1 double, 4 double/single; all en suite
TERMS €37 pps; child reduction

## DINGLE PENINSULA

## Barnagh Bridge

Camp, Dingle Peninsula, Co. Kerry
Tel: 066 713 0145 Fax: 066 713 0299
Email: bbguesthouse@eircom.net
Website: www.barnaghbridge.com

Barnagh Bridge stands in eight acres of well-landscaped gardens, an elevated position overlooking Tralee Bay and the Maharee Peninsula. The house was designed by architect Michael Williams and is delightful in every way. Just about everything has been thought of for guests' comfort. The warm attentive hosts offer a house with all the facilities of a hotel at modest prices. The spacious bedrooms, each with an individual wild flower theme, have high standards of décor and furnishings; all have great views. A conservatory has been added, a wonderful spot in which to relax after a busy day. Heather Williams takes great pride in her cooking, which includes a daily breakfast special, featuring tasty dishes such as mushrooms, kippers, smoked trout, French toast, a wide choice of cereals and fruit, yoghurts, fresh squeezed orange juice, home-made jams and marmalade. A traditional Irish breakfast is also on the menu. The lounge leads out to a patio area and the gardens, which guests are welcome to enjoy on fine days. The ambience is warm and informal, and Heather Williams is very helpful and accommodating. This is a perfect combination for folks looking for a taste of luxury in a beautiful 'get away from it all' setting. Visa and Access accepted.

OWNER Heather Williams OPEN March 15–November 7
ROOMS 2 double, 3 twin; all en suite
TERMS €23–35.50; child reduction; single supplement €6.50–10

## GLENBEIGH

**Mountain View**
Mountain Stage, Glenbeigh, Co. Kerry
Tel: 066 9768541 Fax: 066 9768541
Email: mountainstage@eircom.net

This yellow bungalow lives up to its name: the setting is spectacular–it stands in an elevated position with magnificent views all round.
Bedrooms are colourful and immaculately maintained; three are on
the ground floor. The TV lounge overlooks the view. Breakfast and
dinners, if ordered in advance, are served in the bright dining room.
Owner Anne O'Riordan, a very helpful, accommodating lady, has
been in business for five years. Lassie, the sweet collie, is friendly, fit-
ting the quiet, peaceful location.
  Safe sandy beaches 10 km long are only 2 km away, and there are
mountain and hill walks, fishing and horseback riding in the area, and
the Kerry Way Walk is close by.

OWNER Mrs Anne O'Riordan OPEN April 1–October 31
ROOMS 2 double, 2 single; all en suite TERMS €30; child reduction;
single supplement €6.50 MEALS dinner

**Ocean Wave**
Glenbeigh, County Kerry
Tel: 066 97 68249 Fax 066 97 68412
Email: oceanwave@iol.ie

Ocean Wave, a luxurious property, stands in a superb location,
behind a landscaped garden. It is located on the Ring of Kerry and
has wonderful views of Dingle Bay and the mountains. This peaceful
haven, has the added bonus of the delightful owner, Noreen O'Toole.
Noreen has been in business for over 30 years, just about everything
possible has been thought of for her guest's comfort. Her flair for
décor and style is evident throughout the house. There are many
items of interest, including paintings, photographs, an unusual chaise
lounge, a beautiful chandelier, a mirrored ceiling, and a chess set.
  The house is elegantly furnished, the individually decorated large
bedrooms, three of which have a Jacuzzi, have rich linens, elegant furnishings, and drapes and coronets made by Noreen. All are en suite,
and have TV. The first floor sitting room is a recommended spot
after a busy day of sightseeing; there is also a small balcony. Most of

the rooms have views. There is an extensive breakfast menu, served in the bright dining room, complete with linen tablecloths and napkins.

If you are looking for a special place to stay, Ocean Wave would be an excellent choice.

OWNER Noreen O'Toole OPEN March 1–October 31
ROOMS 3; all en suite TERMS €35-40; single supplement

## GLENCAR

### Blackstones House
Blackstone Bridge, Glencar, Co. Kerry
Tel: 066 976 0164 Fax: 066 976 0164

This spacious award-winning old-style farmhouse is situated at the foot of Carrantuohill, Ireland's highest mountain, beside Blackstone Bridge, Licken Wood, overlooking the Caragh River. Walkers will be interested to know it is on the Kerry Way Walk. The clean and cosy bedrooms, which have floral fabrics and pine furniture, are in the oldest part of the house. The sitting room has antique pine furniture and comfortable easy chairs. Breakfast and pre-arranged four-course evening meals are served; wild salmon and home-produced lamb are often on the menu. Special dietary requirements may be met if pre-arranged. The house has a wine license. Smoking allowed in the lounge only.

The setting is superb, and kindly Breda Breen makes guests feel immediately at home. She offers a hot drink upon arrival. The perfect spot for nature lovers, outdoor activities include nature walks (guides can be arranged), mountain and hill walking, fishing, rock climbing and canoeing. Also of interest are the ruins of an old smelting works, which can be seen in Blackstone. Visa, Self-catering is available. Access and Eurocard accepted.

OWNER Mrs Breda Breen OPEN April 1–October 31
ROOMS 1 double, 2 twin, 2 family, 1 single; 5 en suite
TERMS €25.50; 33% child reduction; single supplement €8.50
MEALS dinner

## KELLS

### Glenville Farmhouse
Gleesk, Kells, Co. Kerry
Tel: 066 947 7625 Fax: 066 947 7625
Email: glenvillefarmhouse@eircom.net

Situated in a delightful position, midway between Glenbeigh and Cahirsiveen on the main Ring of Kerry Road, Glenville is a spacious new country house, with panoramic views of Dingle Bay. The rooms are well-appointed, with an attractive bright décor. There is a comfortable TV lounge. Tasty breakfasts are served in the dining room that overlooks the bay and the mountains. For evening meals, the Thatch Tavern very close by serves a good pint of Guinness, and there is dancing and good craic. A restaurant is within a five-minute drive.

There is hill walking on the farm, and fishing trips on Skellig Bay can be arranged. The famous 18-hole champion course at Waterville is just 19 km away. Visa, Mastercard, Access and Eurocard accepted.

Transfers can be arranged from the airport or train station, and group or individual tours can be arranged if required.

OWNER Marion O'Grady OPEN April 1–October 31
ROOMS 1 double, 2 twin, 1 family; 3 en suite TERMS €30; child reduction; single supplement

## KENMARE

### Ardmore House
Killarney Road, Kenmare, Co. Kerry
Tel: 064 41406 Fax: 064 41406

This luxurious farmhouse is set in beautiful, scenic countryside overlooking the sea. It is warm and inviting and Kathy Mullen is a delightful and pleasant host. Guests are assured of true Irish hospitality. The immaculate bedrooms are well decorated and have comfortable beds. There are two lounges, one with TV and an open fire, and one quiet lounge for chatting and/or reading.

Lake and deep-sea angling, pony trekking and beautiful walks are all available in the area: Kenmare golf course is within 1/2 mile of the house. Scenic farm walks to the cliff and picnic areas can also be taken. Visa, Access and Mastercard accepted.

OWNER Tom O'Connor OPEN March 1–November 30
ROOMS 2 double, 1 twin, 3 double/single; all en suite
TERMS €32 pps; child reduction (50% if sharing); single supplement

Ardmore House

## Muxnaw Lodge

Castletownbere Road, Kenmare, Co. Kerry
Tel: 064 41252
Email: muxnawlodge@eircom.net

This interesting eighteenth-century house enjoys a lovely position, set in 1.5 hectares of beautiful landscaped grounds. The house has an informal, lived-in atmosphere, and is decorated with Laura Ashley wallpapers, a Waterford Crystal chandelier, antique furnishings and many items of interest. The comfortable TV lounge has the original fireplace and window shutters. The spacious bedrooms are refurbished in keeping with the character of the house, which has lovely views, original fireplaces and antique furniture; one bedroom has a brass bed. Telephones are available on request. The all-weather tennis court is available for use by guests.

Evening meals are available by arrangement; vegetarians can be catered for with advance notice. There is no license, but guests may bring their own wine.

A peaceful and relaxing house, this is a wonderful base for touring this beautiful area. A pleasant 10-minute stroll over the bridge takes you into town.

OWNER Mrs Hannah Boland OPEN All year
ROOMS 3 double, 2 twin; all en suite TERMS from €37 pps; child reduction; single supplement MEALS dinner

## O'Donnells of Ashgrove

Ashgrove, Kenmare, Co. Kerry
Tel: 064 41228 Fax: 064 41228
Email: odonnellsofashgrove@hotmail.com

O'Donnells of Ashgrove is a charming, peaceful house set in tranquil surroundings of pasture and woodland, with a view of the Caha Mountains. Lynne O'Donnell is a friendly lady who welcomes guests into her home as friends. In the evening, guests are welcome to relax in the armchairs in front of the fire, or, if preferred, to join the family in their spacious and elegantly furnished TV lounge. There are many antique pieces around and the house is tastefully furnished. Breakfasts are served in the Jacobean-style dining room with its exposed beams, stone fireplace and log fire. Smoking permitted in the lounge only. A range of Lynne O'Donnell's home-made lavender and pot pourri sachets is on display, available to buy.

There is one ground floor room with bath and shower. The twin room is not en suite, but has a private bath two steps away. Guests are encouraged to feel like part of the family, and although there is a guest sitting room, where there is a TV and plenty of books, guests may also join the O'Donnells in their sitting room. Not suitable for babies or children. There are no single rooms, but a double is offered with a supplement.

Of special interest are Kenmare town, the stone circle, sea trips around Kenmare Bay and Gleninchiquin Amenity Area. Terry O'Donnell loves to fish, and is a local award-winning fisherman. He would be delighted to take small groups up to eight on fishing trips; packed lunches, evening meals and accommodation can be arranged for an inclusive price. The fishing is great and the company friendly. German is spoken. Visa and Mastercard accepted.

OWNER Mrs Lynne O'Donnell OPEN Easter–October 31
ROOMS 2 double en suite, 1 twin (private bath), 1 standard
TERMS €32 pps; single supplement

## Whispering Pines
Bell Height, Kenmare, Co. Kerry
Tel: 064 41194 Fax: 064 40813
Email: wpines@eircom.net

Whispering Pines is a delightful place to stay, located a three-minute walk from the town centre, and a five-minute walk from the golf course. This modernised period home with its delightful garden is set back off the road in quiet and peaceful surroundings. The bedrooms are attractively decorated with matching fabrics and duvets. The charming owners John and Mary Fitzgerald make this a wonderful place to stay; fresh baked scones and tea are offered on arrival, and nothing is too much trouble. They are happy to give advice on what to see and do in the area. An ideal location for touring the scenic Ring of Kerry. Pets outside only. Smoking restricted. Private parking. Situated south of town on the N71, five minute walk from the golf course.

OWNER Mary & John Fitzgerald OPEN March 1–November 1
ROOMS 2 double, 2 twin, family; all en suite TERMS €36; child reduction (under 10 years 50%); single supplement

### KILGARVAN

## Sillerdane Lodge
Coolnoohill, Kilgarvan, Co. Kerry
Tel: 064 85359

This inviting bungalow in an 'away from it all' spot is surrounded by beautiful scenery. The bedrooms, all on the ground floor, are light and bright; all have a bright pastel décor. Breakfasts are served in the conservatory-style dining room overlooking the view; the lounge has an open fire. This is wonderful walking country and there is a swimming pool (heated in summer) for guests' use. Evening meals are

available by arrangement, with everything prepared from fresh produce and local ingredients—special diets may also be catered for. The
reputedly highest pub in Ireland is close by.

OWNER Joan McCarthy OPEN May 1–September 30
ROOMS 2 double, 2 twin, 1 family; all en suite TERMS €25.50; child
reduction; single supplement €5 MEALS dinner

## KILLARNEY

### Abbey Lodge
Muckross Lodge, Killarney, County Kerry
Tel: 064 34193 Fax: 064 35872 Email: abbeylodgekly@eircom.net
Website: www.abbey-lodge.com

Abbey Lodge is an attractive building with a stone and brick exteri-
or. It stands in its own grounds a three-minute walk from the town
centre. Recently refurbished, the rooms are of a good size, furnished
and decorated to a high standard. John King was formerly in the
contracting business, and has made creative use of church window
supports in two of the bedrooms, most of which have orthopaedic
mattresses. One bedroom is suitable for disabled visitors. Several
rooms have a bath/shower combination. There are several antique
pieces of furniture; of special interest are the American oak floors.
Throughout the house is a mini art gallery, featuring a fine display of
prints by the artist William Frandison—John King is constantly adding
new prints and paintings to his art collection.
   This charming property with its attentive host, has all the facilities
of a 4-star hotel. Guests would be well advised to leave their car in
the parking lot and walk into town. The guest sitting room has a fire
when chilly, and a good selection of books. Popular with business
people and tourists, this property would be an excellent choice
when visiting the Killarney area. Sightseeing tours can be arranged
and nearby facilities include golf and horse riding. Credit cards
accepted.

OWNER John King OPEN All year except for Christmas
ROOMS 5 en suite TERMS €55 pps; child reduction (50% if sharing);
single supplement

### Fair Haven
Lissivigeen, Killarney, Co. Kerry
Tel: 064 32542
Email: fairhavenbb@eircom.net

Fair Haven is a comfortable, warm country house set in half a
hectare of land in peaceful, scenic surroundings. The simply furnished
bedrooms are spotlessly clean. The lounge has open fires and tea

makers, and guests may help themselves at any time at no extra charge. Smoking is permitted in the guest lounge if other guests have no objection. There is a separate bright dining room where freshly-cooked breakfasts are served. Ann Teahan is an extremely friendly lady who has been welcoming visitors since 1984. Fair Haven was named after the hometown of an American who was the first guest. For guests who would enjoy a rest from driving, Ann Teahan can arrange tours of the Ring of Kerry and Dingle Bay at a modest charge. Buses collect guests at the door. Reservations can also be made for the Killarney Manor House Banquet, an excellent evening of food and entertainment which started in 1990. Golf and fishing are nearby. The postal address for Fair Haven is Fair Haven, Lissivigeen (N22), Killarney.

Fair Haven can be a little tricky to find: it is situated on the eastern side of Killarney on the N22 heading to Cork. One mile from park roundabout, on the right-hand side of the road leaving Killarney, and you will be there.

Guests can be picked up at the property if they would prefer a tour of the Ring Kerry.

OWNER Anne Teahan OPEN May 1–October 31 ROOMS 2 double, 2 twin, 1 family; all en suite TERMS €25.50; child reduction (25% if sharing); single supplement €6.50

## Kathleen's Country House
Tralee Road, Killarney, Co. Kerry
Tel: 064 32810 Fax: 064 32340
Email: info@kathleens.net
Website: www.kathleens.net

Kathleen's Country House is a delightful, family-run guest house where traditional hospitality and courteous personal attention are assured. The house stands in 3 acres of mature gardens, just 1km north of Killarney. It has been completely renovated. Beautifully maintained and very tastefully decorated, improvements to this immaculate property are ongoing. Kathleen's love of art reflects the décor; there is a splendid display of original oil and watercolour paintings, and inspirational verse decorates the walls. The well-appointed bedrooms are elegantly furnished in antique pine with orthopaedic beds. Breakfasts only are served in the spacious dining room at separate tables overlooking the garden. Kathleen's combines the facilities of a 5 star hotel with the comforts and warmth of an Irish home. Children over 2 years welcome. Wine license. Smoking is not permitted.

The house motto of 'Easy to get to, hard to leave' is endorsed by the many repeat visitors who enjoy the traditional hospitality; they may arrive as guests, but they will leave as friends. There are three 18-hole golf courses, plus two 9-hole courses within a five-minute drive, and fishing, lovely country walks, cycling and swimming are all available close by. Special group rates upon request.

OWNER Kathleen & Regan Sheppard OPEN March 17–November ROOMS 19 double/twin/family; all en suite TERMS €110–140 per room; child reduction (50% if sharing with 2 adults); single supplement

## Knockcullen
New Road, Killarney, Co. Kerry
Tel: 064 33915
Email: knockcullen@hotmail.com

Knockcullen, which means 'hill on top', is an immaculate family home in a private location off the main road, situated only a two-minute walk from town and the National Park. Marie O'Brien has been in business for 10 years; she started when the family had grown and she needed to do something to occupy her time and her home. It has become a popular venue; many guests return often for Marie's special hospitality and the warm and welcoming atmosphere. The house is an ideal touring base for this scenic area. Breakfasts only are served, but there are lots of good pubs and restaurants close by. Marie is interested in walking and mountain climbing and is pleased to assist guests with information and/or planned itineraries. Two minutes to town centre and five minutes to bus and railway station.

OWNER Marie O'Brien OPEN March 17–October 31 ROOMS 5 double/twin; all en suite TERMS €28 pps; 33% child reduction under 12; single supplement

## Linn Dubh
Aghadoe Heights, Killarney, Co. Kerry
Tel: 064 33828

A dormer bungalow surrounded by scenic countryside, Linn overlooks Killarney's lakes and mountains. The bedrooms are spotlessly clean and nicely decorated; all have pine orthopaedic beds. Tea making facilities are on the landing and hair-dryers are available on request. Carmella Sheehy is an enthusiastic lady who decided to open up her home when her children were young; B&B allowed her to stay home with her children and still have the opportunity to meet people.

There is a comfortable lounge with a TV, and a large, furnished patio area and a spacious garden for guests' use. This is a peaceful area and golf, fishing and horseback riding are all available close by. For visitors wanting a rest from driving, local tours can be arranged. Visa and Mastercard accepted.

OWNER Carmella Sheehy OPEN March 1–November 30
ROOMS 2 double, 1 twin, 2 family; all en suite TERMS €25.50; child reduction (50% sharing with adults); single supplement €6.50–12.50

## Lohan's Lodge
Tralee Road, Killarney, Co. Kerry
Tel: 064 33871

Lohan's Lodge stands back off the road and is surrounded by a beautiful, well tended garden. Two of the nicest things about the Lodge are the owners, Cathy and Mike Lohan; they are a delightful, warm and friendly couple who love what they do–guests are treated more like friends. The bedrooms, all on the ground floor, are average in size and are colour coordinated. Most have views of the gardens, which guests are encouraged to enjoy, and the patio is furnished. Electric blankets are provided for cool nights. There is an extensive menu for breakfast, which is served in the dining room at separate tables. The elegant, spacious lounge, which has cathedral ceilings, is warmed by a gas fire. This is a wonderful spot for visiting Killarney, a three-minute drive away, after which guests can return to the tranquillity and comfort of Lohan's Lodge. Non-smoking household. Visa and Mastercard accepted. Situated on the N22 Killarney/Tralee Road, 5 km from Killarney.

OWNER Cathy & Mike Logan OPEN March 5–November 5
ROOMS 2 double, 1 twin, single, 2 double/single; all en suite
TERMS €25.50; child reduction; single supplement €10

## The 19th Green Guest House and Restaurant
Lackabane, Fossa, Killarney, Co. Kerry
Tel: 064 32868 Fax: 064 32637
Email: 19thgreen@eircom.net
Website: www.19thgreen-bb.com

The 19th Green is an immaculate, well maintained property situated in quiet and peaceful countryside, just a five-minute drive from Killorglin and Ring of Kerry Road. New owners John and Freda Sheehan maintain high standards. The large bedrooms are tastefully decorated with comfortable beds; one room is suitable for disabled visitors. Smoking is allowed in bedrooms and the TV lounge. The ground floor has been extensively refurbished. The spacious lounge has an open fire in a stone fireplace and overlooks the mountains.

Situated across the road are Killarney's two 18-hole championship courses, sited in mature woodlands. Tee times can be arranged, part of the service extended by the accommodating owners, John & Freda Sheehan. Tours can also be arranged for the Ring of Kerry, Dingle Peninsula, Blarney Castle, etc. John and Freda Sheehan are proud of the personal attention guests receive here, and make every effort to ensure that guests feel welcome and comfortable. The restaurant will offer à la carte dining to residents. The owners are pleased to offer advice on the wide range of restaurants in Killarney. The property is not suitable for children. Visa, Access and Mastercard accepted.

OWNER John & Freda Sheehan OPEN March 17–November 30 ROOMS 13 double/twin/family; all en suite TERMS €50–55 pps; single supplement; child reduction

**Villa Marias**
Aghadoe Heights, Killarney, Co. Kerry
Tel: 064 32307
Email: dgcounihan@eircom.net

A dormer bungalow in a peaceful location, a five-minute drive from the scenic Aghadoe Heights area. The peaceful gardens are a great spot to sit, relax and enjoy views of Killarney's mountains and lakes.

The house is immaculate, the bedrooms well-appointed and comfortable. There is a separate TV lounge with an open fireplace, over which is displayed a fine Waterford Crystal sword. Smoking is allowed in the TV lounge. Mary Counihan has been established for 16 years, prior to which she was in the catering industry; she went into the B&B business to maintain contact with people. Mary is a wonderful host: her first concern is her guests' comfort, and a warm welcome greets everyone. Guests are greeted with a cup of tea or coffee and biscuits upon arrival, even though there are tea makers in the bedrooms. Well located and convenient for all local amenities.

OWNER Mary Counihan OPEN April 1–October 31 ROOMS 3 double, 1 twin; 2 en suite TERMS €25.50–28; child reduction; single room €31.50

## KILLORGLIN

**Grove Lodge**
Killorglin, Co. Kerry
Tel: 066 97 61157 Fax: 066 97 62330
Email: info@grovelodge.com
Website: www.grovelodge.com

This gracious country house stands in 1.2 hectares of mature gardens and woodlands on the banks of the River Laune, and has south-facing views of the McGillycuddy Reeks mountains. The rooms are spacious and the reception lounge has a fully restored antique cast-iron fireplace. The luxurious bedrooms are tastefully appointed. They each have coordinated floral bedding and curtains (one has a lace-canopied four-poster bed), and four have their own balconies. The Lodge is delightful in every way: there are high ceilings, a galleried landing, a colourful patio area and a conservatory. Breakfasts are excellent: guests can help themselves to yoghurt, cereal, fruit and juices followed by pancakes or a traditional Irish breakfast. Smoking is permitted in the lounge only. A superb place to stay when visiting this beautiful region of Ireland, the location is idyllic, peace and quiet above all, and the welcome is wonderful. Blennerville Windmill Centre, Crag Cave and Killorgan Golf Club are all within driving distance. American Express, Access, Visa and Diners Club accepted.

OWNER Fergus & Delia Foley OPEN All year except for Christmas ROOMS 5 double, 1 twin, 4 family; 6 en suite TERMS B&B €30–55 per person; child reduction (50% if sharing); single €32–57

## LISTOWEL

### Ceol na h'Abhann
Tralee Road, Ballygrennane, Listowel, Co. Kerry
Tel: 068 21345 Fax: 068 21345

Ceol na h'Abhann, which means 'Music of the River', is aptly named. This charming thatched house stands on the bank of the River Feale, in a lovely garden with a huge chestnut tree. This is an idyllic setting and guests lucky enough to book in here will not be disappointed.

Niall and Kathleen Stack, the delightful owners, originally had the house built as a home for their retirement, but missed contact with people, and bed & breakfast seemed a fun thing to do. It was hard work, but enjoyable; successful from the beginning, many guests return for the special hospitality extended here.

The immaculately kept bedrooms are individually decorated and have rich, tasteful furniture; they are reached by a staircase with an old cast-iron railing. One bedroom is on the ground floor. Excellent breakfasts are served in the bright dining room, and there is a lounge and sunny conservatory for guests' use. Smoking in sun lounge only. On fine days guests can stroll along the river bank or, for the less energetic, seating is provided. Listowel is within walking distance and there are several venues for evening meals. Credit cards accepted.

OWNER Kathleen Stack OPEN April 1–October 31
ROOMS 4 double; all en suite
TERMS €35 pps; child reduction 10%; single supplement

## SNEEM

### Avonlea House
Sportsfield Road, Sneem, Co. Kerry
Tel: 064 45221

Email: AvonleaHouse@eircom.net
Website: www.sneem.com/avonlea.html

Avonlea is an immaculate, comfortable home in a secluded spot, though only 100m from the village. Mrs Hussey began her bed & breakfast business after a friend asked her to take her overflow guests during high season. Mrs Hussey enjoyed the experience so much that she decided to do B&B full time. A most accommodating host, she is assisted by her children during the summer holidays. The modern bedrooms are warm and comfortable. The TV lounge, with a real fire, has a piano that guests are welcome to play. Guests may also sit outside in comfort to enjoy the lovely gardens.

The house is situated just a two-minute walk from the village, which has several good restaurants and local pubs with entertainment during the season. Ideal spot for the holiday golfer, walker and fishing enthusiast, as all are available nearby. Advance reservations recommended during high season.

OWNER Gerald & Maura Hussey OPEN April 1–October 31
ROOMS 2 double, 3 twin, 1 single; 5 en suite
TERMS €26.50–30pps; single supplement

## Derry East Farmhouse
Sneem, Co. Kerry
Tel: 064 45193 Fax: 064 45193
Email: teahans@eircom.net
Website: www.sneem.com/derryeast.html

Derry East is a working beef farm. This is a botanist's paradise, with its wild mountain landscape background. Derry East has its own hard tennis court and a private fish pond stocked with trout. Guests are welcome to use the facilities and to take farm walks. The bedrooms are warm and comfortable, and the bright, colourful dining room offers views from all windows. Dinner, if arranged in advance, is served featuring home-grown vegetables, with vegetarian and special diets catered for. Smoking is permitted in lounge only.

Derry East is an ideal spot for a relaxing holiday. Mrs Teahan is a caring and considerate host, offering guests a truly warm welcome, ably assisted in the summer by her children, who are happy to play Irish music for her guests.

OWNER Mary & John Teahan OPEN April 1–October 31
ROOMS 1 double, 2 twin, 1 family; all en suite
TERMS from €30 pps; 25% child reduction; single supplement
MEALS dinner from €28

## Hillside Haven

Tahilla, Sneem, Co. Kerry
Tel: 064 82065 Fax: 064 82065
Email: hillsidehaven@eircom.net

This country house stands in an elevated position set in mature gardens with a magnificent view of the sea, mountains and glorious countryside. The bedrooms, all on the ground floor, are spotlessly clean and comfortable.

This is very much a family-run establishment with traditional hospitality and friendly, accommodating owners. Tasty evening meals are served (if pre-arranged) featuring traditional dishes, Irish stew, bacon and cabbage, home-baked breads and desserts; vegetarians are catered for. Breakfasts are served in the dining room, or, if guests prefer, outside in good weather.

Walking is one of Helen Foley's hobbies, and she would be pleased to arrange walking holidays for small groups, and to outline local walks for individual walkers. Complementary tea and coffee is available at any time.

Smoking is only permitted in the lounge. Light snacks are available on request. Credit cards accepted.

OWNER Helen Foley OPEN May 1–September 30
ROOMS 2 double, 2 family; all en suite
TERMS €30-32 pps; child reduction; single supplement


## Old Convent House

Pier Road, Sneem, Co. Kerry
Tel: 064 45181 Fax: 064 45181

Visitors enjoy the old-world atmosphere of the Old Convent House, set in its own grounds on the estuary of a river. The house was built in the middle of the last century as a convent for the Presentation nuns, who taught in the local school until 1891. Since that time it has been in the hands of the O'Sullivan family, who have been careful to preserve the character of the house while offering modern comforts. There are two lounges–one for reading or chatting with other guests, the other a very spacious lounge, and a conservatory. Tea, coffee and biscuits are available at all times in the dining room. Guests are welcome to make use of the large gardens, and there is access to the river. Fishing enthusiasts may take trips on the Bay from Oysterbed Pier, and Sneem with its gaily painted houses is just a pleasant three-minute stroll away. Alice O'Sullivan is an enthusiastic walker and can provide walking maps and assist guests with walking itineraries.

# Old Convent House

OWNER Alice O'Sullivan OPEN March 1–November 15
ROOMS 3 double, 1 twin, 1 family; all en suite
TERMS €30 pps; child reduction (25% if sharing); single supplement

## TRALEE

### Ballingowan House
Mile Height, Killarney Road, Tralee, County Kerry
Tel: 066 7127150 Fax: 066 7120325
Email: ballingowan@eircom.net
Website: www.kerryview.com/ballingowanhouse

An impressive red brick building, standing in its own grounds, with
plenty of parking. The large bedrooms are all en suite, have colourful
throws, TV and hospitality trays. A pleasant sitting room has comfortable leather furniture, TV/video, family portraits, and a real fire
for chilly evenings. The dining room has an unusual sideboard, and
breakfasts are served at separate tables.
The house is bright and clean, there are lots of pine doors, and is
well maintained. Sheila enjoys her business, and has lots of happy
returning guests.

OWNER Sheila Kerins OPEN April 17–September 30
ROOMS 4 double/family/single; all en suite TERMS from €28; child
reduction; single supplement

### Brianville
Clogherbrian, Fenit Road, Tralee, Co. Kerry
Tel: 066 712 6645 Fax: 066 712 6645
Email: michsmit@gofree.indigo.ie
Website: www.brianville-tralee.com

A luxurious modern bungalow situated in half a hectare of landscaped grounds, Brianville stands back off the road behind a beautiful
stone wall entrance, with views of the mountain. The well furnished
lounge has a fireplace, TV and piano. The rooms are well maintained,
have en suite facilities and power showers. All are tastefully fur-

nished, with comfortable beds, hair-dryer, TV and tea makers. There is a lovely antique grandfather clock in the hallway. This is very much a family-run establishment and the owners are helpful and provide literature on what to see and do in the area. All rooms are on the ground floor. There are some excellent seafood restaurants nearby, and golf, fishing, windsurfing and sailing are also within easy reach. The house is situated on the R558, Fenit Road, one and a quarter miles from town centre.

OWNER Mrs Joan Smith OPEN All year ROOMS 2 double, 2 twin, I family; all en suite TERMS €30-35 pps; child reduction; single supplement

## Castlemorris House
Ballymullen, Tralee, Co. Kerry
Tel: 066 718 0060 Fax: 066 712 6007
Email: castlemorris@eircom.net

Castlemorris House, a beautiful ivy-clad Victorian house, stands in its own grounds on the edge of town. Built in 1870 by the local regiment of the British Army and used by the commanding officer as his private residence, the house was purchased by the charming owners, Paddy and Mary Barry, in 1997. They have lovingly restored the residence, carefully combining old-world charm with modern comforts. Many original features remain, such as stained-glass windows and casement shutters. The coving and fireplaces were removed and reinserted after restoration.

A warm and simple elegance pervades, the ambience is unpretentious, and the Barrys are fine hosts. The spacious bedrooms, three with original fireplaces, have king-size beds and are furnished in keeping with the character of the house; two have sloping ceilings and beams, and there several interesting antique pieces about. The peaceful drawing room has an open fire, which is lit at the first sign of a chill in the air. Mary is a trained chef and takes pride in her cooking. Imaginative breakfasts are served at separate tables in the dining room. There is a wine license. Vegetarian and special diets are catered for. Although evening meals are no longer served, there is a wide choice of dining within a short walking distance.

There is plenty to interest the visitor, including Siamsa Tíre (the National Folk Theatre), and Irish music can be heard at local pubs. An Equine Centre is within walking distance of the house. Visa, Mastercard and American Express accepted. The house is a little tricky to find. Take N21 from Limerick, take left off roundabout, signed Dingle/Killorglin, 1/4 mile to T-junction, take a right, the house is immediately on the right.

OWNER Mary & Paddy Barry OPEN January 1–December 20

ROOMS 4 double, 2 twin, 2 family; all en suite
TERMS €35 pps; single supplement

## The Fairways
The Kerries, Fenit Road, Tralee, Co. Kerry
Tel: 066 712 7691 Fax: 066 712 7691

The Fairways is in a tranquil spot with beautiful views of Tralee Bay
and the Slieve Mish Mountains and overlooks cattle grazing pastures
and a 9-hole golf course. The light and airy modern country house is
impeccably maintained and well-appointed. Bedrooms are large and
tastefully decorated, two are on the ground floor. There is an excellent choice for breakfast: guests can have just about anything they
want, including yoghurts, fruits, cereals, home-made brown bread
and/or a traditional cooked breakfast. Evening meals are not available, but there are some excellent restaurants in Tralee. An ideal
spot for golfers and tourists, fishing, sailing and beaches are all close
by. Visa, Mastercard and Eurocard accepted.

OWNER Marion Barry OPEN April 1–October 31 ROOMS 2 double,
1 twin, 1 family; all en suite TERMS €28 pps; child reduction (50%
when sharing); single supplement

## WATERVILLE

## Klondyke House
Cieeran Morris
Waterville, County Kerry
Tel: 066 9474119 Fax: 066 9474666
Email: klondykehouse@eircom.net
Website: http://homepage.eircom.net/~klondykehouse

This handsome two-storey residence is on the edge of the village,
just a three minute walk to all amenities. It stands in its own
grounds, has lovely bay views and is easily located, adjacent to the
Craft Market. The bedrooms, are all en suite, and decorated with
soft colours of gold, pink and creams; all have radio/TV/hair-dryer
and telephone. There is a sun room, and two sitting rooms, one, has
a TV, the other a quiet lounge, a great spot, in which to relax, read,
or plan your day's activities. A real fire burns on chilly evenings. The
house is immaculately kept, and Cieeran Morris is a very hospitable
host. There will be two golf courses in Waterville, the new one
expects to be open by 2005. Trips to Skellig can be organized and
walkers will enjoy the nearby mountains. Fishing can be arranged on
Lough Currane. Credit cards taken. Open all year.

OWNER Kathleen & P. J. O'Connor OPEN All year
ROOMS 6 double/twin/family; all en suite

TERMS €30 pps; child reduction; single supplement

## Seaview

Toor, Waterville, Co. Kerry
Tel: 066 947 4297
Email: jfcurran@eircom.net

Seaview is situated in a 'top of the world' location and has panoramic views of Ballinskelligs Bay, the Ballinskelligs Mountains and Hogs Head. The house is clean and modestly furnished, and the family suite is ideal for a family or friends travelling together. All bedrooms have new carpets and curtains and TV, as well as showers. The hallway now has an attractive wooden floor, the dining room has been redecorated. Very tastefully refurbished, Seaview is maintained to a high standard. This is a friendly, informal house, the welcome is warm, and the owners are very happy to sit and chat with guests. Complimentary tea or coffee is offered on arrival. There is a cosy conservatory which overlooks the view, and there is a good supply of games and books around. Guests are also welcome to share the family lounge. Breakfast only is served, but Margaret Curran is happy to give advice on local places serving evening meals. No smoking.

OWNER Margaret Curran OPEN February 1–November 31
ROOMS 1 double, 1 twin, 1 family; all en suite TERMS €25.50; child reduction (25% if sharing); single supplement €6.50

## Sunset House

Waterville, Co. Kerry
Tel: 066 947 4258

This attractive bungalow overlooks Ballinskelligs Bay on the edge of town. Well kept, clean and comfortable, the house is clean and pleasantly furnished with a spacious dining room and a lounge with TV and piano. There is a pretty furnished patio for guests' use. Mrs Fitzgerald began offering bed & breakfast 20 years ago, adding more rooms for the many guests looking for accommodation. However, she still has to turn people away; advance reservations are recommended, particularly during high season. Evening meals are not available, but the accommodating Mrs Fitzgerald would be happy to recommend local eating places serving good food at reasonable prices. Horseback riding and the beach are close by. The world-famous Waterville golf course is only 1 mile from the house.

OWNER Mrs Patricia Fitzgerald OPEN All year
ROOMS 6 double/twin; 4 en suite TERMS €26 pps; child reduction (25% if sharing); single supplement

## COUNTY WATERFORD

Waterford is probably best known for its crystal factory, which has regular hours for visits. Situated in the southeast of the country, it is reputedly one of the sunniest spots in Ireland. Waterford has a pretty coastline and more rugged interior, with good farmland. The Nire Valley is good for walking and pony trekking, with wonderful views

Waterford city has much of interest to visit. Reginald's Tower, a massive circular fortress, is now the civic museum. Christ Church Cathedral, built in 1779; the French church; the Chamber of Commerce, a lovely Georgian building; and the City Hall, which houses two old theatres, are all worth seeing. The International Festival of Light Opera is held in Waterford in September.

Dunmore East, Tramore, Annestown and Dungarvan are all pleasant seaside spots, particularly Dunmore East, which resembles a Devon fishing village. Farther south is the Irish-speaking village of Ring, where Irish scholars go to study. St Declan's Oratory, built in the ninth century, and St Declan's Well and Temple Disert, can be found at Ardmore. The cathedral dates back to the twelfth century, is known for its sculptured figures.

Seven kilometres from Cappoquin is the Cistercian Abbey of Mount Melleray. The Abbey maintains the tradition of monastic hospitality, so it is quite in order to accept a meal if it is offered.

Lismore, in former times a great centre of learning, was built by King John in 1185 and once belonged to Sir Walter Raleigh. The gardens are open to the public. The medieval Cathedral of St Cathach is most attractive, and was restored in 1633.

## ANNESTOWN

**Annestown House**
Annestown, Co. Waterford
Tel: 051 396160 Fax: 051 396474
Email: relax@annestown.com
Website: www.annestown.com

Annestown House has been in the Galloway family since 1830. The grounds stretch down to a wonderful sandy beach, and there are lovely sea and river views. It is a wonderful old, long narrow structure that was originally three or four houses. One end of the building at one time was the curate's house and the other end housed the village shop. The interior of this lived-in family home, with old family portraits and lots of prints, is on many different levels. It rambles from the billiard room, lined with old books and an open fire, to the small, cosy sitting room and comfortable drawing room. At one time there used to be a restaurant in the house and evening meals, served either at one big table or separate tables, are still available if arranged in advance. The bedrooms, four of which have sea views, all have telephone and tea- and coffee-making facilities. John and Pippa are a delightful, easygoing and interesting couple, and are happy to suggest excursions and activities ranging from golf to hill walking to just exploring the beautiful rugged coastline. Annestown has both a croquet lawn and a grass tennis court. Pets in cars only. Mastercard, Visa and American Express accepted. The house is in the centre of the village.

OWNER John & Pippa Galloway OPEN March 15–November 30 ROOMS 5 double/twin; all en suite TERMS €55; single supplement €15 MEALS dinner €35, supper €6

## ARDMORE

**Ardsallagh Lodge**
Kinsalebeg. Ardmore, Co. Waterford
Tel: 024 93496/0861088683 Fax: 024 93496
Email: info@ardsallaghlodge.com
Website: www.ardsallaghlodge.com

Ardsallagh Lodge stands in a commanding position above the River Blackwater, with wonderful views over the mouth of the river to the sea. The house was acquired in 2004 and has undergone extensive refurbishment to be available for accommodation in 2005. Nearby, visitors can fish, hill walk and enjoy coastal drives. Pets outside only. Major credit cards, except American Express, taken. To reach Ardsallagh from the N25 take a very small road to the west just before the River Blackwater Bridge, on the east side.

OWNER Georgina Annett  OPEN all year ROOMS 3 double, 2 twin; all en suite TERMS €35; single supplement; child reduction

## BALLYMACARBRY

**Cnoc-na-Ri Country Home**
Nire Valley, Ballymacarbry, Co. Waterford
Tel: 052 36239 or 087 9477143
Email: richardharte@eircom.net
Website: homepage.eircom.net/~cnocnaricountryhome/

Cnoc-na-Ri, meaning 'hill of the kings', is a small country home set in a peaceful, quiet spot in the Comeraghs in the heart of the Nire Valley. It has a welcoming, friendly atmosphere and lovely views. Richard and Nora added a wing to their house especially to cater for visitors. The rooms are very comfortable and well equipped with hair-dryers, TV and tea- and coffee-making facilities, and two have views. One bedroom has a jacuzzi bath. Nora, an excellent cook, provides a wide menu for breakfast served at separate tables in the dining room, which overlooks the nicely landscaped garden and patio. The patio is a lovely place to sit and absorb the peace that surrounds Cnoc-na-Ri.

Richard and Nora can provide walking maps and packed lunches, and if needed a local guide is available. Golf, riding and fishing are also popular pastimes in this area, and traditional music and dance is usually to be found in one of the local pubs. Pets in cars or shed only. Visa, Mastercard, Access and Eurocard accepted. The house is five kilometres from Ballymacarbry.

OWNER Richard & Nora Harte OPEN February 1–November 1
ROOMS 1 double, 2 family, 2 twin; all en suite
TERMS €40; single supplement; child reduction
MEALS dinner €30

## Glasha Farmhouse
Nire Valley, Ballymacarbry, Co. Waterford
Tel: 052 36108/086 2443255
Email: glasha@eircom.net
ebsite: www.glashafarmhouse.com

Glasha Farmhouse has won many accolades for its hospitality and quality of accommodation and is a large whitewashed building run by enthusiastic, outgoing, Olive O'Gorman.

Over the years the O'Gormans refurbished the old farmhouse, and today there are 8 en suite bedrooms of different sizes and designs, all equipped with every possible amenity. Some rooms have jacuzzi baths, and two are spacious attic type rooms decorated in bright colours.

Guests have use of an enormous sitting room and sit at separate tables in the dining room. A new conservatory overlooks the patio area, resplendent with an elaborate fountain and potted plants. The dairy farm stretches around the house. Many rooms have views of the Knockmealdown and Comeragh Mountains. Olive is a great cook and provides dinners by arrangement. The property stretches down to the River Nire, where guests like to fish, and the nearest pub is only a three minute walk away.

The Munster Way passes close by and the nearby mountains are a great place for hill-walking. Packed lunches can be provided, and a guide can be made available for those wishing to venture off the beaten track. Most credit cards accepted. No pets. Glasha Farmhouse is signposted from Ballymacarbry.

OWNER: Paddy & Olive O'Gorman OPEN All year
ROOMS 8 family/ double/twin; all en suite
TERMS €50–60 pps; single supplement; child reduction
MEALS dinner €25–35, packed lunches

## Hanora's Cottage

Nire Valley, Ballymacarbry, Co. Waterford
Tel: 052 36134 Fax: 052 36540
Email: hanorascottage@eircom.net
Website: www.hanorascottage.com

An absolute haven of peace and tranquillity, Hanora's Cottage nestles at the foot of the Comeragh Mountains, beside the Nire Church and the old schoolhouse, with the Nire River running alongside. The little cottage was built for Seamus' great grandparents in the late 1800s, and Seamus and Mary, the fourth generation of the family, came to live there in 1967 while it was still a two bedroom cottage. It has come a long way since then. Currently the house has ten spacious, very comfortable bedrooms with every possible amenity. All have jacuzzi baths and king-size beds; while superior rooms have double tubs. All have hair-dryers, telephone, TV and tea- and coffee-making facilities. Breakfasts at Hanora's are quite a feast. There is an exotic array of fruits and Mary's special porridge, local cheeses, smoked salmon and a choice of cooked breakfasts. There are a variety of activities for guests—guided or do-it-yourself walks both strenuous and gentle in the Comeragh Mountains as well as golf and bicycling. Having worked off breakfast, there's Eoin and Judith Wall's dinner to look forward to.

Eoin, Mary's son, trained at Ballymaloe Cookery School and has worked in some renowned restaurants. Later in the evening join the locals at one of the pubs for traditional music, singing and dancing. No pets. Visa and Mastercard accepted. The house is signposted at Ballymacarbry, and is beside the Nire Church by the river.

OWNER Mary Wall OPEN All year except for Christmas
ROOMS 6 double, 4 twin; all en suite TERMS €80–130;
single supplement; not suitable for children MEALS dinner à la carte

## CAPPOQUIN

### Richmond House

Cappoquin, Co. Waterford
Tel: 058 54278 Fax: 058 54988
Email: info@richmondhouse.net Website: www.richmondhouse.net

This substantial house was built in 1704 by the Earl of Cork and Burlington and stands in well maintained parkland. It is a peaceful, comfortable country house, beautifully furnished and decorated with spacious, bright rooms. Paul Deevy trained as a chef at Ballymaloe, and the restaurant at Richmond House has won several awards for the excellence of its cuisine. Dinner is served in two elegant dining rooms, which are also open to non residents, and there is a full bar licence. Guests have use of two sitting rooms and a conservatory overlooking the garden. The comfortable bedrooms are furnished in keeping with the style of the house and have telephone, TV, trouser press, hair-dryers and tea- and coffee-making facilities. Arrangements can be made for salmon fishing on the Blackwater, and trout fishing on the Blackwater, Suir and the Bride. Deep-sea and coarse fishing are also available. Other amenities nearby include pony trekking, walking, mountain rambling and golf. No pets. All major credit cards accepted. Richmond Lodge is half a mile outside Cappoquin on N72.

OWNER Paul & Claire Deevy OPEN January 7–December 22 ROOMS 7 double, 2 single, 1 family; all en suite TERMS €75–120; child reduction; single supplement MEALS dinner €48

## DUNGARVAN

### Gortnadiha Lodge
Gortnadiha, Ring, Dungarvan, Co. Waterford
Tel: 058 46142
Email: gortnadihalodge@eircom.net
Website: www.waterfordfarms.com/gortnadihalodge

Guests will appreciate old-fashioned hospitality at Gortnadiha Lodge, which has been in the Harty family for several generations. Tom and Eileen Harty have relocated their bed and breakfast from Gortnadiha House to the next door Lodge after some eight years. The Lodge, which is surrounded by woodland on an elevated site, has panoramic views of Dungarvan Bay.
Traditionally and comfortably furnished., the Lodge has TV and tea- and coffee-making facilities. The soaps provided are locally made, and until recently the 300 acre dairy farm made Irish farmhouse cheese. Gortnadiha Lodge is only 3 kilometres from Dungarvan, signposted off the main N25 between Dungarvan and Youghal. Pets can be put up in the kennels. Visa and Mastercard accepted.

OWNER Eileen Harty OPEN All year ROOMS 2 double, 1 twin; all en suite TERMS €40 pps; single supplement; child reduction

### Powersfield House
Ballinamuck West, Dungarvan, Co. Waterford
Tel: 058 45594 Fax: 058 45550
Website: www.powersfield.com

Eunice Power trained in the hotel business in Switzerland, came home and married a farmer. With two small children she and Edmund needed to build a house, so they decided to incorporate a family home with a guesthouse and restaurant. The home they built, finished in 2001, is a classical-looking building in the Georgian style, standing about a mile from Dungarvan, just off the Clonmel road. Some land surrounds the house, but most of the dairy and beef farm is a short distance away. Eunice is a bundle of energy and has a love for what she's doing. She's a first class cook, and the small restaurant is open to the public and residents alike. The house is attractively furnished, the decor bright and simple, and the walls adorned with pictures by local artists. The ground floor bedroom is suitable for wheelchair access. The bedrooms have TV and telephone, and tea and coffee can be ordered when required. Pets outside only. Major credit cards accepted.

OWNER Eunice & Edmund Power OPEN All year ROOMS 5 double, 1 twin; all en suite TERMS €50–60; single supplement; child reduction MEALS dinner €27–35 bookable 24hrs in advance

## The Castle Farm
Cappagh, Dungarvan, Co. Waterford
Tel: 058 68049 Fax: 058 68099
Email: castlefm@iol.ie
Website: www.castlecountryhouse.com

Mountain Castle was the principal seat of the McGraths of Sliabh gCua, one of the two Gaelic families that owned land in this country before the arrival of Cromwell. The accommodation is in a restored wing of the fifteenth-century castle, which stands in lovely countryside with fine views. The oldest section, with the original archway, contains the attractive, long, narrow dining room with its 1.25 metre thick stone walls.

Joan Nugent is a very friendly, welcoming lady and has tastefully decorated and furnished the house. It is very comfortable and has a welcoming sitting room where tea and scones are served on arrival. The bedrooms have TV, hair-dryers and tea making facilities. Dinner is available on request, featuring fruit, vegetables, herbs and meats from the family farm, and at breakfast guests are served farm milk and homemade jam. Guests can help themselves to tea or coffee in the kitchen.

There is a hard tennis court, garden walks through the acre and a half of gardens, and fishing on the River Finisk, which flows through the farm. The farmhouse is set on 49 hectares of dairy land, and organised farm groups are accepted. Pets by arrangement. Visa and Mastercard are accepted. Castle Farm is signposted at the N72 and R671.

OWNER Joan Nugent OPEN February–November
ROOMS 2 double, 1 twin, 1 family; all en suite TERMS €40–45; single supplement ; child reduction; MEALS dinner €25–35

## Sliabh gCua Farmhouse

Touraneena, Ballinamult, Dungarvan, Co. Waterford
Tel: 058 47120
Email: breedacullinan@sliabhgcua.com
Website: www.sliabhgcua.com

A warm welcome from Breeda Cullinan awaits the visitor to Sliabh gCua–which literally translated, means the Mountain of the Chieftain. It is an attractive creeper-clad farmhouse, built in the early part of the 20th century. Lovely gardens surround the house, and beyond is the beef farm. Every one of the comfortable bedrooms enjoys views of the garden and the Comeragh and Knockmealdown mountains. Guests have a cosy sitting room for their use, and breakfast is served in the pleasant dining room. Wide planked wooden floors are exposed and overlaid with rugs in much of the house. Sliabh gCua is a good location for touring the Nire Valley, as well as for walking and riding. No pets and no credit cards. The house is signposted off the R672 between Dungarvan and Clonmel, close to the village of Touraneena.

OWNER Jim & Breeda Cullinan OPEN April 1–October 31
ROOMS 1 family, 1 twin, 2 double; all en suite
TERMS €40; single supplement; child reduction

## DUNMORE EAST

### Church Villa
Dunmore East, Co. Waterford
Tel: 051 383390 Fax: 051 383023
Email: churchvilla@eircom.net
Website: homepage.eircom.net/~churchvilla/

This whitewashed period house, one of a row of cottages opposite the Church of Ireland church and adjacent to the Ship Bar and Restaurant, is right in the centre of the attractive village of Dunmore East. The bright bedrooms have been enlarged and redecorated, some retaining their original fireplaces, and they all have TV, hair-dryers and tea- and coffee-making facilities. There is a guest lounge with TV, and breakfast is served in the conservatory. There are plenty of eating places in Dunmore East, including the restaurant next door. Church Villa is ten minutes from the beach and fishing harbour and close to the park where there are caves to explore. There are bicycles for guests' use, and free email access. No pets. Visa and Mastercard accepted.

OWNER Phyllis Lannon OPEN All year except for Christmas
ROOMS 2 double, 2 twin, 1 single, 1 family; all en suite
TERMS €29–33; single supplement child reduction

## McAllister's Bed & Breakfast

Wellington Terrace, Dunmore East, Co. Waterford
Tel: 051 383035
Email: mcallisterbb@hotmail.com
Website: www.indunmoreast.com

McAllister's is part of a terrace, standing in a commanding position, in the middle of the attractive village of Dunmore East, looking over harbour and sea. The front patio is a great place, on a sunny day, to watch the world go by. The house is about 200 years old, and has surprisingly large rooms for its type. A previous owner exposed many of the old stone walls, and stripped a lot of the woodwork, giving the building a somewhat rustic look. The sitting/dining room is a particularly large and pleasing, with a low ceiling and nice views. The family room is apartment-like. Every room except one has a sea view. Carmel McAllister is a friendly lady who gives her guests a warm welcome. No pets. No credit cards.

OWNER Mrs. Carmel McAllister OPEN April 1–October 15
ROOMS 1 family, 1 double/twin, 1 double; all en suite
TERMS €28–32 pps; single supplement; child reduction

## LISMORE

## Buggy's Glencairn Inn

Glencairn, Lismore, Co. Waterford
Tel: 058 56232 Fax: 058 56232
Email: info@buggys.net
Website: www.lismore.com

This delightful old inn was acquired by the Buggys when they decided to leave Kinsale for a quieter life. It has stood at the crossroads in the tiny hamlet of Glencairn since 1720 and has never lost its license to be a pub. Twelve years ago when Ken and Cathleen moved here it needed a lot of work, and they have transformed it into more of a charming restaurant and bar with rooms, than a local pub. It is quaint, cosy and comfortable, decorated with all kinds of knick-knacks, including a collection of Ken's drawings and cartoons.

Upstairs bedrooms have a lot of character, with brass beds and each of the doubles has a claw foot bath in their en suite bathrooms—one twin has an en suite shower. All have TV, tea- and coffee-making facilities and hair-dryers. No pets. Visa and Mastercard accepted.

OWNER Ken & Cathleen Buggy OPEN March 17–1st week November; from November–March mainly weekends
ROOMS 2 double, 2 twin; all en suite
TERMS from €50–62.50; single supplement MEALS dinner from €35

## Park House

Stradbally, Co. Waterford
Tel: 051 293185 Fax: 051 293185

Stradbally Park House is approached up a long driveway through its 300 acres of farmland, a kilometre from the charming little village of Stradbally. A most colourful and beautifully kept garden lies to the front of the house, which dates from the 1800s.

Peg Connors has a good sense of humour and likes to keep an orderly and immaculate home. A long cheerful dining room, where breakfast only is served, lies to one side of the hallway, and a matching size sitting room on the other side. Bedrooms are attractively and simply furnished, mostly in pine with bright, fresh colours. Beaches and good restaurants are nearby. Not suitable for children. No smoking. Pets in stables by arrangement.

OWNER Mrs Peg Connors OPEN Easter–November
ROOMS 2 double, 1 twin, 1 single, 1 family; en suite or with private bathrooms TERMS €35; single supplement

## Cliff House

Cliff Road, Tramore, Co. Waterford
Tel: 051 381497 or 391296 Fax: 051 381497
Email: hilary@cliffhouse.ie
Website: www.cliffhouse.ie

Cliff House, built by its owners, stands in landscaped gardens overlooking the sea. Pat and Hilary are friendly and welcoming and run the guest house in a professional manner. There are now two family suites each consisting of two rooms with en suite bathrooms, and the remaining rooms are well appointed, most having sea views and two are on the ground floor. Bedrooms have TV and hair-dryers.

The large conservatory overlooks Tramore Bay and is a popular place to relax and have a cup of tea or coffee. The extensive breakfast menu has some interesting options. Cliff House is within walking distance of Tramore Golf Club and town centre and adjacent to the new leisure centre. It is a 10 minute drive from the Waterford Glass Factory. No pets. Visa and Mastercard accepted. The house is off R675 as you exit from Tramore to Dungarvan.

OWNER Pat & Hilary O'Sullivan OPEN March 10– start of December
ROOMS 2 double, 2 twin, 2 family; all en suite
TERMS €37–50; single supplement; child reduction

## Glenorney by the Sea

Newtown Hill, Tramore, Co. Waterford
Tel: 051 381056 Fax: 051 381103
Email: glenorney@iol.ie
Website: www.glenorney.com

This attractive looking house on the edge of Tramore was built
twelve years ago and has a nice front garden. It is very well cared for
and has good furniture and decorations. The spacious bedrooms are
clean and bright and most have a sea view, and they each have hair-
dryer, trouser press, telephone, TV and tea- and coffee-making facilities. The nice, bright sitting room has a TV, open fire, piano and sea
views. Double doors lead into the breakfast room, which has separate tables with linen cloths. The sun room, garden and patio area
are great places to sit and admire the view over Tramore Bay. Pets in
cars only. Visa and American Express taken. Glenorney is on the edge
of Tramore and within walking distance of Golf Club and beaches.

OWNER Marie Murphy OPEN All year except for Christmas
ROOMS 2 double, 2 twin, 2 family; all en suite
TERMS €30–40 pps; single supplement; 20% child reduction

## WATERFORD

## Blenheim House

Blenheim Heights, Waterford, Co. Waterford
Tel: 051 874115
Email: blenheim@eircom.net
Website: homepage.eircom.net/~blenheim/

Blenheim House was built in 1763 and stands in 1.5 hectares of
grounds, including a deer park and a children's play area. Most of the
bedrooms have the original Georgian fireplaces and they have tea-
and coffee-making facilities. The large lounge with an open fire overlooks the grounds. The Waterford Glass Factory is close by, and
other local activities include swimming, riding, golf and fishing. Pets
accepted. Blenheim House is 5.5 km from the centre of Waterford
on the Passage East Road, just a seven-minute drive from the ferry.

OWNER Margaret Fitzmaurice OPEN Closed for Christmas ROOMS 2
double, 2 twin, 1 single, 1 family; all en suite TERMS €32; child reduction

## Brown's Town House

29 South Parade, Waterford, Co. Waterford
Tel: 051 870594 Fax: 051 871923
Email: info@brownstownhouse.com
Website: www.brownstownhouse.com

This modest looking, brick-built Victorian town house is on a residential street, only a few minutes' walk into the centre. The house was added to recently, now providing spacious, attractive accommodation with every possible amenity. The en suite bedrooms each have hair-dryer, trouser press, telephone, TV, tea- and coffee-making facilities and mineral water. One room has a rooftop garden, and one is a suite. There is a small sitting room for guests' use and a dining room where excellent breakfasts are served at one table. Waterford's restaurants are within a five-minute walk, as is the Waterford Show. Pets accepted. Visa, Mastercard and Laser accepted.

OWNER Siobhan McConnell OPEN February 1–December 15
ROOMS 4 double, 1 twin, 1 family; all en suite
TERMS €50 pps; single supplement; child reduction

## Foxmount Country House
Passage East Road, Waterford, Co. Waterford
Tel: 051 874308 Fax: 051 854906
Email: info@foxmountcountryhouse.com
Website: www.foxmountcountryhouse.com/

This lovely seventeenth-century house is set in attractive countryside surrounded by its 100-hectare farm, run by David Kent and one of his sons. David and Margaret Kent are a most welcoming, friendly couple, and have been many years in the bed & breakfast business. The drawing room is very attractive with an open fireplace, and is a nice spot to unwind over tea or coffee in front of a warming log fire. Beautifully presented breakfasts are served in the dining room, which overlooks the garden, at separate tables covered in pretty white linen. It is a pleasant stroll to the atmospheric pub under the bridge. Margaret is continuously updating the furnishings and décor. All rooms have hair-dryers. Guests are welcome to use the hard tennis court and to play table tennis. Pets only in cars. To get to Foxmount from Waterford take the Dunmore East Road; after three miles take Passage East Road.

OWNER David & Margaret Kent OPEN March 10–November 1
ROOMS 3 double, 2 twin; all en suite TERMS €55; single supplement ; child reduction

Foxmount Country House

### Sion Hill House & Gardens

Ferrybank, Waterford, Co. Waterford
Tel: 051 851558 Fax: 051 851678

This house has a fascinating history and a wonderful, charming atmosphere. It stands high above the river Suir overlooking the city of Waterford, it was built about 1730 for the founder of the famous Pope (shipping) family. The present owners, George and Antionette Kavanagh, are most delightful and attentive hosts and enjoy relating interesting stories of the house and gardens.

Sion House is full of books and pictures and has a grand piano in the lived in drawing room, and a beautiful grandfather clock dating from 1750 in the hall. The wooden floors in the dining room have recently been renovated.

The Kavanaghs, who are avid gardeners, were lucky enough to have not only the old plans of the gardens, dating from 1763, but also to inherit the old gardener, now in his 80s. Through these two sources they have been able to restore the lovely garden, which is full of rare and interesting plants, trees and ferns, and which is open to the public. A great iron bell made locally and hanging at the side of the house is sounded on New Year's Eve.

The pleasant, comfortable bedrooms overlook the gardens or river, and have TV and tea- and coffee-making facilities. Pets outside only. Visa and Mastercard accepted. Sion Hill is 800-900m from Waterford Bridge Roundabout, between Ard Rí Hotel and Shell petrol station on N25 Wexford-Rosslare Road.

OWNER George and Antoinette Kavanagh
OPEN All year except for Christmas & New Year
ROOMS 1 double, 3 family; all en suite
TERMS from €45 pps; single supplement

## WOODSTOWN

### Gaultier Lodge

Woodstown, Co. Waterford
Tel: 051 382549
Email: castleffrench@eircom.net
Website: www.gaultier-lodge.com

Gaultier Lodge, an 18th century family home, hidden behind a high stone wall in the small village of Woodstown borders the beach, and has wonderful views from practically every room. It is a lovely old house, which although modernised with large, well appointed bathrooms, still retains its family home atmosphere. One room is particularly impressive with a massive four-poster bed. Tropical looking gardens surround the house, and inside pictures of hunting scenes hang on the walls. Breakfast is served in the basement room, just off the kitchen, and the sitting room is a comfortable place to relax. Sheila Bagliani lives part of the time in Galway and in North America, but guests are well looked after in her absence. Dogs by arrangement. Visa and Mastercard accepted.

OWNER Sheila Bagliani OPEN 1 April–31 October ROOMS 3 double, 1 twin; all en suite TERMS €70 single supplement

## COUNTY WEXFORD

The most southerly county and one of the main gateways, through the port of Rosslare, Wexford is also the warmest part of the whole country, an area of gentle hills, fertile farmland and a coastline of sandy beaches. Much of Wexford history is associated with the Norman invasion and the 1798 rebellion.

The Wexford Opera Festival, which takes place in October, is world-renowned and features top international singers. The town throbs with an influx of opera lovers, and many fringe events take place during the festival. It is an attractive town, with narrow, winding streets, and the Maritime Museum and the twelfth-century ruins of Selskar Abbey are of particular interest.

The castle at the attractive market town of Enniscorthy houses the county museum, with an interesting folk section. Worth a visit are the thirteenth-century castle at Ferns, the old town of New Ross, and Dunrody Abbey, dating from 1182, near Campile. Nearby at Dunganstown is the Kennedy ancestral home.

### ARTHURSTOWN

**Dunbrody Country House Hotel**
Arthurstown, New Ross, Co. Wexford
Tel: 051 389 600 Fax: 051 389 601
Email: dunbrody@indigo.ie
Website: www.dunbrodyhouse.com

This beautiful Georgian house in a wonderful park-like setting opened to the public in the summer of 1997 as a country house hotel and restaurant. Dunbrody House was built in 1830 for Lord Spencer Chichester, and remained in the family until recently. Kevin and Catherine Dundon have done an outstanding job renovating the house and transforming it into an elegant and comfortable small hotel, where guests can sample the best of Irish hospitality.

Kevin, a master chef, specialises in contemporary Irish cuisine. Beautifully-presented dishes are served in the enormous dining room, which was previously both the drawing and dining rooms. It is like a stage setting, with extravagant flower arrangements, an interesting mix of old and contemporary furnishings and well spaced out tables. The attractive bar has doors out to the garden, and also leads into a comfortable sitting room. Each bedroom has the same high quality of individual décor and facilities, including hair-dryer, CD/DVD players, telephone, bathrobes, fresh fruit and mineral water. What varies is room size and outlook. For those wanting a lazy morning, breakfast can be served in bed. Land around the house runs to the river; there are horses, a nursery garden and well-tended gardens containing many unusual plants and flowers. Any number of special packages can be arranged, as well as conferences and weddings.

The Dunbrody Cookery School opened in 2002: housed in part of the old stable block it offers day, weekend and longer courses under the direction of Kevin. The newly-opened Spa wing, also housed in the stable block, caters exclusively for residential guests. Visa, American Express, Diners and Mastercard are accepted.

Dunbrody is on the R733, 11 kilometres from Waterford via the Passage East car ferry and 19 kilometres south of New Ross.

OWNER Catherine & Kevin Dundon OPEN All year except for Christmas ROOMS 10 double, 7 twin, 4 single; all en suite TERMS €120; single supplement; child reduction MEALS dinner €50, bar lunch €15, afternoon tea €15

## Glendine Country House
Arthurstown, Co. Wexford
Tel: 051 389258, 051 389500 Fax: 051 389677
Email: glendinehouse@eircom.net
Website: www.glendinehouse.com

Built in 1830 as the dower house to Dunbrody, Glendine stands above the village of Arthurstown, where the ferry runs to Passage East It is surrounded by 50 acres of farmland and has lovely views over the estuary. Annie Crosbie, who is a lovely, friendly, cheerful young mother of three sons, inherited the house from her grandparents. The Crosbies did a lot of renovation when they took over the house and have managed to preserve many original features. These include the pine floors, wide back passageway which runs the length of the house, and the old shutters. It has the feel of a family home and is simply decorated and furnished. A recent addition is four luxury bedrooms all with sea views. Annie grows all her own herbs, strives to serve organic food, and runs a coffee shop in the dining room during July and August. Apart from the 50 acres surrounding the house Tom works another farm five miles away and has horses, sheep and cattle. There are self-catering units in the converted stables. One dog allowed per party—otherwise pets have to be outside. All major credit cards accepted.

OWNER Annie Crosbie OPEN All year except for Christmas and
New Year ROOMS 3 double, 3 twin, 2 family; all en suite
TERMS €45–50; single supplement; child reduction

### Marsh Mere Lodge
Arthurstown, New Ross, Co. Wexford
Tel: 051 389186/087 2227303
Email: stay@marshmerelodge.com
Website: www.marshmerelodge.com

Marsh Mere Lodge stands in a commanding position overlooking
Arthurstown, the bay and small harbour. The front porch is a great
place to enjoy a cup of coffee or tea on arrival and watch the world
go by. The house was built fifty years ago, but it has the feel of an
older home and is full of wonderful pieces–furniture, pictures and
mementoes. The lounge for guests is on the first floor, a large, beautifully furnished room overlooking the water; a relaxing place to set-
tle down with a good book. Marsh Mere is run by Maria McNamara
and her daughter Claire. Maria bakes the bread for breakfast and
Claire can take guests for horse-drawn carriage rides around the
immediate area, if requested ahead of time. They breed labrador and
corgi dogs. The house is dog friendly and dogs can be accommodated in outbuildings. Charming en suite bedrooms have antique furniture, and each is named after a picture, which hangs in the room.
One bedroom is on the ground floor. Marsh Mere Lodge is just
down the road from the Passage East Car Ferry, and within easy
reach of Rosslare. Visa and Access accepted.

OWNER Claire McNamara & Maria McNamara OPEN all year
ROOMS 4 double/twin, all en suite TERMS €40; single supplement

## BUNCLODY

### Meadowside B&B
Bunclody, Co. Wexford
Tel: 054 77459 or 054 76226

Meadowside catches your eye as you drive through Bunclody on the
main N80 road. A colourful, flower decked, old stone building at the
southern end of town, it has been owned and run by Phil Kinsella
since the late 1980s. Phil is a friendly, organised lady with a lot of
energy, who also runs the adjoining flower shop and boutique. The
house is spotless with simple bedrooms, a guests' lounge and breakfast room. All four bedrooms are on the first floor–the two front
ones, with private bathrooms, get the road noise, whilst the two en
suite rooms at the back of the house have a rural aspect. No pets.
All major credit cards taken.

OWNER Phil Kinsella OPEN all year ROOMS 4 double/twin; 2 en suite, 2 with private bathrooms TERMS €35–40; single supplement

## Kilmokea Country Manor & Gardens
Great Island, Campile, Co. Wexford
Tel: 051 388109 Fax: 051 388776
Email: kilmokea@eircom.net
Website: www.kilmokea.com

Kilmokea was built in 1794 as a Church of Ireland rectory, eventually acquired by David Price in 1947, who was responsible for creating the seven acres of gardens. In 1997 Mark and Emma Hewlett bought the property and spent an enormous amount of energy renovating and restoring it back to its original charm. They have succeeded in creating a peaceful and elegant retreat. Each room has its own character and theme and offers, to a lesser or greater extent, vistas and glimpses of the magnificent gardens. The downstairs loo, which was formerly a bathroom, has been decorated and equipped with pictures, photographs and literature, encouraging a long visit! Kilmokea Gardens, which include a formal walled garden full of rare species from all over the world, and a woodland garden with exotic plants, are open March to October, with the exception of Mondays. The Pink Tea Cup Café is the venue for lunch and dinner, and there is a gym, sauna, and aromatherapy sessions available for guests. Two ground floor rooms are suitable for guests with pets. Visa and Mastercard are accepted. From New Ross take the R733 to Campile and follow the signs to Kilmokea Gardens.

OWNER Mark & Emma Hewlett OPEN March 1–November ROOMS 5 double, 1 twin, 1 single, 1 family; all en suite TERMS €80–130; single supplement MEALS Lunch, dinner à la carte

## Ballinkeele House
Ballymurn, Enniscorthy, Co. Wexford
Tel: 053 38105 Fax: 053 38468
Email: john@ballinkeele.com
Website: www.ballinkeele.com

Built in 1840, this impressive country house still belongs to the Maher family four generations later. Approached up a sweeping avenue through game-filled parkland, it is set in 140 hectares of farmland. Apart from such modern conveniences as bathrooms and heating, the restored house remains much as it was built, with a distinctively Victorian flavour, thanks to the fourth generation. The master bedroom, which has a four poster bed, is the same shape as the

Ballinkeele House

drawing room below. The bedrooms are very large and furnished and decorated to a high standard; all have hair-dryers, as well as bottled water and a glass of sherry. The Mahers are a friendly, welcoming couple, and Margaret produces delicious dinners (if booked in advance), which include produce from the garden and fresh local ingredients. Meals are served by candlelight in the elegant dining room, and the house has a wine licence. Breakfast, which is organised by John, can include hot pancakes and homemade jams. The former billiard room has reverted to a big drawing room with TV. Visitors are welcome to walk around the old walled garden, the lake and grounds. There is also a croquet lawn. Pets can be accommodated in the stables, or kept in their owners' cars. Visa and Mastercard accepted. To reach Ballinkeele from N11, turn in Oilgate at signpost.

OWNER John & Margaret Maher OPEN February 1–November 30 ROOMS 5 double/twin; all en suite TERMS €70–90; single supplement MEALS dinner €40

## Clone House
Ferns, Enniscorthy, Co. Wexford
Tel: 054 66113 or 087 2670164 Fax: 054 66113
Email: tbreen@vodafone.ie

This attractive, creeper-covered, 300 year old farmhouse is in a quiet location on nearly 120 hectares of mixed farmland. Guests can fish on the Bann River, which runs through the property, feed the lambs, see calves born or just go for wonderful walks. The Breens bought the property about 40 years ago, and gradually did it up. Betty is particularly gifted at landscaping and has created a lovely garden.

Guests are treated as friends and enjoy such luxuries as breakfast in bed, served at any time, using home-grown or reared produce. The house is very comfortable and has been attractively furnished. Two of the rooms have balconies, which are very popular with guests, and they have hair-dryers and most have TV. There is a comfortable sitting room and dining room. Baby-sitting is available, and there is a

Clone House

pony for children to ride. Many guests come to buy horses, others to visit a local herbalist, others to hunt, or just to relax. Pets by arrangement. Smoking is permitted in the living room and on the bedroom balconies. Clone House is signposted on the N11 at Ferns, 3 km away.

OWNER Mrs Betty Breen OPEN April 1–September 30
ROOMS 3 family en suite, 1 twin, 1 family with private bathrooms
TERMS €40; single supplement; child reduction

## Salville House
Enniscorthy, Co. Wexford
Tel: 054 35252 Fax: 054 35252
Email: info@salvillehouse.com
Website: www.salvillehouse.com

This lovely old house, built in the mid-nineteenth century, stands in its own grounds (with grass tennis court and croquet lawn) over-looking the River Slaney and the Blackstairs Mountains. The interior is light and bright with spacious, simply furnished rooms and wooden floorboards. The bedrooms have hair-dryers and tea- and coffee-making facilities. Salville House has a good reputation for its food, and dinner, by arrangement, is served at one long table in the dining room. Guests are welcome to bring their own wine, and they have use of a comfortable drawing room.

The house is just outside the cathedral town of Enniscorthy, noted for its thirteenth-century castle. There are a number of golf courses in the area, good hill walking on the Blackstairs Mountains and fine beaches along the Wexford coastline. There is also a self-catering unit available.

To find Salville House from Enniscorthy take the N11 towards Wexford, after a mile take the first left after the hospital, go up the hill and turn left. The house is the third on the left.

OWNER Gordon & Jane Parker OPEN All year ROOMS 2 double/twin, 2-bedroom suite; 2 en suite, 1 private bathroom TERMS €45–55; single supplement; child reduction MEALS dinner €30

## The Old Deanery

Ferns, Enniscorthy, Co. Wexford
Tel: 054 66474/ 054 66978 Fax: 054 66123
Email: deanery@indigo.ie
Website: indigo.ie/~deanery

The Sinnotts bought this lovely old house in 1996, primarily because their daughter wanted to run the Garden Centre at the end of the driveway.

Originally built in 1735, the house was extended in 1812 to accommodate the then incumbent's 11 children, and the front door was moved to the side of the house. There is a lovely central hall both on the ground floor and the upper floor.

In spite of all the work to the house itself, Valerie is most proud, and justifiably so, of the five delightful self-catering coach houses, which have been beautifully designed and equipped, and are excellent value. The rate per person includes a continental breakfast tray.

The old gate lodge is now the flower shop, which complements the garden centre, and there are lovely gardens surrounding the house. At night the floodlit abbey and cathedral are particularly picturesque. Pets are allowed in the cottages, at an extra charge. Visa and Mastercard accepted.

OWNER Valerie Sinnott OPEN Easter–October
TERMS €50; self-catering accommodation

## Woodbrook

Killanne, Enniscorthy, Co. Wexford
Tel: 054 55114 Fax: 054 55671
Email: fitzherbert@eircom.net
Website: www.woodbrookhouse.ie

Woodbrook is a lovely, large, Georgian house, first built in the 1770s, but damaged in the rebellion of 1798. Giles and Alexandra FitzHerbert, who both have ties to South America, have lived here with their four children since 1998, and have worked on improvements to the house. The rooms are spectacularly large, and the first floor central corridor is particularly impressive, with the two outstanding features of the house being the 'flying staircase' and the enormous drawing room.

Set in lovely parklands, gardens and woods and part of a farm that provides a house cow and a small herd of pure bred Hereford cattle. The FitzHerberts on occasion arrange opera performances in the grounds, there is a grass tennis court, and the walled garden produces organic fruit and vegetables for sale, and for home consumption. Good home-cooked dinners are available if booked in advance, and the house carries a selection of wines. There are lovely walks on the nearby Blackstairs Mountains, and riding, fishing and golf are all available in the area. Major credit cards are accepted. Woodbrook is 2 miles from Kiltealy and 2 miles from Killanne, off R730.

OWNER Giles & Alexandra FitzHerbert OPEN May–September, and for Wexford Festival (October) ROOMS 3 double, 1 twin; 3 en suite, 1 private bathroom TERMS €65–75; single supplement; child reduction MEALS dinner €35

## FOULKSMILLS

**Horetown House**
Foulksmills, Co. Wexford
Tel: 051 565771 Fax: 051 565633
Email: poloxirl@iol.ie

Horetown House is a lovely, seventeenth century Georgian manor house situated in beautiful parklands and tranquil countryside, amidst 100 hectares of mixed farming. The process of renovating the house is gradual, and more recent improvements include the addition of en suite bedrooms and a wine bar, which is open for light meals and snacks. The entrance hall is lined with the heads of deer and other animals, and the rooms have old fashioned functional furnishings. The bedrooms are spacious and comfortable, and guests can relax in the drawing room in front of the log fire. There is a separate TV room.. The Cellar Restaurant–open to the public–has a good reputation.

Lawn croquet and table tennis are available, and small conferences and business lunches can be catered for. The equestrian centre covers dressage instruction, polocrosse, escorted ride-outs and instruction for beginners, and it has two large all weather indoor arenas. No pets, and no smoking in the dining room. Visa and Mastercard accepted. To find Horetown House, take the right fork at the bottom of Foulksmills for approximately one and a half kilometres, pass a country pub and sharp bend and it is the next turn left.

OWNER Ivor Young OPEN March 1–October 31
ROOMS 10 double/twin, 2 triple; 10 en suite, 2 public bathrooms
TERMS €38–44.50; single supplement €15; child reduction
MEALS lunchtime snacks, dinner from €21–28.50

## INCH

**Perrymount House**
Inch, Gorey, Co. Wexford
Tel: 0402 37387 Fax: 0402 21906
Built by Colonel Perry in 1798, Perrymount has been in Peter's family for the last 100 years. The Donnellys' offer delightful hospitality with both comfortable en suite bedrooms in the house and very pretty self-contained cottages in the courtyard. Peter runs the most

picturesque dairy farm, sometimes with the help of their three young sons. This is a paradise for children. They are made very welcome and there are all sorts of safe play areas for them. They can ride a pony and play with all sorts of pets. There is a lovely view over the hills and walks down to a large pond full of ducks and geese. Anne is an enthusiastic and very successful gardener, and provides delicious food which is traditionally Irish, and mostly home produced. No pets. Visa and Mastercard accepted. Perrymount is signposted off the N11, just south of Inch.

OWNER Peter & Anne Donnelly OPEN April 1–November 1 ROOMS 1 double, 2 family; all en suite TERMS €35; single supplement; child reduction

## KILLURIN

### Healthfield Manor
Killurin, Co. Wexford
Tel: 053 28253 Fax: 053 28253
Website: www.healtfield.8k.com

The story runs that back in the 1400–1500s there was a plague in Wexford, and consequently the water was undrinkable. Healthfield, which has its own well, was the nearest place to the city with good water–hence the name. Built in 1820, this country house is reached up a long driveway through its 40 hectares of farmland, which supports organically-reared sheep, and is bordered by mature shrubs and wonderful rhododendrons. At the top there are spectacular views over the river Slaney. The entrance to the house is through a small conservatory, and beyond is the very large drawing room. The bedrooms are incredibly spacious–the 'Five Acre Suite' has its own sitting room and two bedrooms. All but one room has the lovely front view over the grounds to the river. Packed lunches can be prepared with notice, and pets can be accommodated in the stables. Smoking is permitted in the drawing room. Healthfield is eight kilometres from Wexford, and is signposted on the Killurin road.

OWNER Mayler & Lorette Colloton OPEN All year except for Christmas ROOMS 2 double/twin, 1 family; 1 en suite, 2 private bathroom TERMS €35–45 pps; single supplement; child reduction

## KILMORE

### Ballyhealy House
Ballyhealy Beach, Kilmore, Co. Wexford
Tel: 053 35035 Fax: 053 35038
Email: ballyhealyhouse@eircom.net

Once the seat of Wexford's High Sherriff, this house is very close to the sea and a pleasant beach. The present owner, Betty Maher-Caulfield, acquired the then ruined eighteenth-century house eight years ago, and has created the sort of holiday house of childhood dreams. There are horses and ponies to ride (there is a certified riding school), swimming and sea fishing, and a feeling of freedom and happiness for people of all ages. The bedrooms are very spacious, some with enough beds for a family of four or five, and all have a sea or castle view. Dinner is served at 8 p.m., and must be booked in advance. Children and pets especially welcome. Visa and Mastercard accepted. The house is two miles from Kilmore.

OWNER Betty Maher-Caulfield OPEN All year ROOMS 4 family; all en suite TERMS €40; single supplement; child reduction MEALS dinner €30

## NEW ROSS

### Creacon Lodge Hotel
New Ross, Co. Wexford
Tel: 051 421897 Fax: 051 422560
Email: info@creaconlodge.com   Website: www.creaconlodge.com

This charming, long, low whitewashed house, built in the 1840s, is covered with climbing plants and is set in a very pretty, sheltered garden. Some of the attractive bedrooms are in the main house, tucked under the roof, three are in the old byre and two in the former greenhouse. All rooms have hair-dryer, telephone and TV. The drawing room is full of comfortable chairs and sofas and has a log fire to relax in front of with a drink before or after dinner. The very popular restaurant serves wonderful food, and there is a large bar for both residents and non-residents. Josephine Flood is a most imaginative and attentive host, and her slogan 'Well worth the trouble of finding us' is true.

The John F. Kennedy Memorial Park is a ten-minute drive away, and nearby is the Hook Peninsula, with secluded beaches and coves and the oldest lighthouse in Europe. No pets. Visa and Mastercard accepted. To find Creacon, take the R733 signposted to John F. Kennedy Park and after five kilometres turn left for the house.

OWNER Mrs Josephine Flood OPEN All year except Christmas ROOMS 4 double, 3 twin, 1 single, 2 family; all en suite TERMS from €49; single supplement; child reduction MEALS dinner

### Oakwood House
Ring Road, Mountgarrett, New Ross, Co. Wexford
Tel: 051 425494 Fax: 051 425494
Email: susan@oakwoodhouse.net   Website: www.oakwoodhouse.net

Susan Halpin and her husband built Oakwood House as a guest

house some ten years ago. It is neat and immaculately kept, enjoys lovely views of the Barrow Valley and is located on the ring road (N 30) above New Ross.

The accommodation offers a small, comfortable sitting room, and an extensive, sunny breakfast room which has the view. The bedrooms are simply furnished in pine and have TV, hair-dryers and tea- and coffee-making facilities. It is a 15-minute walk into town—somewhat longer on the way back up the hill—and a nearby pub offers evening meals, snacks and Irish music at the weekend. No pets allowed. Visa accepted.

OWNER Susan Halpin OPEN April 1–November 1
ROOMS 2 double, 1 twin, 1 family; all en suite
TERMS €35 pps; single supplement €15

## ROSSLARE HARBOUR

### Laurel Lodge
Rosslare Harbour, Co. Wexford
Tel: 053 33291

This attractive, low, modern house is down a quiet country lane in the village of Kilrane. The bedrooms are clean, simply furnished and have TV and tea- and coffee-making facilities. There is a guest lounge, and the dining room, where breakfast is served, overlooks a small patio at the back of the house.

There are four hotels and two pubs within walking distance. No smoking and no pets. Mastercard, Visa and Access accepted. Laurel Lodge is signposted off the main road and also in the village.

OWNER Mr & Mrs O'Donoghue OPEN March 1–October 31
ROOMS 2 double, 2 twin; all en suite
TERMS €26.50–30; single supplement; child reduction

### O'Leary's Farmhouse
Killiane, Kilrane, Rosslare Harbour, Co. Wexford
Tel: 053 33134
Email: polearyfarm@eircom.net

O'Leary's Farmhouse is well worth negotiating the narrow lanes from the main N25 road (from where it is signposted). Parts of the original 200-year-old farmhouse were destroyed by fire some thirty years ago—various pieces have been added since, resulting today in a substantial building orientated to the sea, a mere five-minute stroll away. The attractions here are many, most importantly the cheerful mother and daughter team who own and run the farm. Surrounded by its 100 acres of farmland (beef and barley) and with sweeping sea views, it is a peaceful place well off the beaten track. The farm's free range hens provide eggs for breakfast, jams and marmalades are home-made, and sausages and bacon are produced locally. Bedrooms are simply furnished and breakfast is served in the spacious but cosy dining room at separate tables. The old coach house, which, during its lifetime, has also been the turnip house (where turnips were mangled) and potato house, has recently been converted into a charming small self-catering unit–which has its own beach access. Dogs and cats are accepted–cats must be in their own cages.

OWNER Phil O'Leary OPEN closed for Christmas ROOMS 2 double, 2 twin, 2 family, 1 single; all en suite TERMS €27–35; single supplement

## TAGOAT

### Churchtown House
Tagoat, Rosslare, Co. Wexford
Tel: 053 32555 Fax: 053 32577
Email: info@churchtownhouse.com
Website: www.churchtownhouse.com

Set in 3.25 hectares of park-like grounds, this attractive house dates from 1703. Patricia and Austin Cody have worked miracles in trans-forming Churchtown House to what it is today. When they bought it, it had been inhabited by one old man, who used a kitchen with stairs up through a cupboard to one room above. The spacious rooms have been tastefully decorated and furnished, and a bedroom on the ground floor is suitable for wheelchairs. All have telephone, TV and hair-dryers. There are two comfortable drawing rooms and three dining rooms, one is a conservatory like room with windows all around looking out over the garden.

Good old-fashioned cooking and local ingredients are what make dinners at Churchtown House memorable. These need to be booked in advance, and there is a wine license.

Activities such as bird watching, golf, fishing, swimming, walking and riding are available locally. No pets, smoking in garden lounge only. Most major credit cards accepted. Churchtown is on R736.

OWNER Patricia & Austin Cody OPEN March–November
ROOMS 5 double, 5 twin, 1 family, 1 single; all en suite
TERMS from €60–90; single supplement MEALS dinner €39.50

## WEXFORD

### Broom Cottage
Rosslare Road, Drinagh, Wexford, Co. Wexford
Tel: 053 44434

This attractive, creeper-clad, eighteenth-century farmhouse set back a little from the main road is part of a 56-hectare beef, sheep and tillage farm. Eleven hectares of the land lie around the house, three kilometres from the centre of Wexford on Rosslare road.

Broom Cottage has been in the same family for the last 200 years and an extension was built on 25 years ago. It offers comfortable, clean, well-equipped bedrooms, and guests have use of a TV lounge and conservatory. Breakfast only is served in the dining room. No pets. The accommodation is good value and it is convenient for the Rosslare car ferry.

OWNER John & Theresa Devereux OPEN May–September 30
ROOMS 4 double/twin; all en suite
TERMS €30; single supplement; not suitable for children

## Clonard House
Clonard Great, Wexford, Co. Wexford
Tel: 053 43141  Fax: 053 43141
Email: info@clonardhouse.com   Website: www.clonardhouse.com

This elegant Georgian farmhouse, part of a 48 hectare dairy farm, is set in idyllic surroundings with a clear view of Wexford harbour. Clonard House was completely renovated and retains many of its original features, such as cornices, ceiling roses and the dining room fireplace. Since then there has been a continuous programme of updating and refurbishing to maintain its already high standard.

The bedrooms are extremely attractive, with traditional and antique furnishings, and they have TV, hair-dryers, tea- and coffee-making facilities, and some have four poster beds. The lounge has plenty of room to relax in after a busy day's sightseeing. There is a games room in the basement for guests.

Clonard House

This is a lovely, peaceful house with a lot of character (and a stairway to nowhere!). Visa and Mastercard accepted. No pets. It is signposted off the N11 ring road, one kilometre away.

OWNER Kathleen Hayes OPEN May–November
ROOMS 3 double, 3 twin, 1 single, 1 family; all en suite
TERMS €35–40; single supplement; child reduction

## Darral House

Spawell Road, Wexford, Co. Wexford
Tel: 053 24264 Fax: 053 24284

This attractive looking town house was built in 1803 and is set back a little from the road. The Nolans, who are a welcoming couple, renovated the building in 1994, making it warm and comfortable while retaining the elegance of the period. It has very spacious rooms with high ceilings in the dining room and lounge. Bedrooms are very comfortable and thoughtfully equipped, with hair-dryers, TV and tea- and coffee-making facilities. Darral House has plenty of parking and a pleasant back garden, which guests are welcome to use. No pets. Visa and Access accepted. The house is a few minutes' walk to the centre, and offers good value.

OWNER Sean & Kathleen Nolan OPEN All year except for Christmas
ROOMS 1 double, 3 family; all en suite
TERMS €40; single supplement; child reduction

## Killiane Castle

Drinagh, Wexford, Co. Wexford
Tel: 053 58885 Fax: 053 58885
Email: killianecastle@yahoo.com
Website: www.killianecastle.com

This eighteenth-century house is attached to the tower of a fourteenth-century castle and is part of a dairy farm. Killiane Castle is down a quiet country lane and is very handy to the Rosslare ferry, which is only a ten minute drive away. The Mernaghs are constantly striving to keep up standards, and regularly redecorate the house, which is attractively furnished.

The first floor bedrooms are particularly large and they all have TV, hair-dryers and tea- and coffee-making facilities. Coffee or tea are available in a small ground floor lounge, and another sitting room is a nice place to relax in. For those catching early morning ferries, breakfast is provided.

There is a hard tennis court and four self-catering apartments at the back of the house. No pets. Visa and Mastercard are accepted. Killiane Castle is signposted on the N25 between Wexford and Rosslare.

OWNER Jack & Kathleen Mernagh OPEN March–November
ROOMS 3 double, 3 twin, 2 family; all en suite
TERMS €40; single supplement; child reduction MEALS supper

# COUNTY CLARE

Two hundred castles and 2,300 stone forts dating to pre-Celtic times testify to County Clare's turbulent past. Although Shannon Airport lies on the southern border, most of the county is under-populated by tourists. Scenery varies from the barren terrain of the Burren, in Spring covered in a profusion of northern and southern plants, to the scenic lakes and hills of Slieve Bernagh, wonderful walking country, and the towering Cliffs of Moher.

The county is bordered by the sea to the west, and the Shannon Estuary to the south and east. One of the principal sights of the county capital Ennis, situated on a bend of the River Fergus, is the Franciscan Ennis Friary, noted for sculptures and decorated tombs.

A bridge crosses the Shannon at Killaloe. Nearby is a twelfth-century cathedral built on the site of an earlier church. It has a magnificent door and splendid views from the top of the square tower.

Across the Shannon lies Bunratty Castle, well known for its medieval banquets. Dating from 1460, it was once occupied by the father of William Penn, founder of Pennsylvania. A Folk Park in the castle grounds displays examples of houses from the Shannon area. Iniscealta island on Lough Derg can be reached by boat from the attractive village of Mountshannon. There are five old churches, a round tower, saints' graveyard, hermit's cell and a holy well.

Moohaun Fort, one of the largest Iron Age forts in Europe, is to be found at Newmarket on Fergus. Both Knappogue Castle, another venue for medieval banquets, and Quinn Abbey are venues close to Craggaunowen.

Of special interest to both botanists and historians is the Burren. Once densely populated, this savagely rocky area is rich in prehistoric and historic monuments. Its limestone holds a wealth of exquisite, delicate plant life thriving in a myriad of tiny crevices.

The Burren Display Centre explains the fauna and flora of these 500 square kilometres and the remains of ancient civilisation. The ruined Leamaneh Castle is near Kilfenora, which is on the edge of the Burren. Between Kilfenora and Ballyvaughan is Ballykinvarga, one of Ireland's finest stone forts, and southeast of Ballyvaughan is Aillwee Cave, which dates to 2 million B.C.

The road from Lisdoonvarna, Ireland's foremost spa town, leads to the impressive Cliffs of Moher, which stretches for nearly 8 km. Liscannor is famous for the Holy Well of St Brigid, which is an important place of pilgrimage.

Lahinch is a small seaside resort best known for its championship golf course, and to the south is Spanish Point, where many ships of the Spanish Armada were wrecked.

Around the village of Quilty, seaweed can be seen drying on the stone walls. The coast south of Kilkee is every bit as spectacular as the Cliffs of Moher, with caverns and strange rock formations.

## Dolmen Lodge

Tonarussa, Ballyvaughan, Co. Clare
Tel: 065 707 7202 Fax: 065 707 7202
Email: dolmenlodge@eircom.net

This elegant, modern farmhouse stands in open scenic countryside and has stunning views of the Burren and Galway Bay. It is part of a working cattle farm, and there are some interesting rock formations on the land. The bedrooms are large and have dainty duvets and a light pastel décor. The dining room, where breakfasts are served at separate tables, has lace tablecloths; this room overlooks the view, as does the lounge. This is a non-smoking establishment. There are some interesting antiques about, including a grandmother clock in the hallway. Dolmen Lodge offers luxurious, high-quality accommodation at modest prices. It is a superb choice for guests touring this beautiful area. Breakfast only is served, but Ballyvaughan is only I km away. Philip and Mary Kyne have created a friendly, homely atmosphere, and will be happy to assist with choosing venues for evening meals, and also to give advice on what to see and do in the area. Sign-posted on N67 Ballyvaughan-Galway Road.

OWNER Philip & Mary Kyne OPEN March 17–October 20
ROOMS 2 double, 2 twin; I family; all en suite TERMS €32 pps;
child reduction; single supplement (seasonal) Credit cards accepted

## Bunratty Grove

Castle Road, Bunratty, Co. Clare
Tel: 061 369579 Fax: 061 369561
Email: bunrattygrove@eircom.net

Bunratty Grove is ideally placed for visits to nearby Bunratty Castle. Bookings for the famous banquets at the Castle can be made here. The house is within minutes of Shannon Airport, as well as the tourist favourites of fishing, golf courses and Irish heritage sites. All bedrooms are equipped with multi-channel TV, hair-dryer and telephone, as well as tea- and coffee-making facilities.

OWNER Joe and Maura Brodie OPEN All year ROOMS 4 double, 3 twin,
2 family; all en suite TERMS €32 pps; single supplement; child reduction

## Tudor Lodge

Hill Road, Bunratty, Co. Clare
Tel: 061 362248 Fax: 061 362569
Email: tudorlodge@esatclear.ie

This gracious and elegant home stands in a secluded, peaceful, wooded setting where guests awaken to the sound of birds singing. The house was in a derelict condition when it was purchased seven years ago. It has been beautifully restored into a comfortable and quite luxurious home. The tiled entryway is full of plants and the bedrooms are furnished and decorated to a high standard. The bathrooms are large and have powerful showers. There is a very comfortable lounge, with blue leather furniture, which leads out to a conservatory overlooking the well tended garden. An added bonus are the accommodating and helpful owners, Carmel and Michael Dennehey, both local people who provide lots of information for guests on what to see and do in the area. Reservations can be made for the medieval banquet at Bunratty Castle, within walking distance, as is Durty Nellie's pub, which serves lunch and dinner. Shannon Airport is a 15-minute drive from the house. Visa and Mastercard accepted. Situated in Bunratty, 500 m up the hill on the right.

OWNER T.M. Dennehy OPEN February 1–November 30
ROOMS 5 double/twin/triple; all en suite TERMS €35 pps;
child reduction; single supplement

## DOOLIN

### Atlantic Sunset House
Cliffs of Moher Road, Doolin, County Clare
Tel: 065 7074080 Fax 065 707 4922
Email sunsethouse@esatclear.ie
Website: www.atlanticsunsetdoolin.com

You can be sure of a warm welcome at this comfortable house, which stands in its own grounds, one mile from Doolin Village, where Irish music can be heard most nights. Brid has been in business for over 15 years. People feel very much at home here, witness one guest's comment: "Your home is a pleasure".

The large bedrooms, all with pine furniture, have TV and tea makers. The rooms are decorated with soft pastels, and have pretty quilts of pinks, blues and cream. The dining room, where delicious breakfasts are served, feature kippers, French toast, cheese plate, yoghurt, omelette, and traditional fare.

The Moher stone floors are of special interest, as are the many items on display: there are several harps made by Brid's father-in-law, various pots and dolls. A sitting room is also available. This would be an ideal spot from which to visit the Cliffs of Moher, The Burren, and Lisdoonvarna. Credit cards taken.

OWNER Brid and Val Egan OPEN All year except for Christmas
ROOMS 6 double/twin; all en suite TERMS €32–45 pps; single supplement; child reduction

## Carramore Lodge

Roolagh, Killaloe, Co. Clare
Tel: 061 376704

This spacious country house stands in one and a half acres of land-scaped grounds, overlooking Lough Derg. The good-sized, bright and fresh bedrooms are, luxuriously furnished, immaculately maintained, and have either a mountain or lake views. All rooms have en suite facilities, TV and tea-making facilities.

Carramore Lodge is popular with tourists and outdoor enthusiasts, there are lovely walks close by, and is convenient to golf, horse riding, and fishing. Evening meals are not served, but there are several restaurants, and pubs, in Killaloe, within walking distance. Imaginative, tasty breakfasts are served, at separate tables, in the dining room/lounge, and include smoked salmon, home-baked brown bread, fruit, a good choice of cooked items and plenty of tea and coffee. Eileen Brennan loves her business, and is a thoughtful and considerate host.

This is a non-smoking property. Visa and Mastercard accepted. Situated 30 minutes from Shannon airport, and easily located on the Limerick to Ballina Road, just before the village.

OWNER Eileen Brennan OPEN March 1–October 31 ROOMS 4 double/twin/family; all en suite TERMS €25.50; child reduction; single supplement €9

## Clarke's Bed And Breakfast

Killimer Road, Kilrush, County Clare
Tel: 065 90552250 Fax: 06590552250
Email clarkekilrush@hotmail.com
Website: www.clarkekilrush.com

Set back from the main road, behind a black wrought iron gate, and extensive garden, this Georgian two-storey house offers quality accommodation in a peaceful setting. Hospitality begins on arrival, with an offer of a drink and home-baked cakes, continuing on throughout the stay. Good-sized bedrooms have colourful bedding, attractive curtains, and comfortable beds. Two rooms are en suite, two share a bathroom. All have TV, clock radio, hospitality tray and hair-dryer. Rooms to the back of the house overlook the Shannon Estuary. The extensive breakfast menu includes fresh squeezed orange or grapefruit juice, Irish muesli or porridge, fresh fruit, yoghurts, omelettes with Kilrush mushrooms, a cooked variety is also offered. Breakfast can be taken in the dining room or conservatory, which leads out to the gardens, and terrace. There is also a TV lounge.

Michael and Mary Clarke are happy to share their knowledge of the area, and a video on West Clare is available to guests. Opposite the house are the The Vandeleur Gardens. Situated on the N67, a short drive to the Tarbert Ferry. Credit cards taken.

OWNER Michael & Mary Clarke OPEN All year
ROOMS 4 double/twin; 2 en suite
TERMS from €29 pps; single supplement; child reduction

## Old Parochial House
Cooraclare, Kilrush, Co. Clare
Tel: 065 905 9059 Fax: 065 905 9059
Email: oldparochialhouse@eircom.net
Website: www.oldparochialhouse.com

Old Parochial House, built in 1871, was formerly the parish priest's residence, and stands in 1.25 hectares of grounds in an unspoiled area ideal for walking. The house has been tastefully restored, and is non-smoking. It has great views and all-modern comforts, yet retains the character and ambience of a bygone era. There are high ceilings, polished wood floors, original fireplaces and stripped pine doors; the house is furnished in keeping with its character, and is well maintained by Alyson O'Neill, who made all the curtains. She is an informal, congenial lady who takes excellent care of her guests.

The bedrooms are large, and one of the public bathrooms has an original Victorian bath. The spacious sitting room has a bay window overlooking the view, and the dining room, where a varied breakfast is served, has an original black marble fireplace. There is a snooker room, play room and play area, as well as a fish tackle room for lake fishing. There are also local bog walks, ring forts, ancient prayer sites and an old church close by. There are pubs and restaurants in the immediate area for meals. The stables have been converted to provide comfortable self-catering accommodation. Visa and Mastercard accepted. The house is 200 m from Cooraclare and on car ferry route.

OWNER Alyson & Sean O'Neill OPEN May 1–September 30
ROOMS 2 double, 1 twin, 1 family; 3 en suite TERMS B&B €35-45 pps; child reduction under 12 years; single supplement

## LAHINCH

## Auburn House
School Road, Lahinch, County Clare
Tel: 065 7082890
Email: auburnhse@eircom.net   Website: www.auburnhouse.ie

This large attractive, corner house, stands in its own grounds, with ample parking, across from a popular surfing beach. In summer, hanging baskets and flowering tubs abound. Safe sandy beaches can be found very close by. Guests can expect a high standard of furnishings and comfort. The en suite, bright, spacious bedrooms, (three with sea views) have a light pastel décor and comfortable beds, TV is available on request. A freshly-prepared breakfast, with home-baked brown bread, is served in the dining room/sitting room overlooking the sea. The sun room is a great spot in which to relax, as it has sea views.

The owners, a delightful young couple named Cathy and Nanno formerly ran a hotel, but went into the bed & breakfast business to extend a more personal service. The ambience here is warm and friendly. The couple have two lovely children, Laoise, and Emma the baby. Two minutes' walk from the town, with the Lahinch Golf Course close by. French, German and Dutch spoken.

OWNER Cathy and Nanno Vuyk OPEN All year ROOMS 7 twin, double, family; all en suite TERMS €25-35 pps; single supplement; child reduction

**Moy House**
Lahinch, Co. Clare
Tel: 065 7082800 Fax: 065 7082500
Email: moyhouse@tinet.ie

A classic country house, with views of beautiful Lahinch Bay, approached up a long drive, peacefully set in 15 acres of park-like grounds, and mature woodland. Built in the eighteenth century as home to Sir Augustine Fitzgerald, it overlooks beautiful Lahinch Bay. Before the restoration, which took place over a three-year period, Moy House stood empty for ten years, and was derelict. Antoin O'Looney, purchased the house and undertook the daunting job of restoration. The results are stunning, the original oak floors were used, and part of the stone stable wall can be seen. The house is beautifully maintained. The bedrooms are luxurious and individually designed, using a combination of styles from past and present. All have TV, tea makers and hair-dryer. All bedrooms are furnished and decorated with beautiful fabrics, most have working log-burning fire-places, and all but two have sea views. The bathrooms, are equipped with toiletries, dressing gowns, large fluffy towels, and most have shower/bath combination. One bedroom features the original well, from which the water was drawn. Not suitable for children under 12 years. Gourmet candlelit dinners are served in the elegant dining room which overlooks the bay. Everything is prepared with fresh local produce, fish meats, mouth watering home-made desserts, pre-sented with flair and style. The gracious drawing room, has a real fire, where guests can enjoy a pre- or after-dinner drink. Moy House pampers and spoils her guests, Bernadette is the perfect host, who has thought of everything possible to ensure guest's comfort and satisfaction. Situated on the coast road, one and half miles from Lahinch Golf Course. Smoking is permitted in the drawing room.

OWNER Antoin O'Looney OPEN All year except Christmas ; from November-March 1 weekends only ROOMS 8 twin/double/family; all en suite TERMS €200-250 pps double; €155 single MEALS dinner

## The Greenbrier Inn
Ennistymon Road, Lahinch, Co. Clare
Tel: 065 7081242 Fax: 065 708 1247
Email: gbrier@indigo.ie
Website: www.greenbrierinn.com

This impressive five year old property offers first class accommodation. Situated on the main road, it has views of the Atlantic Ocean and the Golf Course 250 yards away. The spacious, tastefully decorated bedrooms have pine furniture, white cotton sheets and bedspreads, multi-channel TV and direct dial phones. Guests have use of a large sitting room, a comfortable place from which to plan your daily activities, and unwind after a busy day. The Greenbrier Inn is non-smoking. Special diets can be accommodated at breakfast. Evening meals are not served, but there are plenty of venues for evening meals within walking distance. The Burren and the Cliffs of Moher are within driving distance. Visa and Mastercard accepted.

OWNER Margaret & Victor Mulcahy OPEN March 1–December 20; December 27–January 10 ROOMS 14 double/twins/family; all en suite TERMS €46-82 pps; child reduction; single supplement

## LISDOONVARNA

## Fermona House
Bog Road, Lisdoonvarna, Co. Clare
Tel: 065 707 4243    Email: fermona@eircom.net

This pleasant cream and green bungalow is set back off the road in a quiet location close to Spa Wells. It is just a five-minute walk from town. The bedrooms and en suite facilities are quite spacious, and are individually decorated in soft colours of blue and peach. There is a small, cosy TV lounge with a stereo which guests may use. The house is exceptionally well maintained and everything is spotlessly clean. Breakfasts are served at separate tables and there are several establishments in town for evening meals. Vera Fitzpatrick is an excellent host and is happy to provide information on sightseeing. Doolin, the Cliffs of Moher and the Burren, golfing, pony trekking and hill walking are all nearby. Visa and Mastercard accepted.
OWNER Vera Fitzpatrick

OPEN April–October ROOMS 2 double, 2 twin, 1 family; all en suite TERMS €28–35 pps; child reduction; single supplement

# COUNTY DONEGAL

County Donegal is a large county with a spectacular variety of scenery and an indented coastline of bays, beaches, cliffs and peninsulas set against a backdrop of mountains, moors and lakes. It has many archaeological sites and much evidence of the old Irish culture and traditions. Irish is still spoken in areas north and west of Killybegs, an important fishing port. Donegal takes its name from the fort the Vikings established: Dún na nGall, the Fort of the Foreigners. The town built by Sir Basil Brooke is on the estuary of the River Eske, a busy place good for buying tweeds. The castle with its great square tower, once the stronghold of the O'Donnells, was refurbished by Brooke in 1610. Bundoran is one of Ireland's best-known seaside resorts with a good golf course and famous beaches. Farther north is Ballyshannon, long a centre of importance because of its river; the town winds up a steep hill above the River Erne. Rossnowlagh beach stretches for 4 km.

Beyond Killybegs, the coastal scenery becomes wild and spectacular. Kilcar is a centre for the hand-woven tweed industry, as is Ardara. The scenery at Glencolumbkille is magnificent, with its blend of hills and sea. The late Father MacDyer organised a cooperative movement to keep young people from emigrating, and also established a folk museum. Portnoo and Narin are other popular seaside towns for holidaymakers. Letterkenny is the largest town in Donegal, dominated by St Eunan's Cathedral, built in the modern Gothic style between 1890 and 1900. The winding road approaching Doocharry from Fintown is known as the 'corkscrew' and brings you through the Gweebarra Glen to the sea. Aranmore Island is the most populated and largest of a series of islands, which can be reached by ferry from Burtonport, an attractive, unspoilt fishing port. Gweedore, situated in the spectacularly wild country, is a major holiday centre. Follow the road of remarkable scenic beauty by Loughs Nacung and Dunlewy into the Derryveagh Mountains.

The Irish-speaking areas of Gortahork and Falcarragh are good places from which to start a climb of Muckish Mountain. There is a fine beach at Dunfanaghy, a good place to explore the granite promontory of Horn Head. Between Creeslough, attractively situated on Sheephaven Bay, and Carrigart is the romantic Doe Castle, almost surrounded by the sea.

Rosapenna, a resort town with a good golf course, is on the way to the beautiful Rosguill Peninsula, with wonderful views of Melmore Head, Horn Head and Muckish Mountain. Milford is a pretty town from where the Fanad Peninsula with its sandy beaches can be explored. The tranquil village of Rathmullan, famous for its historical associations, is beautifully situated with a sandy beach. The road between here and Ramelton is also in a lovely location and is a planned Planter's town, begun early in the seventeenth century.

The Inishowen Peninsula, which lies between the waters of Lough Foyle and Lough Swilly, is quite different from the rest of Donegal. The centre is very hilly, Slieve Snaght at 615m being the highest point. From the Buncrana to Clonmany and Cardonagh road, there are fine views of sea and mountains, and a road runs right to the tip of the peninsula at Malin Head. One of the best views to be had of this part of Donegal is from the Grianan of Aileach. It is 250 m high and consists of a cashel, or stone fort, enclosed within three earthen banks. Cardonagh's chief glory is St Patrick's Cross, which dates from the seventh century, making it one of the very important Christian crosses.

Glenveagh lies in a deep gorge and is the setting for a fairytale castle, as well as wonderful gardens that were developed by Henry McIlhenny. The garden and the estate are now a national park, and Mr McIlhenny had bequeathed the castle to the nation. Gartan, Kilmacrenan and Raphoe, which has a fine old cathedral, are all associated with St Columba.

## ARDARA

### Rosewood Country House
Edergole, Killybegs Road, Ardara, Co. Donegal
Tel: 074 9541168
Email: jmecon@gogreen.indigo.ie

Guests continue to enjoy this two-storey house situated on the edge of Ardara. It is run in a friendly manner by Susan McConnell, who lived in New York for 11 years. Formerly a bungalow, a second storey was added in 1990; the very large lounge/dining room is in this part of the house, and has lovely views of the river. Susan McConnell is an excellent host; nothing is too much trouble for her guests' comfort, and a hot drink is offered to guests upon arrival. Breakfast only is served, but there are good choices in Ardara, and Susan would be happy to make recommendations. Visa and Mastercard accepted.

OWNER Susan McConnell OPEN February 1–December 1 ROOMS 4 double, 2 twin; all en suite TERMS €27 pps; child reduction; single supplement

### Woodhill House
Ardara, Co. Donegal
074 9541112 Fax 074 9541516
Email: yates@iol.ie
Website: www.woodhillhouse.com

Woodhill House is in a wonderful position up a valley from Ardara. It is an historic country house, standing on a site dating from the seventeenth century, overlooking the Donegal Highlands. It was formerly the home of the Nesbitts, Ireland's last commercial whaling family. The present owners bought the house about 13 years ago, and improvements are ongoing: six more rooms are to be added for 2005 season. The two front rooms are large, simply furnished and have wonderful views. There is a friendly informal atmosphere, and the house is surrounded by more than 1.5 hectares of gardens, including a walled garden, open to guests. Pets can be kennelled.

The high-quality restaurant is open from March to the end of October, and there is a licensed, smoking bar. Excellent French-style cuisine is served, using fresh Irish produce and fish from Killybegs, Ireland's principal fishing port. There are several places to eat in Ardara and Irish music is often heard at most of Ardara's 13 bars. The area is well known for its Donegal tweeds and woollen goods. Salmon and trout fishing, shooting, pony trekking, golf and excellent bathing beaches are to be found in this area. The Wildlife Reserve should be of special interest.

Mastercard, Eurocard, American Express and Diners accepted.

OWNER John & Nancy Yates OPEN All year except November-December
ROOMS 6 double, 8 twin, 1 family, 2 single; all en suite
TERMS double, twin, family €55 pps, €35 single; child reduction; single supplement MEALS lunch and dinner €38

## BALLYSHANNON

### Inis Saimer House
Portnason, Bundoran Road, Ballyshannon, Co. Donegal
Tel: 071 985 1418
Email: inissaimer@holidayhound.com
Website: www.inissaimer.com

This charming, listed Victorian residence, of terracotta colours and colonnades, has river or ocean views from all rooms. Woodland walks can be taken from the garden, where the wall dates back to the 1600s. The orchard provides fruit for the home-made jams served at breakfast. There is plenty of old world charm here, the furnishings are mostly antique, and some of the bell pulls are in working order. After eight years of restoration, Inis Saimer opened for business in 1997.

The ambience is relaxed, peaceful and informal. Sharon, a delightful lady, thoroughly enjoys chatting to her guests, and is helpful in every way. The large bedrooms have rich Victorian colours, TV and hospitality trays, one has an original Victorian bath, and shower. The room with private bathroom, has a "loo with a view". There is a drawing room, with TV and a fireplace, and a separate dining room, where guests order from the menu: the smoked salmon and home-baked bread are a treat, and Sharon's delicious omelettes are the house speciality. There is plenty to keep you busy in the area—Belleek Pottery, golf, fishing, and coastal walks. Ballyshannon town is a ten minute drive.

OWNER Mrs Sharon McGuinness OPEN March 1-November 1 or upon request ROOMS 4 double TERMS €30–35 pps single supplement; child reduction

## BRUCKLESS

**Bruckless House**
Bruckless, Co. Donegal
Tel: 074 9737071 Fax: 074 9737070
E-mail: bruck@iol.ie
Website: www.iol.ie/~bruc/bruckless.html

This classic eighteenth-century house stands in a secluded spot in an award-winning garden and cobbled yard, and is a well-known Connemara Pony Stud Farm. It offers gracious living and guests are encouraged to sit around and chat with the owners, who are happy to share their knowledge of the area. The bedrooms are large and elegantly furnished. The spacious drawing room and dining room overlook green lawns and the sea. Both rooms have turf fires, which are lit at the first sign of a chill in the air. Most guests are happy with this house's 'TV-free zone'.

In this beautiful and unspoiled area of Ireland's Atlantic coast, there are many archaeological sites to explore. Fishing, golf and horseback riding are also available. Eurocard, Mastercard, American Express and Visa accepted. Bruckless House is 12 miles west of Donegal town.
OWNER Joan & Clive Evans OPEN April–September
ROOMS 2 double, 2 single; 2 en suite TERMS B&B €55-60

## BUNDORAN

**Bay View Bed and Breakfast**
Main Street, Bundoran, County Donegal
Tel: 071 9841 237

This impressive red brick Victorian House faces the sea, and has safe lockup parking. The property is well maintained and several original features remain, including, marble fireplaces, cornices and a ceiling rose. The bedrooms have coordinated colourful bedding, direct dial phones, TV, hair-dryers, and electric blankets. Tea makers are available, as are ironing facilities, cots and fax facilities. The McGraths take pride in their business, and rooms are upgraded as needed. They are an amiable and helpful couple, and are happy to recommend places for evening meals. Information on the area is provided. Some of the bedrooms, have sea views, as does the large bright dining room and lounge. Golf concessions are available.

OWNER Vincent and Ann McGrath OPEN All year except for Christmas ROOMS 25 double/twin/family; ground floor rooms en suite, varied standard or en suite TERMS €28-35 pps; single supplement; child reduction

## Casa Mia

West End, Bundoran, Co. Donegal
Tel: 071 9841684

Casa Mia is a large, two-storey house within walking distance of the beach and town. This continental-style house is run by Mary Hamrogue, a friendly, bubbly lady. The bedrooms, all with Sky TV, are bright and cheery with yellow, purple and green duvets. Smoking is only allowed in the bedrooms. The guest lounge is spacious and is comfortably furnished. Breakfast only is served, but there is a good choice of eating establishments in town, which is within walking distance. Close to Belleek, horse-riding, golf and fishing.

OWNER Mary & Malachy Hamrogue OPEN All year except Christmas ROOMS 2 twin, 2 family; all en suite TERMS €30 pps double/twin, €40 single; child reduction

## CARRICK

## Rockville Bed & Breakfast

Roxborough, Coast Road, Carrick, Co. Donegal
Tel/Fax: 074 9739107 Mobile: 087 6235582
Email: rockvilledonegal@eircom.net

This friendly four-bedroom bungalow stands in an elevated position, with panoramic views of Donegal Bay and Ben Bulben. The cliffs at Bunglas, the highest marine cliffs in Europe, are 5km away. This is a popular destination for tourists from many parts of the world, and energetic Maureen Hughes arranges walking tours in the Kilcar area. Teelin, an Irish-speaking area, lies close by and attracts people who wish to learn to speak the Irish language. The house is a kilometre from the closest beach and the village of Carrick. The family room has wonderful views, as does the lounge, which has a dining table at one end and sliding doors onto the patio, which has a barbecue. Smoking is only allowed in the lounge. The well-appointed bedrooms are small, spotlessly clean, and are all on the ground floor. Laundry facilities are available.

Evening meals are no longer available, but Maureen Hughes has an arrangement for meals for her guests at the village restaurant. Tasty substantial meals are served on plates made for Rockville House at a local pottery. A four-bedroom self-catering cottage is also available. From Carrick take the Coast Road, Rockville is one mile from Carrick on the left hand side.

OWNER Maureen Hughes OPEN All year ROOMS 1 double, 1 twin, 1 family; 2 en suite (1 with bath) TERMS €75 family, €58 double/twin; child reduction; single supplement No credit cards accepted.

## CARRIGANS

**Mount Royd Country Home**
Carrigans, Co. Donegal
Tel: 074 9140163
Email: jmartin@mountroyd.com
Website: www.mountroyd.com

An attractive creeper-clad country house, set back off the road, standing in a large landscaped garden, with pet Jacob's Sheep in the field. The large bright rooms are on the first floor, beautifully decorated with coronets, coordinated colours of blue/pink/white and cream, rich fabrics and duvets, and antique furniture. All bedrooms have tea makers and TV, as well as views of the rolling hills, and the River Foyle. For guests who prefer a bath to a shower, a combination bathroom is available.

The cosy, predominantly red, sitting room, with a real fire, offers a pleasant spot to unwind after a busy day. Breakfasts are a banquet: there is a help-yourself starter buffet, followed by a wide menu choice, i.e. smoked salmon, omelettes, French toast, plus a well-presented traditional Irish breakfast. Home-made scones and cakes are available in this beautifully maintained house.

As one guest commends: "does it get any better than this?" Little wonder that Josephine was voted 'Landlady of the Year'.

This is extremely good value, and if you are planning on spending time in this area, Mount Royd would be an excellent choice. Book in for several days and enjoy the hospitality, good food and first class accommodation. Evening meals are not served, but there is a pub and restaurant within a mile.

This is a family friendly house, and a cot and highchair are available. Guests have use of the garden. Be sure to visit the Grianan of Aileach prehistoric stone fort, which dates from 2000 B.C., Moonreach Presbyterian Church, one of the oldest in Ireland, and Lifford Visitors Centre. The Giants Causeway is just an hour's drive away. Historic Derry City, with its famous walls, is just a 15 minute drive. Smoking in designated area only.
From Derry, take A40 to Carrigan house on left on the R236. Also signposted off the A139 and A14.

OWNER Josephine Martin OPEN February 1–November 30
ROOMS 3 double, 1 family; all en suite
TERMS from €30 pps; child reduction; single supplement

**Belle View**
Ballyshannon Road, Donegal Town, Co. Donegal
Tel: 074 9722167

Belle View is an attractive bungalow standing in half a hectare of grounds, in a peaceful location overlooking Donegal Bay and the Bluestack Mountains. The house has been upgraded since last edition.

Mary Lawne is an attentive host who welcomes guests with a hospitality tray featuring tea and home baking. The bedrooms have comfortable beds and good-sized bathrooms. Breakfast only is served, and the dining room has tea-making facilities. There is a wide choice of eating establishments in Donegal town.

The guest lounge, which overlooks the mountains and the bay, has an open fire and tea makers. There are some lovely walks close by and boating and water sports are available at nearby Lough Eske, and there is a pitch and putt course adjacent to the house. The nearby Donegal Craft Centre is of special interest.

On the N56 Ballyshannon–Sligo Road, situated near the Craft Village.

OWNER Mrs Mary Lawne OPEN April–November ROOMS 2 double, 2 family; 2 en suite TERMS €25.50–26.50; child reduction; single supplement €6.50 MEALS light meals can be provided

**Island View House**
Ballyshannon Road, Donegal Town, County Donegal
Tel: 074 9722411
Email dowdsb@indigo.ie

Island House stands in an elevated position, in three-quarters of an acre of grounds, one kilometre from the town centre. Bernadette is a friendly host, and the house is beautifully kept. The spacious family room, has an oversized shower. All bedrooms are individually decorated in Victorian colours, and have rich bed covers of white, green, yellow and red.

The ground floor room has a pine wood floor and ceiling; all have en suite facilities, TV, hair-dryer and tea makers. Tasty breakfasts are served on fine china, and lace tablecloths, at separate tables.

Vegetarian and special diets catered for with notice. There are books and puzzles for guests' use. The well furnished lounge overlooks the sea.

OWNER Bernadette Dowds OPEN All year except Christmas
ROOMS 2 double, 1 twin, 1 family; all en suite
TERMS €30–35 pps; single supplement; child reduction

**St Ernan's House Hotel**
St Ernan's Island, Donegal, Co. Donegal
Tel: 073 21065 Fax: 073 22098
Email: res@sainternans.com
Website: www.sainternans.com

St Ernan's, a classic Georgian house, was built in 1826 by John Hamilton, a nephew of the Duke of Wellington. It is situated on what was an island; the island is now linked to the mainland by a short causeway and covers some 3.25 hectares. It is an elegant, lovely country house in a beautiful location, offering peace and tranquillity in wonderful surroundings. It was converted into a hotel in 1983 and has been in the O'Dowds' hands since 1987; it is licensed. The individually styled bedrooms are beautifully proportioned and very spacious; most bedrooms have views of sea and countryside. Two new suites are available. Dinner featuring fresh produce is beautifully presented in the large dining room, and the elegant drawing room, with a log fire, is an informal spot in which to relax after a busy day. Smoking is not permitted in the dining room, and cigar- and pipe-smoking are not allowed on the premises. For guests who are seeking quality accommodations combined with peace and tranquillity, St Ernan's is an excellent choice. Not suitable for children under six years. Access, Visa and Mastercard accepted.

OWNER Brian O'Dowd OPEN Easter–October 31
ROOMS 10 twin/ double, 2 suites; all en suite TERMS from €260-420 per room, including breakfast; child reduction(only children over 6 years); single supplement MEALS dinner from €42

## DUNFANAGHY

**Rosman House**
Dunfanaghy, Co. Donegal
Tel: 074 9136273 Fax: 074 9136273
Email: rosman@eircom.net

Rosman House, an attractive modern dormer bungalow, stands in a superb spot with spectacular views of Horn Head, Muckish Mountain and Sheephaven Bay. It has a large well-landscaped garden, and is within walking distance of the village. Roisin McHugh, formerly a teacher, takes great pride in her establishment, and her husband runs the 40-hectare dairy and sheep farm. Improvements are ongoing and the house has been freshly-decorated. The spacious lounge, where smoking is permitted, opens onto a patio and gardens.

The bedrooms are individually decorated with coordinated floral colour schemes. There are four ground floor rooms. Breakfast and pre-arranged dinners are served in the elegant dining room on separate tables, overlooking Horn Head. There are some enjoyable scenic walks nearby and an 18-hole golf course. Pet accommodation is available. Visa and Mastercard accepted.

Through Dunfanaghy village on the Falcarragh Road, turn right, immediately after Art Gallery.

OWNER Mrs Roisin McHugh OPEN All year ROOMS 1 double, 2 twin, 2 family; all en suite TERMS €30 pps, family prices on request; single €45–50; child reduction

## GLENCOLUMBKILLE

**Corner House**
Cashel, Glencolumbkille, Co. Donegal
Tel: 074 9730021

Corner House is situated in the centre of the village and, as the name implies, located on the corner. Mrs Byrne is a pleasant and considerate host who also runs the adjoining shop, and her son runs the pub.

The house looks quite modest from the outside but is surprisingly spacious inside. It has an enormous dining room and a small upstairs lounge. The house is well maintained; the bedrooms are average in size, are immaculate, fresh and bright. Smoking is allowed in the lounge and the bedrooms.

The surroundings are beautiful and a great spot for hill-walking. A lovely old grandfather clock stands in the hallway. There is an interesting doll collection displayed in a cabinet on the landing.

OWNER Mrs J.P. Byrne OPEN June 1–end September
ROOMS 2 double, 2 twin; all en suite TERMS €54-60 double/twin, €38 single; child reduction; single supplement; no credit cards

## GWEEDORE

**Min-a-Locha**
Brinaleck Post Office, Bloody Foreland, Gweedore, Co. Donegal
Tel: 074 9532279
Email: minalocha@eircom.net

This purpose-built modern bungalow, although it does have a second storey, overlooks what is said to be the best views in Ireland, the Bloody Foreland and the Atlantic Ocean. The house was purpose-built for B&B and offers every comfort in a peaceful and tranquil setting. The bedrooms have a medieval décor and are of a good size, as are the bathrooms. The beds have attractive colourful duvets. All of the curtains and bed covers were made by Kathleen Duggan, who extends a warm welcome and prides herself on personal attention to her guests' needs. The spacious lounge has a Victorian-style fireplace where turf fires burn on cool evenings; guests may smoke in lounge only. Breakfasts are served in the bright and airy dining room, overlooking the view, and include home-baked bread and scones.

There are sandy beaches, hill and coastal walks, cycling and day trips to the Islands. This is a perfect place from which to explore this dramatic and rugged area. A baby-sitting service can be arranged. Traditional Irish music can be found at several local venues. All credit cards accepted. Call for driving directions.

OWNER John & Kathleen Duggan OPEN April 1–October 31 ROOMS 3 double, 1 twin, 1 family; 4 en suite TERMS from €28 pps; child reduction; single supplement

### Fernbank

Redcastle, Lifford, Inishowen, Co. Donegal
Tel: 074 9383032 Fax: 07493 83164

Fernbank, built in 1970, with later additions, is extremely good value and is situated in an elevated position with spectacular views of Lough Foyle. Elizabeth, who is from Buncrana, has been offering her special brand of hospitality for 30 years; there is a home-away-from-home atmosphere and the house is immaculate.

A hot drink is available at just about any time, and Elizabeth is happy to give advice on what to see and do in the area. The bedrooms are all on the ground floor and some have lough views. The sitting room and dining room have pine ceilings and the rooms are bright and cheery. Smoking permitted in lounge only. Greencastle, with its maritime museum and award-winning fish restaurant, is 11 km away. Situated on the main Derry–Moville Road, 9 miles from Muff.

OWNER Elizabeth McLaughlin OPEN All year ROOMS 3 double, 1 twin; all en suite TERMS €30pps, €32 single; child reduction

### McGrory's

Culdaff, Inishowen, Co. Donegal
Tel: 074 9379104
Email: mcgr@eircom.net
Website: www.mcgrorys.ie

McGrory's is a family-run establishment that was totally refurbished in 1999, and provides first-class accommodation. The bedrooms are all of a good size, most have cherry wood furniture, comfortable beds, attractive fabrics and duvets. All have TV, direct dial telephone, hair-dryer, tea makers and luggage rack: rooms in the oldest part of the house have exposed stone walls.

McGrory's is also a pub and a restaurant. The McGrory family are all musical, and Mac's Backroom Bar has earned an excellent reputation as one of Ireland's finest live music venues. Opening acts from around the world have appeared at Mac's, as well as Ireland's top performers, Altan and Paul Brady, The Saw Doctors, and Kieran Goss to name but a few.

Concessions are given to McGrory's residents who attend a gig at the Backroom Bar. Live music is performed every Wednesday and Saturday—quite a success story for a village in Donegal with a population of just 200 people.

The Front Bar hosts traditional sessions on Tuesday and Friday. Fresh local sea food features heavily on the menu in the restaurant, as well as steaks and lamb. Vegetarian and special diets are catered for. Angling and golf are close by; special golfing rates have been negotiated with Ballyliffen Golf Club. Mastercard and Visa accepted. McGrory's is easily located in Culdaff village.

OWNER McGrory Family OPEN All year
ROOMS 17 double/twin; all en suite
TERMS from €45 pps; child reduction; single supplement

## St John's Country House
Fahan, Inishowen Peninsula, Co. Donegal
Tel: 074 9360289 Fax: 074 9360612
Email: stjohnsrestaurant@eircom.net
Website: http://homepage.eircom.net/~st.johnscountryhouse/

St John's was built in 1785, and lovingly restored by the owners in 1980. The idyllic setting is two acres of lovely grounds and landscaped gardens on the shores of Lough Swilly. The spacious bedrooms have large en suite bathrooms, most with bath and shower, and large fluffy towels.

The five double bedrooms are beautifully and luxuriously furnished, with the perfect blend of modern comforts, including telephone, TV and hair-dryer, and the charm of a bygone era. They have king-size beds, with crisp white cotton sheets, warm duvets, rich drapes and carpets, and an added bonus of Lough Swilly and mountain scenery.

The elegant restaurant overlooking the view has won international fame for its imaginative, freshly-prepared food. As the restaurant is open to the public, guests planning on dinner should reserve in advance. There is also a non-smoking dining room. Log fires burn in the bar lounge, an excellent spot for a pre- or after-dinner drink. St. John's is not suitable for children. The ambience is informal and inviting, the owners, who have been here for over 20 years, are charming and helpful.

St John's would be an excellent choice for exploring this unspoilt corner of Ireland. Owner, Reg Ryan, comments he found "his little corner of heaven" and after staying here, am sure you will agree with him.

As the locals say: "up here it's different". A boat is available for folks interested in fishing: golfers are well catered for, with six courses close by. The prehistoric ring fort of Grianan of Aileach dates from around 1700 B.C., and is well worth a visit. Visa and Mastercard accepted. Situated in the village of Fahan on the main Derry to Buncrana Road, R238.

OWNER Reg Ryan & Phil McAfee OPEN March–end October ROOMS 5 double; all en suite
TERMS from €65–105 pps; single supplement MEALS Dinner €45

## INVER

### Cloverhill House
Cranny, Inver, Co. Donegal
Tel: 074 9736165 Fax: 074 9736165

Cloverhill House is approached by a private drive bordered with high yew hedges and is an attractive long, low, modern whitewashed house in an elevated position which has lovely river views.

The extensive gardens are beautiful and there are fruit trees and strawberry fields. There is an enormous and very pleasant sitting/dining room with a turf fire. The bedrooms are spacious and well furnished; three are on the ground floor. An annex bedroom with en suite bathroom is available, ideal for guests who prefer more privacy. Evening meals are available if ordered in advance, and can be enjoyed with a glass of wine. Home-cooked evening meals use fresh fruit and vegetables from the House garden. A ten minute walk brings you to a sandy beach and fishing river. Fishing, golfing and mountain climbing activities are available locally.

OWNER Terry & June Coyle OPEN February to November ROOMS 3 double, 2 twin, 1 single; 2 en suite TERMS €26-28 pps double/twin, €30 single; child reduction.

## KILLYBEGS

### Bannagh House
Fintra Road, Killybegs, Co. Donegal
Tel: 074 9731108
Email: bannaghhouse@eircom.net
Website: www.bannaghhouse.com

This modern house stands in an elevated position in a small front garden and has wonderful views of the harbour, town and near and distant hills. Killybegs is a large fishing port, and the harbour always seems to be full of enormous fishing boats, making this an ideal place for fresh fish.

Melly's Café does an excellent fish and chip meal in vast portions. The lounge and dining room also have bay views. Smoking is permitted in the TV lounge. The bedrooms, all on the ground floor, are well-appointed and tastefully furnished. Phyllis Melly works hard at creating a comfortable home for guests, and is happy to give advice on local activities and to recommend local restaurants.

OWNER Phyllis Melly OPEN April–October ROOMS 2 double, 1 twin, 1 family; all en suite TERMS from €33 pps; child reduction; single supplement

## Hollycrest Lodge
Donegal Road, Killybegs, Co. Donegal
Tel: 074 97 31470
Email: hollycrest@hotmail.com

Guests continue to enjoy the relaxing atmosphere and warm welcome found here at this attractive Georgian-style house, which sits off the road in a large, well-maintained garden. Guests are welcome to make use of the garden, which is a pleasant spot in which to relax on fine days. Anne Keeney is a very personable lady who enjoys meeting people, and nothing is too much trouble to ensure her guests are comfortable. The house is well-maintained and decorated and furnished to a high standard. The colour-coordinated bedrooms are on the ground floor and one has a brass bed.

There is a guest lounge with TV and a separate dining room where filling breakfasts are served. Smoking is allowed only on the sun porch. Evening meals are not served, but there are plenty of eating establishments close by. Credit cards accepted.

N56 from Donegal to Killybegs, situated on right-hand side, on road 2km from Killybegs.

OWNER Ann Keeney OPEN February 1–November 30 ROOMS 3 double, 1 twin, 1 single; 3 en suite TERMS €30 pps; en suite, €28 standard pps; child reduction; single supplement

## Hillcrest
Ballyshannon Road, Laghey, Co. Donegal
Tel: 074 9721837 Fax: 074 9721674
Email: sheilagatins@unison.ie

Hillcrest is a pleasant place to stay–the welcome is warm and friendly, a hot drink usually greets guests upon arrival and the house is spotlessly clean. It is a modern bungalow and stands on the side of a hill in an attractive garden. All the bedrooms, which are on the small side, have pretty front-facing views and are located on the ground floor. The small TV room has comfortable chairs and a piano, which guests are welcome to play. Smoking in lounge only. From Ballyshannon on the N15, Laghey signposted on left, turn right at

Esso station, left at the junction. Hillcrest is the third house on right.

OWNER Mrs Sheila Gatins OPEN Easter–September
ROOMS 3 family rooms; 2 en suite TERMS €31 pps, €36 single;
child reduction; single supplement No credit cards

## LETTERKENNY

### Hillcrest House
Lurgybrack, Sligo Road, Letterkenny, Co. Donegal
Tel: 074 9122300
Website: www.hillcresthousebb.com

Hillcrest is a friendly house, where a warm welcome is extended and
guests are greeted with a complimentary hot drink and cakes upon
arrival. The house is situated on the main Sligo Road, a kilometre
from Letterkenny. The house is potentially noisy, but there are great
water, mountain and town views. The Maguires are a friendly and
helpful couple who have five children. They take excellent care of
their guests, and are helpful in every way. All rooms, although a little
small, are spotlessly clean and comfortable; four of them are on the
ground floor. Hillcrest offers good value and a high standard of
accommodation.

   Breakfast only is served at separate tables in the bright dining
room, and there is a wide choice for evening meals close by. The
Maguires are happy to recommend places to eat and to assist guests
with daily activities. Visa, Mastercard and American Express accepted.

OWNER Larry & Margaret Maguire OPEN All year
ROOMS 2 double, 2 twin, 2 family; 5 en suite TERMS €21.50–23;
child reduction; single supplement €6.50–12.50

### Rinneen Country Home
Woodlands, Ramelton Road, Letterkenny, Co. Donegal
Tel: 074 91 24591
Email: rinneencountryhome@eircom.net

Rinneen, which means 'little plot of land at the top of the hill', has
panoramic views of Lough Swilly, the mountains and green fields,
where contented sheep graze. Major renovations have transformed
this house into a bright, modern, attractive country home. Three of
the rooms are upstairs; two of these command a fantastic view of
woodlands and water. Mrs McBride was selected as winner of the
'Lyons Tea Irish Welcome of the Year'.

   There is a real fire in the cosy lounge, which overlooks the view. An
additional bonus is Mary McBride, a congenial and helpful host,
almost always on hand to assist with itineraries, and who is particularly interested in literature. Excellent breakfasts are served in the

dining room; dinners are not available, but Mary is happy to make suggestions for local pubs and restaurants for evening meals. Visa and Mastercard accepted.

OWNER Mrs Mary McBride OPEN February 20–December 20 ROOMS 2 double, 1 family, 1 single TERMS €27.50 pps, €80 family (2 adults, 2 children), €35 single; child reduction

## White Gables
Derry Road, Letterkenny, Co. Donegal
Tel: 074 9122583

White Gables is a spacious house in an elevated position overlooking the river and the town. There is a pleasant view from the dining room/lounge, which has a small sitting area and a table for breakfast which faces the window. Smoking is allowed in designated area. The small bedrooms are clean and simply furnished; two are on the ground floor. There is a pleasant garden where guests may sit on fine days, and a conservatory with comfortable wicker furniture.

OWNER Cabrini McConnellogue OPEN All year ROOMS 3 double, 2 twin, 2 family, 1 single; 3 en suite TERMS double/twin €25 pps, family room €60, single €30; child reduction

## LIFFORD

## The Hall Green Farmhouse
Port Hall, Lifford, Co. Donegal
Tel: 074 9141318 Fax: 074 9141318
Email: jeanmckean@eircom.net

This traditional farmhouse dates back to 1611 and is situated on a working beef farm. The house has views over the River Foyle and on to the Sperrin Mountains. Salmon fishing is available on the River Foyle which runs through the farm. The bedrooms are tastefully decorated and have electric blankets, hairdryers and other extras. The house is mainly furnished in antiques with marble fireplaces in the dining and drawing rooms. The house is centrally heated with modern conveniences throughout yet is one of the oldest inhabited houses in Ireland and retains the charming architecture of the past.

Guests are welcome to relax in the garden or go for a walk on the banks of the River Foyle. The farmhouse is in a good central position for touring Donegal, Glenveagh Castle and National Park, Slieve League, and the Giant's Causeway in County Antrim.

Golf, walking, bird-watching and a fully equipped leisure centre are close by. A visit to the Lifford Old Courthouse, Visitor and Clan Centre is worthwhile. This is a friendly, non-smoking house with a home-away-from-home atmosphere and the hosts will gladly help organise your itinerary and advise on local restaurants for your evening meal. Guest arrive as strangers but will leave as friends.

Visa, Mastercard accepted. From Lifford take N14 for 3 km, then R265 for 2 miles.

OWNER Mervyn & Jean McKean OPEN January 6–December 15 Off season by request. ROOMS 1 double, 2 family, 1 double/single; 2 en suite TERMS €29–31 pps; child reduction; single supplement

## MOVILLE

### Admiralty House
Carrownaffe, Moville, Co. Donegal
Tel: 074 9382529

Admiralty House, a beautifully restored Georgian house, was in a derelict condition when it was purchased by the McFeelys.

Restoration took over two years: the result is a beautiful country house set in a pleasant wooded garden, with views of Lough Foyle. The entryway is very attractive, and has marble floors as does the lounge. There are rich colours throughout and stained-glass windows depicting various sea scenes. A bonus at Admiralty House is the warmth of the friendly owners. The house is furnished in keeping with its character; most of the pieces were found by the owners at various venues around the country. The bedrooms are individually decorated and are warm and comfortable. The conservatory, with its wicker furniture, is the only new addition to the house. The owners are extremely helpful and provide a portfolio of places to visit.

Breakfasts only are served, but there are plenty of places to eat in Moville, an eight-minute walk away. Of local interest is Greencastle Maritime Museum, a Norman Castle and Napoleonic fort.

Mastercard, Visa accepted. Take the Derry Road from Moville. The house is yellow and white, and overlooks Lough Foyle.

OWNER Suzanne McFeely OPEN June 1–September 30
ROOMS 2 double, 1 twin, 1 family
TERMS €25 pps; child reduction; single supplement

## RAMELTON

### Ardeen
Ramelton, Co. Donegal
Tel: 074 9151243 Fax: 074 9151243
Email: ardeenbandb@eircom.net
Website: www.ardeenhouse.com

This splendid country house built in 1845 is situated in its own grounds overlooking Lough Swilly. It stands in a well-tended pleasant lawned front garden in a peaceful and tranquil spot. Improvements are ongoing, and since last edition a new bathroom and an upgraded shower are complete. The spacious bedrooms are individually and elegantly decorated in lemon, blue and buttermilk; all have patch-work quilts made by the owner, Anne Campbell. The drawing and dining room are furnished with antiques and have open fires.

The house at one time belonged to a private nurse of King George V and, more recently, to two doctors. Anne Campbell is an excellent host who knows just how to make her guests feel at home. She formerly ran a village shop, but now concentrates on running her very successful bed & breakfast. Self-catering is available. There is a tennis court for guests' use. There are three self-catering cottages available from Easter-October.

There are several places for an evening meal in Ramelton, which has been designated a National Heritage town, and is a pleasant, short stroll away. The county Genealogical Centre is located in the old Meeting House, which is one of the oldest Presbyterian churches in Ireland. Visa and Mastercard accepted.

OWNER Mrs Anne Campbell OPEN Easter–October
ROOMS 2 double, 1 twin, 1 family, 1 single; 3 en suite
TERMS €30-40 pps; child reduction; single supplement

## Crammond House
Market Square, Ramelton, Co. Donegal
Tel: 074 9151055

Crammond House is easily located in this unspoiled historical village. Its origins date from 1760, and has been a grocery and hardware shop, as well as a wholesale tea importers. It was home to the same family for four generations, and of special interest are the old photo-graphs of the old shopfront, which the warm and welcoming present owner, Ena Corry, is happy to show guests. The house has undergone a tasteful restoration; the rooms are well furnished and it has all modern comforts and is spotlessly clean. Smoking is not permitted in the dining room.

The bedrooms are bright, decorated mostly with floral wallpapers, and the non–en suite rooms all have sinks. There is a pleasant and friendly atmosphere, and recommendations on places to eat in the village, as well as information on what to see and do in the area, is provided. A hot drink is offered upon arrival, and at other times on request. Easily located in the town square.

OWNER Mrs Ena Corry OPEN April 1–October 30
ROOMS 1 double, 1 twin, 1 en suite family
TERMS from €25 pps ; child reduction; single supplement

## COUNTY GALWAY

Galway contains the widely renowned area of Connemara, which stretches northward from Galway city up to Killary Harbour and is bordered on the east by beautiful Lough Corrib, which boasts an island for every day of the year.

Galway, the 'city of the tribes', and the nearby popular resort of Salthill, which overlooks the famous Galway Bay, have lovely beaches, a promenade for walking and lots of restaurants, making this an ideal holiday spot. Wild Connemara has inspired song and poetry. Today, Galway, Connemara and the west of Ireland are a haven for ancient customs and culture. You will hear lilting and evocative Irish music in the pubs and often the Irish language being spoken. Travel offshore and you become immersed even deeper into Ireland's traditional way of life, with trips to Inishbofin, County Clare, Achill and the Aran Islands. There's plenty to see and do in the west of Ireland: pony trekking, dramatically located golf courses, angling (which is well catered for, with abundant salmon and trout in clean waters).

If you are interested in sixteenth-century castles, visit the ruins of Ardamullivan Castle, 7.5 km south of Gort, an O'Shaughnessy stronghold. Fiddaun Castle, 7.5 km south southwest of Gort, is another of their strongholds.

Clarinbridge is a popular place in September, when it hosts the Oyster Festival. Portumna, a market town, is at the head of Lough Derg. For the more adventurous, a climb up the Slieve Auchty Mountains is well worth the view. Two castles worth seeing are Derryhivenny Castle, 4.5 km northeast of Portumna. Built in 1653, it is well preserved, as is Pallas Castle, 9 km from Portumna on the Loughrea Road.

Ballinasloe's well-known October Horse Fair lasts for eight days, and includes carnival events and show-jumping exhibitions.

### ANNAGHDOWN

**Corrib View Farm**
Annaghdown, Co. Galway
Tel: 091 791114
Website: www.corribviewfarm.com

This 100-year-old, friendly farmhouse, situated in a peaceful area near Lough Corrib, offers good old-fashioned hospitality. It has received the Agri-Tourism Regional Award. The bedrooms are clean and comfortable and have big fluffy towels. The lounge is warm and there is a separate dining room where breakfasts are served at separate tables. For guests who prefer a continental breakfast, there is a reduction in price. Evening meals are no longer available, but Regina's Pub, 3km away, serves light meals and full dinners. This is a family-run bed & breakfast and guests are made to feel immediately at home.

OWNER Mary Scott Furey and Family OPEN April 1–October 31
ROOMS 2 double, 2 twin, 1 family, 1 single; 3 en suite
TERMS €35pps; child reduction; single supplement €10

### Ard Mhuiris
Kilronan, Aran Islands, Co. Galway
Tel: 099 61208
Email: ardmhuiris@eircom.net

This friendly and warm house, with stunning Galway Bay views, is situated in a peaceful location. Cait, a hospitable lady, was born on the island, and is happy to outline local walks, and share her knowledge. She enjoys painting, and there are several pieces of her work on display. There is a sitting room, which has a TV and tea-making facilities. The en suite rooms are neat and clean.

Guests will enjoy the open countryside, and the convenience of the restaurants and pubs at the Harbour, which is a three minute walk. Guests arriving at the Harbour can be met with prior notice. No credit cards accepted.

OWNER Cait Flaherty OPEN March 1–November 1
ROOMS 6; all en suite, 4 on ground floor
TERMS €35 pps; €60 single ; child reduction

### Man of Aran Cottage
Kilmurvey, Inish Mor, Aran Islands, Co, Galway
Tel: 099 61301 Fax: 099 61324
Email: manofaran@eircom.net
Website: www.manofarancottage.com

Man of Aran Cottage has a thatched roof, and stands on an acre of ground. It was built by Robert Flaherty, and used as the film set for *Man of Aran*. There is plenty of Old World charm, and the cottage is well maintained, and the accommodation comfortable. The sitting room is a good place for guests to gather and share their day's experiences.

Excellent breakfast and pre-booked dinners are on offer, and feature fresh organic vegetables from the garden. Joe and Maura are adept at making guests feel at home, and are happy to help in any way to ensure guests have a comfortable stay. No credit cards accepted.

The house is approximately 4 miles from the harbour.

OWNER Joe and Maura Wolfe OPEN March to November
TERMS from €35 pps; single supplement; child reduction

**Screebe House**
Camus, Connemara, Co. Galway
Tel: 091 574110 Fax: 091 574179
Email: bookings@scribehouse.ie
Website: www.screebehouse.ie

This secluded, magical, rugged, listed Edwardian estate comprises 32,000 acres, and stands in the beautiful, wild Connemara country-side. It overlooks Camus Bay, has its own harbour, and, lovely gardens. Although primarily a fishing and shooting lodge, there is lots of on offer for all outdoor enthusiasts. Walks can be taken, where you may see the red deer, rare flora and many birds.

The nine spacious bedrooms, all en suite, other than the two top floor single bedrooms, have antique furniture, and comfortable beds. There are three large, public rooms, a library/sitting room, drawing room and separate dining room. There are several items of interest about, including some original paintings of interest. Food is a specialty of the house—the chef prepares imaginative evening meals, featuring fresh seafood, meats, and fresh local produce, followed by home-made desserts. Special diets catered for with advance notice.

MANAGER Marcus Carey OPEN May 1-September 30
ROOMS 9 double/ twin/family/single; all en suite, except for two singles on top floor sharing a bathroom
TERMS from €70 pps; single supplement; not suitable for children

**Cashel House**
Cashel, Connemara, Co. Galway
Tel: 095 31001 Fax: 095 31077
Email: info@cashel-house-hotel.com
Website: www.cashel-house-hotel.com

Situated at the head of Cashel Bay, this gracious, nineteenth-century country house is set in 20 hectares of award-winning gardens and woodland walks. It has gained an international reputation for good food and luxurious comfort in a quiet, relaxing atmosphere. General and Madame de Gaulle spent two weeks of their Irish holiday here in 1969. Carefully cooked fresh garden and sea produce, such as lobsters, clams, mackerel, salmon and scallops, are its specialities. There is a carefully chosen wine list. Meals are tastefully presented in the elegant dining room with open turf fires. Special diets may be catered for with advance notice. Luxury and tranquillity combine with the romantic setting to create a magical experience: Cashel House is an excellent choice for a special occasion or honeymoon.

The house is furnished with antiques and other fine treasures, and

Cashel House

the bedrooms are beautifully appointed. There are several areas in which to sit, including a conservatory and patio area. Smoking is permitted in designated areas only. Guests may walk along the seashore, through woods and streams, or drive through beautiful scenic Connemara. All major credit cards accepted. Driving 1 1/2 miles west of Recess, turn south of N59–Cashel House signposted from there.

OWNER Dermot & Kay McEvilly OPEN February 5–January ROOMS 35 double/twin/family; 32 en suite TERMS €170-310 per room; child reduction; single supplement (seasonal) MEALS full dinner and lighter meals

## CLARINBRIDGE

**Springlawn B & B**
Stradbally, Clarinbridge, Co. Galway
Tel: 091 796045 Fax: 091 796045
Email:springlawn2@hotmail.com
Website: www.surf.to/springlawn2.com

This attractive house with dormer windows stands in a hectare in the heart of oyster country. Clarinbridge holds an annual Oyster Festival on the weekend of the 2nd Sunday in September.
  There is a wooded area behind the house, and the sea is within walking distance. The good-sized bedrooms maintain a high standard and have modern comfortable furnishings. Maura McNamara, who has been running her successful bed & breakfast for 11 years, takes a personal interest in her guests and is happy to provide information on golf, fishing and pony trekking, all of which are within a 15-minute drive. This non-smoking house has a TV lounge and a separate dining room where breakfasts and light meals are served at modest prices. For evening meals, there are several restaurants close by. There is no public phone, but guests may use the owners' on request. All major credit cards accepted. Springlawn is one mile off the N18 on the Limerick side of Clarinbridge village.

OWNER Maura McNamara OPEN March 1–November 30 ROOMS 3 double/twin/family; all en suite

TERMS €27.50-31 pps; child reduction; single supplement

## CLIFDEN

**Ardmore House**
Sky Road, Clifden, Co. Galway
Tel: 095 21221 Fax: 095 21100
Email: info@ardmore-house.com
Website: www.ardmore-house.com/

This luxurious farmhouse is set in beautiful scenic countryside over-looking the sea. It is warm and inviting and Kathy Mullen is a delight-ful and pleasant host—guests here are assured of true Irish hospitali-ty. The immaculate bedrooms are well decorated and have comfort-able king- and queen-size beds—three of the bedrooms are suitable for disabled guests. This non-smoking house has two lounges; one with TV and an open fire, another mainly for chatting or reading.

Sea-food is a speciality for evening meals—light meals are also avail-able. Special diets can be catered for. Credit cards accepted. Lake and deep-sea angling, pony trekking, beautiful walks and golf are all available in the area. There are scenic farm walks to the picnic areas, and private cliff walks can also be taken.

OWNER John & Kelly Mullen OPEN April 1—September 30
ROOMS 2 double, 1 twin, 3 family; all en suite
TERMS €35 pps; child reduction; single supplement

**Mallmore House**
Clifden, Co. Galway
Tel: 095 21460
Email: info@mallmore.com

This lovingly restored Georgian house (formerly the home of the Darcy family, the founders of Clifden, and his excellency, the Archbishop of Tuam), is set in 14 hectares and is within walking dis-tance of the sea. The house overlooks the bay, and most of the bed-rooms have lovely views. All bedrooms are on the ground floor, spa-cious and comfortable, tastefully decorated in period paper and paint. The large lounge has a turf fire and is a peaceful place in which to relax after a busy day, or smoke. Award-winning breakfasts are served in a separate dining room, and for other meals there are sev-eral establishments in Clifden.

Kathleen Hardman is a considerate and helpful host and guests are assured of personal attention. The world-famous Connemara ponies are bred at Mallmore and can be seen in the grounds, and the wood-land is a haven for a great variety of wildlife. 1 mile from Clifden on the Ballyconneely Road.

OWNER Alan & Kathleen Hardman OPEN March 7–October I
ROOMS 3 double, 2 twin, I family; all en suite TERMS €32-35 pps;
child reduction; single supplement

## Ocean Villa

Sky Road, Kingstown, Clifden, Co. Galway
Tel: 095 21357 Fax: 095 21357
Email: oceanvilla@eircom.net
Website: oceanvillaireland.com

Ocean Villa is situated in a wonderful position overlooking sea and
hills. The house is immaculately maintained and the welcome is warm
and friendly. Carmel Murray is a most hospitable host who greets
guests with a hot drink upon arrival, and is happy to spend time
assisting guests in every way. The bedrooms are warm, of a good
size, have level access, comfortable beds and tea-making facilities.

  This is a peaceful and tranquil location and there is plenty to see
and do from here. Three cats, a horse, cows and calves reside on the
property. Golf, mountain climbing, pony trekking, fishing, and beach
walks, all of which can be arranged by your hosts. Home-cooked
meals are on offer, fresh fish is often on the menu, and special diets
can be catered for with advance notice. Evening meals can be prepared, for a minimum of four guests.

  There are two lounges, one with TV. Smoking is permitted in designated areas only. Take a left turn at centre of Clifden for Sky Road,
pass Abbeyglen Castle Hotel, drive for five more miles on upper Sky
Road, then following finger signs for Ocean Villa.

OWNER Mrs Carmel Murray OPEN March I–October 31
ROOMS 6 double/twin/family; all en suite TERMS €28–32 pps; child
reduction; single supplement MEALS dinner

## Sunnybank House

Sunnybank, Clifden, Co. Galway
Tel: 095 21437
Email: info@sunnybankhouse.com
Website: www.sunnybankhouse.com

This charming period house of character, whose history is part of
Clifden town, commands an elevated position in well-tended landscaped grounds over-looking Clifden town. Sunnybank would be an
ideal base for exploring this beautiful area of Ireland.

  The immaculate, well-appointed bedrooms are tastefully decorated
and furnished to a high standard. Smoking is not permitted in bedrooms. There are two ground floor rooms with their own sitting
rooms. There is also a spacious lounge which has some antique
pieces, including a grandfather clock and soft, comfortable furnish-

ings, and there is an additional lounge with TV. The house is bright and decorated mostly with pastel shades.

There is a heated swimming pool, a sauna, tennis courts and mature gardens for guests' use.

The house is not suitable for children. Visa and Mastercard accepted. N59 from Galway, turn right at Esso station, pass church, take first left, house is 200m on the right.

OWNER Shane O'Grady OPEN March 1–November 1 ROOMS 6 double, 4 twin, 1 single; all en suite TERMS €50-65 pps; single supplement €15

## The Quay House
Beach Road, Clifden, Co. Galway
Tel: 095 21369 Fax: 095 21608
Email: thequay@iol.ie Website: www.thequayhouse.com

Quay House is the oldest building in Clifden, built over 200 years ago for the Harbour Master. Since that time it has been a Franciscan Monastery, and a convent. It is now run by a charming couple, Paddy and Julia Foley, and the ambience is informal and comfortable. The house is non-smoking. The spacious bedrooms are individually themed, with antique furniture, original paintings, and large bathrooms, with both shower and bath. Several bedrooms have working fireplaces, most of them overlooking the harbour. The studios have balconies, and small fitted kitchens. All bedrooms have TV, phone and tea makers– two ground-floor bedrooms have wheelchair access.

Quay House is full of items of interest, including family portraits, and period furniture, and other treasures. The house was in a dilapidated condition until a decade ago, when Paddy and Julia undertook the job of tastefully refurbishing the house, skilfully combining modern amenities with old world charm. A tiger's head greets guests in the entry hall, and Buster, the pug, also resides here. This is a wonderful place to stay, as guests have every comfort. The house has a good selection of wines.

Breakfast is served in the conservatory overlooking the garden, a great spot from which to start the day. Special diets can be catered for at breakfast. There are several establishments in the area for evening meals. Visa and Mastercard accepted.

OWNER Paddy & Julia Foyle OPEN mid-March–end October
ROOMS 14 rooms double/twin/family; all en suite
TERMS from €150 per room; child reduction; single supplement

### Ballykine House

Clonbur, Co. Galway
Tel: 094 9546150 Fax: 094 9546150
Email: ballykine@eircom.net
Website: www.ballykinehouse-clonbur-cong.com

Ballykine House is situated on the road between the picturesque villages of Cong and Clonbur, and is known as the gateway to Connemara. The house continues to maintain its high standard and offers good value accommodation. It overlooks the famous fishing lake of Lough Mask.

Approached via a long private driveway, it has its own private grounds of gardens and lawns, surrounded by beautiful woodlands. The oldest part of the house belonged to the Guinness family; the house and the land were purchased by the family in 1940, with an addition in 1992: there is a wine license. Mr and Mrs Lambe are a very congenial couple who have created a warm and inviting atmosphere. There is a cosy sitting room and open fire, and a conservatory to relax in with tea and coffee makers provided. The house is beautifully maintained, and all bedrooms have TV. Smoking is only permitted in the conservatory.

There are wonderful forest walks (guides can be provided) as well as walks to the summit of magnificent Benlevi. The immediate area is a fisherman's paradise. There is a very pleasant lakeside walk available. Restaurants are within walking distance of the house. Golf is available at famous Ashford Castle and Ballinrobe. Take N84 from Galway to Cong; from Cong take R345 to Ballykine House.

OWNER Ann Lambe OPEN April 1–November 1
ROOMS 5 twin/family/double; all en suite
TERMS from €30 pps; child reduction; single supplement

### Cregg House

Galway Road, Connemara, Co. Galway
Tel: 095 21326 Fax: 095 21326
Email: cregghouse@eircom.net

This immaculate dormer bungalow stands in an elevated position on half a hectare of grounds. The house has a spectacular view of Roundstone Bog and the mountains beyond. Mary O'Donnell continues to maintain her high standards and the bedrooms are prettily and individually decorated with soft pastel colours. The O'Donnells have been offering their special brand of hospitality for over 13 years; guests feel very much at home here, and enjoy chatting round the turf fire, which is lit at the first sign of a chill in the air. Excellent breakfasts include fresh fruit, home-made yoghurt and soda bread. An ideal base from which to tour Connemara, there is a fishing river less than five minutes away and golf and horseback riding are also available. Visa accepted. On N59, main Galway Road.

OWNER Mary O'Donnell OPEN Easter–November 1
ROOMS 3 double, 2 twin, 1 family; 5 en suite
TERMS €24-32 pps; child reduction; single supplement €7.50

**Killary House**
Leenane, Connemara, County Galway
Tel: 095 42254
Email: kingkillaryhouse@eircom.net

Killary House has lots of character, and is situated on 800 acres, part of a working sheep farm, overlooking Killary Harbour. This is an idyllic location for families, and folks interested in outdoor activities. Leenane is a small village which served as the location for *The Field*, a film starring Richard Harris. Evening meals are not served, but there are plenty of establishments close by that serve good food. Special diets are catered for at breakfast. The bedrooms are all spacious, and furnished with antiques. Tea-making facilities are available in the bedrooms. Smoking is permitted only in designated areas in the house. There is also a very large sitting room with TV. The welcome here is warm, guests return here often, enjoying the informal ambience and Fiona's hospitality. There are lovely views all round the property, and pleasant of walks can be taken from the farm. Sign-posted at Leenane.

OWNER Fiona King OPEN March–October
ROOMS 7 double/family/twin; 4 en suite
TERMS €30 pps; reduction for children; single supplement €6.50

**Lakeside Country House**
Oughterard, Connemara, Co. Galway
Tel: 091 552846 Fax: 091 552846

This warm and friendly, immaculately kept house is in a superb position on the shores of Lough Corrib with panoramic views of the lake and its many islands. This is a working farm of sheep and cattle, and there is also a donkey and a Connemara pony. An additional bonus are the delightful and charming owners, Josie and Mary O'Halloran—little wonder guests return here often to enjoy their special brand of Irish hospitality. The bedrooms, all on the ground floor, are of a good size and have patchwork quilts or Country Diary duvets. Smoking is permitted in the sitting room only. There is a bog on the property which provides the turf for the fireplace in the sitting room. Breakfasts only are served in the dining room with pine furniture, and there are several options for evening meals close by. Josie can easily be persuaded to take guests up the river, and there is an angling centre almost adjacent to the property.

There is a picnic area by the lake and in the garden by the fountain/waterfall. You may arrive here as a guest, but you will leave as a friend. It is a wonderful spot from which to explore this beautiful area. Travel down Golf Course–Aughnanure Castle Road and follow signs for Lakeside Country House.

Visa and Mastercard accepted.

OWNER Mary O'Halloran OPEN March 1–November 30 ROOMS 2 double, 1 twin, 1 family; all en suite TERMS €32 pps; child reduction; single supplement €10

## The Convent Guest House
Leenane, Connemara, County Galway
Tel: 095 42240

As the name implies this was formerly a Convent, although for the last twenty years, it has been a comfortable bed and breakfast. Situated two minutes walk to the village, the convent with its sunny exterior is easily located. All the rooms, including the comfortable sitting room and dining room have views of Killary Harbour. The en suite, good size bedrooms. All have TV and tea makers. The dining room was originally used for Mass; there are still pews in the room, as well as original beautiful stained glass windows. Special diets are catered for, although breakfast only is served: the owners of the Convent Guest House own a restaurant in the village, and there are several other venues for evening meals. The house is warm, and the owners friendly. Leenane was the setting for the film *The Field* starring Richard Harris. This is a very scenic area, and Aasleagh Falls is a fifteen-minute walk from the property.

OWNER Sean & Mary Hamilton OPEN March–November ROOMS 5 twin/double; all en suite. TERMS €30 pps; child reduction; single supplement

## Waterfall Lodge
Oughterard, Connemara, Co. Galway
Tel: 091 552168
Email: kdolly@eircom.net
Website: www.waterfalllodge.net
This superb period residence stands in a secluded setting, only a minute's walk to the village. A mature garden with rare shrubs and plants, the beautiful grounds are ablaze with colour in spring and summer, and a cascading waterfall. The river Owen Riff runs through

the property, and private game fishing for salmon and trout is available to guests. A visit to the Glengowla Silver and Lead Mines, Ireland's only show mine, is well worth a visit.

The house is furnished with antiques, including a grandfather clock, and the tastefully furnished bedrooms are reached by a pitch pine stairway. The extensive breakfast menu is available only in the elegant dining room at separate tables, and the spacious TV lounge has a cast-iron and marble fireplace. tea- and coffee-making facilities are in the lounge and guests may help themselves at just about any time. All bedrooms have TV.

Kathleen Dolly is a delightful lady and is very knowledgeable about the area. The atmosphere is friendly and informal—this is a non-smoking house. This is a popular bed & breakfast establishment and early reservations are recommended.

Take N59 from Galway city to Oughterard; Waterfall Lodge is the first house on the left after the bridge.

OWNER Kathleen Dolly OPEN All year ROOMS 6 double/twin/family; all en suite TERMS €40 pps; child reduction; single supplement €6.50

## CORRANDULLA

### Cregg Castle

Corrandulla, Co. Galway
Tel: 091 791434 Fax: 091 793238
Email: creggcastle@indigo.ie
Website: www.creggcastle.com

Cregg Castle, the last fortified castle to be built west of the Shannon, sits in a peaceful and tranquil spot on 67 hectares of wildlife preserve, also home to several other animals, such as pet sheep, dogs, a donkey and chickens. This is a very lived-in, casual, informal property, and there are no strict rules here: it is a real castle, lived in by real people. Dogs. cats, sheep, cattle and a donkey live on the property. Guests may walk in the woods and spot the wildlife, or go farther afield and take a walk by the river. Breakfasts, which include free-range eggs and home-baked bread, are served

Cregg Castle

until noon, with light meals available by arrangement. Smoking is permitted in the Great Hall only.

The emphasis at Cregg Castle is on relaxation, and guests are encouraged to get to know each other, enjoying conversation and the occasional traditional musical evening. This is an ideal place for those who want to be involved in Irish music. The owners are experienced musicians and are delighted to play with or for guests. Most of the bedrooms are of a good size and have comfortable beds—five rooms feature four-poster king beds.

This is a unique property with many original features, such as the huge locks and security bars, the foot scraper with the rampant black cat of the Blake's crest and the shutters on the big windows. The Blake crest is also on the fireplace with its black marble. Outside in the courtyard is a Queen Anne bell tower; in the inner yard is the original forge and the remains of an oven for firing pottery. A spring well provides the castle with water. Cregg Castle's welcome, as described in their brochure, is exactly right—"Hail Guest, we ask not what thou art; if friend we greet thee hand and heart; if stranger, such no longer be, our friendly faith shall conquer thee."

Cregg Castle is a place to capture Ireland's history and culture, in the warm and informal ambience of a real castle. Visa, Access and Mastercard accepted.

Directions from Dublin/Limerick: take Tuam/Sligo turn off at Oranmore roundabout (five miles from Galway). Turn right for Tuam at Claregalway and then first left for Corrandulla.

OWNER Pat & Ann-Marie Broderick
OPEN All year except for Christmas
ROOMS 9 double/twin/family; all en suite
TERMS €70 pp double occupancy; child reduction; single supplement

## GALWAY

### Dun Roamin
30 Beach Court, Gratton Road, Salthill, Galway, Co. Galway
Tel: 091 582570

The Bogan family named their modern, attractive, red brick house after their decision to stay put and enjoy Galway and the beautiful scenic countryside. The house has a warm and welcoming atmosphere and the rooms are clean with comfortable beds and warm duvets. The guest lounge is cosy and breakfasts only are served in a separate dining room, consisting of cereals, fruit and a traditional Irish platter. Smoking is only allowed in the lounge. Dun Roamin is located less than two minutes from the beach, restaurants and other amenities. Jo Bogan is a down-to-earth, friendly lady, and a helpful and considerate host. Guests are welcomed with a hot drink upon arrival.

OWNER Mrs Jo Bogan OPEN January–October
ROOMS 2 double, 2 twin; all en suite
TERMS €30 pps; child reduction; single supplement €10

## Killeen House
Bushy Park, Galway, Co. Galway
Tel: 091 524179 Fax: 091 528065
Email: killeenhouse@ireland.com
Website: www.killeenhousegalway.com

This charming house, built in 1840, is approached by a tree-lined
driveway. It nestles in 10 hectares of beautifully landscaped gardens
that extend down to Lake Corrib. Catherine Doyle is a wonderful
host with a flair for décor and a passion for antiques.

The house has been tastefully refurbished, combining all modern
comforts without detracting from the original ambience. The elegant
drawing room has the original marble fireplace and an interesting
teapot collection. The rooms are enormous and luxuriously appointed. One room reflects the Victorian era, another the Edwardian. As a
guest once commented: "These must be the most comfortable beds
in Ireland." There are direct dial telephone and tea-making facilities
in all bedrooms, all with bath and shower.

A varied breakfast is tastefully presented in the dining room. For
those who enjoy gracious living in a tranquil atmosphere, Killeen
Lodge is an excellent choice. Smoking is only permitted in the drawing room. The house is not suitable for young children. A path from
the house leads down to the shores of Lough Corrib. All major
credit cards accepted. Situated on the N59 four miles from Galway
city centre.

OWNER Catherine Doyle OPEN All year
ROOMS 6 double/twin/family; all en suite
TERMS double from €140-160; single supplement €30-45

## Delphi Lodge
Leenane, Co. Galway
Tel: 095 42222 Fax: 095 42296
E-mail: info@delphilodge.ie   Website: www.delphilodge.ie

This magnificent 1830s house was beautifully restored in 1988, and
exceptionally maintained, is now one of the finest sporting lodges in
Ireland. Set in 400 hectares with three loughs in a stunning lakeside
location, and surrounded by ancient woodlands and towering mountains, it is the ultimate Connemara retreat.

The house has antique pine furniture and the bedrooms have lovely
views, seven with views of the lake. Some rooms have been upgrad-

ed, and most have new furnishings.

Originally the sporting estate of the Marquis of Sligo, Delphi is now the home of Jane and Peter Mantle. Jane is a Cordon Bleu cook who specialises in local seafood. The Lodge has a strong emphasis on salmon and trout fishing, and Delphi is one of the finest game fisheries in Ireland.

Fly-fishing for salmon is available, but must be pre-booked. The fishing season runs from spring to September. Outside the fishing season the lodge is popular with shooting parties, ramblers and golfers. Horseback riding and hunting can also be arranged.

Superb, safe and uncrowded beaches are within a 20-minute drive, and the Lodge is conveniently placed for visiting Westport and all the sites of Connemara. A huge snooker room and a magnificent library are open to guests. Smoking is restricted.

Evening meals are served at an old oak table and the wine cellar is extensive. Not suitable for children under 10 years. French spoken. There are four charming country cottages available for self-catering. Visa and Mastercard accepted.

OWNER Peter Mantle OPEN January 6–December 20
ROOMS 6 double, 6 twin; all en suite
TERMS from €150–250 per room; single supplement €30
MEALS dinner

### Glen Valley House
Glencroff, Leenane, Co. Galway
Tel: 095 42269
Email: gvhouse@yahoo.com

This friendly, award-winning, modest farmhouse is found down a rather bumpy road in a remote location amidst lovely countryside. Nestled in the foothills of Lettershanbally Mountain, this is a working farm and a warm, friendly, non-smoking house. The rooms are spacious, clean and filled with old-fashioned furniture. The small, cosy lounge has turf fires.

This is an ideal base for those who enjoy hill walking. Pony trekking is available on the farm, which is run by Mrs O'Neill. Substantial breakfasts are provided, and Mrs O'Neill is happy to make recommendations and dinner reservations for the restaurants which can be found a short drive away. N59 Clifden Road, four and half miles from Leenane Village.

OWNER Josephine O'Neill OPEN May 1–November 30
ROOMS 2 double, 2 twin, 1 family; 3 en suite, 1 private bath
TERMS €30 pps; child reduction; single supplement €12.50

**Moycullen House and Restaurant**
Mountain Road, Moycullen, Co. Galway
Tel: 091 555566 Fax: 091 555566
Email: info@moycullen.com
Website: www.moycullen.com

Moycullen House lies on a narrow, quiet road, on one of the highest points in the area overlooking Lough Corrib. It is on the edge of Connemara, making it an ideal location for touring, trips to the Aran Isand and Lough Corrib. It was built in the 1930s by Lord Campbell, and has great oak doors with the original iron locks. The servants' bells still exist in the sitting room. During the time of remodelling for the new dining room and restaurant, two stone fireplaces were exposed.

The restaurant on the premises, which is open to the public has full bar facilities, and an outstanding wine list. The award winning restaurant is run by Marie's son Richard, who is the chef, and his wife, Louise. Dinners are not served on Wednesday, table d'hote and an à la carte menu is available. The house stands in 12 hectares of rhododendrons and azaleas, and a pure spring provides the house with water. The bedrooms are large, tastefully decorated and well furnished, most with period fireplaces.

There is an elegant and comfortable sitting room which has an old stone fireplace, and also a conservatory. Philip and Marie are charming hosts who can organise coarse, trout and salmon fishing as well as boats on Lough Corrib. There are four 18-hole golf courses within a half hour's drive. Credit cards accepted.

OWNER The Casburn Family OPEN mid-March–early January
ROOMS 2 family/double/twin; 1 en suite, 1 private bath
TERMS double €45–50 pps; child reduction; single supplement
MEALS full à la carte & table d'hote

**Corrib View Farmhouse**
Lough Corrib, Oughterard, County Galway
Tel: 091 552345 Fax: 091 552880
Email: corribvw@gofree.indigo.ie

This secluded, 200 year old Georgian style farmhouse, bordered by shrubs and trees, stands in lovely gardens, with panoramic views of Lough Corrib. This is a wonderful place, where you can unwind, and enjoy the stunning scenery. The pitted rock formation, created over thousands of years by acid water, and the beautiful summer lilies, are an added bonus. The bedrooms are of a good size, and the family room is very large, all have en suite facilities. The rooms have comfortable, old fashioned furniture, and the ambience is warm and friendly. There is a guest sitting room, and private tennis courts are available. Fishing boats and boatman can be hired, Oughterard Golf Club, and pitch and putt courses, are a few minutes walk. The ruins of Aughnanure Castle are close by, and a boat ride will take you to the fifth-century monastic ruins. Credit cards taken.

OWNER Ethel and Rita Lea OPEN February 1-November 30
ROOMS 6 double/twin/family; all en suite
TERMS €30–35 pps; single supplement

## Corrib Wave Guest House
Portacarron, Oughterard, Co. Galway
Tel: 091 552147 Fax: 091 552736
Email: cwh@gofree.indigo.ie
Website: www.corribwave.com

Corrib Wave House has been upgraded to a three-star guest house with wine license, situated in picturesque surroundings overlooking the lake and Connemara mountains.

This is a peaceful and tranquil spot, part of a working sheep farm of 10 hectares. The bedrooms, all of which overlook the view, have been upgraded with sturdy seating, made by owner Michael Healy, and have good-sized bath-rooms. The lounge, where smoking is permitted, has an open fire and there is a separate dining room where breakfasts and excellent evening meals, if pre-arranged, are served. This is an ideal spot for people who enjoy the outdoors; there are lovely walks close by, and salmon, trout and coarse fishing. There are boats for hire, and ghillies can be arranged. Swimming can be enjoyed on the lake, and there is an 18-hole golf course within a kilometre. The house is conveniently located near Galway and Connemara. Corrib Wave Guest House, off the N59, 1.5 km east of Oughterard. Visa, Mastercard, Eurocard accepted.

OWNER Michael & Maria Healy OPEN February–November
ROOMS 3 double, 4 twin, 3 family; all en suite
TERMS €35–40; child reduction; single supplement
MEALS dinner €24

## ROUNDSTONE

### Errisbeg Lodge
Errisbeg, Roundstone, Connemara, County Galway
Tel: 095 35807
Email: errisbeglodge@eircom.net
Website: www.errisbeglodge.com

Errisbeg Lodge, named after the mountain, stands on 30 acres, amid several acres of Traditional, Connemara Gardens. Situated on the mountain slopes, overlooking two Atlantic Beaches, it is nature lovers paradise. There are Connemara Ponies, rare wild flowers, plenty of beautiful walks, and for the artists an opportunity to capture the local beauty on canvas. The ground floor, well maintained, en suite bedrooms, are equipped with clock radios, hair-dryers and an information pack.

Some of the rooms have king-size beds, and are of a good size. There is a sitting room, and although Errisbeg Lodge, is a TV free zone, there is a video and plenty of books available.

Shirley King is a friendly and helpful lady who enjoys her bed and breakfast business. She is happy to offer advice, and recommend things to do and places for meals. French is spoken. Shirley has been in business for seven years, and has built up a steady clientele: advance reservations are highly recommended.

OWNER Shirley King OPEN February 1-November 30
ROOMS 5 twin/double; all en suite
TERMS €35–42.50 pps; single supplement; child reduction

## The Angler's Return
Toombeola, Roundstone, Connemara, Co. Galway
Tel: 095 31091 Fax: 095 31091
Email: lynnhill@eircom.net

Nestled at the foot of Derrada Hill, between the mountains and the sea, and overlooking a fresh water tidal pool, The Angler's Return dates back to the 1900s. The longest running bed and breakfast in Connemara, it has thick stone walls, log fireplaces and an interesting history.

First built as a single-storey cottage known as 'The Fishery', John Robertson, a Scottish gentleman, leased the building and started a salmon cannery on the small island in the Owenmore River. It was rebuilt as a hotel in 1839, and has been run as a guesthouse by the same family since 1964. It stands in five hectares, with woodlands and colourful gardens.

The lounge, with terracotta tiles, has a log fireplace, and is a good spot in which to relax, a TV-free zone with plenty of books to read. The ambience is free and easy, there are no petty rules, and guests are well taken care of. The spacious bedrooms have lake and garden views: they are not en suite, but do have wash basins, and there are two bathrooms exclusively for guests. One new bedroom has its own shower and toilet. Breakfasts feature mostly organic produce: home-made yoghurt, honey, home-baked bread, home-made marmalade and apple jelly and free-range eggs. Smoking is permitted in the lounge.

Lynn is happy to describe places of local interest. It is an artist's and hill walker's paradise. Sea fishing can be arranged locally and brown trout lakes can be fished at no charge to guests.

Connemara is one of the most unspoilt and beautiful landscapes in Europe. Golfing, beaches, restaurants and pubs are a short drive away. From Galway take N59 Galway/Clifden Road, turn left on R341 at Roundstone/Ballynahinch Road Castle sign, 4 miles from there.

OWNER Lynn Hill OPEN March 1–November 30
ROOMS 2 double, 2 twin; 1 en suite with own bathroom
TERMS €45 pps; single supplement
MEALS dinner, snacks

## SALTHILL

### Atlantic View
4 Ocean Wave, Salthill, Co. Galway
Tel: 091 582109 Fax: 091 528566 Mobile: 086 8524579

This detached, attractive white house faces the seafront. The front bedrooms overlook the sea; all are colour-coordinated and spotlessly clean, and two have orthopaedic beds. There is a balcony for guests' use and a small TV lounge.

The house is a five-minute walk from the town centre and directly across from the beach. Mrs Breda Treacy is an accommodating host and there is plenty of information provided on what there is to do and see in the area. This is good value accommodation in a central position. All major credit cards accepted.

OWNER Breda & Jennifer Treacy
OPEN All year except December 23–27
ROOMS 5 twin/double/family; all en suite
TERMS from €30–99 pps; 50% child reduction; single supplement

### Carraig Beag
1 Burren View Heights, Knocknacarra Road, Salthill, Co. Galway
Tel: 091 521696
Email: thelydons@eircom.net
Website: www.dirl.com/galway/salthill/carraigb-beag.htm

This luxurious, red brick house is just off the promenade and has peek views of the bay. The bedrooms are a good size and are furnished with every comfort in mind. The house is under constant upgrade, is well furnished, with a beautiful dining room where freshly-prepared breakfasts, may be enjoyed. There are attractive, rich wood doors and a handsome staircase.

Breakfasts are served at separate tables in the elegant dining room, which has a beautiful crystal chandelier and marble fireplace. The owners, Paddy and Catherine Lydon, are an added bonus. They are a very helpful and accommodating couple, and superb hosts: they often take walks along the promenade in the evening; guests may join them, but beware, you might find it hard to keep up!

This good value bed & breakfast offers a high standard of accommodation at modest prices, and it is well situated for all of the local amenities. Mastercard accepted.

Follow the promenade from Galway to Salthill. First building after the seafront is the Spinnaker House Hotel, on your left. Turn right after the Spinnaker into Knocknacarra Road; Carraig Beag is the second house on the right, and is signposted.

OWNER Catherine & Paddy Lydon OPEN March 1—October 1
ROOMS 2 double, 2 twin, 1 family; all en suite
TERMS €32–40pps; child reduction; single supplement

## Mandalay by the Sea

10 Gentian/ Blake's Hill, Upper Salthill, Co. Galway
Tel: 091 524177 Fax: 091 529952
Email: mandalay@esatclear.ie

This beautiful, new Georgian-style house is in a superb location overlooking the bay and the Aran Islands. Mandalay is furnished and decorated to extremely high standards; there are rich wood furnishings and antiques. The rooms are spacious, two have balconies and all have views. The entry hall and the kitchen have Liscannor stone floors from the Burren. There are two lounges, one with a piano and TV. There are lots of plants and dried flower arrangements throughout the house. Excellent breakfasts are served in the bright dining room.

For nature lovers there are some very pleasant walks close by, and a bird sanctuary can be seen in front of the house. Visa and Mastercard accepted. Mandalay by the Sea can be found off 336 Coast Road, 2 miles from Galway city.

OWNER Sean Darby OPEN All year
ROOMS 2 double, 2 twin, 2 double/single; all en suite
TERMS €34 pps; child reduction; single supplement

## Rose Villa

10 Cashelmara, Knocknacarra Cross, Salthill, Co. Galway
Tel: 091 584200 Fax: 091 584200
Email: kevin.ohare@ireland.com
Website: www.rosevilla.utvinternet.ie

This handsome large, bright and airy house, stands in a peaceful spot on the road to Connemara, with views of the Bay and Bird Sanctuary. The bedrooms are individually decorated, well furnished, have comfortable beds, and Dormer duvets. All have en suite bathrooms, tea makers, and TV. Hairdryers are available on request.

Kevin and Maire work as a team, to maintain their high standards. Excellent breakfasts include fresh fruit, yoghurt, and a freshly-cooked version, served at separate tables in the bright, sunny dining room.

Of interest is a selection of prints of the Custom House Trinity College which are on display. There is a comfortable lounge, where a gas fire is lit at the first sign of a chill in the air, and a balcony for guests' use. Kevin usually greets guests, and provides lots of local information available, and is also happy to share his knowledge of the area.

OWNER Kevin and Maire O'Hare OPEN All year ROOMS 4 double/twin en suite
TERMS €30 pps; single supplement; child reduction

## The Connaught
Barna Road, Salthill, Galway, Co. Galway
Tel: 091 525865 Fax: 091 525865
Email: tcconnaught@eircom.net

This pleasant, friendly residence is set back off the road in a quiet position. Galway town is within walking distance, or you can take a city bus, which runs at 30 minute intervals. It is a well-maintained house, redecorated throughout to a high standard. The well-appointed bedrooms are nicely furnished, and all have new comfortable orthopaedic beds with electric blankets, TV and hospitality trays. The lounge has rich red carpeting and there is a bright dining room where an extensive menu of substantial, freshly-prepared breakfasts can be enjoyed. The sitting room is a TV-free zone, and a pleasant place in which to relax.

An extremely cordial and helpful couple, the Keaveneys do everything to ensure their guests are comfortable and well taken care of. There is a warm and friendly atmosphere and guests feel relaxed and very much at home here. There are lots of interesting family photographs on display, as well as other items of interest.

The Connaught offers visitors good value bed & breakfast, and this would be an ideal place from which to explore this diversified and beautiful area. Drive along the promenade in Salthill, with Galway Bay on the left. Continue on until you reach the T-junction, and turn left at Barna Road. House is approximately 500 yards on the right-hand side.

OWNER Colette & Tom Keaveney OPEN March 15–November 15 ROOMS 3 double, 1 twin, 2 family; all en suite TERMS from €30-32.50 pps; child reduction; single supplement

## Ard Mhuirbhi

Aille, Inverin, Spiddal, Co. Galway
Tel: 091 593215 Fax: 091 593326
Email: ardmhuirbhi@eircom.net

Ard Mhuirbhi, which means 'seashore height', offers quality accommodation. The house is located on the sea side of the coast road on a small, peaceful road, and stands in extensive landscaped gardens. The entrance to the house is through a small porch full of colourful potted plants and flowers. The bedrooms, all on the ground floor, are large and well furnished. They have large wardrobes, soft pastel colours and coordinated fabrics, and two have excellent views of the Burren and the bay. All bedrooms have TV and electric blankets.

The lounge is well furnished and breakfast is served on the patio on fine days. The house is immaculately maintained and is delightful in every way. Owner Rita Feeney has thought of just about everything for her guests' comfort and is an attentive, courteous host.

This is a tranquil place to return to after a busy day and guests can enjoy walks on the beach three minutes from the house, or the moors and bog, which are just a five-minute drive away. Convenient for touring Connemara and for trips to the Aran Islands. Credit cards accepted. Situated 5 km west of Spiddal village on the R336 coast road.

OWNER Rita Feeney OPEN March 1–October 31
ROOMS 2 double, 1 twin, 2 family; 4 en suite
TERMS €30 pps; child reduction; single supplement

## Cala 'n Uisce

Greenhill, Spiddal, Co. Galway
Tel: 091 553324 Fax: 091 553324
Email: moyafeeney@iolfree.ie
Website: geocities.com/spiddalgalway

Cala 'n Uisce means 'little harbour', which is apt, as the house is in a picturesque setting facing the bay. The house was designed by owner Pádraig Feeney and has leaded windows and a red brick exterior. High standards are found here, and the house continues to be exceptionally well maintained. This is a non-smoking establishment. There are three ground floor bedrooms, attractively decorated with coordinated fabrics; all bedrooms have tea-making facilities and TV. Many interesting paintings of local scenes, by Mrs Feeney and other family members, are on display throughout the house. The lounge, which has a turf fire, leads out onto a patio. The dining room, where tasty breakfast is served on linen table-cloths and pretty china, overlooks the bay.

Pádraig Feeney's father was a cousin of John Ford, who directed

*The Quiet Man.* This is an Irish-speaking area, and the Feeney family speaks Irish. Cala 'n Uisce is a most comfortable and peaceful place; it stands in half a hectare of landscaped gardens, and there are beautiful bog areas and sea walks close by. No smoking in the bedrooms. No pets. Credit cards accepted. Situated 2.5 km west of Spiddal village.

OWNER Moya Feeney OPEN April–October ROOMS 5 double/ twin; all en suite TERMS from €30 pps; child reduction; single supplement

### Cloch na Scith – Thatched Cottage
Kellough, Spiddal, Co. Galway
Tel: 091 553364 Fax: 091 553890
Email: thatchcottage@eircom.net
Website: www.thatchcottage.com

This cosy, 130-year-old, traditional thatched cottage, part of a working farm, has played host to actress Julie Christie and the Swedish ambassador. There are thick stone walls, uneven floors, plenty of history and an old-world charm. Owner Nancy Hopkins-Naughton offers one of the warmest welcomes in Ireland. She is a delightful, down-to-earth host and guests are greeted with a hot drink on arrival, often with home-made cake. The family are Irish speaking and into Irish music. The lounge/ dining room has turf fires, and a Galway wedding shawl which belonged to Nancy's grandmother hangs on the wall. Breakfast, and four-course home-cooked dinners if ordered in advance, are served on old pine tables and blue willow china. Guests may bring their own wine to dinner. Nancy is an absolutely delightful lady; there are no petty rules here and guests are treated as friends, so it is little wonder that many guests are repeat visitors. Smoking is not permitted. Bedrooms are comfortable with firm beds; two are on a lower floor and one room is quite large with its own bathroom. The beach is two minutes away and there are maps provided for folks interested in walking. Cloch na Scith has been featured on TV's *Holiday* programme. A one-bedroom, self-catering cottage is available.

OWNER Nancy Hopkins-Naughton OPEN All year except for Christmas ROOMS 1 double, 1 twin, 1 single; all en suite TERMS double €32 pp; child reduction; single supplement

### Col Mar House
Salahoona, Spiddal, Co. Galway
Tel: 091 553247 Fax: 091 553247

This comfortable secluded country home stands in mature gardens and private woods, 150 yards off the road. The rural and peaceful setting is close to the sea and the beach. Bog walks with lovely views can be taken. Col Mar House is well maintained, with new windows recently installed. Special diets can be catered for at breakfast. Dinners are not served, but there are plenty of venues for evening meals close by. Credit cards taken.

Irish is spoken in this non-smoking house. The bedrooms are of a good size, have comfortable beds, and are furnished in keeping with the house; tea-making facilities are provided in rooms. Children are welcome here: there is a playground, cot, and a highchair available. Guests are welcome to enjoy the garden.

There is a sandy beach, golf and fishing nearby, and this location is handy for touring Connemara. Maureen Keady is a warm and hospitable host, a hot drink is offered on arrival, and there is a good supply of information on what to see and do in the area. Situated 1.5km west of Spiddal.

OWNER Maureen Keady OPEN May–September
ROOMS 5 double/ twin/family; all en suite
TERMS €30 pps; child reduction; single supplement

## Suan Na Mara
Stripe, Furbo, Spiddal, Co. Galway
Tel: 091 591512 Fax: 091 591632
Email: brian@suannamara.com Website: www.suannamara.com

A most attractive custom-built dormer bungalow, designed to high standards, stands in grounds with a lawned garden, complete with fish pond, old water pump, and seating for guests. The house is luxuriously furnished, and there is a ground floor bedroom, which has a colourful patchwork quilt.

Home-made pies or scones are available on arrival. All rooms have extras, such as fruit bowls, bottled water, and a choice of drinks, along with TV, hair-dryer, tea- and coffee-making facilities, and power showers. High chair and baby cot can be provided. Irish films are shown in the evening, with a viewing system available in all bedrooms. There is a sitting room, with a fireplace, plenty of comfortable seating, and a bright dining room where imaginative breakfasts and dinners are served. Fresh flowers adorn the tables when possible, and meals are served on fine china on linen tablecloths. Just about everything has been thought of to provide the finest in accommodation. Laundry and ironing facilities are available.

Brian Clancy is a qualified chef, who has worked in many fine hotels; his superb meals can now be enjoyed at Suan na Mara. Dinners have to be booked in advance and any special dietary requirements made known. The menu is in five languages; Irish, English, German, French and Italian. This award winning property is situated 8 miles from Galway, and just a few minutes walk to the beach. This non-smoking house is an ideal base for touring the west of Ireland, and there is pony trekking, golf and fishing nearby. Trips to the Aran Islands can be arranged.

OWNER Brian and Carmel Clancy OPEN All year except January ROOMS 4 double/twin; 3 en suite TERMS from €39 pps; child reduction; single supplement MEALS dinner

## TUAM

**Gardenfield House**
Tuam, Co. Galway
Tel: 093 24865

This rambling, comfortable period house dates from 1860 and is part of a 26-hectare working farm of sheep and cattle. The atmosphere is casual, friendly and welcoming. The house is in a tranquil setting and is approached up a gravel drive through fields dotted with sheep. The rooms are all good-sized, and are individually decorated in burgundy and gold, and a mixture of soft pastel shades. There are tall ceilings, and the dining and sitting rooms have the original casement shutters. Free-range chickens provide the eggs for breakfast and Esther, who is a good cook, prepares excellent evening meals, with plenty of organic vegetables; lamb from the farm is often on the menu. Vegetarians can be catered for with advance notice. Both the small, snug sitting room and the lounge have coal fires. There are two self-catering units available.

OWNER Mrs Esther Mannion OPEN All year ROOMS 1 double, 1 twin, 1 family; 2 en suite TERMS €35 pps child reduction; single supplement €6.50 MEALS dinner

## COUNTY LIMERICK

Bordered on the north by the expanses of the Shannon, Limerick a peaceful farming county with its fair share of relics from the past. Limerick city's origins go back to the days of the Vikings. Always a principal fording point for the Shannon River, it has played an important part in Irish history, particularly during the 1690s. Old English Town and the old Irish area across the river are the most interesting parts of the city to explore, particularly the Georgian architecture around St John's Square. The most noteworthy sight to visit is the Granary, a restored eighteenth-century warehouse, which houses the tourist office as well as restaurants, shops and an exhibition gallery. King John's Castle with its massive rounded tower, St Mary's

Cathedral, dating from 1172, and the Hunt Collection at the National Institute for Higher Education can also be visited.

Adare has some splendid ruins to see, the finest one being the Franciscan Friary. Others include the Trinitarian Abbey, the Augustinian Abbey and St Nicholas Church. It is a most attractive town, with pretty thatched cottages and lovely views of Desmond Castle and Adare Manor on the river. It is thought the 'limerick' may well have come from Croom, which was the meeting place of eighteenth-century Gaelic poets, who wrote extremely witty verse.

## ADARE

### Adare Lodge
Kildimo Road, Adare, Co. Limerick
Tel: 061 396629 Fax: 061 395060
Email: info@adarelodge.com
website: adarelodge.com

New owners took over the Lodge in May 2004, a pleasant and hospitable couple, offering general all round quality and excellence. Totally refurbished, the house boasts new furnishing, linens, a subtle décor, and attractive drapes made by a family member.

Guests have free use of a gym and Jacuzzi. The lounge has a wide screen TV, and open peat fire. The owner has a nearby farm, and horseback riding can be arranged. Excellent breakfasts are served in the attractive dining room, and there is conservatory lounge. All the bedrooms are on the ground floor.

This mock Tudor house is on a quiet side street, surrounded by an award-winning garden. The picturesque centre of Adare village, with its thatched cottages, is just a two-minute walk away. Evening meals are not available, but there are plenty of venues for food in the village.

On pleasant days guests can enjoy a cup of tea on the patio. Adare Lodge is licensed. Credit cards taken.

OWNER Richard Carter and Ella Fitzpatrick
OPEN All year except for Christmas
ROOMS 13 double/twin/family; all en suite
TERMS €37.50-40 pps; single supplement

### Carrabawn House
Killarney Road, Adare, Co. Limerick
Tel: 061 396067  Fax: 061 396925
Email: carrabawn@indigo.ie
Website: www.carrabawnhouseadare.com

Carrabawn House, situated on the edge of Adare Golf Course, just a few minutes from the picturesque village of Adare, stands in beautiful gardens, and is delightful in every way. Bridget Lohan takes immense pride in her guesthouse, and is the proud recipient of several awards, including the prestigious "Environmental Award" for the Best Kept Business Premises. The bedrooms, some with garden views, have individual décor, and are named after local counties;Limerick, Donegal, Cork, Tipperary, Leitrim and Kerry etc. They are tastefully decorated with rich pastels, cream colours, have quality furnishings, and four-star amenities; satellite TV, direct dial telephone, and tea makers. The en suite bathrooms are fully tiled and have power showers. Freshly-prepared breakfasts are served in the conservatory dining room, overlooking the garden, and there is also a comfortable sitting room.

Bridget enjoys her guests, and is happy to sit and chat, and give advice on places of local interest. The hospitality here is of the highest standard, and this would be a great choice from which to explore this area. There are several venues for dinners in the village, and Bridget would be happy make recommendations and or reservations. Credit cards taken.

OWNER Bridget Lohan OPEN All year except for Christmas
ROOMS 8 double/twin/family; all en suite
TERMS €40–50 pps; single supplement;
child reduction (not suitable for young children)

### Clonunion House
Limerick Road, Adare, Co. Limerick
Tel: 061 396657  Fax: 061 396657
Email: clonunionhouse@eircom.net

This traditional eighteenth-century farmhouse is 100 m off the main road in tranquil surroundings, and is part of a working sheep, beef and tillage farm. At one time it was the stud farm belonging to Lord Dunraven, and interested guests can see the Horse Cemetery, with its horse-shoe- shaped headstones, where several famous stallions were buried.

The house is furnished in keeping with its character; three bedrooms have the original fireplaces, and one a high bed. They are clean and comfortable. Breakfast only is served, but there are plenty of venues for evening meals and Irish music in Adare, Ireland's prettiest village, which is just 2 km away. American Express, Visa and Access accepted.

Take right at the roundabout Croom Road for 200 metres, first entrance on left.

OWNER Mary & Michael Fitzgerald OPEN April 1–October 31
ROOMS 1 double, 1 twin, 1 family; all en suite
TERMS €32.50-35 pps; child reduction; single supplement

## Glin Castle
Glin, County Limerick
Tel: 068 34173  Fax: 068 34364
Email: knight@iol.ie
Website: www.glincastle.com

This magical property, although a castle, with all the delights of living in a bygone era, is first and foremost a home. People do live here, and the ambience is welcoming, and informal. From the moment of arrival, when a member of staff warmly greets you, you know they are happy to have you as their guest.

Glin Castle stands on the banks of the River Shannon, surrounded by 500 acres of woodland, gardens, and a dairy farm.

It has been in the FitzGerald family for over 700 years; originally built as a long thatched house, throughout the years it is transformed into an impressive castle. The interior has a large assortment of portraits, paintings, prints and many other works of art. Of special interest are a set of bayonet holders decorated with the FitzGerald arms, an embroidered settee, the work of Veronica FitzGerald, a mahogany games table dating from 1750, and a fine example of mid-eighteenth century Irish seat furniture, an upholstered armchair and chair with shepherd's crook arms. This is only the tip of the iceberg. When making a reservation, be sure to allow time to enjoy all the treasures to be found in the castle. The luxurious, beautifully furnished bedrooms range from standard to superior, but whichever your choice, you will not be disappointed. All rooms have all modern amenities, quality toiletries, large fluffy towels, and bathrobes. There is a library, a handsome drawing room and a charming dining room, where gourmet meals are served. All diets catered for, reservations are required. For the discerning visitor looking for that special place, Glin Castle has to be a first choice. Located half an hour from Shannon Airport, and Ballybunion Golf Course. No children under 10.

MANAGER Bob Duff OPEN March 1–October 31
ROOMS double/twin
TERMS from €280 per room; child reduction

## Clonmacken House
Off Ennis Road, Limerick, Co. Limerick
Tel: 061 372007  Fax: 061 327785
E-mail: clonmack@indigo.ie

A large, purpose-built, attractive yellow-and-green-trim guest house standing in its own grounds in a quiet setting, just a five-minute drive from Limerick City. Brid McDonald thoroughly enjoys her bed & breakfast business; guests receive a warm welcome in this friendly and hospitable house. Excellent standards of décor prevail and the house is comfortably furnished. The bedrooms are standardised and have attractive rose-patterned duvets, and multichannel TV. The comfortable lounge has soft furnishings and dainty wallpapers. Bunratty Castle is a 10-minute drive and Shannon Airport is a 15-minute drive. Breakfast only is served, but a pub serving evening meals is just 200 m away. Visa, Mastercard accepted.

OWNER Brid & Gerald McDonald OPEN All year
ROOMS 3 double, 3 twin, 2 family, 2 double/single; all en suite
TERMS €23–28.50; child reduction; single supplement from €7.50

### Trebor
Ennis Road, Limerick, Co. Limerick
Tel: 061 454632 Fax: 061 454632
Email: treborhouse@eircom.net
Website: homepage.eircom.net/~treborhouse/index.html

Trebor, which is the name of the owner's son spelt backwards, is a well maintained, comfortable turn-of-the-century townhouse. The bedrooms are spotless and tastefully decorated with colour coordinated wallpapers and fabrics. Breakfast includes freshly-squeezed orange juice, muesli or porridge and home-made breads, followed by a cooked breakfast. Mrs Joan McSweeney takes excellent care of her guests and is happy to give advice on what to see and do in the area. Trebor is popular with cyclists. Drying facilities are available. Evening meals are available (vegetarian and special diets catered for) if arranged in advance. Credit cards accepted.

OWNER Mrs Joan McSweeney OPEN April 1–November 1
ROOMS 2 double, 1 twin, 2 family; all en suite
TERMS €23 pps; child reduction; single supplement €11

## MUNGRET

### Shanville B&B
Loughanleach, Mungret, Co. Limerick
Tel: 061 353887
Website: www.shanville.ie

Shanville, a two-storey red brick house, with colonnades to the front, stands in its own grounds, with an attractive front and rear garden. Noreen Walshe takes care of the garden, which guests are welcome to enjoy on warm days. A friendly host, she takes excellent care of her guests, and is happy to help in every way.
The house is well maintained and offers good value accommodation.

The rooms are decorated in warm colours, terracotta etc., and the large family room has a double and two single beds. All bedrooms have en suite facilities, hair-dryers, and tea makers. The family room has a TV. Breakfasts consist of fruit, yoghurt, cheese, home-made brown bread, and traditional fare. The cosy dining room/sitting room has a real fire lit on chilly evenings. There are several venues for evening meals within a short drive.

OWNER Noreen Walshe OPEN All year except Christmas
ROOMS 3 double/twin/family; all en suite
TERMS €30pps, €40 single; child reduction

## NEWCASTLE WEST

### Ballingowan House
Newcastle West, Co. Limerick
Tel: 069 62341  Fax: 069 62457
Email: ballingowanhouse@tinet.ie

This light and airy Georgian house, known to locals as the "pink house", stands back a good distance from the road behind a well-landscaped front garden. The bedrooms are quite spacious, are colourfully coordinated, and have multichannel TV. Two have a bath and shower and the rear rooms overlook peaceful countryside. One bedroom is on the ground floor. The lounge is bright with a blue and terracotta décor, interesting coving, and a marble fireplace. The conservatory area, which is full of colourful potted plants in summer, is a good spot in which to relax with a book and a cup of tea. Breakfast only is served at a large table, and tea is offered upon arrival and by request at other times. The owners are most accommodating and guests receive lots of personal attention; there is plenty of information on what to see and do in the area. Self-catering units are also available.

OWNER Carmel O'Brien OPEN All year
ROOMS 2 double, 1 twin, 1 triple, 1 double/single; all en suite
TERMS €26.50-30 pps; child reduction; single €39-42.50

## TARBERT

### Knights Haven
Tarbert/Glin, County Limerick
Tel: 068 34541
Email knightshaven@eastclear.ie
Website: www.knightshaven.com

This large country house stands in a peaceful position overlooking the River Shannon, and rolling hills. It is part of a working dairy farm where children are welcome to explore.

This is a child friendly property: three delightful children, James, Hazel and Patrice live here, as does Tiny the dog, and swings and slides are available. The bright and clean bedrooms, have white furniture, patchwork or blue and white quilts, one has a king-size bed, and two have river views. Four of the rooms are en suite, one has a private bathroom; all have TV, radio and tea makers. There is also a guest lounge. Breakfasts feature fresh eggs from the farm's chickens. Tony Jacklin, the golfer, and family enjoyed the friendly ambience, and appreciated the use of the barbecue.

Glin Castle, and the Equestrian Centre, is adjacent to the farm and the Tarbert Ferry is 3 km away.

OWNER John and Josephine O'Donovan OPEN All year
ROOMS 5 family/twin/double; 4 en suite, 1 with own bathroom
TERMS €32 pps; single supplement; child reduction

## COUNTY MAYO

County Mayo is a maritime county, with the Atlantic Ocean making deep inroads into its coastline on the west and on the north. The sea influences the shape of its beauty, from the long, narrow fjord of Killary Harbour to the island-studded Clew Bay. Castlebar is the country town of Mayo and a good centre for touring. The most interesting building in the town is now the art centre and the education centre—it was formerly a chapel, the cornerstone of which was laid by John Wesley in 1785.

Westport is a gem of a town. The architect is unknown—some locals believe him to be a French architect left behind from Humbert's expedition in 1798. The main feature is the Octagon, a fine piece of planning. In the centre stands a Doric pillar, mounted on an octagonal granite base, on which the statue of George Glendenning once stood. Innisturk Island can be visited from Roonah Point. It is an exceptionally attractive island with a lovely harbour; there is a glorious beach on the south side. Killary Harbour is a striking example of a fjord. Its 8 km sweep cuts deep into the surrounding mountains.

Knock Fold Museum pays tribute to the area's forefathers. The collections and exhibitions on show help us to understand what life was like for our ancestors.

An area and attraction well-worth visiting is The Céide Fields Centre, which recreates the life of a Stone Age farming community, overlooks spectacular cliffs on the north Mayo coast. At over five thousand years old, this one of the world's most ancient field systems. Mayo's blanket bogs have preserved many elements of life in that far-off era.

**Aquila**
Sraheens, Achill Island, Co. Mayo
Tel: 098 45163
Email: kay.sweeney@aquila-house.com

This cosy, clean, modern bungalow is situated in an elevated position, with magnificent views of Achill Sound and the Corraun Mountains. The bedrooms are well-appointed, prettily decorated and have comfortable beds. One very popular room is the converted attic room, but it is not for everyone, as the approach is via a very narrow staircase. There are four rooms on the ground floor. Cots are available. Smoking is permitted in the bedrooms.

There is a comfortable sitting room and lounge with TV/VCR and an open turf fire. The house is located near five 'Blue Flag' beaches, and two Outdoor Pursuit Centres. Self-catering is available. Drive onto Achill Island, take the second left turn; house is signposted.
OWNER Mrs Kay Sweeney OPEN March 1–September 30
ROOMS 2 double, 1 twin, 1 family, 1 single; 4 en suite
TERMS €32 pps; single supplement €6.50 MEALS tea and scones

**Belvedere House**
Foxford Road, Ballina, Co. Mayo
Tel: 096 22004

This spacious, modern two-storey house stands in its own grounds, a 10-minute walk from the town centre. Bedrooms are of a good size, attractively decorated and clean, with orthopaedic beds. There is a very large dining room and lounge with TV and fireplaces. The owners are attentive and work hard to maintain the high standards. Breakfast only is served, but there are many fine eating places in the area.

Ballina is situated on the lower reaches of the River Moy, directly between Lough Conn/Cullen and Killala Bay. Bicycles are available for hire locally. For guests who would like a day trip to Dublin, there is a good local bus service. Ballina is a bustling town and there are several venues where traditional Irish music can be heard. On main Dublin Road–N6 heading to Ballina.

OWNER Mary Reilly OPEN January 3–December 15
ROOMS 2 double, 2 twin, 2 family; 5 en suite
TERMS from €26.50; child reduction; single supplement €7.50

**Kingfisher Lodge**
Mount Falcon, Foxford Road, Ballina, Co. Mayo
Tel: 096 22718
Email: kingfisherlodge@eircom.net

This family-owned charming country house stands in extensive grounds 6.5 km from Ballina. It is nestled between two mountain ranges and surrounded by unspoiled beaches. It opened in 1990 and has been successful since the beginning; many guests are repeat visitors. Kingfisher Lodge has fast become known as one of the premier guest houses in the area. An extension, combining 2 family rooms, has been added. There is a sitting room and reading room with a real fire. The bedrooms are beautifully decorated; one has a four-poster bed with a floral and lace canopy. This is exceptionally good value, the perfect combination of superb hosts, pleasant surroundings and comfortable accommodation.

Kingfisher Lodge is an ideal base for anglers; Kevin Gallagher, a full-time fishing guide with 25 years experience fishing the River Moy, will assist with all the arrangements for a fishing holiday and secure the correct permits. Ghillie service is available upon request. There are five golf courses in the area and Ballina is a lively town where traditional Irish music can be found most nights. Early reservations are recommended at this popular establishment.

Take the Foxford to Ballina Road, turn left after Mountfalcon Castle. Kingfisher Lodge is signposted at the end of the road.

OWNER Kevin & Bernadette Gallagher
OPEN March 1–September 30 ROOMS 2 double, 2 twin, 4 family; all en suite TERMS €30.50; child reduction; single supplement €9

## BALLYCASTLE

**Ballyglass B&B**
Ballycastle, Co. Mayo
Tel: 096 43343

This old stone house was totally gutted for the purpose of building a holiday home for the down-to-earth owners, Jim Hennelly and Carmel Kelleher, but with more tourists visiting this beautiful and interesting region, they opened the house as a bed & breakfast instead.

This is good-value, clean, no fancy frills accommodation; the bedrooms are simply furnished. Jim cooks breakfast and takes care of guests, Carmel works outside the home, but helps out when she can. The dining room is adjacent to the cosy lounge with its turf fires. Jim also makes clocks from pine, yew and oak, which are on display, and are available for purchase. There are archaeological digs going on and Jim will take interested people along to see them, and to the second tallest stone in Ireland, which is close by. An ideal spot from which to visit the unique Ceide Fields, fifteenth-century Moyne abbey or Belderrig prehistoric farm, or take a walk on the Western Way.

OWNER Jim Hennelly & Carmel Kelleher OPEN May 4–October 1
ROOMS 2 double, 1 twin, 1 family; 2 en suite
TERMS €19; child reduction; single supplement €12.50

## Keadyville
Carrowcubbic, Ballycastle, Co. Mayo
Tel: 096 43288

Keadyville is in a beautiful location overlooking Downpatrick Head and the sea. Mrs Kelly went into business as more tourists came to the area to visit the interpretative centre of the fascinating Ceide Fields, which are older than the pyramids. The top floor, all in pine, was added to the property in 1992 and a conservatory was added in 1997. The rooms are average in size and are clean and comfortable, and all offer scenic views. One bedroom is on the ground floor. The friendly owners are local people and greet guests with a cup of tea, and are happy to provide information on the area. There is a cosy lounge/dining room where a fire is lit on chilly days; smoking is only allowed in the lounge. There are self-catering units available. Take the Ballycastle/Belderrig Road; house is signposted.

OWNER Michael & Barbara Kelly OPEN All year except Christmas
ROOMS 2 double, 2 twin; all en suite TERMS €25 pps;
child reduction; single supplement €5

## BELDERRIG

## The Hawthorns
Belderrig, Co. Mayo
Tel: 096 43148 Fax: 096 43148
Email: camurphy@indigo.ie

Located in the picturesque village of Belderrig (between Ballina and Belmullet), beside the sea and small fishing port, this clean and cosy bungalow stands in an open area with wonderful views of Ben Head and the Twang Mountains. There are cliff walks close by and the sea is a five-minute walk. Owner Carmel Murphy is a local lady who enjoys sharing her knowledge of the area with interested guests. The house is within driving distance of the Ceide Fields. The bedrooms, all on the ground floor, are spotlessly clean. Smoking is permitted in the bedrooms. The lounge has a turf fire, which is lit on cool days, and breakfasts, dinners and light meals are served in the bright dining room. Vegetarians can be catered for; all meals must be ordered in advance. This is a pleasant family home–the Murphys have three children. Self-catering is available. Baby-sitting can be arranged.

OWNER Carmel Murphy OPEN All year ROOMS 2 double, 1 twin; 2 en suite TERMS €25 pps; child reduction; single supplement €9 MEALS dinner, light meals

### Primrose Cottage
Pontoon Road, Castlebar, Co. Mayo
Tel: 094 9021247

If you are looking for that 'special place' to stay, Primrose Cottage, standing behind a very pretty garden, would be a good choice. Sisters Monica and Teresa Nealon are a delightful team, taking excellent care of guests in a home-from-home ambience. They are both retired, and having travelled extensively, wanted to ensure that all the comforts they found lacking, during their travels, were provided. There are lots of items of interest throughout the house, including paintings of local scenes, candles, dolls and books. Although the house is non-smoking, it is not suitable for children. The bedrooms are of a good size, with pine furnishings, electric blankets and comfortable beds. Tea makers, hair-dryers and a portfolio on what to see and do in the area complete the facilities. The ground floor room has a king-size bed. Two rooms have en suite, one its own adjacent luxury bathroom. Warm terry-towelling bathrobes are provided in all rooms.

There is an imaginative breakfast menu, prepared to order, and home-made scones and preserves are offered on arrival. The guest lounge has a real fire, and there is lots of Irish literature to read. Monica and Teresa are knowledgeable about the area, and are happy to assist guests with itinerary planning. Evening meals are not served, but there several venues for evening meals in Castlebar. Situated on the edge of town off R310.

OWNER Monica & Teresa Nealon OPEN January 1–December 18 ROOMS 2 twin, 1 double; 2 en suite, 1 own bathroom TERMS €32-33 pps; single supplement €8

### Windermere House
Westport Road, Islandeady, Castlebar, County Mayo.
Tel: 094 9023329
Email windermerehse@eircom.net

Although situated on the main N5 Westport Road, this country house stands well back off the road, in a large well-tended garden. The entry porch has a splendid array of colourful flowers in spring and summer. The bright and cheerful bedrooms have pretty pastel shades, and pine furniture. All have en suite facilities, TV, clock radios, and tea makers. A sitting room, with rich Victorian colours, and a coal fire, provides a cosy spot in which to relax after a busy day. Kay, is a pleasant host, and is happy to help in every way. Windermere House is well maintained, and provides good value accommodation. Guests are welcome to enjoy the garden on fine days, and there is secure parking. Located four miles from Castlebar, and just over five miles from Westport. Plenty of venues close by for evening meals. Dixie, the dog is friendly. Angling and boat hire are available.

OWNER Kay and Peter McGrath OPEN All year ROOMS 5 twin/double/ family/single; all en suite TERMS €30 pps; single supplement; child reduction

## CHARLESTOWN

**Ashfort**
Galway/Knock Road, Charlestown, Co. Mayo
Tel: 094 9254706
Email: ashfort@esatclear.ie

Ashfort is an impressive two-storey Tudor-style house set off the road in spacious grounds. The bedrooms are well-appointed, and have rich wood furnishings. The house is decorated to a high standard throughout; there are plush carpets and a luxurious lounge for guests to relax in.

This is an ideal base from which to explore the unspoiled area of the west of Ireland, and there are lots of things to see and do in the area. Owners Carol and Philip O'Gorman are a delightful couple who are always happy to assist guests with itinerary planning, and to make recommendations for evening meals. Guests are greeted with a hot drink upon arrival. The bedrooms are roomy and comfortable.

Ashfort is modestly priced for the comfort and high standards found here; guests would be well advised to book in for several nights and use this as a base. Knock Shrine is a 20-minute drive.

Situated on the N17/N5, 5 miles from Knock Airport.

OWNER Carol & Philip O'Gorman OPEN March 1–December 31
ROOMS 2 family, 3 double/single; all en suite
TERMS €25.50; child reduction; single supplement €6.50

## CROSSMOLINA

**Kilmurray House**
Castlehill, Crossmolina, Co. Mayo
Tel: 096 31227

Kilmurray House is a large, attractive, welcoming farmhouse on 22 hectares of dry stock farm-land, beautifully situated under Nephin

Mountain. It is hard to believe that the house was a ruin before Joe and Madge lovingly restored the interior, cleverly combining modern conveniences and a traditional setting.

The original oak staircase and wooden doors have been retained, as has the fireplace in the lounge, made by a local craftsman. The house is the recipient of two awards: the "Farmhouse of the Year" and the "BHS and Bord Fáilte Award." Smoking is permitted in bedrooms only. The bedrooms are large, tastefully decorated with matching fabrics and comfortably furnished. All rooms have a double and single bed; the two single rooms share a close-by bathroom.

A turf fire burns brightly in the lounge on chilly days. It's an ideal base from which to explore this scenic area, and a fisherman's delight—the farm has its own boats for guests' use on Lough Conn.

Breakfast only is served, but there are several restaurants and pubs in the area for evening meals. Very enjoyable Irish musical evenings are less than 0.5 km away. The Heritage Museum for tracing ancestry is 2.5 km away. Baby-sitting is available. Sign-posted from Crossmolina town.

OWNER Madge & Joe Moffat OPEN April 1–October 1
ROOMS 2 double, 2 twin, 2 family, 2 single; 4 en suite
TERMS €30 pps; child reduction; single supplement €8.50

## ERRIS

### Hillcrest House
Main Street, Bangor, Erris, Co. Mayo
Tel: 097 83494

This is a modern, cosy bungalow, located in the centre of the village, very close to the Owenmore River. Mr and Mrs Cosgrove are a very congenial couple, and Mr Cosgrove was born in the village. The restaurant, which is part of the house, is very popular with the locals. Special diets are catered for if pre-booked. Mrs Cosgrove, who does all the cooking, has built up an excellent reputation for providing good food.

The bedrooms are comfortable and hot water bottles are provided. The property is non-smoking. This is a popular spot with fishermen, with river and lake fishing close by. Credit cards accepted. On the N59 from Mulrany to Belmullet.

OWNER Evelyn Cosgrove OPEN All year ROOMS 2 double, 2 twin
TERMS €28–30 pps; child reduction; single supplement €6.50
MEALS dinner, high tea

## Beach View House
Ross, Killala, Co. Mayo
Tel: 096 32023

Beach View House as the name indicates has views of the bay, and is within a two-minute walk of Blue Flag beaches. This quiet, peaceful spot is ideal for bird-watching and outdoor activities. Mary is a congenial host; her guests are well taken care of, and made very much at home in the cosy ambience. The bedrooms, all on the ground floor, have soft pastel colours of green, blue and pink, with coordinated duvets and curtains all made by Mary. Hairdryers are available. All the rooms have garden views.

There is a turf fire in the cosy lounge, which has a TV and VCR, and tea is available on request. Smoking is only allowed in the lounge. Dinners have to be pre-booked, with special diets catered for, and there are plenty of choices for food within a very close drive. Mary has been offering her special brand of hospitality since 1981, with many visitors returning for yet another peaceful break. A garage is available for pets.

Northbound from Killala, take the first right off R341.

OWNER Mary O'Hara OPEN All year
ROOMS 4 double/twin/family; all en suite
TERMS from €26.50 pps; child reduction; single supplement
MEALS dinner (if booked)

## Ashford Manor B & B
Claremorris Road, Knock, Co. Mayo
Tel: 094 9388514
Email: omgreal@oceanfree.net

Ashford Manor is a large, attractive house with hanging baskets, potted plants, and leaded windows. The house is beautifully maintained and immaculately kept. The entryway has rich carpets, and the relaxing sitting room has tasteful furniture and rich red carpet. The bedrooms are of a good size and are well furnished.

Breakfasts are excellent and are cooked on the Aga. On fine days guests can enjoy a cup of tea outside where seating is provided.

OWNER Olivia McGreal OPEN February–November
ROOMS 2 double, 2 twin, 2 family; all en suite
TERMS €30 pps; child reduction; single supplement

**Rivervilla**
Shraugh, Louisburgh, Co. Mayo
Tel: 098 66246 Fax: 098 66246
Website: www.rivervilla.com   Email: rivervilla@eircom.net

Rivervilla is a bungalow situated in a peaceful and secluded spot along the banks of the Runrowen River, on a 10-hectare sheep farm. The house is non-smoking. Salmon and trout fishing are available as well as lovely river-side walks. A real home-away-from-home atmosphere pervades here, and home-baked breads are a feature. Evening meals are no longer served, but there are several excellent restaurants nearby.

The bedrooms are tastefully decorated; some have glorious views of Shreffy Mountain and Croagh Patrick. Of special interest is the Great Famine and Granville Interpretive Centre. There are some excellent places for evening meals in Louisburgh. Visa, Eurocard accepted. Sign-posted on Louisburgh/Westport Road R335 or via Chapel Street, Louisburgh, pass Spar shop: continue past O'Malleys Builders, the house is signposted from there.

OWNER Mary O'Malley OPEN May 1–September 30
ROOMS 1 double, twin, 1 family, 1 single; 2 en suite
TERMS €28-31 pps; child reduction; single supplement

**Altamont House**
Altamont Street, Ballinrobe Road, Westport, Co. Mayo
Tel: 098 25226

Altamont House is a pre-Famine wisteria-covered farmhouse situated within a five-minute walk of the town centre. The standards continue to improve at this pleasant, welcoming house; established as the first guest house in the area, it has an excellent reputation for offering good service at reasonable prices.

The spotless bedrooms are prettily decorated, and the rooms to the rear of the house overlook the lovely garden, as does the lounge, which has an open fire. A sun-lounge and patio has been added. The prize-winning gardens are a popular spot with guests.

Breakfasts are served in the attractive dining room, where a silver service is employed, and when possible there are fresh flowers on the table. Evening meals can be had at several good pubs and restaurants close by.

Sadly, Rita Sheridan who had been in the B&B business for over 40 years, has passed away. She will be missed by all the folks who had stayed at Altamont House. Mary, who had assisted with the business for 20 years will run the establishment. The same high standards will continue, and the welcome will continue to be warm and inviting.

OWNER The Sheridan family OPEN March–November
ROOMS 2 double, 3 twin, 1 family, 2 double/single; 5 en suite
TERMS €29-31 pps; child reduction; single supplement

## Ben Gorm Lodge
Murrisk na Bol, Westport, County Mayo
Tel: 098 64791
Email gormlodge@eircom.net
Website: bengormlodge.com

Situated ten minutes east of Westport, this country house, with a
green and white exterior, stands in an elevated position, and has sea
and mountain views. It is close to Croach Patrick and Clew Bay.
Outside seating is provided for picnics, or just to unwind, and enjoy
the scenery. The house has lots of pine, light neutral colours, and all
rooms have sea views. The well-maintained bedrooms are en suite,
and there is sitting room on the first floor which has TV, and a fireplace.
   Mary was formerly in the catering trade, and prepares an excellent
breakfast, including fresh home-baked scones. A short walk takes you
to the beach, and for the hardy, there are mountains to climb. Pubs
and restaurants for evening meals can be found close by. Discounts
available for long stays. Secure parking available.

OWNER John and Mary Gavin OPEN Easter–October
ROOMS 1 double, 1 twin, 1 family; all en suite
TERMS from €30 pps; single supplement; child reduction

## Bertra House
Thornhill, Murisk, Westport, Co. Mayo
Tel: 098 64833 Fax 098 64968
Email bertrahse@anu.ie
Website www.bertrahse.com

This modern bungalow, set at the foot of Croach Patrick, known as
Ireland's Holy Mountain, has fine views overlooking Clew Bay. Five
minutes brings you to a Blue Flag sandy beach, with hill walking, golf
and fishing close by. This is a very peaceful location, there are cattle
in the fields, and the ambience is friendly. The inviting bedrooms, are
tastefully decorated with pretty wallpapers, and have firm beds.
Margaret makes all the curtains and bed covers. The Sunshine Room,
is yellow and gold; all have en suite facilities, TV, hair-dryer and tea
makers. Two rooms have sea views as does the dining room and sitting room. Breakfasts include home-baked soda bread, yogurt, cereals
and fruit, followed by a cooked variety, and served family style.

Margaret is an attentive host, who has been in business for over 21 years. Guests enjoy the beautiful surroundings and the informal atmosphere. Visitors are welcomed with a hot drink on arrival. Credit cards taken.

OWNER Margaret Gill OPEN March 1 to October
ROOMS 4 double/twin/family; all en-suite
TERMS from €30 pps; single supplement; child reduction

## Brook Lodge
Deerpark East, Newport Road, Westport, Co. Mayo
Tel: 098 26654
Email: brooklodgeb&b@eircom.net

This spacious house is situated in a quiet residential area 2.5 km from the town centre. This is a relaxed and friendly house, and guests are encouraged to make themselves at home. Owners Michael and Noreen Reddington are extremely pleasant, and early breakfast can be provided if required, or if you prefer, a cooked breakfast is available until 10 a.m.

The lounge has a turf and coal fire in the restored Victorian fireplace, a pleasant spot in which to unwind after a busy day. Smoking is only allowed in the lounge. The bedrooms are good-sized, have a soft pastel décor and are tastefully furnished. There is a good choice of pubs and restaurants in town, a five-minute walk away. Visa and Mastercard accepted. Third turn to right after petrol station on N59 to Newport.

OWNER Michael & Noreen Reddington
OPEN March 1– November 30 ROOMS 4 twin; all en suite
TERMS €30 pps; child reduction; single supplement

## Cloneen House
Castlebar Street, Westport, Co. Mayo
Tel: 098 25361

Easily located in the heart of Westport, Cloneen House has a terracotta, deep south exterior and large colourful display of flowers on the balcony and at the front of the house.

The bedrooms are decorated with warm autumn colours, coordinated fabrics and bedspreads, made by Mrs Reidy. All have TV, telephone, hair-dryer, and ironing facilities. Well-presented breakfasts are served at separate tables in the bright dining room: there is also a very large lounge with comfortable furnishings. Smoking is allowed only in the lounge. The Irish Museum close by should be on your list of things to see.

OWNER Mrs C. Reidy OPEN All year
ROOMS 16 double/twin/ family; all en suite
TERMS €35–42.50 pps; child reduction; single supplement

## Moher House

Liscarney, Westport, Co. Mayo
Tel: 098 21360
Email: moherbandb@eircom.net
www.westportireland.ws/moherhouse/

Marian O'Malley is a delightful lady who knows just how to make
her guests feel at home, offering a cup of tea and some of her delicious home-baked scones upon arrival. Marian is the recipient of the
'Irish of the Welcomes Award'. The house stands in an award-winning
garden. All en suite bedrooms are well maintained, with duvets, electric blankets and hot water bottles. Excellent breakfasts and dinners
are served, using the best cuts of meat provided by a local butcher.
The cosy sitting room has a real fire burning in the marble fireplace.
   There are four designated walks for dedicated walkers–Moher
House is located off the Western Way Walking Trail, and a pickup and
drop service is available to the trail. The more adventurous can climb
Croagh Patrick Mountain, with its magnificent view of 365 islands.
   Fishing is available in Moher Lake across the road from the house.
Transport to the pub in the evening is also offered. Visa accepted.
Take N59 heading south out of Westport on Westport/ Clifden
Road.

OWNER Marian O'Malley  OPEN March 17–October 31
ROOMS 1 double, 2 twin, 1 family; all en suite
TERMS €30 pps; child reduction; single supplement

## Riverbank House

Rosbeg, Westport Harbour, Co. Mayo
Tel: 098 25719

An inviting, spacious house with attractive black shutters, flower baskets and window boxes, situated in a peaceful spot adjacent to a
river. The rooms are a good size and are clean and comfortable with
modern furnishings. New windows and wooden floors have been
installed since the last edition. There is a relaxing guest lounge with
an open fire. Kay O'Malley is pleased to help guests plan activities or
day trips. Freshly-prepared tasty breakfasts with home-baked bread
are served in the sunny dining room; evening meals are not available,
but there are several choices for evening meals close by. Local
amenities include shooting at the Tirawley Game Reserve, bathing,
boating, trout and salmon fishing and golf. Visa and Mastercard
accepted. On T39/ R335, turn left at the harbour.

OWNER Kay O'Malley OPEN April 1–October 30
ROOMS 4 double, 2 twin, 2 family; 6 en suite
TERMS €30 pps; child reduction; single supplement

**Seapoint House**
Kilmeena, Westport, Co. Mayo
Tel: 098 41254 Fax: 098 41903
Email: info@seapointhouse.com
Website: www.seapointhouse.com

Seapoint House is situated in a beautiful, unspoiled setting overlooking an inlet of Clew Bay. The new owner has taken over from her mother-in-law, and has refurbished the house to provide quality, comfortable accommodation. Two deluxe bedrooms, are now available, one has a Jacuzzi bath, and a third room has been renovated to provide disabled access. Most of the rooms have views of the sea and mountains. There is a very large lounge and a fireplace, a reading room, and a tastefully-decorated dining room, which leads out onto a sun porch. The upgraded bedrooms are functional and spotlessly clean and self-catering is available. This is a non-smoking house.

Fishing, sailing, walking and an 18-hole golf course are available nearby and there is a pony for children to ride. Baby-sitting can usually be arranged. Visa and Mastercard accepted.

OWNER Carol O'Malley OPEN April 1–October 31 ROOMS 2 double, 2 twin, family; all en suite TERMS €32 pps; child reduction; single supplement

## COUNTY SLIGO

County Sligo is located in one of the most beautiful and least explored regions of Ireland, surrounded by rugged mountains and rolling hills. The landscape is a patchwork of picturesque lakes, lush forests and sparkling rivers, its coastline dotted with peaceful coves. Sligo's seaside resorts stretch along the coast from Innishcrone to Mullaghmore, with sandy beaches, fishing, golfing, beautiful walks and horseback riding–there is so much to do in this uncrowded corner of Ireland.

Explore the Glenriff Horseshoe, the Ladies Brae, visit Lissadell House, and for the more adventurous, climb to the summit of Queen Maeve's Cairn. Tour the loughs–Arrow, Gill, Easky, Gara, Glencar, Templehouse and Talt–and feast your eyes on Sligo's beauty. W. B. Yeats, the poet, is buried at Drumcliffe. He called Sligo "The Land of Heart's Desire," and after you have visited, you will too.

## Temple House

Ballymote, Co. Sligo
Tel: 071 9183329 Fax: 071 9183808
Email: guest@templehouse.ie
Website: www.templehouse.ie

Temple House is approached through an impressive gateway bordered by white iron railings. The drive meanders through parkland to this large Georgian mansion. It is set in 400 hectares of farmland and woodland, and there is a large garden where organic vegetables are grown for the evening meal. The estate has been in the Perceval family since 1665, the present house having been redesigned and refurbished in 1864. The entrance through a portico leads to a large entry hall with tiled floor and shooting gear. This in turn leads to a second, larger hall, off which is an enormous dining room and three sitting rooms, all with open fires. The larger room has lovely views over the garden to the lake and ruins of a castle built by the Knights Templar in 1200. The enormous bedrooms are furnished with antiques and family portraits. Some have original bathroom fittings, curtains and carpets, which are faded and worn, but this all lends charm and atmosphere to the house. The Percevals are very friendly people. Mrs Perceval does all the cooking and Mr Perceval runs the farm, which is stocked with sheep, Kerry cattle and poultry, providing the kitchen with fresh meat, bacon, eggs, vegetables and fruit. Almost everything is home-grown and home-made, including yoghurt, jams and cream cheese. Evening meals, if pre-arranged, are served at 7:30 p.m. Please note Mr Perceval is chemically sensitive, so guests are asked to avoid all perfumed products. Mastercard and Visa cards accepted.

OWNER Roderick & Helena Perceval OPEN April 1–November 30 ROOMS 3 double, 1 twin, 1 single; 4 en suite TERMS €65–85 pps; child reduction; single supplement MEALS dinner €35

## Villa Rosa

Bunduff, Cliffoney, Co. Sligo
Tel: 071 9166173 Fax: 071 9166173

This friendly family home has wonderful views of the Donegal Mountains and Bunduff Beach, and overlooks a bird sanctuary and megalithic tombs. The property is well-maintained and is decorated to a high standard. It offers clean and comfortable accommodation. There is a TV lounge and an en suite bedroom on the ground floor.

There are several sea and hill walks locally, as well as a nearby golf course and diving facilities. John and Beatrice pride themselves on the personal touch, doing everything possible to ensure guests enjoy their stay. Guests feel very much at home. The house is nestled in its own grounds and the ever-changing scenery and views are superb—an excellent choice for folks looking for a peaceful and tranquil holiday. American Express, Visa and Eurocheque accepted.

OWNER Beatrice McLoughlin OPEN May 1–August 30
ROOMS 2 double, 1 twin, 2 family; 4 en suite
TERMS double/twin €30 pps; single €35

## COOLLOONEY

**Union Farm**
Coollooney, Co. Sligo
Tel: 071 9167136

This 300-year-old house, painted pale blue, stands in a very neat front garden in quiet, peaceful countryside and has lovely views. The house is part of a 20-hectare cattle farm and is well-kept, with an old-fashioned parlour-like lounge, which has a piano and TV. There is a separate dining room where freshly-prepared, tasty breakfasts are served.

Low doorways and thick walls abound, and the small, spotlessly clean bedrooms are modestly furnished. Evening meals or high tea are served at 7 p.m. if arranged in advance. Union Farm offers good value accommodation, and fishing is available on the property, which is inhabited by sheep and swans.

OWNER Des & Tess Lang OPEN March 1–October 15
ROOMS 2 double, 2 twin, 1 single TERMS €25-30 pps, single €35; child reduction; single supplement No credit cards

## DRUMCLIFFE

**Benbulben Farm**
Barnaribbon, Drumcliffe, Co. Sligo
Tel: 071 9163211 Fax: 071 9173009
Email: hennigan@eircom.net

This large, modern house nestles in the foothills of Benbulben Mountain in a well tended landscaped garden, surrounded by a 36-hectare sheep farm. There are unparalleled views and 250 square kilometres of beautiful Yeats country—his last resting place is Drumcliffe churchyard, which is within view of the farm.

This is very much a family home, and the Hennigans are very congenial people, offering a hospitality tray upon arrival. The rooms are spotlessly clean and simply furnished with fitted wardrobes and firm beds, and most have views. This is perfect walking country (there is a nature walk on the farm), and there are 30 mapped hill walks in the vicinity. Transport can be arranged to take visitors to starting points and back to base in the evening. If you're looking for a tranquil holiday, you may wander round the farm, visit the small museum on the property and enjoy some local lane walks. There is a TV lounge and a bright dining room where breakfasts are served.

Sligo has some fine early megalithic tombs. Benbulben Farm would be a good base from which to explore this scenic area. Visa and Mastercard accepted. Take the N15 from Sligo, turn right at Drumcliffe Creamery. Signposted.

OWNER Anne Hennigan OPEN April 1–October 1
ROOMS 3 double, 2 twin; 5 en suite
TERMS from €30 pps; single supplement

**Urlar House**
Drumcliffe, Co. Sligo
Tel: 071 9163110

This Georgian house is approached up a private drive in a peaceful location. The house is spacious and well maintained. The TV lounge, where smoking is permitted, has an original marble fireplace and two archways with the original Wedgwood figure design. Bedrooms vary in size; there is a family suite, consisting of double and twin rooms with en suite facilities, ideal for friends or family travelling together.

Mrs Healy is the proud recipient of the northwest Agri-Tourism Award and a Galtee Breakfast Award. Excellent breakfasts are served family-style on a large antique table, and consist of yoghurts, stuffed pancakes, omelettes, or traditional Irish breakfast. There is an enclosed sun porch for the children to play in, which leads onto the garden.

OWNER Mrs Gemma Healy OPEN May 1–September 1
ROOMS 5 double, 3 twin, 2 family TERMS double/twin €36 pps; single €44; child reduction; single supplement

## RIVERSTOWN

**Coopershill**
Riverstown, Co. Sligo
Tel: 071 9165108 Fax: 071 9164266
E-mail: ohara@coopershill.com

Approached through parks and woodland, a long drive winds its way to this Georgian mansion, which has been home to the O'Hara family for seven generations since it was built in 1774. Peacocks strut on the front lawn and there are splendid views over woods, hills and the River Arrow, which runs through the property. The house has been restored by the present owners to an extremely high standard, without in any way detracting from its ambience. Much of the furniture is original, family portraits adorn the walls: the rooms are extremely large and luxurious.

Candlelit dinners are served in the elegant dining room, which has enormous sideboards with gleaming family silver. There is a lounge and a spacious drawing room with a log fire. Five of the bedrooms have four-poster or canopy beds.

Walks can be taken on the 200-hectare estate, where there is an abundance of wildlife. Coarse fishing is available on the River Arrow, and a boat is available for trout fishing on nearby Lough Arrow. There is a championship golf course nearby, beautiful uncrowded beaches and megalithic monuments. If you are looking for somewhere to stay for a special occasion, Coopershill would be an excellent choice.

OWNER Brian & Lindy O'Hara OPEN April 1–October 31
ROOMS 7 double, 5 twin; 7 en suite
TERMS double/twin €101–114 pps; child reduction negotiable; single supplement €19 MEALS dinner €45-50, afternoon tea €4

**Ross House**
Riverstown, Co. Sligo
Tel: 071 9165140 Fax: 071 9165140

This 100-year-old country house in peaceful surroundings is approached down a quiet country lane. Mrs Hill-Wilkinson is a friendly woman who enjoys baking and welcomes guests into her kitchen. Home-cooked meals are available on request from 7.30 pm and a cup of tea is available later in the evening: special diets can be catered for if pre-arranged. It is a comfortable family home. Guests have use of a TV lounge with a turf fire. Smoking is allowed in the lounge only. One of the bedrooms is small; the other three are average in size, clean and comfortable.

There are two large en suite bedrooms on the ground floor, suitable for guests with disabilities. There is a tennis court for guests' use. This is a wonderful place for children; there is a donkey, haymaking and cattle on this mixed 48-hectare farm. Many visitors come to Lough Arrow for the fishing. Fishermen can hire boats, tackle and engines at the farm.

There are beautiful beaches close by and many ancient monuments to visit throughout County Sligo, at Creevykeel and Deerpark for instance. The archaeological sites at Carrowmore and Carrowkeel are of special interest.

OWNER Nicholas & Oriel Hill-Wilkinson
OPEN March 16–November 1
ROOMS 1 double, 2 twin, 2 family, 1 single; 2 en suite
TERMS €35 pps; child reduction; single supplement €7.50
MEALS dinner

## Serenity B & B

Doonierin, Kintogher, Rosses Point, County Sligo
Tel: 071 9143351
Email: serenitysligo@eircom.net

This is a haven of tranquillity, a wonderful 'away from it all' property. It stands in extensive grounds, surrounded by magnificent scenery, with stunning views of the Bay, and the Benbulben Mountains. You will receive a warm welcome from Brendon Kelly, a local history buff, who enjoys sharing his knowledge about local events. He has a great sense of humour and is an entertaining gentleman. Ask him to share the history of St. Columba's Church at Drumcliffe, final resting place of William Butler Yeats, whose great-grandfather was Rector in the early years of the nineteenth century. This 'little bit of heaven' provides a high standard of accommodation, with curtains and quilts made for the house. The largest bedroom has Georgian and Victorian furniture and patchwork quilts. Breakfast, with home-baked bread, ordered off the menu, is served at separate tables in the conservatory. Secure parking.

OWNER The Kelly family OPEN March–October
ROOMS 2 double, 2 twin; all en suite
TERMS €33-40 pps single supplement

## Aisling

Cairns Hill, Sligo, Co. Sligo
Tel: 071 9160704
Email: aislingsligo@eircom.net

This immaculate bungalow, whose name means 'Irish Dream', stands in its own grounds in an elevated location on the south side of Sligo. The bedrooms are average in size and are comfortably furnished. They are all on the ground floor and now have TV and dressing gowns. Des and Nan are a very congenial and accommodating couple who work together as a team. Nan cooks breakfast while Des enjoys chatting with guests and helping them plan daily activities. Breakfast only is served, but there are plenty of eating establishments in Sligo. There is a comfortable lounge with a coal fire.

OWNER Des & Nan Faul OPEN All year
ROOMS 2 double, 2 twin, (double, single bed in each room)
TERMS €66 per room, €45 single

## Lissadell
Mail Coach Road, Sligo, Co. Sligo
Tel: 071 9161937

This red brick new house is within walking distance of the town centre and offers a high standard of accommodation. The rooms are of a good size, well furnished and tastefully decorated. Mary formerly ran a bed & breakfast establishment by the same name in the area for several years and brings her expertise to this new property. Mary is friendly and accommodating and is willing to help her guests in every way to ensure they have a comfortable stay. Freshly-prepared breakfasts only are served, but there are several establishments within walking distance for evening meals. Lissadell is a good base from which to explore Yeats' country.

OWNER Mary Cadden OPEN All year ROOMS 2 double, 1 twin; all en suite TERMS from €33 pps; single supplement

## Lough Gill House
Pearse Road, Sligo, County Sligo
Tel:071 9150045 fax 071 9150639
Email: loughgillbandb@eircom.net
Website: www.loughgillhouse.com/

This ivy-covered modern, two-storey house, with its home-from-home ambience, is within walking distance of town centre. The house is comfortably furnished and the four pleasantly decorated bedrooms are all en suite, have TV and tea makers. Guests are welcome to join the owners, Shane and Florrie Gilmartin in their sitting room. Breakfasts are served on cobalt blue china at separate tables in the dining room. Situated on N4 Dublin/ Galway Road. Parking available.

OWNER Florrie Gilmartin OPEN All year except for Christmas ROOMS 4 double/twin/family/single; all en suite
TERMS from €34 pps; single supplement

## Tree Tops
Cleveragh Road, Sligo, Co. Sligo
Tel: 071 9160160 Fax: 071 9162301
Email: treetops@iol.ie
Website: www.sligobandb.com

This well-maintained, spacious, modern, attractive house stands in a secluded location with an interesting garden and fishpond. An eight-minute walk will take you to the town centre. The immaculate bedrooms are large, tastefully decorated and well furnished, with orthopaedic beds. This tasteful home has a large collection of Irish prints and paintings on display. Wholesome breakfasts are served in the dining room/ lounge, which has period furniture. There are some lovely walks and views close by. Tree Tops would be a good choice as a base from which to explore this interesting area. Credit cards accepted.

OWNER Doreen MacEvilly OPEN January 10–December 20
ROOMS 2 double, 1 twin, 2 family; all en suite
TERMS double/ twin €34 pps, family €93, single €46.50; child reduction 20%; single supplement

## STRANDHILL

### Mardel B & B
Seafront, Strandhill, County Sligo
Tel: 071 9168295

Breathtaking sunsets from can be observed from Mardel B & B, which stands in a peaceful position overlooking the sea and the golf course. In spring and summer the terrace is ablaze with a colourful array of hanging baskets and flowering tubs. Anne, an attentive host, also does the decorating, reflected in the bright and cheerful bedrooms, with colours of terracotta, cream, peach, green, yellow and blue; all have sea or mountain views. Rooms have TV, tea makers and en suite facilities. Guests have use of a lounge, and sun terrace. A substantial breakfast is served, and there are lots of venues for evening meals within walking distance. The Celtic Seawood Baths, are adjacent, and advance reservations can be made through Anne. Five minutes from Sligo Airport. A private car park is available.

OWNER Mrs Anne Marie Kelly OPEN mid-March–mid-October
ROOMS 2 double, 2 twin; all en suite
TERMS from €30 pps; single supplement; child reduction

## TUBBERCURRY

### Cruckawn House
Ballymote Road, Tubbercurry, Co. Sligo
Tel: 071 9185188 Fax: 071 9185188
Email: cruckawn@esatclear.ie
Website: www.sligotourism/cruckawn

This friendly, welcoming home is set back off the road and stands in its own grounds overlooking a golf course; there are clubs and caddies for hire, and the green fees are moderate. Maeve Walsh is a friendly, outgoing lady who knows how to make her guests feel at home, and greets them with a complimentary hospitality tray. Maeve is also director of the North West Tourism Organisation and an expert on local attractions. The rooms are a little small, but are spotlessly clean and comfortable. There is a pleasant TV lounge and a separate dining room where freshly-prepared, substantial breakfasts are served. Evening meals are no longer served, but there are several establishments close by for evening meals. Separating the dining room from a small sun lounge are sliding glass doors with the family crests of the owners' families engraved in the middle of each door. Laundry facilities are provided. Local amenities include salmon and trout fishing, game shooting, mountain climbing, horseback riding and pony trekking. Tubbercurry is quite a lively place: traditional Irish music and dance can be enjoyed Tuesday and Thursday and on weekends from May to September. Visa, Access and Mastercard accepted.

OWNER Joe & Maeve Walsh OPEN Easter–November ROOMS 5 double, 2 twin, 2 family; all en suite TERMS €30-35 pps; single €40; child reduction

## Pine Grove
Ballina Road, Tubbercurry, Co. Sligo
Tel: 071 9185235

This attractive, large house has been repainted white and green and has had Georgian-style windows installed. It stands in a pretty front garden on the edge of town on the Ballina Road. Mrs Kelly is a good cook and breakfasts are served in a large dining room overlooking a patio. The wonderful breakfasts are substantial. The house is simply furnished with old-fashioned furniture. There is a TV lounge with an open fire. There is no license, but guests are welcome to bring wine if they wish. This is a popular venue and reservations are recommended. On pleasant days guests are welcome to use the garden. Visa, Mastercard and Eurocard accepted. Situated on Ballina Road, 300 m off N17. Knock Airport is 11 miles away.

OWNER Teresa Kelly OPEN All year
ROOMS 1 double, 2 twin, 2 family; all en suite
TERMS €32 pps; child reduction; single supplement

## COUNTY CARLOW

One of the smallest counties in Ireland, Carlow lies just below
Wicklow and is in an area of rich farmland.

The county town, Carlow, has had an eventful history, which
includes being captured by Cromwell in 1650. Now the town manu-
factures beet sugar and has quite a few noteworthy sights, including
the ruin of a Norman castle, a Gothic Revival Catholic church, the
Carlow Museum and the fine courthouse with a Doric portico fashioned after the Parthenon.

There is a ruined twelfth-century church at Killeshin, with a fine
Romanesque doorway, and fourteenth-century Ballymoon Castle,
which has apparently never been occupied.

## BAGENALSTOWN

### Kilgraney House
Bagenalstown, Co. Carlow
Tel: 059 97 75283 Fax: 059 97 75595
Email: info@kilgraneyhouse.com
Website: www.kilgraneyhouse.com

Bryan Leech and Martin Marley have created a most delightful fanta-
sy world in their charming Georgian house, overlooking the lovely
Barrow valley. Kilgraney Country House is full of wonderfully chosen
pieces of fabric, furniture and art from all around the world, with a
strong Philippine influence, and each of the six comfortable bedrooms is furnished and decorated with unique imagination. This is a
delightful place to spend a weekend, and in fact Bryan and Martin
specialise in creating memorable weekend getaways. Guests can
experience wonderful home-cooked six course dinners using both
exotic products and home-grown fruits, herbs and vegetables.
Breakfast, served in the sunlit morning room, offers both traditional
and healthy options. There are two courtyard suites, which can be
used for B&B or self-catering. Massage and aromatherapy can be
arranged with advance notice. The house has a wine licence. No
pets. Kilgraney House is unsuitable for small children. Access, Visa
and Mastercard accepted. Just off the R704, Kilgraney is halfway
between Bagenalstown (Muine Bheag) and Borris.

OWNER Bryan Leech and Martin Marley
OPEN March–November
ROOMS 6 double/twin/single; all en suite; 2 courtyard suites
TERMS €55–85
MEALS dinner €45

## Lorum Old Rectory

Kilgreaney, Bagenalstown, Co. Carlow
Tel: 059 9775282 Fax: 059 9775455
Email: enquiries@lorum.com
Website: www.lorum.com

Dating from the eighteenth century, Lorum Old Rectory is set in 7.5 hectares nestling beneath the Blackstairs Mountains. It is surrounded by open countryside, with views as far as Tipperary.

Lorum Old Rectory

The bedrooms are spacious, furnished with antiques, and all have their original fireplaces, hair-dryers, telephone and tea- and coffee-making facilities. Five-course imaginative dinners are available, by prior arrangement, with home-grown organic vegetables, and the house does have a wine licence. There is a tiny snug room with fire-place in addition to the drawing room. The atmosphere is comfort-able and informal, and Bobbie Smith is a friendly person. Cycling holi-days can be arranged. Guests have use of a croquet lawn. Pets out-side only. Access, Mastercard, Laser and Visa cards accepted. The Old Rectory is 6.5 kilometres from Bagenalstown on R705 Borris road.

OWNER Bobbie Smith OPEN February 1–November 30
ROOMS 3 double, 2 double/twin; all en suite
TERMS €65–70; single supplement; child reduction
MEALS dinner €38

## BALLON

## Sherwood Park House

Kilbride, Ballon, Co. Carlow
Tel: 059 9159117 Fax: 059 9159355
Email: info@sherwoodparkhouse.ie

This lovely Georgian house is set in peaceful countryside, and has a large garden and pleasant views. Patrick and Maureen Owens are a most welcoming, gentle couple and have friendly dogs. Sherwood Park has an especially beautiful winding staircase, and an unusual raised hallway features an old, flat-topped piano. The drawing room also has a piano, and excellent, home-cooked five-course dinners are elegantly served by candlelight in the very large dining room.

Guests may bring their own wine, and dinner must be ordered in advance. The bedrooms are spacious and comfortable and some have lovely furniture, including several four-poster beds. Families are well catered for, and the rooms have en suite bathrooms with both baths and showers. They each have a hair-dryer, trouser press and tea- and coffee-making facilities. Pets in cars only. Visa, Mastercard and American Express are accepted. Altamount Gardens are nearby, and golf, fishing and riding can be enjoyed locally. The house is just off N80.

OWNER Patrick & Maureen Owens OPEN All year
ROOMS 2 double, 2 family; all en suite TERMS €50;
single supplement; child reduction; MEALS dinner €35

## BORRIS

### The Step House
Main Street, Borris, Co. Carlow
Tel: 059 9773209 Fax: 059 9773395

This early Georgian town house stands right in the centre of Borris. It ws originally the dower house to the castle, the entrance gates to which are on the opposite side of the street. The drawing room and the dining room leading from it have ornate fireplaces. Most of the bedrooms, all with TV, lie at the back of the house, some with nice views, and one has a four-poster bed. They are spacious, comfortable and attractively furnished and decorated.

Cait Coady is a cheerful, energetic host, and some of her recent additions to the house are the covered side porch with tables and chairs, and the nicely landscaped, extensive back garden. Borris is close to the Leinster Way and there are great walks along the River Barrow. Pets by arrangement. Visa and Mastercard accepted.

OWNER James & Cait Coady OPEN 17 March–20 December
ROOMS 3 double, 2 twin; all en suite
TERMS from €45; single supplement; not suitable for children

## CARLOW

### Barrowville Town House
Kilkenny Road, Carlow, Co. Carlow
Tel: 059 9143324 Fax: 059 9141953
Email: barrowvilletownhouse@eircom.net
Website: www.barrowvillehouse.com

A friendly welcome, professional service and comfort in a lovely in-town setting are what visitors can expect at this attractive, eigh-teenth-century townhouse. The Dempseys, experienced in hotel ownership, did the whole house up (which was a major undertak-ing), and created a place of elegance and comfort. The en suite bed-rooms have hair-dryers, telephone, TV, shoe shine and tea- and cof-fee-making facilities. Exquisitely presented, sumptuous breakfasts are served in the attractive conservatory overlooking the lovely, private back garden. There is also a small sitting room, which has a TV and tea- and coffee-making facilities and a door out to the garden, which is a nice place to take a stroll. Barrowville House never fails to live up to its high standards. It is on the main Kilkenny road, just a three-minute walk from the centre of town. No pets. Smoking permitted only in the sitting room. Visa, Access and American Express accepted.

OWNER Randal & Marie Dempsey OPEN All year
ROOMS 2 double, 2 twin, 21 single, 2 family; all en suite (5 have bath and shower) TERMS €37.50–42.50; single supplement

## COUNTY CAVAN

Cavan is an undiscovered county, an angler's delight with its unlimit-ed opportunities for coarse and game fishing. Large areas of Cavan seem to have more water than land. The undulating landscape and picturesque settings are dotted with wooded islands providing much of the county's delightful scenery. There is plenty to see and do, including a museum in Virginia, which has 3,000 items dating back to 1700. Saint Killian's Heritage Centre and Fore Abbey are other sites of interest. Cavan Crystal can be bought in the factory shop on the outskirts of Cavan town. Derragara Museum is situated on the Annalee River, and exhibits a full-size mud and wattle homestead.

### BELTURBET

**Rockwood House**
Cloverhill, Belturbet, Co. Cavan
Tel: 047 55351 Fax: 047 55373
Email: jbmac@eircom.net

A charming country house standing in three of secluded woodland gardens. The house was built in the style of an older house that pre-viously stood on the property, using the original stone and wood in the building of the new house.
   The house is furnished with a mixture of modern and antique pieces, and the good-sized bedrooms have comfortable beds and pastel duvets. Bedrooms do not have TV, but there is one in the guest lounge where fires burn on cool evenings.

Traditional freshly-prepared breakfasts are served in the dining room, which overlooks the garden. Tea and coffee are available on request. Guests are well taken care of at Rockwood House by Susan MacAuley who enjoys having people in her home. Plenty of information is provided on what to see and do in the area.

Visa and Mastercard accepted. Situated on the N24 two miles from Butlersbridge and six miles from Cavan.

OWNER James and Susan MacAuley OPEN closed 2 weeks over Christmas ROOMS 2 double, 2 twin; all en suite
TERMS from €38 single, €60 double/twin; child reduction 25%

## MOUNTNUGENT

### Ross Castle
Mountnugent, Co. Cavan
Tel: 043 81286
Email: book@ross-castle.com
Website: www.ross-house.com

This fascinating castle is situated amidst majestic trees and has magnificent views of Lough Sheelin, a lake famous for its brown trout. The castle was built in the sixteenth century, and later fell into a derelict condition. It was restored in 1864 by Anna Maria O'Reilly, a lineal descendant of Myles O'Reilly (known as 'The Slasher'), who used the tower in the castle the night before being killed by Oliver Cromwell's troops.

It has a fascinating history and offers unique and interesting accommodation. It is entered through a gateway to an inner courtyard and surrounded by a stone wall. On the ground floor is a large entrance hall connecting the tower and the sitting room. There is an open fireplace, and French windows offer a beautiful view across the lake. One double bedroom has access to its own terrace. The tower is ideal for friends or family travelling together; there are two double en suite bedrooms, plus an additional toilet, and a sitting room—access is by 65 winding stone steps. The rooms are furnished with antiques and the ambience is peaceful. Tea makers are available in the sitting room and evening meals can be taken at nearby Ross House. In addition, guests are able to make use of the rest of the facilities such as boat hire, tennis court, sauna and jacuzzi for a modest charge. A self-catering cottage is also available. Under new management, smoking is permitted.

This is exceptionally good value accommodation: early reservations are highly recommended. Visa, Mastercard and Eurocheque accepted.

OWNER Benita Walker OPEN All year
ROOMS 1 double, 2 twin, 1 family; 4 en suite TERMS €45 pps; children under 3 free, under 12, €35; single supplement €10

**Ross House**
Mountnugent, Co. Cavan
Tel: 049 8540218 Fax: 049 8540218
Email: rosshouse@eircom.net
Website: www.ross-house.com

This charming, Virginia creeper–covered old manor house dates from the 1600s and stands in beautiful grounds on the shores of Lough Sheelin. It was built as a dormer house and belonged to the Nugent family, who were the Lords of Delvin.

The spacious bedrooms, centred around the courtyard, are in the tastefully restored carriage houses. They have antique furniture, and three rooms have a conservatory and four have their own fireplace. All rooms have TV and telephone. Smoking is permitted in specific bedrooms and the dining room. After a busy day sightseeing, guests may, for a modest charge, enjoy the sauna and/or jacuzzi.

This is a wonderful place and must be one of the best value bed & breakfast properties in Ireland. A Christmas package is available, but very early reservations are essential.

Guests have access to a sandy beach which provides safe bathing. The private pier with boats for hire gives fishermen the opportunity to fish waters of this well-stocked lake. Ross House is fast being recognized for its fine Equestrian Centre, part of the 145-hectare farm which offers pony trekking, a horse-back riding arena and a tennis court.

Ulla Harkort is a very congenial and accommodating host. Delicious four-course dinners are prepared, if ordered in advance, using fresh produce and local meats; vegetarian and light dinners are also available. If you are looking for high standards, good food and a tranquil setting with lots of old-world charm, then Ross House should be your first choice. Mastercard and Visa accepted.

OWNER Ursula Liebe-Harkort OPEN All year
ROOMS 4 family, 2 double/single; all en suite
TERMS from €35 per person sharing; child reduction–
free up to 2 years, 30% thereafter; single supplement
MEALS €20 dinner; wine license

## VIRGINIA

**The White House**
Old Castle Road, Virginia, Co. Cavan
Tel: 049 8547515 Fax: 049 8547515
Email: mchugo@esatclear.ie

This warm, traditional-style house is in a lovely situation adjacent to the beautiful Deerpark Lakeland Forest, a well-known spot for hiking, horseback riding, golfing, fishing and water sports. It stands in a large garden where there is a display of old farming implements from Mr McHugo's father's farm in Galway. The bedrooms are clean and tidy with bright wallpapers and comfortable beds. Satellite TV and tea-making facilities in all bedrooms.

There is a conservatory and lounge for guests' use. Smoking is only allowed on the patio. Breakfasts are excellent and feature smoked salmon and scrambled eggs, fresh fruits and yoghurts or a full Irish breakfast. Emily pampers her guests, with nothing being too much trouble to ensure their stay is comfortable. Tea and scones are served on your arrival.

This is a popular venue for fishermen and tourists. Cavan has 365 lakes, one for every day of the year, so if fishing is your interest you have come to the right place! A visit to Cavan Crystal is worthwhile and the local museum has 3,000 items dating back to 1700. Credit cards accepted.

OWNER Emily McHugo OPEN January 1–December 1
ROOMS 1 double, 3 family; all en suite
TERMS €30 pps €40 single; child reduction 25–50%; single supplement

## COUNTY KILDARE

County Kildare is famous for horse breeding and training, which takes place on the Curragh, a great plain leading into the Bog of Allen. Many horse-race meetings are held here, including the Irish Derby, the Irish 2000 Guineas, the Irish Oaks and the Irish St Leger. Kildare town is the centre for horse breeding and has a well-pre-served Church of Ireland cathedral and round tower.

At Robertstown, the eighteenth-century buildings along the Grand Canal have been restored to look as they did when this was a great water thoroughfare. Here is it possible to visit Europe's largest fal-conry. Two of Ireland's greatest Georgian houses, Carton and Castletown, are located at Celbridge. A music festival takes place in June at Castletown, as does one of the hunt balls held during the Dublin Horse Show week.

The very pretty village of Leixlip has many associations with the Guinness family; the twelfth-century Norman castle belongs to Desmond Guinness.

Remains of a Franciscan Abbey can be seen at Castledermot, and Athy has many historic sights worth exploring, including the six-teenth-century Woodstock Castle, just out of town. Moone High Cross, one of Ireland's most beautiful high crosses, is at Moone Abbey, 12 km from Athy.

## Coursetown Country House

Stradbally Road, Athy, Co. Kildare
Tel: 0509 8631101 Fax: 0509 8632740
Email: coursetown@hotmail.com

Pride of ownership and attention to detail are prevalent at Coursetown House, originally a 200 year old farmhouse. What remains of the old brickworks that stood beside the house is a church like bell in a mini tower, still in use. The farm consists of 200 acres of arable land and an immaculately maintained and interesting garden surrounds the house. One room has been designed specifically with the wheelchair user in mind. The remaining rooms are upstairs and have every possible amenity including a full range of toiletries. The plainly furnished breakfast room has doors out to a patio and pretty garden, where breakfast is served on fine days. The lounge has a full range of books to appeal to the tourist. Pets by arrangement. Visa and Mastercard accepted. Coursetown House can be found off the R428 3 km from Athy.

OWNER Iris & Jim Fox OPEN February 1–December 20
ROOMS 3 double, 1 twin, 1 single; all en suite
TERMS €55; single supplement; not suitable for children

## Moate Lodge

Athy, Co. Kildare
Tel: 059 8626137 Fax: 059 8626109
Email: marypelin@moatelodge.com  Website: www.moatelodge.com

Mary and Raymond Pelin offer a warm welcome to guests at their neatly kept stone built 300-year old farmhouse., surrounded by farmland and reached off the N78 road down a couple of narrow lanes. When Mary started her b&b business it was a hobby in comparison to the importance of farming, but these days it has taken on a more significant role. And now the Pelins have renovated one side of the attractive farm buildings courtyard into three well equpped self catering units. Bed & breakfast guests have a choice of four simply furnished bedrooms in the house. Breakfast in summer time is served in the conservatory at the back of the house, and at other times in the formal dining room, where home cooked dinners are also served. Visa and Mastercard accepted, and pets are welcome. The house is signed off the N78 about 5 kilometres from Athy heading towards Kilcullen.

OWNER Mary & Raymond Pelin OPEN all year ROOMS 1 single, 1 twin, 2 double; 3 en suite, 1 private bathroom
TERMS €28; single supplement; child reduction MEALS dinner €20

## Tonlegee House

Athy, Co. Kildare
Tel: 059 8631473 Fax: 059 8631473
Email: marjorie@tonlegeehouse.com
Website: www.tonlegeehouse.com

Set in a quiet country position, Tonlegee House was built around
1790 and stands in 2 hectares of grounds. Marjorie did a great job
restoring the house, which previously had been flatlets, into a place
of character and comfort. The drawing room is especially large and
pleasant, and the bar has nice old furniture and prints. The bedrooms
are comfortable and attractively decorated and have TV, telephone
and mineral water. Tea or coffee is served upon arrival.

However, it is the food that draws people here. Organic vegetables
and salads come from the walled garden, and fresh fish and game are
specialities. Visa, Mastercard and American Express accepted. No
pets. Tonlegee is signposted off Castlecomer to Kilkenny road.

OWNER Marjorie Molloy
OPEN All year except Christmas, New Year and Hallowe'en
ROOMS 2 single, 2 twin, 8 double; all en suite
TERMS €65 pps; single supplement; child reduction
MEALS dinner from €25

## CASTLEDERMOT

## Kilkea Lodge Farm

Castledermot, Co. Kildare
Tel: 059 9145112 Fax: 059 9145112
Email: kilkealodgefarm@kildarehorse.ie

Kilkea Lodge, which has belonged to the Greene family since 1740, is
approached down a long driveway and is set in rolling parkland with
a pleasant, rural aspect. Godfrey runs the 105-hectare farm with livery yard.

It is very much a family home, a typical old country house with
guests sharing some of the facilities with family members, and it has
a relaxed, informal atmosphere.

The comfortable drawing room has a piano and fireplace, and traditional food is served in the dining room. The family room is an enormous studio, converted from an old barn, with its own entrance,
four beds, a small loft and a sitting area in the middle—ideal for families or small groups. Kilkea Lodge is not suitable for young children.

Kilkea Lodge is suited to those who enjoy country life and animals.
Dinner by arrangement for groups of minimum of six people. Pets
outside only, and no smoking in the bedrooms. American Express
accepted.

OWNER Marion & Godfrey Greene OPEN All year except for
Christmas and January
ROOMS 4 double/twin/family; some with private bathrooms
TERMS €44.50; single supplement €12.50 MEALS dinner from €25

## Springfield
Celbridge, Co. Kildare
Tel: 01 6273248  Fax: 01 6273123

This substantial Georgian house with Victorian flavours is set in five
hectares of fields and gardens with horses, dogs and cats. It was the
childhood home of Aidan Higgins and is referred to in his book
*Langrish, Go Down*, and was at one time gutted by fire and rebuilt following the original plans.

The house is luxuriously decorated with six large en suite bedrooms. There is one family room up a narrow spiral staircase, and
another has four bunk beds. The master bedroom has a stereo system, jacuzzi for two, a shower with two jets, and an extra large four-
poster bed. All rooms have TV, video, telephone, hair-dryers and tea-
and coffee-making facilities.

Libby has six children, and welcomes families. Visiting children muck
in with the family and are fed all together in the enormous kitchen,
which was originally the old milking rooms and is also available to
guests for take-out food, etc. Breakfast is served in the traditional
dining room at one large table, or after 12 p.m. in the kitchen. There
is a selection of 150 videos, a one kilometre track in front of the
house for runners, and exercise machines. No pets. For directions
from Celbridge, cross the Liffey bridge, keep left and follow the main
road south for about 2 km. The house is on the right behind elec-
tronically controlled gates. Access, Visa and American Express accepted.

OWNER Libby Sheehy OPEN All year
ROOMS 4 double, 2 family; all en suite TERMS €76; child reduction

## Ballinagappa Country House
Clane, Co. Kildare
Tel: 045 892087
Email: ballinagappahouse@eircom.net
Website: www.ballinagappa.com

Beside a quiet country road, Ballinagappa is a comfortable farmhouse
dating from the mid-19th century, and extensively renovated in
recent years. It is still part of a small farm, mostly beef rearing, and
also has an equestrian centre. The two family en suite rooms are

spacious and well-equipped, and have views over the surrounding farmland. Guests have use of a small formal drawing room with baby grand piano, leading out to a new conservatory. Breakfast is served in the dining room, which has access to the colourful back patio area and hot-tub. It is a 20-minute stroll to Clane, the nearest village. Dogs are catered for.

OWNER Myles Doyle OPEN all year
ROOMS 2 family en suite TERMS €44; single supplement

## KILDARE

### Castleview Farm B&B
Lackagh, Kildare, Co. Kildare
Tel: 045 521816 Fax : 045 521816
Email: castleviewfarmhouse@oceanfree.net
Website: www.kildarebandb.com

A warm and friendly welcome awaits you at Castleview Farm. The present farmhouse was built twenty years ago just after Liz and Ned Fitzpatrick got married. The simply furnished guest bedrooms are all on the ground floor. One room has an extra attached bedroom, and with both rooms en suite it is perfect for extended families. The original farmhouse, an old attractive thatched roof building, was recently opened as a cosy self catering cottage. It adjoins the farm buildings, which are used to run the 136 acre mostly dairy farm. Castleview is in a quiet, rural setting, just off the Kildare to Monasterevin road, and adjoins an old ruined church. Visa and Mastercard accepted. Pets outside.

OWNER Liz Fitzpatrick OPEN March 1–October 31
ROOMS 1 double, 2 family, 2 en suite, 1 private bathroom
TERMS €25–30

### Fremont
Tully Road, Kildare, Co. Kildare
Tel: 045 521604

Fremont is a modern bungalow in a private setting, with just a three-minute walk to the town centre and the twelfth-century cathedral. The house is in good decorative order, and the ground floor bedrooms are spotlessly clean, with modern furnishings, shower units and hair-dryers. The comfortable TV lounge has a Leitrim stone fireplace and there is a display of Waterford, Galway and Cavan crystal in the bright dining room.

Mrs O'Connell is a considerate host who enjoys meeting people, and she extends a warm welcome to everyone. The Irish Stud and Japanese Gardens can be reached in 15 minutes on foot. Pets outside only and smoking is allowed in the TV lounge. Fremont is sign-posted from the centre of town.

OWNER Frieda O'Connell OPEN March 17–October 30
ROOMS 2 double, 1 twin; 1 en suite, 2 public bathrooms
TERMS €24; single supplement €5

MAYNOOTH

**Moyglare Manor Hotel**
Moyglare, Maynooth, Co. Kildare
Tel: 01 6286351 Fax: 01 6285405
Email: info@moyglaremanor.ie
Website: www.moyglaremanor.ie

A lovely long driveway flanked by majestic trees, and to each side fenced fields with horses and sheep grazing, leads to this impressive eighteenth-century stone built mansion. A series of small reception rooms and hallways stuffed with antique furniture, ornaments and flowers gives it a rather dark and sombre air. The bedrooms are spacious and comfortable,  with hair-dryers, telephone and mineral water.

  The cuisine at Moyglare attracts many visitors. Beautifully presented food is served in the two elegant dining rooms by candlelight, and there is an extensive wine list. Small conferences can be catered for.

  There are several golf courses in the vicinity, and riding and hunting can be arranged. No pets. The property is 2 km from the church in Maynooth. Moyglare is the nearest country house hotel to the airport. All major credit cards accepted.

MANAGER Nora Devlin, Shay Curran OPEN All year except for Christmas ROOMS 16 double or twin; all en suite
TERMS €125; single supplement MEALS dinner €55

MONASTEREVIN

**Cloncarlin Farmhouse**
Nurney Road, Monasterevin, Co. Kildare
Tel: 045 525722
Email: marie@cloncarlinhouse.com

This 200 year old attractive house was built by Lord Drogheda to entertain his guests, and is reached up a long tree-lined driveway. It is set in pretty countryside in an elevated position, part of a 68-hectare mixed farm. When the McGuinnesses bought it ten years ago it was pretty derelict. The comfortable bedrooms have pleasant views, and there is a lounge and dining room.

  Fishing is available on the Barrow River, and there are riding stables close by. The Japanese Gardens and National Stud are a 15 minute drive away. Pets outside only. The house is signposted off the Dublin/Cork road.

OWNER Marie McGuinness OPEN January 1–December 15
ROOMS 1 single, 3 twin, 1 family; all en suite
TERMS €23–25.50; single supplement; child reduction

### Barberstown Castle
Straffan, Co. Kildare
Tel: 01 6288157 Fax: 01 6277027
Email: barberstowncastle@ireland.com
Website: www.barberstowncastle.com

Dating from the early thirteenth century, this historic castle was one of the first great Irish country houses to open for guests, becoming a hotel in 1973. The castle keep is a venue for banquets, and larger groups are entertained in the sixteenth-century banqueting hall.

The Elizabethan part of the castle dates from the second half of the sixteenth century, and the Victorian house was built in the 1830s. It is said that a man is interred between the top of the stairs and the roof of the tower. His family did this to prevent their eviction as tenants, as the lease stated that if he was put underground, it would expire.

The bedrooms are spacious and comfortable and each is individually decorated. All rooms have hair-dryer, trouser press, telephone, TV and modem line. In 2004 a new wing was added increasing the number of bedrooms and the conference facilities.

Barberstown has a good reputation for its food, which is creative and beautifully served.

It is an interesting and relaxing place to stay, within easy reach of Dublin and the airport. No pets. Major credit cards accepted.

From Dublin exit the N4 for Maynooth and Straffan.

OWNER Kenneth C. Healy OPEN February–December
ROOMS 60 double/twin; all en suite
TERMS €110; single supplement; child reduction
MEALS dinner, à la carte

### The K Club
Straffan, Co. Kildare
Tel: 01 601 7200 Fax: 01 601 7299
Email: hotel@kclub.ie
Website: www.kclub.ie

The ultimate in luxury, elegance and service, The Kildare Hotel & Golf Club is a superb country mansion standing in gracious parklands and manicured gardens. Its 18-hole Arnold Palmer-designed championship golf course, is the venue for the 2005 Ryder Cup. The 700 acres stretch to the River Liffey—the island in the river can be reached by a series of paths and bridges.

The origins of the house go back to 550 AD, and the present building was restored and opened in 1991 as a luxurious hotel and country club. No expense has been spared with the refurbishment of public rooms and bedrooms alike. The highest quality materials have been used, interesting paintings hang on the walls, Waterford glass is used from chandeliers to tooth mugs and every possible comfort and thought has gone into bedrooms and bathrooms.

The service is impeccable, the staff efficient, and The K Club has a friendly and relaxing atmosphere. The amenities are endless, and every taste and activity is catered for, from golf to salmon fishing, indoor tennis, health and leisure club with indoor swimming pool, snooker, bicycling, squash, clay pigeon shooting and horseriding. All major credit cards accepted. Wheelchair facilities. The property is signposted in the village of Kill and can be found on the way to Straffan.

OPEN All year ROOMS 69 twin/double/suite, 25 garden apartments TERMS €295–3800 MEALS all available

## Windgate Lodge
Barberstown, Straffan, Co. Kildare
Tel: 01 6273415

This attractive, modern, red brick house is set back off the road in half a hectare of landscaped gardens. The house is in good decorative order, and there are two bedrooms on the ground floor.

Pat Ryan is a friendly lady and is always eager to offer assistance to guests. Good home-cooked breakfasts are served in the dining room, and there is a TV lounge. A self-catering unit is also available. Close by there are country walks, golf, riding, a butterfly farm and steam museum. Smoking is permitted downstairs only.

With the motorway all the way to the centre of Dublin, this is a good location for either Dublin or the airport. Cars can be left at the railway station three kilometres away at Maynooth, from which there is a good train service into town, and buses also run frequently. To reach Windgate Lodge from the N4 westbound, take the Maynooth exit, turn left and the house is 5 km on the left.

OWNER Patricia Ryan OPEN All year ROOMS 1 double, 1 twin, 1 family; all en suite TERMS €31.50; single supplement €6.50; child reduction

## Martinstown House

The Curragh, Co. Kildare
Tel: 045 441269 Fax: 045 441208
Email: info@martinstownhouse.com
Website: www.martinstownhouse.com

This unusual house was built as a shooting lodge for the second Duke of Leinster, and was constructed in the 'Strawberry Hill' Gothic style 200 years ago. It is set in 70 hectares of park-like grounds and farmland and has a wonderful walled garden full of flowers, fruit and vegetables, and a hard tennis court. At the back of the house is an unusual gothic stable yard. Mrs Long has had some interesting decoration done to the house. The entryway has a faux mural, giving one the feeling of the entrance to a church, and then opens out to countryside views. The house is very comfortable, and furnished with some lovely furniture in a simple, unfussy way. There is a smaller sitting room, and grander, more formal drawing room with a high, decorated ceiling.

The bedrooms are spacious and the bathrooms newly tiled, one or two reached up a narrow winding staircase. Dinner, served in the attractive, intimate dining room and cooked by a French chef, is available if arranged in advance. No pets or small children, and no smoking in the bedrooms. American Express, Visa and Mastercard accepted. Martinstown House can be found from the N7 in Kildare by passing the Japanese Gardens, forking right and following the signs.

OWNER Mrs Thomas Long OPEN All year except for Christmas and Easter ROOMS 2 double, 2 twin; 2 en suite, 2 private bathrooms TERMS €89; single supplement €12.50 MEALS dinner €38

## COUNTY KILKENNY

Kilkenny, the county town, is one of the oldest and most interesting towns in Ireland. It comes alive at the end of August during the Kilkenny Festival, which is one of Ireland's foremost cultural festivals. Kilkenny Castle dominates the town centre, and just opposite are the Kilkenny Design Centre workshops, which can be visited.

The cathedral stands on the site of a monastery built by St Canice in the sixth century and from which the city took its name. The Kilkenny Archaeological Society houses its collection in a most interesting Tudor merchant's house–Rothe House–and the City Hall, built in 1761, was formerly the Tolsel or Toll House. The well-known writers Swift, Berkeley and Congreve, were educated at Kilkenny

College, a fine Georgian building.

The Kilkenny countryside is pretty and compact, and places of interest to visit are the attractive town of Thomas-town, near Dysart Castle, former home of George Berkeley, after whom the city and oldest campus of the University of California is named. Near to Callan on the King's River is Kells, a fortified, turreted and walled collection of early ecclesiastical buildings, and near Urlingford are the ruins of four castles.

## CALLAN

**Ballaghtobin**
Callan, Co. Kilkenny
Tel: 056 7725227
Fax: 056 7725712
Email: catherine@ballaghtobin.com
Website: www.ballaghtobin.com

Ballaghtobin, its origins dating back to the twelfth century, has been in the Gabbett family for 450 years. Today's house covers different periods, the most recent being the front entrance area, which was rebuilt by Mickey Gabbett's parents. Set in parkland and its 500 acres of farmland, it is surrounded by gardens, which include the ruins of a Norman church, a hard tennis court and croquet lawn.

Mickey and Catherine are a delightful and very friendly couple and are delighted to welcome guests to their beautiful home. Flair and imagination has been used in renovating the guests' quarters, which include the drawing room, a small sitting room off which is found the attractive conservatory, and the delightful bedrooms, two of which have sofa/stools that fold out to become extra beds. All have hair-dryers, trouser press, TV, tea trays and local reading material. Pets accepted. Visa and Mastercard are taken. Ballaghtobin is off the R699 road between Callan and Knocktopher, but it is as well to get precise directions.

OWNER Catherine Gabbett OPEN February–end October
ROOMS 1 twin, 1 family, 1 double; all en suite
TERMS €50 pps; single supplement; child reduction

## GRAIGUENAMANAGH

**Ballyogan House**
New Ross Road, Graiguenamanagh, Co. Kilkenny
Tel: 059 972 5969
Fax: 059 972 5016
Email: info@ballyoganhouse.com
Website: www.ballyoganhouse.com

Peace and quiet in a beautiful country setting are what attract and entice people back to Ballyogan House. Easy-going hosts Fran & Robert Durie like to make sure their guests are comfortable and well cared for. The attractive mid-nineteenth century house has magical views over the colourful garden to the trees lining the valley and to the Blackstairs Mountains. It was the River Barrow which drew the Duries to Ballyogan. Fifty acres of woods and fields stretch down to its banks and along it to a waterfall.

The bedrooms, two of which are on the first floor, and two on the second, are named after different plants and have their own colours and décor styles. The plant-filled conserevatory is a favourite place for guests to unwind, leading off the pleasant sitting room. Packed lunches can be provided, and pets, including horses, are catered for. Most major credit cards accepted. Ballyogan is off R705 between Graiguenamanagh and New Ross.

OWNER Fran & Robert Durie OPEN April 1–October 31 ROOMS 1 double, 2 twin, 1 family, all en suite shower rooms TERMS €40 pps; single supplement

**Cullintra House**
The Rower, Inistioge, Co. Kilkenny
Tel: 051 423614
Email: cullhse@indigo.ie
Website: www.indigo.ie/~cullhse/

This attractive, ivy-covered, 200-year-old house is approached by a long driveway through a park of grazing cattle, and has been in Patricia Cantlon's family since the turn of the century. It is an animal and bird sanctuary, and there are a great many friendly cats and a local fox who comes to eat dinner in the garden every evening. The rooms, including a garden conservatory and a converted barn, reflect Patricia's artistic talents. She is also an accomplished cook and serves dinner by candlelight in an unhurried fashion. Guests should bring their own wine.

Breakfast can be taken as late as you wish. The studio/conservatory with a small kitchen for making drinks is available for guests and can also be used as a small conference room. There are 93 hectares of farmland, and a private path leads to beautiful Mount Brandon, the ancient Cairn and Lady Annely's Wood. Pets by arrangement, no smoking in the dining room. Cullintra House is signposted off the R700 New Ross to Kilkenny road, 6 miles from New Ross.

OWNER Patricia Cantlon OPEN All year
ROOMS 6 double/twin; 3 en suite, 2 public bathrooms
TERMS €35–45; single supplement; child reduction
MEALS dinner €35

**Garranavabby House**
The Rower, Inistioge, Co. Kilkenny
Tel: 051 423613

This attractive country house, parts of which date back to the seventeenth century, is set in a pretty garde,n and is part of a large mixed farm, mostly sheep and cattle. There are ornamental pheasants, chickens to provide eggs, and lovely views. It is an excellent spot for fishing, hill walking, riding and shooting.

Garranavabby is a nice, comfortable, well lived in family home, with some faded furnishings, but a welcoming atmosphere pervades. Guests have use of a comfortable sitting room, and breakfast is served in the pleasant dining room with a sideboard full of silver. Pets by arrangement. No smoking in the bedrooms.

OWNER Johanna Prendergast OPEN All year
ROOMS 1 double, 1 twin, 1 family; 2 public bathrooms
TERMS €28.50; single supplement €6.50

**Grove Farmhouse**
Ballycocksuist, Inistioge, Co. Kilkenny
Tel: 056 7758467
Email: grovefarmhse@unison.ie

In a rural setting this 200 year old farmhouse is surrounded by its beef, sheep and corn growing farmland. With a small, pretty, colourful garden to the front, the house both inside and out is immaculately maintained. The South Leinster Way passes through the farm, which has belonged to the same family for generations. The dining room, where breakfast only is served is particularly large, and there is a pleasant living room. No smoking. Pets by arrangement. All major credit cards accepted. Grove Farmhouse is well signed from the R700 Thomastown to Inistioge road.

OWNER Nellie Cassin OPEN April 1–October 31
ROOMS 1 double, 2 twin, 1 family; all en suite
TERMS €27; single supplement; child reduction MEALS Light meals

## KILKENNY

**Berkeley House**
5 Lower Patrick Street, Kilkenny, Co. Kilkenny
Tel: 056 7764848 Fax: 056 7764829
Email: berkeleyhouse@eircom.net
Website: www.berkeleyhousekilkenny.com

The house was renovated about twelve years ago by previous owners. It dates from the 1800s and is right in the very centre of

Kilkenny, close to the castle. It offers well equipped, nicely decorated bedrooms, recently refurbished, which have phones and TV, and is efficiently, and professionally run. There is an attractive small breakfast room and car parking is available behind the house. No pets. Major credit cards accepted.

OWNER Vincent Quan OPEN All year
ROOMS 2 double, 2 twin, 6 double/twin; all en suite
TERMS €40–55; single supplement; child reduction

### Burwood Bed & Breakfast
Waterford Road, Kilkenny, Co. Kilkenny
Tel: 056 7762266

This modern bungalow with old fashioned hospitality is set back off the main road with a small front garden. Joan Flanagan is a most accommodating host and is proud of the personal attention she gives guests. A cup of tea or coffee is offered upon arrival and in the evening.

The small bedrooms are all on the ground floor and are simply decorated. They have tea- and coffee-making facilities and hair-dryers. There is a comfortable TV lounge for guests and breakfast only served in the dining room. The large rear parking area has 24-hour surveillance. Neither smoking nor pets allowed.

Burwood can be found on the Waterford road, one kilometre from the centre of medieval Kilkenny.

OWNER Joan Flanagan OPEN May–October
ROOMS 3 double, 1 twin; 3 en suite, 1 private bathroom
TERMS €25.50; single supplement €7.50; child reduction

### Danville House
New Ross Road, Kilkenny, Co. Kilkenny
Tel: 056 7721512 Fax: 056 7721512
Email: treecc@iol.ie

This 200 year old Georgian house is set in open countryside, with a pretty garden and a long driveway up from the main road. The house has been split into two, with one half taken up with care of the farm. Kitty is a friendly, cheerful hostess, and the house has a relaxed atmosphere. One bedroom is on the ground floor, and they all have hair-dryers. The TV lounge is combined with the dining room, which has a large table where breakfast is served.

In summer croquet is set up on the lawn, and there is a walled kitchen garden.

Fishing, golf and riding are available nearby. No pets. Danville House is one kilometre from Kilkenny on the New Ross road.

OWNER Kitty & Dan Stallard OPEN March 1–October 31
ROOMS 5 double/twin/single; 4 en suite, 1 private bathroom
TERMS from €32; single supplement

## Dunromin

Dublin Road, Kilkenny, Co. Kilkenny
Tel: 056 7761384 Fax: 056 7770736
Email: valtom@oceanfree.net
Website: www.dunrominkilkenny.com

The standard of maintenance is exceptionally high throughout the
public rooms and bedrooms of this house. There is a wonderful,
friendly atmosphere and tea or coffee is offered on arrival. The bedrooms have recently been completely refurbished in bright cheerful
colours, and are immaculately clean.

Dunromin

Guests enjoy the secluded, landscaped garden, and there are views
of the golf course to the front. Dunromin is well known for its informality and great musical evenings, set off by Tom Rothwell playing
the accordion. Breakfasts include home-baked breads and home-
made preserves. The house is on the edge of the town, reached off
N10. No pets. No smoking. Visa and Mastercard accepted.

OWNER Valerie & Tom Rothwell OPEN April 1–November 30
ROOMS 5 double/twin; all en suite
TERMS €32–36; single supplement; child reduction

## Hillgrove

Bennettsbridge Road, Kilkenny, Co. Kilkenny
Tel: 056 7751453 or 7722890
Email: hillgrove@esatclear.ie
Website: homepage.eircom.net/~hillgrove

This delightful family home is set back off the New Ross Road, three
kilometres from Kilkenny. Margaret Drennan used to work for the
Irish Tourist Board and knows everything there is to know about

Kilkenny. She is happy to suggest itineraries and help with planning your stay.

The house is furnished in a mixture of old and reproduction furniture and the en suite bedrooms all have hair-dryers and tea- and coffee-making facilities. There is a TV lounge and a varied breakfast menu. No pets.

OWNER Margaret & Tony Drennan OPEN February 1–December 12
ROOMS 2 double, 2 twin, 1 family; all en suite
TERMS €32; single supplement; child reduction

## Newlands Country House
Sevenhouses, Danesfort, Kilkenny, Co. Kilkenny
Tel: 056 7729111 Fax: 056 7729171
Email: newlands@indigo.ie
Website: indigo.ie/~newlands

The Kennedys originally owned Shillogher House in Kilkenny, then decided to move out into the countryside and designed and built Newlands moving in the mid 1990s. It is set in 28 hectares of farmland, supporting cattle and sheep, and Seamus breeds greyhounds. Although the house has every comfort, and wonderful food, it is the personalities and hospitality of Seamus and Aileen that make a stay here so memorable. The house is very well built and insulated, so one hears no noise from other guests. Bedrooms are very comfortable, with lavish décor; four have whirlpool baths, and they all have telephone, TV, trouser press, hair-dryers, fridges and tea- and coffee-making facilities. Outstanding breakfasts, orchestrated by Seamus, are served in the conservatory style dining room, which has bright, cheerful colours and an attractive tiled floor. There are special weekend packages available, which include an eight course dinner on Saturday night. These are very popular with people wanting to get away for peace and quiet in comfortable surroundings. Kilkenny is but a short drive away, with all its historical attractions and variety of restaurants. No pets and no smoking. Visa, Mastercard and Access accepted. To find Newlands take the N10 Waterford road from Kilkenny and turn right at the Harvester Pub–the house will be on right-hand side in about half a mile.

OWNER Seamus & Aileen Kennedy OPEN All year except Christmas
ROOMS 3 double, 3 double/twin; all en suite
TERMS €31.50–38; single supplement in summer €19
MEALS dinner on Saturday evenings, & sometimes Wednesday

## Blanchville House

Dunbell, Maddoxtown, Co. Kilkenny
Tel: 056 7727197 Fax: 056 7727636
Email: info@blanchville.ie
Website: www.blanchville.ie

This elegant Georgian country house stands in its own grounds and is approached by a tree and shrub lined private drive. It has a warm and friendly atmosphere and is beautifully furnished with antiques. The large, comfortable bedrooms overlook the lovely green countryside and have hair-dryers, tea- and coffee-making facilities, TV, and some rooms have trouser press. The spacious drawing room with the original wallpaper and service bells has a TV, grand piano and an open fireplace.

Light suppers which may be booked in advance, are served in the atmospheric dining room, tastefully prepared with home-grown produce. Guests are welcome to bring their own wine. There is a hard tennis court for guests' use and a billiard and games room. Local amenities include golf, racing, fishing and flying at Kilkenny Air Club. There are a wide range of archaeological and historical attractions. Blanchville is at the centre of a Craft Trail incorporating five prominent studio workshops in Co. Kilkenny.

A recent addition to the establishment are three most attractive and well-appointed self-catering units, skilfully converted from the ruins of the Victorian coach house. They are well suited for families with children. Pets by arrangement. Most major credit cards are accepted.

To reach Blanchville take the first right one kilometre after the Pike Pub off the N10 Dublin road. Then left at next crossroads and the entrance is 2 kilometres on the left.

OWNER Tim & Monica Phelan OPEN March 1–November 1
ROOMS 3 double, 2 twin, 1 family; all en suite
TERMS €55–60; single supplement; child reduction
MEALS light supper €6–15

Blanchville House

**Abbey House**
Jerpoint Abbey, Thomastown, Co. Kilkenny
Tel: 056 7724166 Fax: 056 7724192
Email: abbeyhousejerpoint@eircom.net
Website: www.abbeyhousejerpoint.com

Abbey House is an attractive building located opposite Jerpoint
Abbey. The house may have been built as early as 1540, and a mill
here dates from the twelfth century. Ruins of the old mill, which
Helen Blanchfield would love to restore, lie behind the house. The
house itself was in very bad condition when the Blanchfields bought
it in 1988, and only one original wall is left after doing the restoration work.

Helen is an amusing, chatty lady with a lot of energy who genuinely
cares for her guests' well-being. The house is spacious, with a drawing room, and simply furnished bedrooms all equipped with hair-dryers, telephone and TV. The pleasant dining room has small individual
tables and views over the old mill. Dogs allowed in baskets in bedrooms. Visa, Access, Mastercard and Eurocard accepted. Abbey House
is on the N9.

OWNER Helen Blanchfield OPEN All year except for Christmas
ROOMS 6 double/twin/single; all en suite
TERMS €35–40 pps; single supplement; child reduction

**Ballyduff House**
Ballyduff, Thomastown, Co. Kilkenny
Tel: 056 7758488
Email: baclyd@eircom.net

This attractive eighteenth-century manor house is set in lovely
peaceful countryside, reached down a series of country lanes and
entered through a gateway and up a long pot-holed driveway. It
stands just above the River Nore and enjoys views of the river and
hills.

Mrs Thomas is a charming young widow with two children, and is a
kind and thoughtful hostess. Ballyduff is a wonderful old family home,
with an interesting collection of family portraits. The bedrooms are
huge and comfortably furnished and have good-sized bathrooms.

Breakfast is served in the dining room, and guests also have use of
a wonderful library and drawing room with TV. Arrangements can be
made for guests to fish on the estate's own stretch of the River
Nore.

Hunting is available. No smoking in bedrooms. Visa and Mastercard
accepted.

OWNER Mrs Breda Thomas OPEN All year
ROOMS 2 double, 1 twin; all en suite
TERMS €45; child reduction

**Belmore**
Jerpoint Church, Thomastown, Co. Kilkenny
Tel: 056 7724228

Belmore House is full of character, as are its owners, Joseph and Rita
Teesdale, and their son, Henry. First built as a shooting lodge by the
Earl of Belmore, the house has a lovely atmosphere and is full of
interesting pictures and books, many about the history of Jerpoint
Abbey and other sites dating from the Norman conquest.

The family rooms are mostly in the servants' quarters with vaulted
ceilings and flagstone floors. The guest rooms mostly have elegant
rounded ceilings, are well-appointed and have hair-dryers, etc.

The Teesdales have owned the house since 1953, and farmed their
two farms on both banks of the River Nore. Trout and salmon fishing is free for guests. Pets are welcome in stables. Visa, Mastercard
and American Express accepted.

OWNER Rita & Joseph Teesdale OPEN All year except Christmas
ROOMS 2 double, 1 twin; all en suite
TERMS €35; single supplement; child reduction

## URLINGFORD

**Springview House**
Urlingford, Co. Kilkenny
Tel: 056 8831243
Website: www.springviewbb.com

Springview House is most people's ideal of an Irish country farmhouse. Full of peace and comfort it was probably built in the late
1700s or early 1800s, and originally the upper rooms were accessed
one room through another. Later a corridor was built and now
there are three delightful family rooms, each with a double and single bed and private or en suite bathroom. The Joyce family have lived
here since 1916, Mr Joyce running their two farms with dairy cows
and beef cattle, and Eileen Joyce is a charming, friendly hostess.
Springview offers good value and can be found 600 metres off the
Urlingford to Kilkenny R693 road.

OWNER Mrs Eileen Joyce OPEN April 1–November 1
ROOMS 3 double/twin; 2 en suite TERMS €30 pps; child reduction

## COUNTY LAOIS

Both Laois and Offaly lie in the central part of Ireland, with the River Shannon forming their western border.

Clonmacnoise is an important name in Irish history. St Ciarán founded a monastery here in A.D. 548, which became one of Ireland's best-known religious centres. A pilgrimage is held here each September on the feast of St Ciarán.

### BORRIS-IN-OSSORY

**Ballaghmore Country House**
Borris-in-Ossory, Co. Laois
Tel: 0505 21266 Fax: 0505 23669
Email: ballaghmorehse@eircom.net
Website: www.ballaghmorecountryhse.com

This modern cream-and-green shuttered farmhouse sits way back off the road in a large landscaped garden with a pond and a small waterfall. It is part of a 30-hectare mixed farm and there is new coarse fishing lake on the property; the land runs adjacent to an 18-hole golf course. Beautifully maintained with tasteful décor, the bedrooms are reached by a split mahogany staircase, and have cast-iron beds, lace canopies, and restful pastels of peach, cream, lemon and grey. Excellent breakfasts and pre-arranged high tea or evening meals are served in the inviting dining room and there is a turf fire in the lounge, the only smoking room in the house.

The warm hospitality shown to guests and the extremely high standards found at Ballaghmore House make this an excellent choice for touring this unspoiled area. Specialist in package activity holidays: fishing, golfing, walking and cycling. American Express, Visa and Mastercard accepted. On N7 half-way between Limerick and Dublin, between Roscrea and Borris-in-Ossory.

OWNER Carole England OPEN January 2–December 21
ROOMS 6 double/twin; all en suite
TERMS €36 pps; child reduction; single supplement
MEALS dinner €12-25

### KILMINCHY

**Chez Nous**
Kilminchy, Co. Laois
Tel: 0502 21251

Chez Nous is a classic Irish vernacular design residence, situated in a quiet spot in a peaceful cul-de-sac. Guests who book in here are treated as friends and enjoy first-class accommodation. The luxuriously-appointed bedrooms are very tasteful, the sunshine suite has a half tester canopied bed, and all are tastefully decorated in soft pastels of pink sorbet, peach blossom, and lavender blue. The family suite has two double rooms and a separate single, ideal for families or friends travelling together. Just about everywhere you look is decorated with bows, ribbons and pretty curtains.

Breakfasts are a banquet, and include sugar-rimmed orange juice, edible flowers, potato cakes, pan-fried trout, home-baked brown bread, home-made preserves and marmalade, or for those who prefer, a traditional Irish breakfast. There is a conservatory with a blue and yellow décor, where guests may help themselves to tea and coffee, and cosy log fires in the sitting room. Evening meals are served, if arranged in advance, but there are options for eating out at several venues close by. The house was featured in Select, a yearly magazine which features houses and furnishings of special interest. Not suitable for children under 10.

OWNER Audrey & Tony Canavan OPEN All year
ROOMS 2 double, 2 twin, 2 family; all en suite
TERMS €23.50–25.50; child reduction; single supplement €6.50
MEALS dinner

## RATHDOWNEY

### Castletown House
Donaghmore, Rathdowney, Co. Laois
Tel: 0505 46415 Fax: 0505 46415
Email: castletown@eircom.net
Website: www.castletownguesthouse.com

Castletown House has been awarded for the third time the prestigious Agri-Tourism Provincial Award. This warm and welcoming nineteenth-century farmhouse stands in scenic countryside surrounding an 80-hectare beef and sheep farm, on which the ruins of a Norman castle remain. The house is approached via a private drive through open fields full of grazing sheep.

The house is spotlessly clean, with a comfortable and relaxed atmosphere. Improvements are ongoing; the hallway, kitchen and dining rooms have newly tiled floors, and TV and hair-dryer are available in all bedrooms.

Castletown House

This must be one of the best value accommodations in Ireland; the bedrooms are all a good size, and there are several pieces of antique furniture. Fresh farmhouse breakfasts and pre-arranged light evening meals are served in the dining room, which has a marble fireplace; there is also a sitting room with TV and information on what to see and do in the area. Smoking is only permitted in the lounge. Guests enjoy gathering in the family kitchen for a cup of tea and a chat with the friendly owners. A conservatory games room is available to guests and there is an open farm on the property with star billing going to the three donkeys Mollie, Donna and Wilkie.

The nearby Donaghmore Famine Museum is undergoing restoration, and is well-worth a visit. Donaghmore provided the setting for the film *All Things Bright and Beautiful*, starring Gabriel Byrne. A new Designer outlet has opened in Rathdowney ( only 5 miles drive from Castletown House) and a new Golf Driving Range and Pitch and Putt Course opened in Cullaun, Knock, Roscrea. Access, Mastercard, Eurocard and J.C.B. accepted.

OWNER Moira Phelan OPEN March 1–November (other dates may be arranged) ROOMS 2 triple, 1 family, 1 single; all en suite TERMS €30 pps, €35 single; child reduction MEALS light meals

## STRADBALLY

### Tullamoy House
Stradbally, Co. Laois
Tel: 059 8627111 Fax: 059 8627111
This impressive stone-built house, part of a working sheep and cattle farm, stands in tranquil surroundings, 5km from Stradbally. Families are welcome, baby-sitting can be provided, and there is cot and high chair available. The rooms are quite large and are furnished in keeping with the character of the house.

Breakfast and home-cooked dinners are available, by prior arrangement; children's meals can also be provided. Special diets can be catered for if pre-arranged. The ambience is friendly, your hosts, very helpful and they are happy to give advice on activities in the area.

This is a good location from which to visit this scenic region, and there is fishing, horse riding, a forest park, pitch and putt course, golf and the Curragh race course close by. Guests are welcome to explore the farm and make use of the pleasant garden. There is a sitting room and separate dining room. Smoking in lounge only.

Tullamoy House can be found 5km off the N80, 20 km north of Carlow.

OWNER Pat & Caroline Farrell OPEN March–October
ROOMS 4 double/family; all en suite
TERMS from €29; child reduction; single supplement €6.50
MEALS dinner

## COUNTY LEITRIM

Leitrim is a county of charming beauty, with distinctive hill formations and lovely lakes. This long, narrow county is divided in two by
Lough Allen, one of the many lakes of the River Shannon. The county
is a very popular place for anglers, and the main topic of conversation everywhere seems to be fishing.

Dromahair is a pretty village, located about 12 km from
Manorhamilton. The road from here is superbly scenic, with views of
Lough Gill and beautiful wooded countryside.

Fenagh, which is located in the hills, has the ruins of a Gothic
church, all that remains of the monastery which St Columba founded
as a school of divinity. You can fish to your heart's content in this
area, which is full of lakes, beautiful scenery and wildlife.

Carrick-on-Shannon is the centre of river cruising on the Shannon.
There is a large marina, several cruising companies, and lots of
restaurants and pubs, which during the season have traditional Irish
music.

### BALLINAMORE

### Glenview
Aughoo, Ballinamore, Co. Leitrim
Tel: 071 9644157 Fax: 071 9644814

Glenview is a most attractive farmhouse on the new Shannon–Erne
link, 500m from lock 4, beside the Woodford River. This is a delightful rural setting; there are extensive gardens, and there is a small
museum on the premises. A games room and pool table are available
for guests' use. The house is efficiently run and guests are always
made to feel part of the family. The residence has undergone extensive renovations and there is now a fully licensed restaurant offering
the meal of the house and a table d'hôte menu. The lounge has a
marble fireplace where log fires burn on cool days, and an antique
chaise longue. There are many lakes close by and guests are advised
on the best places to fish. A tackle shed, cold room and bait service
are provided. Teresa Kennedy has been very successful with her bed
& breakfast business for the past 14 years, and is the proud recipient
of the BHS Agri-Tourism Award. Three self-catering bungalows are
available, two of which have full wheelchair facilities. There is plenty
to keep the visitors busy, including barge cruises, walking, golfing,
horseback riding, canoeing, a Genealogy Centre and traditional Irish
music in the local pubs. Access, Visa and Mastercard accepted.

OWNER Teresa Kennedy OPEN March 1–October 31
ROOMS 5 twin, 1 family; 5 en suite
TERMS from €30 pps; child reduction; single supplement
MEALS dinner

## Riversdale Farm Guesthouse

Ballinamore, Co. Leitrim
Tel: 071 9644122 Fax: 071 9644813

This large, spacious country residence surrounded by an 32-hectare farm overlooks the new Shannon-Erne waterway, which borders the farm for 1km and is adjacent to Aughoo lock. All of the rooms have views and are furnished to a high standard. There are two lounges, one with TV, and both have open fires. Breakfast and excellent dinners are served in the conservatory dining room, which is furnished with chestnut and beech furniture made by a local craftsman. This is a wonderful spot for an all-purpose holiday—in the courtyard of the farm there is a small leisure complex which consists of a heated pool, sauna, and squash court. The cut-stone hay barn has been converted to a large games room, which could also be used for small seminars. The Ballinamore-Ballyconnell canal, which is based at Riversdale Farmhouse, also offers barging holidays; the barges are a modification of the traditional narrowboat, but are wider and offer more living space and comfort. Full details are available from Riversdale Farm, which is run by a member of the Thomas family. Cooking is done by the Ballymaloe-trained family and there is a wine licence.

There is a 9-hole golf course at Ballinamore and five minutes away is Drumcoura City Western Riding Centre. Special breaks are available. Access, Mastercard and Visa accepted.

OWNER Raymond Thomas OPEN All year
ROOMS 10 double/twin/ family; all en suite
TERMS €28; child reduction 25%; single supplement €9
MEALS dinner

## The Old Rectory

Fenagh, Glebe, Ballinamore, Co. Leitrim
Tel: 071 9644089
Email: theoldrectoryleitrim@eircom.net
Website: www.theoldrectoryireland.com

The Old Rectory dates from the nineteenth century, and stands in 50 acres of private woodland, overlooking Fenagh Lake. The perfect place for folks wanting to get away from the hustle and bustle of city life, it is furnished with antique pieces. The rooms are well-maintained and comfortable. All bedrooms are en suite, with TV and tea makers.

Dinners are available, using local produce, meats, and home-made desserts. Pre-booking, is essential, and vegetarians are catered for with advance notice. Situated next to Fenagh's historic Abbey. Guests can enjoy walks through the woodland and there is plenty of wildlife to be seen.

This is good value, non-smoking accommodation. Golf, fishing and horse riding are all close by. Visa and Mastercard accepted.

OWNER Mrs Julie Curran OPEN January 10–December 1
ROOMS 4 single/twin/family; all en suite
TERMS €34 pps; child reduction; single supplement

## CARRICK-ON-SHANNON

### Ard na Greine
St Mary's Close, Carrick-on-Shannon, Co. Leitrim
Tel: 071 9620311

Ard na Greine is an ideal property for people looking for an angling holiday–this well-maintained house is situated in a quiet cul de sac, yet is within walking distance of the River Shannon and a choice of 41 fishing lakes. Helen Dee is a most welcoming lady who runs her B&B in a friendly but efficient manner and serves a hearty breakfast. Evening meals are not served, but there are several establishments within walking distance. The rooms are spotlessly clean in this comfortable modern house, and the guest lounge has a video and TV. Guests are welcome to return at any time during the day and Helen is happy to help with things to see and do in the area–there is a heated swimming pool, sports complex tennis courts, and a 9-hole golf course, and for folks interested in a little night life there are several local bars and hotels that provide music. Visa accepted.

OWNER Helen Dee OPEN All year
ROOMS 4 double, 4 twin, 2 family; 2 en suite, 3 shower only
TERMS €36 pps; child reduction; single supplement

### Caldra House
Carrick-on-Shannon, Co. Leitrim
Tel: 071 9623040 Fax: 071 9623040
Email: info@caldrahouse.ie

This family-run, beautifully restored Georgian house offers the highest standards of hospitality and good home-cooked food. It stands in a secluded spot in 30 hectares of farmland overlooking the Shannon Waterways and is an ideal location for visiting local beauty spots. Guests are made to feel immediately welcome; tea or coffee is offered upon arrival. In addition to the lounges, there is a conservatory, which is a delightful spot in which to relax on pleasant days, and both the dining room and lounges have fires on chilly days. Smoking in designated areas.

There are boats and a bait and tackle room for guests' use. There are 41 coarse fishing lakes within an 8 km radius. Traditional music can be enjoyed in local pubs. Most major credit cards accepted. Pass the Shannon Valley Hotel and take the first left; the lodge is signposted from there.

OWNER Anabella Jackson OPEN All year
ROOMS 3 double, 1 twin, 1 family; all en suite
TERMS €26.50; child reduction; single supplement €4

## Corbally Lodge
Dublin Road, Carrick-on-Shannon, Co. Leitrim
Tel: 071 9620228 Fax: 071 9620228

Corbally Lodge is a country-style house furnished with antiques, set in an attractive garden in a peaceful spot. The bedrooms are well-maintained and are spotlessly clean and comfortable; two are on the ground floor. The comfy lounge has turf fires and a TV.

Mrs Rowley is a friendly, hospitable lady who takes excellent care of her guests. Smoking is allowed in the sitting room. Tasty breakfasts and pre-arranged home-cooked dinners are served in the bright dining room, featuring fresh vegetables, home-baked bread and excellent desserts.

The River Shannon is close by and there are numerous lakes in the area. Golf, swimming and local boat hire are also available. Visa, Mastercard accepted. Sign-posted at Carrick-on-Shannon.

OWNER Valerie & P. J. Rowley OPEN March–October
ROOMS 2 double, 3 twin; 3 en suite
TERMS €24; child reduction 25%; single supplement €6.50
MEALS dinner

## KESHCARRIGAN

## Primrose House
Letterfine, Keshcarrigan, Co. Leitrim
Tel: 071 964 2960

Set in a peaceful spot, with stunning views of Loch Scur and the Iron Mountains, this blissful country house is an ideal choice when visiting this scenic area. Andy had been fishing in the area for fifteen years, before he and Gil decided to make this their permanent home.

There is plenty of seating outside overlooking the view, tea is available on request, and you may be fortunate to sample Andy's speciality, Christmas or Chocolate Cake. Andy does most of the cooking, he prepares an excellent breakfast, with free range eggs from their chickens, with black and white pudding on offer.

Home-cooked dinners can be arranged, and vegetarians and special diets catered for with notice. Meals are served in the large family kitchen, or, on nice days, on the patio.

The cheerful bedrooms are mostly furnished with pine and have strong showers. There is a sitting room, and guests are also welcome to join Gill and Andy in their sitting room.

The owners enjoy chatting to guests, and offering advice on what to see and do in the area. There are several restaurants and pubs for food.

OWNER Andy and Gill Johnson
OPEN Open all year, including Christmas
ROOMS 2 double, I family, I twin, I single; all en suite
TERMS from €25 pps; single supplement; child reduction
MEALS dinner by arrangement

## ROOSKEY

### The Moorings
Rooskey, County Leitrim
Tel: 071 9638359
Website: www.mooringsguesthouse.com

Fishermen and lovers of the outdoors will certainly feel at home at The Moorings: it is situated just of the N4, on the banks of the River Shannon.

All the public rooms have river views. There is a spacious lounge, small sitting room, and a stylish blue dining room, leading out to the terrace. From here guests can soak up the scenery, spot the wildlife and watch the cruisers sail gently by.

Recently refurbished, with stylish bright colours, the cosy ground floor bedrooms, are named after local loughs: Bofin, Scannel, Grange and Carnadoe. Four are en suite, one has a private bathroom; all have TV and tea makers. Small boats can be hired, and a fisherman's log cabin with fridge for tackle and bait, can be ordered in advance.

Breakfasts are a banquet, home-made scones, pancakes, omelettes, potato cakes, fresh squeezed orange juice, or a traditional fry up, with fresh cafetiere coffee are available daily. Dinners can be arranged, special diets catered for with notice, and barbecues on the terrace can be arranged. For guests who prefer to eat out, there are several venues in the village for food. Edwin is a fun, helpful host, who enjoys his work. Transfers from the train station can be arranged. Credit cards taken.

OWNER Edwin and Pat McWilliams OPEN All year
ROOMS 3 double, I twin, I family; 4 en suite, one private bathroom
TERMS €40–45 pps; single supplement; child reduction

## COUNTY LONGFORD

The most central county in Ireland, Longford lies in the basin of the
Shannon. The landscape is consequently low and flat, interspersed
with small streams and lakes dotted with islands. Longford has
strong associations with writers, particularly Oliver Goldsmith,
Padraic Colum, Maria Edgeworth and Leo Casey, and is a popular
place for coarse fishing.

The town of Longford is spaciously laid out with wide streets, a
Renaissance-style court house and a nineteenth-century cathedral,
which is built of grey limestone and has impressive towers. Close to
Newtonforbes is beautiful Castleforbes, a fine seventeenth-century
castellated mansion. St Patrick is said to have founded a church at
the old village of Ardagh in a pretty wooded setting, the ruins of
which can still be seen.

### DRUMLISH

### Cumiskey's Farmhouse
Ennybegs, Drumlish, Co. Longford
Tel: 043 23320
Email: kc@iol.ie
Website: www.iol.ie/~kc

Cumiskey's farmhouse is in a rural location, surrounded by stone
walls, an excellent choice from which to explore the many places of
interest in the area. There is a slab stone entryway, arched doors,
leaded windows, and a beamed ceiling. The drawing room has a large
stone fireplace with turf fires, and a medieval-themed light. A galleried landing in the lounge is approached via a spiral staircase which
leads to the library area. Smoking is permitted only in sitting room.
A luxury suite is ideal for 'romantic getaways'; it has a king-size bed,
sitting room, corner bath and shower, dressing gowns and slippers,
telephone and fridge. All the bathrooms have power showers.

Antique furnishings include a sideboard and chaise longue in the
sitting room. Four course evening meals can be taken; vegetarian
choices are also on offer, but, must be pre-booked. Breakfast
includes buffet starters, followed by a traditional cooked breakfast.

Musical evenings take place on occasion and there is a piano available to play. Guests may enjoy a glass of wine with their meal as the
house has a wine license. There is a Regional Theatre in Longford
and a championship Pitch and Putt Course. Horse riding can be
arranged. Access, Visa and Mastercard accepted. Once in the general
area, this interesting, well-maintained house is well signposted.

OWNER Patricia Cumiskey OPEN March–October
ROOMS 6 double/twin/family; 5 en suite, 1 own bathroom
TERMS €25.50–51; child reduction; single supplement €7.50–12

## Sancian House
Dublin Road, Longford, Co. Longford
Tel: 043 46187

Sancian House has been welcoming guests for many years; they return often to enjoy the warm and informal atmosphere and high standards found here. A pot of tea and scones is offered upon arrival. The rooms are spotlessly clean and simply furnished. The house sits back off the main road, the front garden is full of roses and there are colourful window boxes.

Anna McKeon is a friendly, outgoing lady who is very knowledgeable regarding family heritage, and is willing to assist guests who are interested in tracing their family history. An 18-hole golf course is located across the street, and it is a five-minute drive to the lovely village of Ardagh.

OWNER Anna McKeon OPEN All year
ROOMS 2 double, 1 twin, 2 single; 3 en suite
TERMS €23; child reduction;
single supplement €6.50 (double room)

## Eden House
Newtownforbes, Co. Longford
Tel: 043 41160

This large Tudor-style red brick house is easily located when reaching Newtownforbes, Although in the village, it is set back off the road double glazing keeping traffic noise to a minimum. The owners built the house for their retirement, but soon decided to open for business and offer rooms for travellers. En suite facilities were added, and the ground floor room has an adjacent bathroom.

The rooms are well-appointed and have coordinated fabrics. Soft colours predominate, and there is a blue, green, and yellow room, known as the sunshine room. The lounge has a real fire, lit at the first sign of a chill, and the very welcoming hosts offer scones and tea on arrival. Smoking in sitting room only.

Breakfasts are excellent, pancakes, French toast, as well as traditional cooked fare, are on offer, This is a very comfortable home, guests feel immediately at ease. Bike storage is available. There are plenty of venues for evening meals in the village.

OWNER Eileen Prunty OPEN All year except for Christmas
ROOMS 5 double/twin/family; all en suite TERMS €26.50;
child reduction; single supplement €7.50

## COUNTY MONAGHAN

Monaghan is a sportsman's paradise, with many lakes and small roads winding round the hills and through Monaghan's pastoral landscape. It is an unspoilt area, rich in farming land, and ideal country for outdoor activities and exploring.

Among the prettiest lakes are Lake Muckno, Glaslough Lake, Lough Emy and the Dartry Lakes. Monaghan is a market town, and is home to an award-winning museum which houses the Clogher Cross, a fine example of early Christian metalwork.

In July, Monaghan hosts the Fiddler of Oriel Festival of Irish dance and music.

### CARRICKMACROSS

**Shanmullagh House**
Killanny Road, off Dundalk Road, Carrickmacross, Co. Monaghan
Tel: 042 966 3038 Fax: 042 966 1915
Email: flanagan@esatclear.ie

Shanmullagh House is an attractive, modern, red brick house in a rural setting with countryside views. With nothing in sight but green fields and mature trees, it is a peaceful and tranquil "away from it all" spot. The property is adjacent to the well-known Nurenmore Hotel and Country Club with its excellent golf course. The house is tastefully decorated throughout and has pine floors, immaculately kept bedrooms and power showers.

Mr Flanagan runs a gift shop in town and Margaret Flanagan takes care of the bed & breakfast–and her three delightful young daughters. Excellent breakfasts are served in the dining room which overlooks the view, allowing a peaceful start to the day. Smoking in lounge only. The owners are a congenial and friendly couple who obviously enjoy what they do, and guests are well taken care of here. Visa accepted.

OWNER Margaret Flanagan OPEN All year
ROOMS 2 double, 2 twin, 2 family; 5 en suite
TERMS €30 pps; twin/ double €60 single €40;
child reduction; single supplement

### CASTLEBLANEY

**Rockville**
Dundalk Road, Castleblaney, Co. Monaghan
Tel: 042 9746161 Fax: 042 9740266
Email: rockvillehouse@hotmail.com
Website: www.dirl.com/monaghan/rockville-house.htm

Rockville is situated on the outskirts of town on the N2 Dublin–

Derry Road. It is set back off the main road, stands in its own grounds, and double glazing keeps traffic noise to minimum.

Joan Loughman is a welcoming lady, the ambience is friendly and informal. Tea is offered on arrival, and nothing is too much trouble to ensure guests have everything they need. There is a separate dining room, with an attractive wood ceiling, and a spacious lounge, which has a real fire when chilly. Smoking is permitted in the lounge only. The rooms are furnished, with a mixture of modern and traditional, and colour coordinated with dainty wallpapers; all rooms have TV.

Lough Muckno Park, with fishing, golfing, horse riding, tennis and water-skiing is within walking distance. There are also several venues for evening meals in town. There is seating in the pretty garden for guests' use.

OWNER Joan Loughman OPEN All year except for Christmas
ROOMS 2 double, 2 twin; 3 en suite
TERMS double/twin €30pps, family €80, single €35; single supplement

## NEWBLISS

### Glynch House
Newbliss, Co. Monaghan
Tel: 047 54045 Fax: 047 54321
Email: mirth@eircom.net

Glynch House is an impressive Georgian residence set in beautiful countryside, part of an 80-hectare farm where they raise calves and a beef suckling herd. The house has spacious rooms, furnished in keeping with its character, and there is an original marble fireplace in the lounge, where peat fires burn on chilly days. Smoking is only allowed in the study. The original casement shutters are still in working order.

Most of the bedrooms overlook peaceful countryside and a fairy fort. John O'Grady can easily be persuaded to tell guests stories about the fairies. An additional bonus of staying at Glynch Farm are the owners themselves–a down-to-earth, friendly and hospitable couple who have created a wonderful, informal atmosphere, and have a great sense of humour. John obviously enjoys chatting with guests and sharing his knowledge of the area.

The house was originally built for a member of the Hugonuck family. Newbliss is an artist's colony; Richard Morris, a well-known architect, left his home for use by artists and musicians. More details on this interesting aspect can be obtained from John O'Grady.

Excellent, freshly-prepared breakfasts are served family-style, with special diets catered for by arrangement. There are several eating establishments close by for evening meals. Credit cards accepted. Take R183 Clones Road–Glynch House is on the left-hand side when the overhead bridge comes into view. The bridge is 4 miles from Clones.

OWNER John & Martha O'Grady
OPEN February 1–September 30 (other dates by arrangement)
ROOMS 1 double, 2 twin, 1 family, 1 single; 3 en suite
TERMS €50 pps; child reduction

## COUNTY OFFALY

Offaly lies in the central part of Ireland, with the River Shannon forming their western border. There is an attractive castle at Clononey, and Anthony Trollope first started writing novels whilst living at Banager, a pretty little village on the canal. At Birr, the gardens of the castle are open to the public.

### BIRR

**Minnocks' Farmhouse**
Roscrea Road, Birr, Co. Offaly
Tel: 0509 20591 Fax: 0509 21694
Email: Minnocksfarmhouse@eircom.net

This Georgian-style house with colonnades, Georgian doors, windows, ceiling rose and cornices was cleverly converted from a farmhouse in 1991. It is part of a 40-hectare working dairy farm. There are two ground floor bedrooms, which have firm beds and are individually decorated with matching fabrics and curtains. All rooms include telephone. Breakfasts include freshly-made scones, potato bread, eggs, bacon, cream and milk from the farm; special diets catered for at breakfast by arrangement. There are some good value restaurants close by, which Veronica will be happy to give you information on. Smoking is allowed in the lounge, if other guests do not object.

Veronica Minnock is a gracious host and has been awarded the Golden Thoughts Tourist Award, an accolade for 'service above and beyond the call of duty'. A cup of tea is offered upon arrival–in fact, at Minnocks' farm, the kettle is rarely off the boil! Visa accepted. The farm is close to the new Telescope and Science Centre. Directions from Birr town: N62 heading south, situated on left side of the road, 3km from Birr.

OWNER Veronica Minnock OPEN All year
ROOMS 1 double, 2 twin, 2 family, 1 single/double; all en suite
TERMS €25.50; child reduction; single supplement €8.50
MEALS dinner

## The Ring Farmhouse

Birr, Co. Offaly
Tel: 0509 20976
Email: carmel@irishfarmhouseholiday.com
Website: www.irishfarmhouseholiday.com

This family-run dairy farm stands on the site of Loretto Castle in peaceful countryside. From an aerial view it resembles a Tara Brooch: geologists and historians are mystified as to the origins of the perfect circle. Carmel will share information and photos of the ring.

The ground floor bedrooms are decorated with a medley of pastel shades in blues, pinks and green. Rooms have multi-channel TV. Breakfast is served in the sunny conservatory which overlooks open countryside, and there is a sitting room.

The area has monastic sites, gardens, scenic walks, golf and fishing. Birr, designated a Heritage Town and home to several public houses, is within 2 km. The Thatch, an award-winning pub, is in walking distance.

OWNER Carmel Carroll OPEN All year except for Christmas
ROOMS 4 double/twin/family; 3 en suite
TERMS €30 pps; single supplement; child reduction

## FERBANE

## Wynne's B & B

Dealbhna, Eathra, Gallen, Ferbane, Co. Offaly
Tel: 090 64 54044 Fax: 090 64 54044
Email: jcwynne@eircom.net

The hosts are welcoming and very helpful at this immaculately kept red brick two-storey house. Marie enjoys her bed and breakfast, which she has run for five years. The rooms in light pastel colours have quality furniture, high beds and comfortable mattresses, and all have TV, tea makers and en suite facilities. The family accommodation is very large, and comprises two rooms, one with two single beds and a cot.

Marie cooks an excellent breakfast, well-presented in the dining room, and there is a TV lounge. The photo on the landing was taken when Offaly won the 1971 All Ireland Championship football award. John and Marie can be spotted in the photograph. Wynne House is delightful in every way, with charming hosts and first class accommodation.

OWNER Joe and Marie Wynne OPEN All year
ROOMS 5 twin/double/family; all en suite
TERMS €25 pps; single supplement; child reduction

**Rahan Lodge**
Killina, Rahan, Tullamore, Co. Offaly
Tel: 0506 55796 Fax: 0506 55606
Email: bnb@rahanlodge.com
Website: www.rahanlodge.com

This lovely old Georgian house stands in 20 acres of land in the countryside away from the noise of traffic. There are no petty rules or areas declared off-limits—guests arrive as strangers and leave as friends. The house has original wood floors, and several items of interest including old desks with inkwells, an original portico and fanlight.

There are no en suite bathrooms, but there are three bathrooms exclusively for guest use. The drawing room has the only TV. There is a piano, which guests are welcome to play, and contribute to musical evenings.

Carole McDermott is a very happy lady, who enjoys cooking: pre-arranged meals are offered, with vegetarian and special diets catered for with notice. Fresh garden produce is used when available, and breakfast includes free-range eggs from Carole's chickens. Ponies live in the field along with Princess the donkey. If you are tired of hearing an alarm clock, this friendly retreat wakes you with bird song.

OWNER Carole McDermott OPEN All year
ROOMS 5 double/twin/family TERMS from €25 pp

**Ballinamore Farm**
Tullamore, Co. Offaly
Tel: 0506 51162

This attractive two-storey farmhouse is part of a 160 acre working arable and cattle farm. Guests are welcome to explore the farm, and spend time in the well-tended mature garden. The rooms all have TV, and are individually colour-coordinated with bright colours of coral and blue. The cosy lounge has a real fire which is lit when chilly.

Of special interest are the pieces of petrified wood from the bog. The sun porch to the front of the house overlooks the garden, and is a pleasant spot in which to relax and read. Agnes Mealiffe is a super host, the house is spotlessly clean and comfortable, and Milly the dog is a friendly source of guest entertainment.

The house is ¹/₂ mile north of Tullamore, signposted on main road. There is plenty of choice for evening meals, with 23 restaurants in the town.

OWNER Larry and Agnes Mealiffe OPEN March–October

ROOMS 3 double, I twin, I family; 4 en suite, I with own bathroom
TERMS €30 pps; single supplement; child reduction

**Loughmore Lodge**
Clonminch Road, Tullamore, Offaly
Tel: 0506 20808

This white double-fronted Victorian house stands in its own grounds
behind a black wrought-iron gate, adjacent to the Court Hotel. The
rooms are colourful, with old-fashioned furniture, new beds and
power or electric showers. A tasty breakfast is served—guests can
have just about whatever they want. Famous architect Fergal
McCabe once lived here. Tullamore town is within walking distance.

OWNER Mary Doheny OPEN All year except for Christmas
ROOMS I treble, 2 double, 2 twin; 3 en suite
TERMS €38 pps; single supplement; child reduction

## COUNTY ROSCOMMON

County Roscommon is an island county 60 km in length. Two-thirds
of the county is surrounded by water. In the north are the largest
lakes: Lough Key, Lough Gara and Lough Boderg. The great Lough
Ree is in the east. The limestone foundation of the county and the
numerous lakes make it a fisherman's paradise. Large areas of arable
land are to be found in the centre of the county, and the principal
occupation is raising cattle and sheep.

Roscommon is a county of abbeys and castles. You can visit
Clonalis House, Castlerea, once the home of two of Ireland's high
kings in the twelfth century; Strokestown Park House, with its
records of Famine-ridden Ireland; prehistoric Rathcroghan; St John's
Interpretative Centre; medieval Boyle and picturesque Lough Key
with its forest park. For those interested in contemporary art, the
Glebe House Gallery is situated midway between Boyle and Carrick-
on-Shannon at Crossna, Knockvicar.

### BOYLE

**Abbey House**
Boyle, County Roscommon
Tel: 071 9662385
Email: abbeyhouse@eircom.net

Abbey House is a charming spacious Victorian house, nestled
between the twelfth-century Abbey and the River Boyle. Although in
a peaceful spot, with old farm implements and beech copper trees,

and large garden, it is within walking distance of the town. The original casement shutters and marble fireplace are still in working order, and the house is furnished with antiques. Breakfast is served at a large refectory table in the dining room, which has a chaise longue.

Rich Victorian colours are very much in evidence and the bedrooms are well appointed and comfortable. This is a warm and friendly house. Christine Mitchell, has been in business for over 26 years, and takes excellent care of her guests. She is happy to assist with what to see and do in the area, and recommend venues for evening meals. For folks wanting to step back in time, Abbey House would be a good choice. Three self-catering cottages also available.

OWNER Christine Mitchell OPEN March 1–October 31
ROOMS 6 double/single/family/twin; all en suite
TERMS from €28–30 pps; single supplement; child reduction

## CARRICK-ON-SHANNON

### Avondale House
Roosky, Carrick-on-Shannon, Co. Roscommon
Tel: 071 9638095

This attractive house stands in its own grounds 500 m from the River Shannon. This friendly, family-run establishment has a relaxing, cosy atmosphere. Carmel Davis was formerly in the hotel trade but missed the personal contact with people and decided to open her own bed & breakfast establishment. Carmel and her husband were successful from the beginning and soon added on additional bedrooms. The bedrooms are clean and comfortable with orthopaedic beds. The cosy TV lounge has a turf fire, and smoking is permitted here only. Excellent home-cooked evening meals are available if ordered in advance, and there is a new hotel within walking distance which has an excellent restaurant and bar food.

Avondale is a good base for anglers; there is a tackle room with fridges and drying facilities are also available. For people who enjoy walking there is a pleasant river walk close by. Guests are well-taken care of at Avondale and are assured of personal attention from the pleasant owners. Visa and American Express accepted.

OWNER Carmel Davis OPEN All year ROOMS 2 double, 2 twin, 1 family; all en suite TERMS €31.50; child reduction; single supplement €6.50 MEALS dinner

### Glencarne House
Ardcarne, Carrick-on-Shannon, Co. Roscommon
Tel: 071 9667013

This charming Georgian house, approached up a private drive, is located in scenic countryside with lovely views overlooking green fields and grazing sheep. A very warm welcome awaits you at Glencarne House. Agnes Harrington has won several awards, including the Galtee Breakfast Award and the Agri-Tourism National Award. Special diets may be catered for if pre-arranged. The house is well-maintained and freshly-decorated. It is warm and relaxed, and the bedrooms have every comfort, including armchairs, hot water bottles and electric blankets, and some have antique brass beds. There is a peaceful, old-fashioned lounge with a marble fireplace which, along with the dining room, has a real fire on chilly days. Smoking is allowed in TV lounge only.

Agnes Harrington is an excellent cook; if pre-booked, evening meals are prepared fresh daily and desserts feature some of the best pastry in Ireland. There is a golf course within 1km and lots of outdoor activities and wildlife walks in the nearby 325-hectare Lough Key Park. Many guests have been returning to this special place over the years and early reservations are recommended.
On N4 between Boyle and Carrick on Shannon.

OWNER Agnes Harrington OPEN March 1–October 15
ROOMS 3 double, 1 twin, 1 family, 1 single; all en suite
TERMS €31.50; 25% child reduction; single supplement €6.50
MEALS dinner

## CASTLEREA

### Clonalis House
Castlerea, Co. Roscommon
Tel: 094 9620014 Fax: 094 9620014
Email: Clonalis@iol.ie
Website: http://www.hidden-ireland.com/clonalis/

Clonalis House is an impressive Victorian Italianate mansion, built on a 700-acre wooded estate. It was the home of the O'Conors of Connacht, descendants of Ireland's last High Kings and traditional Kings of Connacht. The house is furnished in keeping with its character; the bedrooms have half tester and or four poster beds, all have their own bathroom. Guests are welcome to browse through the archive and library, dating from the 16th century, and of special interest are the heirlooms, such as Carolan's Harp and the O'Conor Coronation Stone.

Dinners are served, with vegetarian and special diets, if pre-arranged, and for guests staying three or more nights there is a reduction. Clonalis House is a non-smoking establishment. The house is not suitable for children under 14. Guests are welcome to take walks on the estate, and Galway, Sligo and Mayo are within an hour's drive. Visa, Mastercard, Access accepted. On the west side of Castlerea on the N60.

OWNER Pyers and Marguerite O'Conor-Nash
OPEN April 15–September 30 ROOMS 3 double, 1 twin; all en suite
TERMS €73.50; single supplement €12.50 MEALS dinner

## STROKESTOWN

**Church View House**
Strokestown, Co. Roscommon
Tel: 071 9633047 Fax: 071 9633047

This spacious, 200-year-old, rambling country house stands in a scenic location. It has been in the Cox family for four generations and is
part of a 100-hectare working farm. The original structure of a
Famine fever hospital is found on the grounds. The house continues
to be well-maintained, and the good-sized bedrooms are simply furnished. One lounge has the original marble fireplace. Evening meals
including tasty home-made dishes and desserts, are available, but
must be ordered in advance.

Church View House is not licensed, but guests may bring their own
wine. Strokestown Park House, the Famine Museum and gardens are
6 km away. On N4 west from Dublin to Rooskey turn left onto 371
to Strokestown: Church View House is signposted on this road.

OWNER Harriet Cox OPEN June–September
ROOMS 2 double,2 twin, 2 family; 3 en suite
TERMS €35 pps; child reduction; single supplement

## COUNTY TIPPERARY

Located in the centre of the southern part of Ireland, and famous
for the song *It's a Long Way to Tipperary*, it is a beautiful county of
rich farmland. From the top of Slievenamon there is a splendid view.
To the north you can see the Rock of Cashel, a steep outcrop of
limestone topped by impressive ruins–a truly spectacular sight, particularly during the summer when it is floodlit at night. .From early
times the rock was a fortress and seat of chieftains, and later it
became an important religious site. Today you can see the vast ruins
of the gothic cathedral, which dates from the thirteenth century; the
tower of the Castle; the cross of St Patrick, the massive base of
which is said to be the coronation stone of the Munster kings; and
Cormac's Chapel, which dates back to 1130. Cashel Palace Hotel is a
fine Queen Anne-style house, a former Church of Ireland bishops'
residence.

A fine collection of sixteenth- and seventeenth-century books can
be found in the Diocesan Library in the precincts of St John the
Baptist Cathedral. There's a good craft shop where you can buy

Shanagarry tweed. Situated between Thurles and Cashel, Holy Cross Abbey was built in 1110, to house a part of the True Cross, and later became a popular place of pilgrimage.

Cahir, a most pleasant town on the River Suir, has a beautifully restored fifteenth-century castle on an island in the river, and now houses the tourist office. The mountains between Nenagh and Toomvara were the home of Ned of the Hill, the local Robin Hood. Nearby is Nenagh Round, all that remains of a castle built in 1200. Kilcooly Abbey, the Abbey of the Holy Cross and the attractive old church at Fethard are all worth seeing. Ahenny has two elaborately carved eighth-century stone crosses, and Carrick-on-Suir has a fine example of a Tudor mansion, which can be visited by request.

## BANSHA

### Bansha House
Bansha, Co. Tipperary
Tel: 062 54194 Fax: 062 54215
Email: banshahouse@eircom.net
Website: www.tipp.ie/bansha.htm

This impressive Georgian residence is approached by an avenue of beech trees, set in 40 hectares of land. Furnished in keeping with its character, there are several pieces of antique furniture. The bedrooms are large, and two are on the ground floor. The charming lounge has a log fire and leads out onto the gardens. A relaxed and comfortable atmosphere pervades this non-smoking house, and guests can often be found in the kitchen with Mary, chatting about the area's attractions. Cooking is of a very high standard, with home-made breads, tarts and pies. The house holds a wine license.

John and Mary breed racehorses, and their stables-registered Equestrian Centre offers horseback riding, and the farm has an all-weather 1km track. Glorious scenic tours can be taken from here. This is superb place for guests wanting some peace and tranquillity. A self-catering cottage is also available.

Bansha House

Mastercard, Visa, accepted. 1km off main Limerick–Waterford Road. N24 at Bansha. 5 miles to Tipperary town.

OWNER John & Mary Marnane OPEN January 1–December 20
ROOMS 4 double, 3 twin, 1 single; 5 en suite
TERMS €40–45 pps; child reduction; single supplement

## Lismacue House
Bansha, Co. Tipperary
Tel: 062 54106 Fax: 062 54126
Email: lismac@indigo.ie Website: www.lismacue.com

Lismacue House has been in Kate Nicholson's family since it was built in 1813. It is a classic, beautifully proportioned Irish country house, set in its own extensive grounds at the foot of the magnificent Galtee Mountains. The house has one of the most impressive lime-tree avenues in Ireland. The spacious drawing room and library have their original wallpaper. Breakfasts and dinners are served in the imposing dining room; special diets can be catered for if pre-arranged. Traditional log fires burn in the warm and welcoming reception rooms. Special interest holidays are available, such as pony trekking for adults and children and, from November to February, hosted hunting holidays. There is also trout fishing on the estate's own river (tuition available). There are three golf courses and tennis courts close by and the Rock of Cashel and Cahir Castle are just a short drive away. French is spoken here. Visa, Mastercard, American Express accepted. Take N24 from Tipperary through Bansha towards Cahir, entrance just outside Bansha on the left.

OWNER Kate Nicholson OPEN March 17–October 31
ROOMS 2 double, 1 twin, 2 family; 3 en suite
TERMS €57–70; child reduction; single supplement €14
MEALS dinner €33 (except Sunday)

## BORRISOKANE

## Dancer Cottage
Carraghmore, Borrisokane, Co. Tipperary
Tel: 067 27414 Fax: 067 27414
Email: dcr@eircom.net
Website: www.dancercottage.cjb.net

This handsome Tudor-style house stands in its own grounds, within a mile or so of Borrisokane. This is a peaceful location, and the award winning gardens are available to guests. The good sized, en suite rooms have old-fashioned furniture and comfortable beds. The ambience is friendly and informal, and there is plenty to keep visitors busy in the area. Clonmacnoise, an ancient monastic site, is close by, as are museums of old distilleries, the Slieve Bloom Mountains, and within a few minutes is Lough Derg, a lake extending to 30km, where the River Shannon runs through. Excellent breakfasts are served, you can skip lunch, and for guests who like to return after a busy day, dinners can be arranged. Special diets are catered for, and home baking is a speciality of the house. Carmen and Wolfgang are attentive hosts, and are happy to recommend places to eat, and advice on the best place for a glass of Guinness. Dancer Cottage would be a good choice from which to explore the many places of interest in the area. Credit cards accepted.

OWNER Carmen and Wolfgang Rodder OPEN March–October
ROOMS 3 double, 1 treble
TERMS €30-40pps; single supplement; child reduction

## CAHIR

### Ashling
Cashel Road, Cahir, Co. Tipperary
Tel: 052 41601

This pink-washed low building is 2 km outside Cahir, and has lovely views from the front of the house. Breda Fitzgerald is a very friendly, chatty lady who keeps an immaculately clean and tidy house. The rooms are on the small side, but are comfortably furnished. There is a large sitting room off the dining room. Non-smoking house.

OWNER Breda Fitzgerald OPEN All year
ROOMS 2 double, 2 twin; 3 en suite
TERMS €35 pps; child reduction; single supplement €12.50

## CASHEL

### Rockville House
Cashel, County Tipperary
Tel: 062 61760

Rockville House stands in a well-tended garden, within walking distance of Cashel Rock. An informal, comfortable residence, maintained to a high standard by Patrick Hayes and his mother, Anna Hayes. The dining room/sitting room combination has a marble fireplace and a handsome sideboard. The bedrooms have bright blue and white prints, traditional, old-fashioned furniture and comfortable beds. Guests are welcome to make use of the gardens. Cashel Rock can be seen from the house. Secure parking is available.

OWNER Patrick Hayes OPEN All year
ROOMS 6 family/double/ twin; all en suite
TERMS €27 pps; single supplement; child reduction

**Woodruffe House**
Cahir Road, Clonmel, Co. Tipperary
Tel: 052 35243

This spacious and elegant house, set on 110 hectares of mixed farming, is surrounded by a lovely garden full of mature trees and flowers. There are walks through the farm, and Cahir, Cashel and Clonmel are within driving distance. This is a warm and inviting house, and even though it was only built in 1977, it has the ambience of a bygone era. The four spacious bedrooms are beautifully decorated with matching Sanderson wallpapers and fabrics. The house is not suitable for children under five. High tea available.

Guests enjoy the log fires on chilly evenings. Anne O'Donnell is a gracious host who offers complementary refreshments on arrival. Evening meals are available, if pre-arranged. Anne is an excellent cook; a favourite dish with guests is her baked fish with its delicious sauce, and her mouth-watering desserts, such as pavlova with fresh fruit, are equally popular.

OWNER Anne O'Donnell OPEN April 4–September 30
ROOMS 3 double, 1 twin; 2 en suite
TERMS €19–21.50; child reduction; single supplement €6.50
MEALS dinner

**Killaghy Castle**
Mullinahone, Co. Tipperary
Tel: 052 53112 Fax: 052 53561
Email: c.killaghycastle@eircom.net

This Norman castle, whose original owners were Cromwellian Planters, has been added on to and extended over the years. Originally it was just a Motte and Bailey, still visible to the left of the castle. During Tudor times a long house was built on to the rear of the property, and in 1800 two other buildings were added, making Killaghy the castle we see today. It is part of a 96-hectare dairy and tillage farm. The present owners, the Collins family, moved here in 1995 from Cork.

Moira Collins is a down-to-earth and friendly lady, who has created an informal, welcoming atmosphere, adding her personal touch by redecorating and installing new curtains and orthopaedic beds. The house is full of antiques purchased specifically for the house to enhance the old-world ambience. This well-maintained property is non-smoking. The bedrooms are enormous and some have original fireplaces, as do the dining room and the drawing room; the latter is a wonderful spot to relax in and help yourself to tea or coffee.

The drawing room has interesting coving and a terracotta border. The house has glorious views all round. There is a nature trail and walled garden, as well as games and two tennis courts for guests' use. Visa and Mastercard accepted.

OWNER Moira Collins OPEN All year
ROOMS 2 double, 1 twin, 1 double/single; 3 en suite
TERMS €31.50–44.50; child reduction; single supplement €12.50
MEALS dinner €25.50–44.50

## NENAGH

### Otway Lodge Guest House
Dromineer, Nenagh, Co. Tipperary
Tel: 067 24133 / 24273

Otway Lodge is in a lovely position overlooking Lough Derg. Parts of the house, which was formerly part of a barracks, are over 100 years old. It has been extended and tastefully modernised since that time. The modestly-furnished bedrooms are a good size, as are the bathrooms. There is a spacious guest lounge with a peat fire, TV, harp and piano. Frank and Ann work as a team and enjoy their business, and always have a pot of tea on the hob. There is a small shop on the premises offering sweets, lemonade and other snacks. This is an ideal spot for families and water sports enthusiasts as there is wind-surfing, sailing, water-skiing and trout and coarse fishing available. Boats for hire.

OWNER Ann & Frank Flannery OPEN All year
ROOMS 2 double, 4 twin; all en suite
TERMS €23; child reduction; single supplement €7.50

## TIPPERARY

### Clonmore House
Galbally Road, Tipperary, Co. Tipperary
Tel: 062 51637
Email: clonmorehouse@eircom.net

Guests continue to enjoy this immaculate, detached house set back from the main road on the edge of town. The bedrooms are tastefully decorated and colour-coordinated with modern fitted wardrobes.

Breakfasts only are served in the attractive dining room with its pretty lace tablecloths. The spacious lounge overlooks the garden which guests can enjoy. A fire is lit in the lounge on chilly days, and guests may enjoy a hot drink in the evening; a pleasant spot to unwind after a busy day of sightseeing. On fine days the sun lounge is a popular place to sit; it is also the only smoking area in the house.

Mary Quinn is a delightful hostess who prides herself on personal service. She is pleased to advise on good local restaurants. The town centre is a five-minute walk.

OWNER Mrs Mary Quinn OPEN March–November
ROOMS 2 double, 3 twin, 1 family; all en suite
TERMS €30; child reduction; single supplement

**Woodlawn**
Galbally Road, Tipperary, Co. Tipperary
Tel: 062 51272
Email: Woodlawn_tipp@hotmail.com

This traditional-style house, with an English russet brick exterior, stands a good distance off the road in a quiet spot behind a large, landscaped garden. It was built as a family home 12 years ago, and when the two sons left home, the owners used the excess space for a bed & breakfast. It is beautifully maintained, has a tranquil ambience and the rooms to the rear of the house overlook horses grazing in the fields. The bedrooms are individually decorated with restful pastel colours and have plenty of wardrobe space.

Nuala O'Sullivan is extremely hospitable, and goes out of her way to ensure her guests are well-taken care of. Smoking allowed in lounge only. Excellent breakfasts are served and include a wide cereal choice and fresh fruit, followed by a traditional Irish breakfast. One and a half miles from Tipperary on the B662 Galbally Road.

OWNER Nuala O'Sullivan OPEN April–October
ROOMS 2 double, 1 twin, 1 double/single; all en suite
TERMS €25; child reduction; single supplement €6.50

## COUNTY WESTMEATH

Centrally located, this county offers a peaceful and beautiful land-scape, excellent fishing and lots of history.

Lakes are the main attractions. The four largest are Loughs Owel, Ennell, Derravaragh and Lene. Beautiful Lough Sheelin is farther north and there are a number of small lakes too, as well as Lough Ree, an expansion of the Shannon, which is now popular for sailing, cruising and coarse fishing. On many of the islands that dot the lakes are remains of early Christian churches.

Mullingar, the county town, is a thriving commercial centre and attractive market town. One of the best cattle-raising districts of Ireland, it is also a great centre for hunting, shooting and fishing.

Athlone is the largest town in the country. Originally a fording point of the Shannon, Athlone is now a busy market town, major road and rail terminus, and harbour on the inland waterways system. Athlone Castle, now housing a museum dealing with local history, is a strongly fortified building with many interesting features. It has been a famous military post since its original construction in the thirteenth century.

Lough Derravaragh, one of the most beautiful in County Westmeath, is associated with the most tragic of Irish legends, when the Children of Lir were changed into swans by their jealous step-mother and spent 300 years on dark waters.

Tullynally Castle is near Castlepollard. Seat of the Earls of Longford, the castle has a spectacular façade of turrets and towers. Fore is the most historic Christian site in Westmeath. There are several ruins to see, dating from the tenth century, among them St Fechin's Church, an unusual feature of which is the massive cross-inscribed lintel stone.

## ATHLONE

### Cluain-Innis
Summerhill, Galway Road, Athlone, Co. Westmeath
Tel: 090 6494202

Cluain-Innis is a friendly, cosy bungalow situated 4 km from Athlone. The bedrooms are fresh and bright, prettily decorated and are all on the ground floor. Improvements are ongoing and TV and hair-dryers have been added to the rooms. Kathleen is friendly and helpful, she enjoys having people stay, "a real home from home experience". The lounge is tastefully decorated with matching pink and red fabrics, attractive lights and wall lamps, and tea and coffee makers. Smoking is permitted in the lounge. Breakfast only is served but there is a good choice of restaurants and pubs in Athlone for evening meals. This is an ideal location for touring Clonmacnoise and Deer Park. Fishing and golf are close by. Visa card accepted. Situated in a cul de sac on the N6 Galway Road, 3 miles from Athlone town centre. Left-hand side of the road 500 yards, at the end of the dual carriageway.

OWNER Kathleen Shaw OPEN April 1–October 31
ROOMS 1 double, 1 twin, 1 family; 1 en suite
TERMS €28 pps; 50% child reduction; single supplement €4

## Shelmalier House
Cartrontroy, Retreat Road, Athlone, Co. Westmeath
Tel: 090 6472245 Fax: 090 6473190
Email: shelmalier@eircom.net
Website: www.shelmalierhouse.com

Shelmalier House is a spacious, modern house standing in its own grounds with an attractive front garden. The bedrooms, two of which are on the ground floor, are beautifully appointed, recently upgraded, and have firm, comfortable beds. This is very much a family-run establishment, with considerate hosts who extend a very personal service to ensure their guests' comfort. The TV lounge is spacious, and there is a sun porch, where guests may help themselves to complementary tea or coffee at any time. Smoking is allowed in lounge and bedrooms.

Jim and Nancy specialise in coarse fishing holidays, but a warm welcome is extended to all visitors. Evening meals are served with the emphasis on fresh food and home-baking, but they must be ordered in advance. There is an 18-hole golf course on the shores of Lough Ree, trail walks and a heated swimming pool within a 10-minute walk. This is a delightful house with most hospitable hosts. Visa, Access credit cards are accepted. Situated on Retreat Road (Cartrontroy), signposted off R446 and R55.

OWNER Jim & Nancy Denby OPEN January 10–December 20
ROOMS 3 double, 3 twin, 1 family; all en suite
TERMS family €95, twin €95, single €95

## CASTLEPOLLARD

## Whitehall Farmhouse
Castlepollard, Co. Westmeath
Tel: 044 61140

This creeper-covered, nineteenth-century farmhouse is approached up a private drive. It is set among mature trees and a garden, part of a working cattle, sheep and tillage farm. The house is furnished in keeping with its character and retains the original casement shutters. The bedrooms are warm and cosy with attractive bed linens and comfortable beds. There is a good-size TV lounge and a separate dining room where freshly-prepared breakfasts are served.

Abigail, a friendly, outgoing lady, has been running her bed & breakfast establishment for over ten years. Guests enjoy the special warmth and hospitality here and many folks are happy repeat visitors. Guests are welcome to wander around the farm and watch the animals. The ancient monastic village of Fore nearby contains an interesting seventh-century church.

Traditional Irish music can be heard at local pubs and perhaps, too, some of the folklore tales of the area.

OWNER Donagh & Abigail Smyth OPEN April 1–November 1
ROOMS 1 double, 2 twin; all en suite
TERMS €30 pps; child reduction 33%; single supplement €6.50
MEALS dinner

## MOATE

### Cooleen
Ballymore Road, Moate, Co. Westmeath
Tel: 09064 81044

This well-maintained, attractive bungalow with hanging baskets and flower tubs is situated in a country setting of 0.5 hectares. Ethna Kelly is a considerate host and guests are greeted with a hot drink upon arrival. The good-sized rooms are tastefully furnished and decorated, and have comfortable beds. Cooleen is a non-smoking house. Breakfasts are excellent and include fresh, home-baked scones, and are served in the lush conservatory on warm days. There is a lounge where turf fires burn in the evening. Bicycles are available and there are some lovely walks winding past the bog. This is perfect for folks who are looking for an informal, home-away-from-home atmosphere. The house is 2km off N6 on Ballymore Road.

OWNER Ethna Kelly OPEN January 15–December 15
ROOMS 1 double, 2 twin; all en suite
TERMS €30 pps; €35 single; child reduction; single supplement

### Temple Country House
Horseleap, Moate, Co. Westmeath
Tel: 0506 35118 Fax: 0506 35118
Website: www.templespa.ie

This lovely 200-year-old country house sits in a secluded position amidst mature trees and gardens on a 57-hectare cattle farm. It was built on the site of a sixth-century monastery—hence the name. The house has been in the same family for three generations and is full of old-world charm; there are marble washstands and fireplaces, and brass beds. Bernadette is an excellent cook; dinners are served in the large dining room and feature tasty, healthy foods, fresh vegeta-

Temple Country House

bles, local meats and delicious home-made desserts. After dinner, guests gather round the open fire in the lounge, often joined by Bernadette and Declan. A games room and a library were added in the mid-1990s.

Temple House is becoming well-known for its health and leisure facilities. Special packages are offered for individual or small groups in the 'Temple Spa', with sauna, steam room, beauty salon, yoga room, aromatherapy and reflexology. Guided walks are also organised. Fishing and golfing holidays at championship courses can also be arranged. Reservations should be made as far ahead as possible.

Temple House is a haven of peace and tranquillity, the food is excellent and Bernadette and Declan are the perfect hosts. Vegetarian and special diets can be catered for with advance notice. Visa and Mastercard accepted.

OWNER Declan & Bernadette Fagan
OPEN January 15–November 30
ROOMS 2 double, 4 twin, 1 family, 1 single; all en suite
TERMS from €60 pps; child reduction; single supplement €19
MEALS dinner

## MULLINGAR

**Glenmore House**
Dublin Road, Mullingar, Co. Westmeath
Tel: 044 48905

This elegant and informal large Georgian house stands in four acres of secluded woodlands and lawns. The family is interested in sports, and the daughter is a fine horse rider, as evidenced by the display of ribbons. The bedrooms are very spacious, one has a king-size bed, two have en suite facilities, and two share a bathroom. All bedrooms have TV. There are lots of antique furnishings, two marble fireplaces, and a ceiling rose. The lounge is a good spot in which to relax and enjoy the good supply of books. Regina Healy, an artistic lady, is available to help her guests in every way, and happy to share her knowledge of the area. Regina has a good sense of humour, and serves an excellent breakfast, on Royal Doulton china, in the elegant dining room. Glenmore House is an ideal choice for folks looking for a few days "away from it all". Golf, fishing, and horse riding are nearby.

OWNER Regina Healy OPEN January 10–December 16
ROOMS 4 double; 2 en suite, 2 standard
TERMS €30–40 pps; single supplement; child reduction

### Hilltop Country House

Delvin Road (N52 off N4), Rathconnell, Mullingar, Co. Westmeath
Tel: 044 48958 Fax: 044 48013
Email: hilltopcountryhouse@eircom.net
Website: www.hilltopcountryhouse.com

This exceptionally well-maintained, spacious, split-level house is approached by a private gravel drive. The house sits in an elevated position with views of Sheever Lough in the distance and the city at night. The house was specifically designed for bed & breakfast; the bedrooms are all large, with a high standard of décor, and have comfortable firm beds and TV. One of the bedrooms is on the ground floor and has its own entrance. New carpeting has been installed, and a conservatory has been added. Freshly-prepared breakfasts are served in the bright dining room overlooking pretty countryside. Dympna and Sean are extremely hospitable and helpful, and are happy to assist with itinerary planning. Hilltop has facilities for the angler, including a tackler with drying facilities. Boat hire can be arranged. Tea makers are available in the hallway. There are several options in the area for evening meals. Access and Visa accepted.

OWNER Sean & Dympna Casey OPEN February 1–November 30
ROOMS 2 double, 3 twin; all en suite TERMS €35 pps; child reduction; single supplement

### Keadeen

Irishtown, Mullingar, Co. Westmeath
Tel: 044 48440
Website: www.mullingarbandb.com

There is a comfortable, easy-going atmosphere at this well-maintained, extensively refurbished bungalow, situated in a peaceful location on the edge of town. To quote Madge Nolan, "I have never met a guest I didn't like," which could have something to do with her friendly and welcoming personality.

The bedrooms are spotlessly clean and are individually decorated in bright colours, with warm duvets and rich carpets. There is a TV lounge where smoking is permitted.

Breakfasts are served from 7 a.m. to 10:30 a.m. and consist of home-made marmalades, preserves and freshly-baked bread. Dinners are no longer available, but Madge Nolan will be happy to recommend local establishments for evening meals.

Local amenities include golf, swimming, fishing and boating. On the N4 from Dublin take third exit for Castlepollard, turn left, continue to mini roundabout, second exit, signposted from there.

OWNER Madge Nolan OPEN March–October
ROOMS 2 double, 1 twin, 1 family; 2 en suite
TERMS €30 pps; single €35; child reduction; single supplement

**Lough Owel Lodge**
Cullion, Mullingar, Co. Westmeath
Tel: 044 48714 Fax: 044 48771
Email: aideen.ginnell@ireland.com

Lough Owel, over five miles long, is one of Europe's best-known trout lakes. The farmhouse stands in 50 acres, which extend down to the lough shore. Ghillie service is available, as well as boat engines.

Fully refurbished and in excellent decorative order, the en suite bedrooms, which are named after local lakes, offer most comfortable accommodation. This peaceful tranquil setting is the ideal place for fisherman and tourist alike to enjoy all the area has to offer. A hard tennis court, games room, and tackle room is available. Horse riding, tennis and golf can be arranged. Wind-surfing and golf are available close by. Greyhound racing takes place twice weekly. Evening meals and packed lunches are available on request.

Mullingar, a market town, has several venues for meals, and local pubs have musical evenings. For those not coming by car, there are trains and buses to and from Dublin daily.

Guests looking for the perfect place to unwind will be well satisfied with this charming house situated in this secluded, tranquil set-

Lough Owel Lodge

ting. Credit cards accepted. N4 north from Mullingar, signposted just before the road on left.

OWNER Martin & Aideen Ginnell OPEN Open March 1—October 12
ROOMS 1 double, 1 twin, 2 four poster, 1 family suite; all en suite
TERMS from €60 per room; child reduction; single supplement

## Woodlands Farmhouse
Streamstown, Mullingar, Co. Westmeath
Tel: 044 26414

A charming 200-year-old farmhouse, surrounded by ornamental trees, part of a 50-hectare cattle farm. Mary Maxwell has created a

Woodlands Farmhouse

wonderful, informal, welcoming atmosphere–a marvellous spot for families. Guests are encouraged to explore the farm and there are free pony rides for children.

The bedrooms are spacious and there are lots of antique furnishings, including a chaise longue and a lovely dresser. Guests enjoy sitting around in the spacious lounge, which has a grand piano, and musical evenings are encouraged.

Smoking is permitted only in the lounge. Four bedrooms are on the ground floor. Breakfast and pre-arranged dinners are served in the very large dining room; when possible, meals feature fresh, home-grown produce. Vegetarians can be catered for with advance notice.

Take N4 from Dublin, onto N6 going west. At Horseleap turn right at the filling station, and watch for a 'Woodlands Farm' sign.

OWNER Mary Maxwell OPEN March 1—October 1
ROOMS 2 double, 1 twin, 2 family, 1 single; 4 en suite
TERMS family €95, double/ twin from €70, single €40;
child reduction; single supplement

## Mornington House

Multyfarnham, Co. Westmeath
Tel: 044 72191 Fax: 044 72338
Email: stay@mornington@ie Website: www.mornington.ie

Mornington House, a gracious family home, was built in 1854 and extended in 1896. It is surrounded by beautiful trees–the Mornington Oak is over 200 years old. It is within easy walking distance of Lough Derravarragh, 'Lake of the Oaks' in Gaelic legend, one of three lakes where the Children of Lir spent 300 years of their 900-year exile. The grounds are inhabited by foxes, badgers, storks among a wealth of flora and fauna. The house is furnished with much of the original furniture and many family portraits, and retains the ambience of a bygone era, lovingly combined with all modern comforts. Smoking is permitted only in the drawing room. Mornington is an oasis of peace and tranquillity, an ideal location in which to explore the Midlands and the surrounding scenic area; Dublin is within a 90-minute drive. The reception rooms have open log and turf fires.

Anne and Warwick are charming hosts; Anne is an excellent cook, and wonderful dinners are served by candlelight in the Victorian dining room, featuring fresh fruit, vegetables and herbs from the walled garden. Vegetarians can be catered for with advance notice. The bedrooms are large; two have brass beds, one a king size. All rooms have been refurbished, and are beautifully maintained. Children are welcome by arrangement.

Canoes, boats and  bicycles available for hire. All major credit cards accepted. N4 from Mullingar bypass take R394 for 8km to Crookedwood, left at Wood Pub, 2km to first junction turn right; house is 1km on the right.

OWNER Warwick & Anne O'Hara OPEN Easter–October 31
ROOMS 2 double, 1 twin, 1 family, 1 single; 3 en suite TERMS €60-70 pps; €120-140 double room; child reduction; single supplement
MEALS dinner €40

Mornington House

## COUNTY ANTRIM

County Antrim's attractions are many. The city of Belfast lies on the shores of Belfast Lough, in a most attractive setting, surrounded by hills that can be seen from most parts of the city. It became a thriving commercial centre and port in the nineteenth century, and now has a population of over 300,000, about a quarter of the population of Northern Ireland. Among Belfast's many sights are the grand City Hall, the ornate Crown Liquor Saloon, St Anne's Cathedral, W5 at the huge Odyssey complex and the Ulster Museum, which contains the treasures from the wreck of the Spanish Armada vessel, the *Girona*. The town of Antrim is set back from Lough Neagh, the largest expanse of inland water in the British Isles, and famous for its eels. The main fishery is in Toomebridge. County Antrim's coastline is among the most spectacular and scenic in Europe. Carrickfergus to the south, the oldest town in Ireland, is dominated by its castle. Farther north lies Larne, an important port, only a two-and-a-half hour ferry ride from Scotland. Beyond Larne, the Coast Road built in the 1830s affords breathtaking views of the coast and cliffs.

Antrim's Coast Road connects each of the nine famous Glens of Antrim, green valleys running down to the sea, with rivers, waterfalls, wildflowers and birds. From south to north they are: Glenarm, Glencloy, Glenariff, Glenballyeamon, Glenaan, Glencorp, Glendun, Glenshesk and Glentaisie. These names are said to mean: 'glen of the army', 'glen of the hedges', 'ploughman's glen', 'Edwardstown glen', 'glen of the rush-lights', 'glen of the slaughter', 'brown glen', 'sedgy glen', and finally 'Taisie's Glen' (a legendary princess of Rathlin Island).

The resort town of Ballycastle is famous for its "Oul Lammas Fair," which once lasted a week and now takes place over two hectic days at the end of August. Ballintoy is a picturesque, Mediterranean-looking fishing village, one of the prettiest towns on the coast, beyond which is one of the word's most amazing natural wonders. The Giant's Causeway, a legendary mass of some 40,000 tightly packed basalt columns, reaches heights of 12 m. These columns also appear at Staffa Island on the Scottish coast

## AHOGHILL

### Neelsgrove Farm

51 Carnearney Road, Ahoghill, Ballymena, Co. Antrim BT42 2PL
Tel: 028 2587 1225 Fax: 028 2587 8704
Email: msneely@btinternet.com
Website: www.neelsgrove.freeserve.co.uk

In a very rural location surrounded by farmland and an acre of garden, Neelsgrove Farm is a neat, well-kept farmhouse with friendly owners. It offers simple, comfortable accommodation. One of the bedrooms is on the ground floor, and they all have TV and tea- and coffee-making facilities. It is convenient for the Glens of Antrim, and golf, fishing, forest and river walks are nearby. From Ahoghill take B93 Randalstown road for 1/4 mile, first road on right for 2 miles.

OWNER Margaret & Andrew Neely OPEN All year
ROOMS 3 double/ twin; 2 en suite
TERMS from £17–19.50; single supplement; child reduction

## BALLINTOY

**Whitepark House**
Whitepark Bay, Ballintoy, Co. Antrim BT54 6NH
Tel: 028 2073 1482
Email: bob.isles@virgin.net
Website: www.whiteparkhouse.com

Just off the coast road between the Giant's Causeway and Carrick-a-Rede Rope Bridge, Whitepark is a most interesting house. Dating from the 18th century, with later additions, it used to own the beach. Now, across the road, there's a path that leads to lovely, sandy Whitepark beach. The central room of the house with a lovely bowed end is where breakfast is served, and guests like to gather around the fire in the long drawing room, which overlooks the gardens that surround the house. Of the three upstairs bedrooms, one is particularly large with windows all around, and they all share one large bathroom. The house is full of bits and pieces acquired from Sri Lanka and other points east, where Bob and Siobhan like to escape to in the winter. No smoking in bedrooms, pets outside. Major credit cards accepted.

OWNER Bob & Siobhan Isles OPEN All year
ROOMS 2 double, 1 twin; one public bathroom
TERMS £30; single supplement; unsuitable for children

## BALLYCASTLE

**Islandarragh House**
7 Islandarragh Road, Capecastle, Ballycastle Co. Antrim BT54 6HX
Tel: 028 207 62933

Follow a series of narrow lanes inland from Ballycastle, to find Islandarragh, a neat 1920s farmhouse, recently refurbished. Part of the alteriaons added en suite bathrooms to the two front bedrooms, creating an interesting window shape in the upstairs landing. The dining room at the back of the house overlooks the pretty garden and countryside. The guests' sitting room is pleasantly furnished and decorated. Jane Kane is a thoughtful host. No smoking, no pets and no credit cards. Signposted off the A44 three miles from Ballycastle.

OWNER Mrs. Jane Kane OPEN March 1–October 31
ROOMS 1 twin, 1 double; en suite
TERMS £20; single supplement; child reduction

## Colliers Hall
50 Cushendall Road, Ballycastle, Co. Antrim BT54 6QR
Tel: 028 2076 2531
Email: reservations@colliershall.com
Website: www.colliershall.com

This eighteenth-century pebble-dashed farmhouse lies just off the
main road 3 kilometres south of Ballycastle. The bedrooms are spacious, with the washbasins cleverly incorporated into marble washstands, and all have tea- and coffee-making facilities and hair-dryers.
The house is furnished with a mixture of traditional and antique furniture, and one room has a four-poster bed. The large TV lounge has
an original marble fireplace, and dinner, by arrangement for groups
only, is served in the dining room. Recently opened is the hostel, a
renovated barn, offering simple, bright small rooms, all en suite, with
an upstairs lounge/kitchen. These rooms are available for bed &
breakfast guests at the bargain prices. There are lovely walks through
the woods, with views of the Knocklayde Mountains and Glenshesk
Valley. An 18-hole golf course is close by, and it is 3 kilometres to
the ferry terminal serving Ballycastle to Campbelltown in Scotland.
Colliers Hall offers comfort, excellent value and a warm atmosphere. No pets, smoking in TV lounge only. Visa accepted.

OWNER Gerard & Maureen McCarry OPEN April 1–September 30
ROOMS 4 double/twin, 1 family; all en suite
TERMS £18–25; single supplement; child reduction
MEALS dinner £12.50

## BALLYMENA

## Marlagh Lodge Country House
71 Moorfields Road, Ballymena, Co. Antrim BT42 3BU
Tel: 028 2563 1505 Fax: 028 2564 1590
Web: www.marlaghlodge.com

A large Victorian building with well-proportioned rooms and lots of
space. Relaxing, soothing environment apart from busy A36 Larne
Road by the house. Smoking permitted in drawing room and dining
room. The Thompsons are a delightful, musical couple, who previously owned another Bed and Breakfast near Templepatrick. Visa,
Mastercard and Switch accepted.

OWNER Rachel Thompson OPEN all year
ROOMS 3 double/twin; en suite or private bathroom

TERMS £35 MEALS dinner £25

**Harmony Hill Country House**
Balnamore. Ballymoney, Co. Antrim
Tel: 028 276 63459 Fax: 028 276 63740
Email: webmaster@harmonyhill.net
Website: www.harmonyhill.net

Reached up a long driveway, Harmony Hill appears a quite modest building. It was built in the 1760s by John Caldwell near Balnamore Mill, a cornmill, which he developed into a successful business. His two sons were implicated in the rebellion of 1798 and as a result the entire family was exiled to North America. The house continued to be used by mill managers, and today is home to Richard and Trish Wilson.

The renovated west wing of the house accommodates guests, and includes a successful restaurant offering dinner every day, as well as Sunday lunch. Facilities include bar, large, well-proportioned drawing room with doors out to the terrace and gardens, and four ground floor bedrooms. A further cosy room with turf fire is available in the cottage at the end of the driveway. Harmony Hill can be found in the village of Balnamore, nine miles from the coast.

OWNER Richard & Trish Wilson OPEN all year
ROOMS 5 twin/double; all en suite
TERMS £36; single supplement
MEALS dinner, Sunday lunch

**Ravenhill House**
690 Ravenhill Road, Belfast, Co. Antrim BT6 OBZ
Tel: 028 9020 7444 Fax: 028 9028 2590
Email: info@ravenhillhouse.com
Website: www.ravenhillhouse.com

A restored Victorian house convenient for the centre and university, Ravenhill is a comfortable place, and Roger and Olive are a welcoming couple. The bedrooms are bright, spacious and well equipped, and the sitting room and dining room have open fires, a piano and a good selection of reading material.

Breakfast features home-made organic breads and marmalade, and vegetarian dishes. No smoking and no pets. Visa, Mastercard and Switch accepted.

OWNER Olive & Roger Nicholson OPEN closed Christmas
ROOMS 2 double/ twin, 1 family, 1 twin, 2 single; all en suite

TERMS £30 single supplement

## Roseleigh House
19 Rosetta Park, Belfast BT6 0DL
Tel: 028 90 644414
Email: info@roseleighhouse.co.uk
Website: www.roseleighhouse.co.uk

This restored Victorian-style, brick-built house is surrounded by a small garden. It is in a residential area of south Belfast, conveniently located for bus routes leading into the city centre. Roseleigh House is run by Donna McCumiskey, a friendly lady. The bedrooms all have TV, hair-dryer and tea- and coffee-making facilities. A laundry service is available, and both lunch and dinner are served if arranged in advance. No pets. Smoking is permitted in the lounge. There is a car park to the rear of the house. Major credit cards accepted.

OWNER Donna McCumiskey OPEN All year
ROOMS 3 double, 2 twin, 1 family, 2 single; all en suite
TERMS £30; single supplement; child reduction
MEALS lunch, dinner

## BELFAST BT7

## Oakdene Lodge
16 Annadale Avenue, Belfast BT7 3JH
Tel: 028 9049 2626 Fax: 028 9049 2070
Email: booking@oakdenelodge.com
Website: www.oakdenelodge.com

This substantial detached Victorian house is located $2^1/_2$ miles from the city centre, and is popular with business visitors. It offers good, simple accommodation without a lot of atmosphere. Peter Stephens, who runs Oakdene efficiently, took over the business from his father six years ago. Five of the bedrooms are in the original part of the house, which has high ceilings, old fireplaces and tiny bathrooms–the remaining 12 rooms are in the newer additions. One of these rooms is suitable for wheelchairs. There is a smoking and non-smoking lounge as well as breakfast room. Major credit cards accepted.

OWNER Peter Stephens OPEN All year
ROOMS 17 double/twin; all en suite
TERMS £27.50; single supplement £11

**Tara Lodge**
36 Cromwell Road, Belfast BT7 1JW
Tel: 028 9059 0900 Fax: 028 9059 0901
Email: info@taralodge.com
Website: www.taralodge.com

A purpose-built, small hotel/guest house, Tara Lodge was opened in 1998. It is situated on a quiet residential street, close to the University and within easy access of the city centre. It offers well planned, functional, bright bedrooms, simply and attractively furnished with all amenities including hair-dryers, trouser press, telephone, TV and tea- and coffee-making facilities. One bedroom is suitable for disabled guests. There is a small TV lounge on the first floor and a quite extensive dining room for breakfast. There is a large off-street parking area. Tara Lodge is particularly suited to business people. No pets. Some designated smoking rooms. Most major credit cards accepted.

OWNER Conor O'Donnell OPEN All year except for Christmas
ROOMS 19 double/twin/single/family; all en suite
TERMS £35; single supplement; child reduction

## BELFAST BT9

**Ash-Rowan Town House**
12 Windsor Avenue, Belfast BT9 6EE
Tel: 028 9066 1758 Fax: 028 9066 3227
Email: ashrowan@hotmail.com

This late Victorian house stands in its own garden in a quiet, tree-lined avenue in south Belfast. It was once the home of Thomas Andrews, designer of the *Titanic*. He left from here for the ship's maiden voyage. Ash-Rowan is a most attractive house of character, with some original fireplaces, interesting colours and furnishings, antiques and all kinds of knick-knacks

A cosy place with a friendly atmosphere, Sam and Evelyn have thought of just about everything for their guests, combining all the facilities of a hotel with personal service at a reasonable price. There are flowers and newspapers, and a laundry service is available. Bedrooms all have TV, hair-dryers, trouser press, information packs, bathrobes, linen sheets and tea- and coffee-making facilities.

A popular place to sit is the new conservatory, and Ash-Rowan's renowned breakfasts, which include freshly-squeezed orange juice and home-baked bread are served in the breakfast room. Pets in cars only. Visa and Mastercard accepted, Secure off street parking. The house, between the Malone and Lisburn Roads, is ten minutes from the city centre and five minutes from M1 and M2.

OWNER Evelyn & Sam Hazlett OPEN All year except Christmas
ROOMS 5 double/twin/single; all en suite TERMS from £48; single supplement

## Avenue House

23 Eglantine Avenue, Lisburn Road, Belfast BT9 6DW
Tel: 028 90 665904 Fax: 028 90 291810
Email: www.avenueguesthouse@ntlworld.com

This late Victorian terraced brick-built house, which stands on a fairly busy residential tree lined street has been totally renovated. The rooms are spacious and light and furnished with elegant simplicity. The bedrooms vary in size and all have TV, telephone, hair-dryers, trouser press and tea- and coffee-making facilities. Both the breakfast room and drawing room have their attractive, original marble fireplaces, and the rooms are separated from each other by a pull-up wall. A small patio area off the breakfast room is also available for guests, and there is internet access. No pets, no smoking and no credit cards. Avenue House is located between the Malone and Lisburn roads. It is conveniently placed for the University and centre of town, which can easily be reached by bus.

OWNER Stephen Kelly OPEN All year
ROOMS 1 double, 2 twin, 1 family; all en suite
TERMS £25; single supplement

## Camera House

44 Wellington Park, Belfast BT9 6DP
Tel: 028 9066 0026 Fax: 028 9066 7856
Email: malonedrumm@hotmail.com

This attractive Victorian townhouse has been a guesthouse for 47 years. It is very charmingly and simply furnished in muted tones with pretty pottery in the dining room. All organic food is served at breakfast time. Camera House is on a quiet tree-lined street close to Queen's University and within easy range of the centre of Belfast. No pets. Major credit cards accepted.

OWNER Paul Drumm & Caroline Malone-Drumm
OPEN All year except for Christmas
ROOMS 12 double/twin/single/triple; 2 en suite
TERMS £26–30; single supplement; child reduction

**The Old Rectory**
148 Malone Road, Belfast BT9 5LH
Tel: 028 9066 7882 Fax: 028 9068 3759
Email: info@anoldrectory.co.uk

When the Old Rectory was built in 1896, it was out in the countryside. Now it is within a comfortable distance of the city
centre–three kilometres–and still has views of the Belfast mountains.
It was designed by the architect Henry Seaver, who was also responsible for the neighbouring Church of St John's (he was the brother
of the then minister, Rev. Richard Seaver). Later in life it became a
nursing home, before becoming the Callan family home. Furnished
and decorated with individual taste, it has some interesting pieces
whilst retaining the feel of a family home. Books and newspapers can
be found in the sitting room, and a complementary 'hot Irish
whiskey' is served each evening. The bedrooms each have TV, hair-
dryer, trouser press and tea- and coffee-making facilities. Guests have
use of a croquet lawn. Malone Road is one of the principal streets
leading into the centre of town and is right on the bus route. Pets in
cars only. No smoking and no credit cards.

OWNER Mary Callan OPEN All year except for Christmas
ROOMS 2 double, 4 twin, 3 single, 1 family; all en suite or private bathroom TERMS £27–32.50; single supplement; child reduction

## BUSHMILLS

**The Bushmills Inn**
9 Dunluce Road, Bushmills, Co. Antrim
Tel: 028 2073 3000 Fax: 028 2073 1048
Email: mail@bushmillsinn.com
Website: www.bushmillsinn.com

At the very centre of the small town of Bushmills, this was originally
a coaching inn. Rescued from dereliction some twenty years ago, it is
now a haven of hospitality, comfort and good food for golfers,
tourists and business people. Bushmills is famous as the world's oldest distillery and is close to the Giant's Causeway and the Royal
Portrush Golf Club.

The original building is a network of atmospheric small dark
rooms, warmed by peat fires: the bar is still lit by gas light. The
restaurant overlooking the garden courtyard is an intimate dining
area, each table its own 'snug'. The ten bedrooms in the old building
are on the small side; the added 22 are big enough for sitting areas
and small dressing rooms, bright and designed in an attractive rustic
style. New buildings transition well into the old. Visa and Mastercard
accepted.

OWNER Roy Bolton OPEN all year
ROOMS 32 twin/double/family/ single; all en suite
TERMS from £49; single supplement; child reduction
MEALS dinner from £28

## Craig Park

24 Carnbore Road, Bushmills Co. Antrim BT57 8YF
Tel: 028 2073 2496 Fax: 028 2073 2479
Email: jan@craigpark.co.uk Website: www.craigpark.co.uk

Craig Park, situated in open countryside, has views of the Donegal
and Antrim hills, and is three kilometres inland from Bushmills. The
original house now has Georgian-style additions, giving it an imposing look. This provides accommodation for guests with three good-
sized bedrooms, a large sitting room and a dining room, where
breakfast only is served. There are great walks, cycling and golf, and
the Giant's Causeway is nearby. Visa and Mastercard accepted. Pets
outside only. No smoking.

OWNER Jan & David Cheal OPEN All year
ROOMS 2 double, I family; all en suite
TERMS £32.50; single supplement; child reduction

## Valley View

6a Ballyclough Road, Bushmills, Co. Antrim BT57 8TU
Tel: 028 2074 1608 Fax: 028 2074 2739
Email: valerie.mcfall@btinternet.com
Website: www.irish-bnb.com/valleyview

This whitewashed, modern house was built by the McFalls and
extended recently to provide more guest accommodation. It is surrounded by its own 24 hectares of farmland, supporting beef and
sheep, and is six kilometres inland from Bushmills. Many of the
north Antrim coast's famous attractions are nearby, including Rathlin
Island, the Giant's Causeway, Carrick-A-Rede Rope Bridge, Dunluce
Castle and Bushmills Distillery.
  Mrs McFall is a cheerful, friendly host with young children, and is
welcoming to families; there is a children's play area. The accommodation is simple and bright. Guests have use of a comfortable sitting
room. Breakfast only is served at separate tables in the dining room.
One room is suitable for disabled guests: all have TV, hair-dryers and
tea- and coffee-making facilities. There is a large self-catering unit
sleeping 8 people. Pets are permitted in cars. No smoking. Visa and
Access accepted. Valley View is signposted off the B67 and B17.

OWNER Mrs Valerie McFall. OPEN All year except for Christmas
ROOMS 3 double, 2 family, 2 twin; all en suite

TERMS £20–22; single supplement; child reduction

## Caldhame Lodge

102 Moira Road, Nutts Corner, Crumlin, Co. Antrim BT29 4HG
Tel: 028 94 423099 Fax: 028 94 423099
Email: info@caldhamelodge.co.uk
Website: www.caldhamelodge.co.uk

Caldhame Lodge is just off the main Moira Road, in its own grounds and just five minutes from the airport. It was built in the early 1990s as the McKavanaghs' family home. Since then it has been adapted to accommodate guests and is comfortable, very well furnished with new furniture, and is meticulously maintained. The rooms have every possible amenity, some bedrooms have jacuzzi baths and four poster beds and one room has a steam/sauna room. The bedrooms all have hair-dryers, trouser press, telephone and irons. Breakfast, lunch, high tea and evening meals by arrangement are served in the dining room/sun lounge, and guests have use of two further lounges, one with TV. Anne Kavanagh runs a very professional business-like establishment and has won accolades for being the best guest house. No pets. There are designated bedrooms for smokers. Major credit cards accepted. Caldhame Lodge can be found on the A26 ten and a half miles from Junction 9 on the M1.

OWNER Anne McKavanagh OPEN All year
ROOMS 4 double, 2 twin, 2 family; all en suite
TERMS £22.50; single supplement £7.50; child reduction
MEALS lunch £7.50, high tea £10, dinner £15

## Keef Halla

20 Tully Road, Nutts Corner, Crumlin, Co. Antrim BT29 4SW
Tel: 028 9082 5491 Fax: 028 9082 5940
Email: info@keefhalla.com
Website: www.keefhalla.com

Keef Halla, meaning 'welcome' in Arabic, acquired its name because Charles Kelly used to work in Saudi Arabia and bought the house with the money he earned there. It is an old country house that has been renovated and recently extended. Charles Kelly, who runs the guest house (Siobhan is a teacher in Belfast), has earned a reputation for the level of comfort and service he provides—borne out by being awarded accolades for the best guest house. The bedrooms all have telephone, hair-dryers, trouser press, TV and tea- and coffee-making facilities. The comfortable sitting room has an open fire, leather sofa and chairs, and leads into the dining room, where meals are available all day long if arranged in advance. Packed lunches can also be provided. One guest arriving by helicopter landed in the garden: Keef Halla claims to be the nearest guest house to the airport. A free internet service is available. Pets can be accommodated in outbuildings. Some rooms are available for smokers. Major credit cards accepted. Just off the main A26 road, five minutes from Belfast International Airport.

OWNER Charles & Siobhan Kelly OPEN All year
ROOMS 2 double, 5 family; all en suite
TERMS £27.50; single supplement; child reduction
MEALS lunch £8, dinner £15

## CUSHENDALL

### Glendale Bed & Breakfast
46 Coast Road, Cushendall, Co. Antrim BT44 ORX
Tel: 028 2177 1495

This white, pebble-dashed house is down a private driveway off the main A2 road in the village of Cushendall. It enjoys lovely views of the Antrim plateau and sea. The O'Neills are friendly and welcoming hosts, attracting a lot of repeat visitors. Mr O'Neill works on the Larne–Cairnryan ferry, and enjoys outlining sightseeing itineraries for guests. The house is well-maintained and comfortably furnished and the bedrooms have hair-dryers and tea- and coffee-making facilities. There are some non-smoking bedrooms. Glendale is within walking distance of the beach and golf course. Pets are accepted. Visa, Eurocard and Mastercard accepted.

OWNER Mrs Mary O'Neill OPEN All year
ROOMS 1 double, 5 family; all en suite
TERMS £18; child reduction

## CUSHENDUN

### The Villa Farmhouse
185 Torr Road, Cushendun, Co. Antrim BT44 OPU
Tel: 028 2176 1252 Fax: 028 2176 1252

Catherine Scally is in her nineties and has lived at the Villa since she married, opening her bed and breakfast business some 40 years ago. Now she is ably assisted by Maggie, who does everything, including the provision and supervision of not only breakfast, but lunch, afternoon tea and dinner. The house is situated way up above the delightful little village of Cushendun, which is owned by the National Trust and contains the smallest pub in Ireland. It has fantastic views of the spectacular coastline, the sea, and is on the Ulster Way. Both house and garden are immaculately kept and guests have use of a charming sitting room full of photographs. This arrangement of family photos and the home was featured in the Australian TV show "Good Morning Australia". The bedrooms have tea- and coffee-making facilities, two have sea views, and the other has views of the hills behind. For the infirm there is a chair lift, and the Coach House is available for self-catering. From Cushendun take Torr Road, at T-junction turn right, after half a mile the Villa is the third road on the left.

OWNER Catherine Scally OPEN February–October
ROOMS 1 family, 2 double; all en suite
TERMS £20; single supplement; child reduction
MEALS lunch, afternoon tea, dinner by arrangement

## PORTRUSH

### Glenkeen Guest House
59 Coleraine Road, Portrush, Co. Antrim BT56 8HR
Tel: 028 70 822279 Fax: 028 70 822279
Email: glenkeen@btinternet.com
Website: www.glenkeenguesthouse.co.uk

Glenkeen is a well-maintained, clean guest house located on the edge of Portrush. It is set back a little, by its car park, from the busy main A29 road. Mrs Little is a friendly and efficient lady who has been in the bed & breakfast business for a number of years, and is most particular about keeping the house in good decorative order. The large comfortable rooms have TV, telephone and tea- and coffee-making facilities. Breakfast is served in the dining room, and the pleasant sitting room has comfortable chairs and sofas. There is a chair lift on the stairs for infirm or disabled guests. Some bedrooms are non-smoking. No pets. Visa, American Express and Mastercard accepted.

OWNER Mrs Roberta Little. OPEN All year
ROOMS 5 double, 2 twin, 3 family; all en suite
TERMS £23; single supplement; child reduction

### Maddybenny Country House
18 Maddybenny Park, Loguestown Road,
Portrush, Co. Antrim BT52 2PT
Tel: 028 7082 3394 Fax: 028 7082 3394
Email: accommodation@maddybenny22.freeserve.co.uk
Website: www.maddybenny.freeserve.co.uk

Maddybenny Country House, meaning "sanctified or holy post", dates from the 1600s. It was built as a plantation house on lands belonging to the Earl of Antrim. The first Presbyterian minister, Rev. Gabriel Cornwall, lived here. Added to over the years, the house floor plan is unusual in allowing one to walk completely around the house from the inside. It is approached up a long track and stands in a wonderful, rural location. It is part of a big complex of buildings consisting of the farm, stables and six self-catering cottages. The riding school is run by Rosemary White's son, and offers tuition to guests by an international rider. Maddybenny Farm is a comfortable, relaxed place, a bright and spacious house with a comfortable drawing room, games room and dining room where breakfast only is served. The bedrooms are very large, and have hair-dryers, TV and tea- and coffee-making facilities. There is a fridge for guests' use and laundry facilities.

Maddybenny Country House

Rosemary White is a marvellous host with a wonderful sense of humour. Her breakfasts are copious and include home baking and fresh trout. Maddybenny is very near the Royal Portrush Golf Club, the Giant's Causeway, the University and beaches. The self-catering cottages are equipped to a high standard and sleep six to eight people. Pets are permitted in cars. No smoking in the dining room. Visa and Mastercard accepted. The farm is signposted on the A29 Portrush to Coleraine road.

OWNER Rosemary White OPEN All year except for Christmas
ROOMS 1 double, 1 twin, 1 family; all en suite
TERMS £25–27.50; single supplement; child reduction

## COUNTY ARMAGH

County Armagh is the smallest and most varied county in Northern Ireland, ranging from magnificent mountain scenery in the south to rich fruit-growing land in the north, interspersed with small lakes and dairy farms.

Armagh, the ancient capital of Ulster and former great centre of learning, has been the spiritual capital of Ireland for 1,500 years and is the seat of both Catholic and Protestant archbishops. The two cathedral churches are prominent features in the city. The Church of Ireland cathedral stands on the hill where St Patrick built his stone church, and the twin spires of the Catholic cathedral, which was finished in 1873, rise from the opposite hill.

In the south of Armagh the mountains of Slieve Gullion contain an unspoilt area of small villages and beautiful scenery.

Crossmaglen has possibly the largest market square in Ireland, and has become the centre of the recently revived lace-making industry. Jonesborough hosts an enormous open-air market every Sunday.

Whilst driving down a country lane, you might come across the great Armagh game; roads bowls, which is shared with County Cork. The object is to hurl a metal bowl weighing 1 kg as far as possible, covering several miles in the shortest number of shots. Children are sent ahead to warn motorists.

The orchard of Ireland, this rich fruit-growing county in the northeast is at its best in May. Apple Blossom Sunday takes place in late May.

## ARMAGH

### Hillview Lodge
33 Newtownhamilton Road, Armagh, Co. Armagh BT60 2PL
Tel: 028 3752 2000 Fax: 028 3752 8276
Email: alice@hillviewlodge.com
Website: www.hillviewlodge.com

Hillview is a modern building about two kilometres outside Armagh, set just back from the road beside a golf driving range, which is under the same ownership. The accommodation is functional and well designed, and the entire house has plain wood-type floors, unalleviated by any rugs. The bedrooms all have hair-dryers, telephone, TV and tea- and coffee-making facilities. One ground floor room is suitable for disabled guests. The dining room, where breakfast only is served, has a sitting area, and there is a further place to sit in the entrance/reception room and conservatory.

Hillview is well suited to business people, or those who want to practise their golf swing. The driving range is floodlit for night use. No pets. No smoking. Visa, Mastercard, Delta and Switch accepted. Hillview is located on the B31 Newtownhamilton road.

OWNER Alice McBride OPEN All year
ROOMS 1 double, 2 twin, 3 family; all en suite
TERMS £25; single supplement; child reduction

**Ni Eoghain Lodge**
32 Ennislare Road, Armagh, Co. Armagh BT60 2AX
Tel: 028 3752 5633 Fax: 028 3751 1246
Email: nieoghainlodge@amserve.com
Website: www.kingdomsofdown.com/nieoghainlodge

Ni Eoghain is a pleasant, secluded country house set in wonderful
gardens. Surrounded by twelve acres of woodland, the three acre
garden has twice received awards. Bedrooms are simply furnished
and decorated and all are on the ground floor. The house is four
kilometres south of Armagh and is signposted off the A29.

OWNER Noel McGeown
ROOMS 3 twin/double, all en suite
TERMS £17.50 pps; single supplement

## RICHILL

**Ballinahinch House**
47 Ballygroobany Road, Richill, Co. Armagh BT61 9NA
Tel: 028 3887 0081 Fax: 028 3887 0081
Email: info@ballinahinchhouse.com
Website: www.ballinahinchhouse.com

This early Victorian house is part of a working arable and beef farm
of 50 hectares. It has an informal, welcoming atmosphere and
Elizabeth Kee is a delightful host. The rooms are spacious and traditionally furnished, the bedrooms comfortable, all with TV and hair-
dryers, and the dining room has its original black slate fireplace.
There is half a hectare of newly landscaped gardens in front of the
house, and the setting is peaceful with lovely walks close by. No pets
and no smoking. Visa and Mastercard accepted. To reach Ballinahinch
House, turn off the A3 onto the B131, take the second road on the
left and continue over the crossroads—the house is approximately
one and a half kilometres down on the left.

OWNER Elizabeth Kee OPEN January–November
ROOMS 4 double/twin/single/family
TERMS from £25; single supplement; child reduction
MEALS by request

## COUNTY DERRY

Derry (or Londonderry) is probably best known for the tune *The Derry Air*, also known as *Danny Boy*. The city of Derry is situated on a hill on the banks of the Foyle. The city acquired the name Londonderry in the seventeenth century when the City of London financed building and resettlement in the city. The seventeenth-century walls, about 1.5-km-round and 5.5-m-thick, have withstood several sieges and are still intact, giving magnificent views of the surrounding countryside.

Derry still preserves its ancient layout, and amongst the historic buildings is the 1633 Gothic Cathedral of St Columb. From the quay behind the Guildhall, hundreds of Irish emigrants left Derry for America during the eighteenth and nineteenth centuries, amongst them the families and ancestors of Davy Crockett and US President James Polk.

The Mussenden Temple, built by the eccentric Earl Bishop of Derry as testimony of his affection for Lady Mussenden, stands on a windswept headland on the coast at Downhill; adjacent, the castle is now in ruins but exudes an aura of romance and grandeur, and is worth visiting. One of Ulster's finest fortified farmhouses can be seen at Bellaghy, and whiskey is produced at Bushmills near Coleraine, the town which St Patrick is supposed to have founded.

### AGHADOWEY

**Greenhill House**
24 Greenhill Road, Aghadowey, Coleraine, Co. Derry BT51 4EU
Tel: 028 7086 8241 Fax: 028 7086 8365
Email: greenhill@btinternet.com

A nice old Georgian house standing in its own grounds of trees, lawns and shrubs, with lovely views over farmland to distant hills. This is a 60-hectare arable and beef farm and the Hegartys have owned the property for nearly two decades. Accommodation has been upgraded, with new furniture, beds and carpets in addition to antique furnishings; two of the bathrooms now have baths and showers, and are well-appointed with every convenience. Two of the rooms have been refurbished with new beds and linens. Smoking is only permitted in designated bedrooms.

Mrs Hegarty, formerly a teacher, now devotes her time to running her successful, very well-maintained bed and breakfast; she is a most friendly and cheerful lady. There is a spacious lounge which overlooks the fields, and a marble fireplace where fires burn brightly on chilly evenings. Breakfasts are served at separate tables. Many venues nearby which serve evening meals. Greenhill House is the recipient of several awards, including the 'Taste of Ulster' and 'British Airways Awards'.

Greenhill House

Take the A29 from Coleraine to Garvagh for seven miles, left of B66 (Greenhill Road) towards Ballymoney for short distance; Greenhill is signed on the right. Visa, Delta, Mastercard accepted.

OWNER Mrs Elizabeth Hegarty OPEN March 1–October 31
ROOMS 2 double, 2 twin, 2 family; all en suite
TERMS from £28 pps

## CASTLEROE

**Camus House**
27 Curragh Road, Castleroe, Coleraine, Co. Derry BT51 3RY
Tel: 028 7034 2982

Camus House was built on the site of an old monastery, and is a listed building, dating from 1685, the oldest house in the area. The house is in a delightful setting, close to the River Bann, and Mrs King owns 2 km of river frontage. Her passion is fishing, and this is a great fishing family; her daughter has represented Ireland. This lovely old ivy-covered house is approached by a private driveway through park-like grounds, and has a pretty front garden.

Mrs King is a most friendly and accommodating lady who runs a warm and comfortable bed & breakfast, and is also a member of the 'Healthy Eating Circle Galtee Breakfast Awards'.

The house has lots of character and is comfortably furnished as a family home. In winter, guests use Mrs King's cosy sitting room, which has an open fire. There is another sitting room, and a dining room where breakfasts only are served. Not suitable for children. Smoking is permitted in bedrooms. Telephone for directions to the house.

OWNER Josephine King OPEN January–December
ROOMS I twin, I double, I family
TERMS from £22.50 pps, £25 single
MEALS packed lunches

### Killeague Farm Lodge
157 Drumcroone Road, Blackhill, Coleraine, Co. Derry BT51 3SG
Tel: 028 7086 8229
Email: killeaguelodge@btinternet.com

Margaret Moore previously ran her bed & breakfast from the farm, which is now lived in by her son. Guests are still welcome to wander around the farm, but the accommodations are now in a beautiful new property built on the land. Two of the luxurious bedrooms are on the ground floor and all are very tastefully decorated: one has a semicircular wall, old pine furniture and a pastel lemon décor; another has mahogany furniture and pine décor; the third large upstairs room is blue, with rich mahogany furnishings. There is a sun lounge and two other lounges for guests' use. Breakfast is a banquet, served on Royal Albert China, in the elegant dining room, with fresh fruit, yoghurts, juice, warm scones, home-made preserves, home-baked bread, and for those with a large appetite a full traditional Irish breakfast follows. Margaret's award-winning hospitality brought this comment from a visitor: "I thought I had died and gone to heaven!"
   Bedrooms have TV, radio and tea makers. Margaret's motto is "Good food, fun and fellowship". Children are welcome. A limited laundry service is available.
   The house is non-smoking. Horse-riding can be arranged. Killeague Lodge is within 30 minutes of Giants Causeway and the North Antrim Coast. From Coleraine, take A29 south to Garvagh and Cookstown, House is approximately 5 miles on this road on the left. Credit cards not accepted.

OWNER Margaret Moore OPEN All year
ROOMS I double, I twin, family; all en suite
TERMS double/ twin £22 pps, family £22;
child reduction–under 5 years free, when sharing up to 10 years;
single supplement MEALS Dinner £12

### The Merchant House
16 Queen Street, Derry, Co. Derry BT48 7EQ
Tel: 028 7126 9691 or 7126 4223 Fax: 028 7126 6913
Email: saddlershouse@btinternet.com

This listed Georgian townhouse, situated in a conservation area, was awarded a Gulbenkian/Civic Trust Award for Restoration, and is within walking distance of most amenities. It has an interesting history; it was built originally for a wealthy merchant, and has been used as a bank and a rectory. There are five good size bedrooms, furnished with period furniture, rich white bedspreads, TV, books, and tea makers. Several original features remain, such as polished wood floors, ceiling coving, and a marble fireplace. An elegant drawing room is available to guests. Breakfasts only are served, and special diets can be catered for. There are several establishments for evening meals within walking distance. Non-smokers are preferred. Spanish is spoken, and off street parking can be requested. Visa, Mastercard accepted.

OWNER Joan & Dr Peter Pyne OPEN All year
ROOMS 5 double/ twin; 1 en suite
TERMS from £28-30 pps; child reduction; single supplement

## The Saddler's House

36 Great James Street, Derry, Co. Derry BT48 7DB
Tel: 028 7126 9691 or 7126 4223
Fax: 028 7126 6913
Email: saddlershouse@btinternet.com

A tastefully restored, and immaculately maintained, 19th-century property townhouse, situated in a conservation area in the heart of Derry. It is the most centrally located bed and breakfast in the city, and is within walking distance of restaurants, shops and most amenities.

The bedrooms, 3 of which are en suite, are furnished with period furniture, all have TV, tea makers and books, and overlook a walled garden. Two are ground floor rooms, one of which is a twin en suite.

Breakfasts are plentiful, with fresh brewed coffee, home-made preserves and marmalade, and a cooked variety, served at separate tables on pretty blue china, in the cosy dining room. Special diets can be catered for at breakfast.

A sitting room is available for guests, and guests are welcome to use the garden. This is popular venue, and early reservations are recommended. Non-smokers are preferred. Spanish is spoken. Off street parking is available. Visa and Mastercard accepted.

OWNER Joan Pyne OPEN All year
ROOMS 7 double/twin; 3 en suite
TERMS from £25; child reduction; single supplement

**Drumcovitt House and Barn**
704 Feeny Road, Feeny, Co. Derry BT47 4SU
Tel: 028 7778 1224
Fax: 028 7778 1224
Email: drumcovitt.feeny@btinternet.com
Website: drumcovitt.com

This impressive house dates back some 300 years, and was built on the land owned by the Fishmonger Company. A round-ended Georgian front was added in 1796, enlarging the house, adding two extra reception rooms and two bedrooms. The views here are stunning, stretching down a wooded valley to Benbraddagh, across to Mullaghash.

This is a working farm, and sheep and young stock graze in the adjoining pasture. The ambience is informal, friendly and relaxing. There are no en suite rooms, but it is such a wonderful house, no-one seems to mind; the two bathrooms and an additional loo provide ample facilities.

Many original features remain, such as the inner hall's sandstone floor, pitch pine floors, window panes and shutters. The spacious bedrooms have king-size beds, TV, telephone and tea makers. The landing has a library nook, and a comfortable drawing room with plenty of seating.

Breakfasts, at which vegetarians are catered for if pre-arranged, and modestly priced home-cooked dinners are served family style. Dinners should be pre-booked. Period furniture decorates the house, and guests return often for the charm, and friendship they found here. While the Sloans are thinking of retiring, their son Christopher will take over, continuing the friendly, charming service so valued by guests over the years.

The beech trees and grounds provide a great habitat for birds and butterflies, and quiet walks can be taken along the lanes. There are many standing stones and Danish Forts to be seen, and Banagher Dam with its surrounding slopes is an Area of Special Scientific Interest. The city of Derry is a 20 minute drive. Self-catering cottages are available. Drumcovitt Barn is a non-smoking house. Visa/Mastercard, American Express accepted. Situated approximately half a mile from Feeny village.

OWNER Frank and Florence Sloan OPEN All year
ROOMS 4 twin, 4 double, 1 family room
TERMS double/ twin £23 pps, family £27 pps;
child reduction

**Ballycarton House**
239 Seacoast Road, Limavady, Co. Derry BT49 0HZ
Tel: 028 7775 0216 Fax: 028 7775 0990
Website: www.ballycartonhouse.com
Email: stay@ballycartonhouse.com

Built in the 1800s, this lovely rambling farmhouse, is nestled at the foot of Binevenagh Mountains, and has wonderful views. It has been a bed and breakfast for over 35 years, ran all that time, by the present owner's parents. It was taken over 5 years ago by Patricia Craig, who has completely refurbished the property, retaining its charm, character, and warm ambience. Patricia offers the same high standards people have enjoyed in the past. Tartan carpets greet guests as they enter, and the five large en suite, well-equipped bedrooms, are tastefully decorated in soft shades, and have pine furnishings. All rooms have TV, clock radio, hair-dryers and tea makers. There is a conservatory and sitting-room, plus a dining room, which has William Morris wallpaper, and many items of interest. A fire burns in the sitting-room on chilly days, and the conservatory overlooking the view is a peaceful spot to relax and plan your days out.

This is the perfect combination of a great house, wonderful hospitality and good food. The imaginative breakfast menu includes French Toast, Pancakes American style, served with maple syrup, croissants, juice, fruit and a full Irish breakfast with home-made soda bread. Special diets are catered for at breakfast. Little wonder Ballycarton House is a recipient of 'Ulster Guest House of the Year' and was rated 4 diamonds from the RAC. Guests have use of the garden, which has a gazebo, and barbecue area. Non-smokers are preferred. When booking, ask for their directional map to be sent.

OWNER Patricia Craig OPEN All year
ROOMS 5 double/twin/single; all en suite
TERMS from £25-37 pps; child reduction; single supplement

**Ballyhenry House**
172 Seacoast Road, Limavady, Co. Derry BT49 9EF
Tel: 028 7772 2657

This large, bright and airy farmhouse is close to the sea between Limavady and Castlerock. It was built around the turn of the century by Mr Kane's grandfather, and the flat and fertile land extends to 140 hectares. The farm is managed by Rosemary Kane's two sons and their uncle; it is a very successful operation, and they have won a variety of awards. Guests are welcome to wander around the farm and watch daily activities. Rosemary Kane is a very friendly lady, who prepares excellent evening meals, if arranged in advance.

The rooms are nicely proportioned and pleasantly decorated and furnished with some interesting antique furniture. A large en suite room has a double and a single bed and its own balcony, and a loft has been converted to provide a self-catering unit that sleeps six. Smoking in lounge only. From Londonderry left at traffic lights before entering Limavady the B69 road, farm is just over 3 miles on this road. From Coleraine 2 miles after Bellarena train crossing turn right onto Seacoast Road.

OWNER Rosemary Kane OPEN All year
ROOMS 1 single, 1 double/twin, 1 family, 1 single
TERMS double/ twin £20-25 pps, single £25; child reduction
MEALS dinner £15

## Streeve Hill

25 Dowland Road, Limavady, Co. Derry BT49 0HP
Tel: 028 7776 6563 Fax: 028 7776 8285
Email: pandjwelsh@yahoo.co.uk

Peter and June Welsh are warm and welcoming hosts, greeting guests with tea and biscuits, and create a relaxed and informal atmosphere in their home. Streeve, which means 'running water' in Gaelic, was built by Conolly McCausland in 1730 and stands in secluded grounds on 500 acres of parkland, woodland and farmland. The three comfortable luxurious bedrooms, are furnished with antiques, have crisp cotton sheets, and lovely views. One very spacious room is ideal for families, all rooms have en suite facilities. The drawing room has a log fire burning on cool days. The emphasis at Streeve is on good food. Breakfasts include a wide range of starters, with home-baked bread, freshly-squeezed juice, fruit, cereals followed by traditional fare, with free-range eggs. Pre-arranged four-course candlelit dinner could include, chilled pimento soup, Irish salmon fillets with a herb crust, zucchini frites, cucumber and dill salad, rocket, new potatoes, Irish cheeses, and mouth-watering desserts. Fresh vegetables and fruit from the garden are used in season. Vegetarians are well catered for. Dinners are available June, July and August, (except Sunday and Monday). Peter cooks breakfast and June is the Master Chef for evening meals. Smoking is allowed in the drawing room only if other guests have no objection. No pets.

There are several golf courses close by and for garden enthusiasts arrangements can be made to visit Drenagh Gardens for a modest fee. American Express, Visa, Mastercard accepted. From Limavady take B119 signposted from Castlerock, follow estate wall on the right, past gate lodge, turn right at the end of the wall.

OWNER Peter & June Welsh OPEN February 1–October 30
ROOMS 3 double/family; all en suite

TERMS £40–50 per person; child reduction if sharing;
single supplement £5
MEALS dinner

## PORTSTEWART

**Oregon Guest House**
168 Station Road, Portstewart, Co. Derry BT55 7PU
Tel: 028 7083 2826

Within walking distance of the town centre, about 1km from the
sea, this well-maintained, well-kept guest house lies on the outskirts
of Portstewart, just off a fairly busy main road. The house has a high
standard of furnishings and fresh, bright rooms, decorated with floral
curtains and bed covers. One double bedroom has a corner bath,
and some are on the ground floor. The small, cosy, panelled dining
room, with fine china and flowers on the table, overlooks the sunny
patio with a pond and small fountain. The lounge is comfortable.
Breakfast and pre-arranged evening meals are served in the dining
room, which is very bright with windows all round. There is plenty of
information for the visitor. Access, Visa, Mastercard, American
Express accepted.

OWNER Mrs Vi Anderson OPEN February 1–October 31
ROOMS 4 double, 2 twin, 1 family, 1 single; all en suite
TERMS £22.50; child reduction; single supplement £8.50
MEALS dinner

# COUNTY DOWN

A county rich in monuments of antiquity, County Down has been subject to many invasions throughout its history, the fiercest of all from the Vikings in the ninth century. Legend has it that St Patrick landed here in A.D. 432 at the place where the Slaney River flows into Strangford Lough. During the 30 years between his arrival and death in A.D. 461, St Patrick converted the pagan Irish to Christianity.

The Ards Peninsula, bordered by Strangford Lough to the west and the Irish Sea to the east, is a narrow strip of land with a bracing climate, reputedly the sunniest and driest part of the North. It has some charming villages and towns that were first settled by the Scots and English.

Bangor was a famous centre of learning from the sixth century, until it was devastated by the Vikings in the ninth century. It was from here that the missionaries St Columbanus, St Gall and many others set off to bring Christianity to the rest of Europe.

The breezy coast road runs from Bangor past Ballycopeland– the only working windmill in Ireland–past the pretty village of Kearney to the attractive town of Portaferry, where the short ferry ride to Strangford affords lovely views of Strangford Lough. The Lough is a famous bird sanctuary and wildlife reserve, and the small rounded hills, called 'drumlins', that cover North Down are to be found in Strangford Lough, appearing as small islands.

Amongst the historic places to visit are Castle Ward, built by the first Lord Bangor in 1765, and Mount Stewart, the childhood home of Lord Castlereagh, a former British Foreign Secretary. Out of the Cistercian Abbeys in medieval County Down, three were built around the Lough: Inch Abbey, Grey Abbey and Comber. Downpatrick, at the southern tip of Strangford Lough, is an attractive Georgian town and contains the burial site of St Patrick, which is in the graveyard of the cathedral.

The Mourne Mountains cover a small area, 22.5 km long and 12 km wide, with 12 rounded peaks. The barren peak of Slieve Donard, climbing steeply to 860 m, dominates this peaceful land-scape, which is a paradise for walkers. From the summit you can see the Isle of Man, the Belfast hills and Lough Neagh.

There are also two artificial lakes or reservoirs that supply Belfast with water. These are surrounded by a huge dry stone wall over 2 m high and 33 km long. The Mourne International Walking Festival attracts thousands of walkers from all over the world each June.

The coast south from Newcastle, a lively seaside resort, was notorious for smuggling in the eighteenth century. Newry was once a prosperous mercantile town with large town houses and public buildings, as well as the earliest Protestant church in Ireland, St Patrick's Church of Ireland.

## Cairn Bay Lodge

278 Seacliff Road, Bangor, Co. Down BT20 5HS
Tel: 028 9146 7636 Fax: 028 9145 7728

Cairn Bay Lodge is a most interesting and substantial house. Built in 1880, it stands in a large and beautifully maintained garden, set back from the shore with uninterrupted views of the sea. There are all kinds of unusual pieces of furniture and décor. The drawing and sitting rooms occupy the front of the house, affording lovely views over Belfast Lough.

The well equipped, spacious, comfortable bedrooms, each with hairdryer, trouser press, TV, tea- and coffee-making facilities, desks and some with telephone, have a yesteryear feel to them.

There is a resident beautician, baby-sitting service, and meals can be served if booked in advance. Visa and Mastercard accepted. Pets in cars only, no smoking.

Cairn Bay is a quiet, peaceful place, just a five-minute walk from the centre of Bangor at the southern end.

OWNER Christopher Mullen OPEN All year
ROOMS 9 double/twin/ single/family; all en suite
TERMS £35; single supplement; child reduction
MEALS dinner £14.50

## Shelleven House

61 Princetown Road, Bangor, Co. Down BT20 3TA
Tel: 028 9127 1777 Fax: 028 9127 1777
Email: shellevenhouse@aol.com
Website: www.shellevenhouse.com

Shelleven House stands one street above the sea front in a small terrace of Victorian buildings. The Westons, who are a friendly, competent couple, acquired the building eight years ago, and have now refurbished the bedrooms and bathrooms.
Some of the bedrooms have sea views, some are on the small side, and the ground floor room is suitable for wheelchair use. The comfortable lounge is separated from the dining room by a slide-up door and evening meals are available with notice.

Shelleven House is fully licensed. There are some smoking areas. Visa and Mastercard are accepted.

OWNER Mary & Philip Weston OPEN All year
ROOMS 3 double, 5 twin, 3 single; all en suite
TERMS £28; single supplement; child reduction
MEALS dinner £25

## Slieve Croob Inn

119 Clanvaraghan Road, Castlewellan, Co. Down BT31 9LA
Tel: 028 4377 1412 Fax: 028 4377 1162
Email: slievecroob@mcmail.com
Website: www.slievecroobinn.com

Under Slieve Croob on a remote country lane this collection of
whitewashed buildings blend well into the landscape. Purpose-built,
they provide one building containing the bed & breakfast accommodation, and others for self-catering and banqueting facilities. The B&B
guests have a lounge and the restaurant for breakfast, lunch and dinner, and bedrooms that are spacious, comfortably furnished and well
equipped with tea- and coffee-making facilities, TV and telephone.
With the mountain behind and the sea view in front the Inn is located in a spectacular position and is a great place for walkers. Slieve
Croob is well signposted from Castlewellan.

OWNER Laurence Kelly OPEN All year
ROOMS 7 double/twin, 1 suite
TERMS £30; single supplement; child reduction
MEALS Sunday lunch £12.95, dinner £22.95

## Ballymote House

Downpatrick, Co. Down BT30 8BJ
Tel: 028 4461 5500 Fax: 028 4461 2111
Email: bandb@ballymotehouse.com
Website: www.ballymotehouse.com

Ballymote House dates from around 1730, and has been owned by
James and Nicola for fifteen years. Returning from London to a
slower paced country life, the renovation process they started
added on to the back of the house, part of which is an enormous
kitchen, and upstairs the three comfortable, nicely furnished guest
bedrooms.

The Manningham-Bullers are an energetic, busy couple. Apart from
offering guests a comfortable retreat, they run an insurance business,
and are heavily involved in the horse world - polo, eventing and
show jumping. The 20 acres surrounding the house are kept for their
own several horses, and their gardens were designed by George
Carter, a Chelsea Flower Show Gold winner. Nicola loves to cook
and takes pride in acquiring only the best of local ingredients. She
will on occasion cook dinner if there are enough guests in the
house. Riding and sailing can be arranged. Kennels can be provided
for dogs and stables for horses. No smoking. Ballymote can be found
off the B176 in the direction of Killough.

OWNER James & Nicola Manningham-Buller OPEN closed Christmas
ROOMS 2 double/twin en suite
TERMS £30–35
MEALS dinner £30

### Denvir's Hotel
English Street, Downpatrick, Co. Down BT30 6AB
Tel: 028 4461 2012 Fax: 028 4461 7002

Established in 1642 this middle of the town old inn is still a hub of
activity. The bar has an unusually high ceiling and is almost square in
shape, above which are six spacious, attractively furnished and decorated bedrooms. The dining room, a bright room of cheerful colours
and gaily coloured tablecloths, is quite separate from the bar.

OWNER Ronnie Martin & Colin Magowan OPEN All year
ROOMS 2 family, 2 double, 2 twin; all en suite
TERMS £27.50; single supplement
MEALS dinner, lunch

### The Mill at Ballydugan
Drumcullan Road, Ballydugan, Downpatrick, Co. Down
Tel: 028 4461 3654 Fax: 028 4483 9754
Email: info@ballyduganmill.com
Website: www.ballyduganmill.com

As a boy, Noel Killen hid a penny in Ballydugan Mill's upper beams,
with the wish that one day he would be able to own and restore it.
Fifteen years ago that dream started to become reality. Abandoned
for 150 years, restoration took twelve years of painstaking work.
There had been a mill on the site since the twelfth century: the
present flour mill building dates from the 18th century, a massive
stone structure six floors high. The fifth floor houses an Exhibition &
History Centre, the first floor the restaurant, the ground floor a bar
and coffee shop, and the remaining floors staff and guest bedrooms,
suites and function rooms.

  The architectural integrity of the building and materials used have
been kept as close as possible to the original. The bedrooms are spacious, unfussily furnished, with lovely views of the attractive countryside. An old steam tower stands next to the Mill, which was used for
energy when the river was low, and a nearby windmill provided wind
power. Noel is now working on ancillary buildings across the massive courtyard, which will eventually house staff members. Very popular for weddings and functions, the Mill is signposted off the A25 on
the Newcastle road. Smoking permitted in the bar. No pets. Most
credit cards.

OWNER Noel Killen OPEN closed for Christmas
ROOMS 8 double, 3 family, 1 disabled room; all en suite
TERMS £37.50; single supplement; child reduction

## Tyrella House
Downpatrick, Co. Down BT30 8SU
Tel: 028 4485 1422 Fax: 028 4485 1422
Email: tyrella.corbett@virgin.net
Website: www.hidden-ireland.com/tyrella

This large, elegant country house, with a porticoed, classical façade, stands in 120 hectares of parkland and farmland that stretches down to the sea and its private sandy beach. Most of the house dates from around the eighteenth century, with the Georgian front added in the early nineteenth century. The grounds include a private eventing course, polo ground and a point-to-point course which is used a couple of times a year. Horses are available for beach, forest or mountain rides, or guests are welcome to bring their own horses. Hunting can be arranged and tuition is available for polo. The house has a welcoming feeling, with a large hallway with open fire, and stairs leading up to the three large bedrooms. Dinner (if pre-booked) is served by candlelight in the elegant dining room. Dogs can be accommodated in the kennels or owner's car. Visa, American Express and Mastercard accepted. Advance booking essential. Tyrella's Gate Lodge with blue gates is seven kilometres from Clough on the Clough/Ardglass road.

OWNER David & Sally Corbett OPEN February 1–November 30
ROOMS 1 double, 1 twin, 1 family; 2 en suite, 1 private bathroom
TERMS from £45; not suitable for children
MEALS dinner £25

## DROMORE

### Clanmurry
16 Lower Quilly Road, Dromore, Co. Down
Tel: 028 9269 3760 Fax: 028 9269 8106
Email: mccorkell@btinternet.com
Website: www.clanmurry.com

Garden lovers would enjoy Clanmurry, a compact Georgian house, surrounded by wild, luxurious gardens, spacious lawns, and shielded from the nearby A1 Belfast/Dublin Road. The previous owner sympathetically enlarged the original 1820 house in the 1960s, adding the attractive entrance hall with dome, and the back of the house, which is now the kitchen. The garden layout is his design, and encompasses some five acres. The guests' drawing room is filled with light and is a comfortable place to sit. John and Sara McCorkell are a quietly welcoming couple, and Clanmurry is a peaceful, relaxing place, only 20 minutes from Belfast, just off A1 between Hillsborough and Dromore. No smoking. Pets are accepted, as are Visa and Mastercard.

OWNER John & Sara McCorkell OPEN all year
ROOMS 2 twin with private bathrooms
TERMS £30; single supplement

## Sylvan Hill House
76 Kilntown Road, Dromore, Co. Down BT25 1HS
Tel: 028 9269 2321 Fax: 028 9269 2321
Email: coburns@sylvanhillhouse.freeserve.co.uk

This listed Georgian house built in 1781 stands in beautiful gardens with mature trees and panoramic views of the Mourne and Dromara mountains. Jimmy and Elise Coburn are solicitous hosts, entertaining their guests either in their well-lived-in sitting room, or in the more formal dining room. They join their guests for dinner, which in summer is sometimes served in the conservatory. Mrs Coburn is a gourmet cook, and all breads and desserts are home-made—a special treat at breakfast is her elderflower marmalade. The three very large bedrooms, all with hair-dryer and tea- and coffee-making facilities, overlook the garden, and the furnishings are a mixture of antique and traditional. Pets are accepted by arrangement. Smoking is limited, and not allowed in bedrooms. To find Sylvan Hill House, turn off the A1 onto the Lurgan road, take the first right (Kilntown Road) signposted to Moira, go 2.5 km to the top of the hill: house is on right.

OWNER Elise Coburn OPEN All year
ROOMS 1 double, 1 twin, 1 family; all en suite
TERMS £30; child reduction
MEALS dinner £16 (including wine)

## HOLYWOOD

## Ardshane Country House
5 Bangor Road, Holywood, Co. Down BT18 0NU
Tel: 028 90 422044 Fax: 028 90 427506

Ardshane means 'hill of John' and is built on the 800-year-old campsite of King John's army. It is a large, Edwardian, brick family home standing in most attractive mature gardens, approached up a long driveway. It is a restful, spacious and elegant house, beautifully appointed with every comfort. There is a TV lounge and an elegant dining room with a marble fireplace. The bedrooms are large, with modern bathrooms, telephone, TV, hair-dryers, trouser press and tea-

and coffee-making facilities. There is a croquet lawn for the enjoyment of guests, and the house is well suited for the disabled.

Pets are accepted by arrangement. Non-smoking bedrooms are available. Ardshane is at the Bangor end of Holywood off the main road.

OWNER Valerie Caughey OPEN All year
ROOMS 3 double, 3 twin, 1 family, 1 single; 7 en suite
TERMS £32.50; single supplement; child reduction


## Rayanne House
60 Demesne Road, Holywood, Co. Down BT18 9EX
Tel: 028 90 425859 Fax: 028 90 425859
Email: rayannehouse@hotmail.com
Website: www.rayannehouse.co.uk

Rayanne House, a substantial brick building dating from the nineteenth century, stands in its own grounds and enjoys lovely views across Belfast Lough to Carrickfergus and the Antrim Hills. It offers a warm welcome, good food and a high standard of comfort and service, and was recently taken over by Anne McClelland's son, Conor and his wife. The bedrooms are charming, each one completely individually decorated and furnished with a lot of flair. They all have large bathrooms, and all the bits and pieces included you can imagine, as well as the more standard amenities of hair-dryer, telephone, trouser press, TV and tea- and coffee-making facilities. The two sitting rooms and the dining room are comfortable, informal and filled with all sorts of china and knick-knacks. Breakfasts are memorable with a wide selection from the menu. No pets, smoking in the lounge only. Visa and Mastercard accepted.

OWNER Conor & Bernadette McClelland OPEN All year
ROOMS 3 double, 3 twin, 1 single, 1 family; all en suite
TERMS £41.25 pps; single supplement; child reduction
MEALS dinner from £20

### KILKEEL

## Heath Hall
160 Moyadd Road, Kilkeel, Co. Down BT34 4HJ
Tel: 028 41 762612 Fax: 028 41 764032
Email: emcglue@hotmail.com

Heath Hall, a turn-of-the-century, stone-built farmhouse has a modern appearance, and is set in 6.5 hectares of farmland with sheep and cattle. It has views of the sea and the Mourne Mountains. The house was completely renovated a few years ago, and some rooms have sea views. All three bedrooms have hair-dryers and tea-making facilities. The TV lounge has the original marble fireplace, and there is also a snooker room. The house was formerly run as a bed & breakfast by Mrs McGlue's mother-in-law, and has a reputation for offering good value meals and accommodation. Lunch must be arranged in advance. Pets outside only. No smoking. Heath Hall is located on the B27, 2.5 kilometres north of Kilkeel.

OWNER Mary McGlue
OPEN All year except for Christmas and New Year
ROOMS 1 double, 1 twin, 1 family; 1 en suite, 1 shared bathroom
TERMS £19–20; child reduction
MEALS lunch

**Hill View House**
18 Bog Road, Atticall, Kilkeel, Co. Down BT34 4HT
Tel: 028 417 64269/07762923731 Fax: 028 41764269
Email: trainor18@btopenworld.com
Website: www.kingdomsofdown.com/hillviewhouse

Just outside the small village of Atticall, a few miles inland from Kilkeel, Hill View is part of a sheep farm. With great hill vews from each side of the house and every bedroom, it is very popular with walkers and cyclists—they can leave their cars at the house and set off on a variety of trails. The Trainors are happy to drop guests off, and supplied with a packed lunch, let them walk back. Guest bedrooms are small and comfortable, and one room serves as sitting area and breakfast room. One farm building has been converted into a high quality self-catering unit for up to 6 people, with its own garden and children's play area. Major credit cards accepted.

OWNER Trainor family OPEN closed for Christmas & New Year
ROOMS 3 double/twin, 1 single; 2 en suite
TERMS £22.50; single supplement

## KILLINCHY

**Barnageeha**
Ardmillan, Killinchy, Co. Down BT23 6QN
Tel: 028 9754 1011

On the edge of tiny Ardmillan village, Barnageeha is reached up a winding driveway, across a small river. A long, low, modern attractive whitewashed building covered in creepers and climbing roses, it is right on the shores of Strangford Lough. The house is very comfortable and pleasantly furnished, has a relaxing atmosphere, and Margie Crawford is a delightful host. All bedrooms are large and en suite. Dinner can be provided if arranged in advance. The property comprises a small sheep farm. The bird-watching attracts a lot of visitors, and with the proximity to the water, watchers can remain in the comfort of the house. There is a tennis court for guests' use. Pets and horses can be accommodated in the stables. Directions are advisable.

OWNER Margie Crawford OPEN Easter–September
ROOMS 3 twin/ double; all en suite
TERMS £30; single supplement MEALS dinner

### The Old Schoolhouse Inn
100 Ballydrain Road, Killinchy, Co. Down BT23 6EA
Tel: 028 9754 1182 Fax: 028 9754 2583
Email: info@theoldschoolhouseinn.com
Website: www.theoldschoolhouseinn.com

The restaurant was the original old school and has been whimsically decorated with knick knacks and bottles, and decorated in warm, dark colours. A guest wing was addded recently in matching brick, offering spacious, comfortable bedrooms, equipped to a high standard, each one named after an American president of Ulster descent. Avril is the head chef, and whilst the food is based on French cooking, she likes to experiment with new combinations. The Inn is next to Castle Espie, which has the largest collection of wildfowl in Ireland, and Strangford Lough is only a few minutes away. No pets. Credit cards, except Diners, taken. From Comber follow signs for Castle Espie: The Old Schoolhouse Inn can be found 1/2 mile beyond.

OWNER Terry & Avril Brown OPEN All year
ROOMS 12 double/ twin; all en suite
TERMS £32.50; single supplement
MEALS dinner £17.95–19.95

## KILLYLEAGH

### Dufferin Coaching Inn
31 High Street, Killyleagh, Co. Down BT30 9QF
Tel: 028 4482 8229 Fax: 028 4482 8755
Email: dufferin@dial.pipex.com
Website: www.dufferincoachinginn.co.uk

Halfway down High Street of historic Killyleagh town, this atmospheric old inn lies between spectacular Killyleagh Castle above and the shores of Strangford Lough below. The Inn has been operating since 1803, and both it and the seventeenth-century castle were originally part of the Dufferin & Ava estate. Kitty Stewart and Morris Crawford are an amazing couple with a lot of energy. They originally owned both the pub part of the inn and the accommodation. This is now separate: and they own the bed & breakfast which has very attractive, spacious and beautifully-decorated bedrooms with large bathrooms. Some have four poster beds. They also own conference facilities which evolved from the courtyard at the back of the building bordered by old stables. The B&B drawing room was once the Ulster Bank. Morris is in the building trade, and he and Kitty also run riding, sailing and golf holidays. The pub offers entertainment and excellent food. Dufferin Coaching Inn is a lively spot with comfortable accommodation and great atmosphere. No pets. No smoking. Most major credit cards.

OWNER Kitty Stewart OPEN All year
ROOMS 4 double, 2 twin; all en suite
TERMS £32.50; single supplement; child reduction

## NEWCASTLE

### Harbour House Inn
4 South Promenade, Newcastle, Co. Down BT33 OEX
Tel: 028 4372 3445/ 3535 Fax 028 4372 3445
Website: www.harbourhouseinn.co.uk

Harbour House Inn stands right beside the harbour at the south end of Newcastle, and it has offered hospitality since it was built over 100 years ago. Very much a family-run and -operated business Frank and Brenda Connolly have been here 25 years, daughter Frances, a cheerful, chatty person, not only helps run the inn, but owns and runs the adjoining Stone Boat fish restaurant. In a superb location with great sea views, just above a sandy beach, the bar and lounge have a welcoming, atmosphere. full of pictures, photos and knick knacks. One night a week live music is played and another is quiz night. All rooms are on the first floor - three have sea views. A baby-sitting service can be made available. There are some non-smoking rooms. No pets. All major credit cards accepted except for American Express.

OWNER Frank & Brenda Connolly & Frances Monteith
OPEN all year ROOMS 7 double/twin; all en suite
TERMS from £25; single supplement; child reduction

### The Briers
Middle Tollymore Road, Newcastle Co. Down BT33 0JJ
Tel: 028 43 724347 Fax: 028 43 726633
Email: michelle@thebriers.co.uk
Website: www.thebriers.co.uk

This 200-year-old former farmhouse, once part of Lord Roden's estate, is set in 0.75 hectares of grounds, including a newly planted aboretum. The original house is a low, whitewashed building. A modern two-storey addition houses guest accommodation. There are two ground floor bedrooms suitable for disabled guests. Bedrooms are en suite, with hair-dryers, TV and telephone. Dinner is available if arranged in advance. No smoking. Pets outside only. Horseback riding and fishing available close by. Most major credit cards accepted.

The Briers is signposted opposite Tollymore Forest Park.

OWNER Michelle Bowater OPEN January–November
ROOMS 7 twin/double; all en suite
TERMS £25; single supplement; child reduction
MEALS dinner from £15

## NEWRY

### Deer Park
177 Tandragee Road, Drumbanagher, Newry, Co. Down BT35 6LP
Tel: 028 3082 1409

Deer Park is a most attractive 18th-century farmhouse, just off the A27 road in the direction of Portadown, . Its elevated position gives wonderful views of the Mourne Mountains and surrounding farmland. Sheila Thompson is a relaxed, friendly lady. Her husband, who runs the farm with their son, is an avid hunt enthusiast– borne out by many pictures depicting hunting scenes. The house is very comfortable and attractively furnished and decorated with one en suite room on the ground floor and the upstairs room uses a splendid bathroom with old fashioned tub, which was converted from a bedroom. Breakfast is served either in the dining room or conservatory. No smoking, pets, or credit cards.

OWNER Sheila Thompson
ROOMS 2 double/twin; 1 en suite, 1 private bathroom
TERMS £25

## NEWTOWNARDS

### Ballycastle House
20 Mountstewart Road, Newtownards, Co. Down BT22 2AL
Tel: 028 4278 8357 Fax: 028 4278 8357
Email: ballycastle@breathemail.net
Website: www.ballycastlehouse.com

A warm welcome always awaits you at Ballycastle House, the comfortable home of the Deerings. The house was built over 150 years ago and is set in 16 hectares of lovely grounds that were once part of the Mount Stewart estate. The bedrooms have some interesting furniture, the guest lounge features the original fireplace, and a conservatory has been added. Mr Deering collects and restores old farm machinery and tractors. The house is minutes from the sea, with lovely walks close by. Pets outside only, no smoking. Ballycastle House can be found one kilometre off the A20, turning left at the Ballywalter signpost, six kilometres south of Newtownards.

OWNER Margaret Deering OPEN All year except for Christmas
ROOMS 2 double/twin, 1 family; all en suite
TERMS £24; single supplement; child reduction

## Ballynester House
Cardy Road, Newtownards Co. Down BT22 2LS
Tel: 028 4278 8386 Fax: 028 4278 8986
Email: geraldine.bailie@virgin.net
Website: www.ballynesterhouse.com

Standing just above the village of Greyabbey, Ballynester House was built by Geraldine Bailie's husband. It enjoys lovely views of Strangford Lough and is surrounded by its own garden. The house is well furnished and decorated, and the three guest bedrooms are all on the ground floor. They all have TV, hair-dryer and tea- and coffee-making facilities. The two front rooms have the water view, and the rear bedroom was the original master, and has a large bathroom. Geraldine Bailie is a charming and friendly person and keeps her home in immaculate condition. Visa and Mastercard accepted. No smoking and no pets. There is an adjacent self-catering lodge. The house is signposted at the roundabout at Greyabbey.

OWNER Geraldine Bailie OPEN Closed Christmas
ROOMS 1 double, 1 twin, 1 family; all en suite
TERMS £25; single supplement; child reduction

## Beech Hill Country House
23 Ballymoney Road, Craigantlet, Newtownards,
Co. Down BT23 4TG
Tel: 028 9042 5892 Fax: 028 9042 5892
Email: info@beech-hill.net
Website: www.beech-hill.net

This long, low, whitewashed house was built 40 years ago in the Georgian style by Victoria Brann's grandmother. Standing on a slight rise surrounded by its own farmland (which is let out), Beech Hill has lovely views over the north. Down countryside. The grounds include a croquet lawn. Beech Hill has a very pleasant country house atmosphere with the public rooms leading from one to another. The elegant dining room and comfortable drawing room are tastefully furnished with antiques, and beyond is the conservatory, which is used for breakfast. The bedrooms are on the ground floor. The beds are made up with Irish linen and all the rooms have TV, hair-dryer, telephone, trouser press and tea- and coffee-making facilities.

Nearby are Mount Stewart House and Gardens, Rowallane Gardens, Dundonald Motte and Greyabbey, with its herb garden and antiques centre. Visa and Mastercard accepted. Pets by arrangement, and smoking is permitted in the drawing room. Beech Hill is ten minutes from the centre of Belfast, and can be reached by taking the A2 and 1½miles from the bridge at Ulster Folk Museum, turn right up Ballymoney Road signed to Craigantlet. The house is 1¾ miles on left.

OWNER Victoria Brann OPEN All year
ROOMS 1 twin/double, 2 double; all en suite
TERMS £32.50; single supplement

**Edenvale House**
130 Portaferry Road, Newtownards, Co. Down BT22 2AH
Tel: 028 9181 4881 or 07798 741790 Fax: 028 9182 6192
Email: edenvalehouse@hotmail.com
Website: www.edenvalehouse.com

Approached up a long driveway, Edenvale is a small Georgian country house located above Strangford Lough. Standing in its own grounds surrounded by fields, Edenvale House is immaculately kept, both inside and out. Diane Whyte is a welcoming host, and the atmosphere is informal and relaxed. The house has been beautifully furnished and decorated with great taste, and there are lovely views from the first floor rooms. One of the bedrooms now has a four-poster bed and a dressing room with room for a single bed if needed. Guests generally prefer to have breakfast, which includes fried potato bread and hot home-made bread, at the big kitchen table.

Edenvale House

Diane's daughter looks after the livery business, and guests are welcome to bring their horses. The beautifully kept stables and barn lie to the side of the house, and within the half a hectare of gardens is a croquet lawn. Mountstewart House is three minutes away by car. Children and pets are very welcome. Visa and Mastercard accepted. Edenvale House is 3 km from Newtownards on the Portaferry road.

OWNER Diane Whyte OPEN All year except for Christmas
ROOMS 1 double, 1 twin, 1 family; all en suite
TERMS £32.50; single supplement; child reduction

## PORTAFERRY

### The Narrows
8 Shore Road, Portaferry, Co. Down BT22 1JY
Tel: 028 4272 8148 Fax: 028 4272 8105
Email: info@narrows.co.uk
Website: www.narrows.co.uk

The Narrows stands at the very end of the Ards Peninsula, and right on the shorefront overlooking the 'narrows' and village of Strangford on the opposite side of Strangford Lough.

Owned by Will & James Brown, two brothers who returned to their father's family home in 1992 and skilfully and sympathetically transformed a series of derelict buildings into a place of charm and rustic simplicity. The original house contains most bedrooms, simply decorated and furnished with telephone, TV and tea- and coffee-making facilities. Every room except the single has a sea view.

Behind the house is the old renovated stone byre, which has a sauna (free for guests). The restaurant building is new and very cleverly designed, still retaining its big arched entranceway, allowing cars to be driven into the small courtyard. Upstairs is a conference/function room with big windows on each side overlooking the sea or charming walled garden. Weekend workshops are sometimes held on such subjects as painting, basket-making and stonewalling (some of the garden walls were rebuilt by students—nothing like being paid to have the work done!).

The very popular restaurant offers deliciously cooked local food, with a strong emphasis on seafood. The floors and furniture are pine, there is a small bar in the corner, the day's menu is posted on a blackboard, and every table enjoys views of the water. Will's wife, Sarah, is the pastry chef, and she is also responsible for the décor in the house. Some of the paintings around the house are Sarah's; paintings and weavings by local artists also hang on the walls.

Equally welcoming to families and functions, The Narrows is a great place for a break in this beautiful and interesting area of Ireland. No smoking in bedrooms. All major credit cards, except Diners, accepted.

OWNER Will Brown OPEN All year
ROOMS 6 double, 5 twin, I single; all en suite
TERMS £45; single supplement; reduction for children
MEALS lunch, dinner–à la carte

## STRANGFORD

**The Cuan**
Strangford Village, Co. Down BT30 7ND
Tel: 028 4488 1222
Email: info@thecuan.com
Website: www.thecuan.com

This quite extensive long, low building comprises bars, restaurant, a
traditional fish and chip shop, and B&B accommodation. Peter and
Caroline McErlean, the very delightful, friendly owners, gradually
acquired the buildings over the last few years, and opened the different pieces along the way. Now it seems they own almost one side of
the charming square, which is where the ferry to Portaferry comes
and goes from.

The bedrooms are well furnished and equipped, and one is suitable
for less able visitors. There are four golf courses within ten miles,
excellent sea angling, lovely walks and, reached by ferry, 'Exploris' a
sea aquarium. No pets, smoking in lounge and bar only. Credit cards,
except American Express, taken.

OWNER Peter & Caroline McErlean OPEN All year
ROOMS 5 double, I twin, I single, 2 family; all en suite
TERMS £39.95; single supplement; child reduction
MEALS food served all day

# COUNTY FERMANAGH

County Fermanagh is lake or land—one third of the county is under water—and is traversed by the Erne River, which meanders its way across the forested county into a huge lake dotted with drumlins. A paradise for fishing, boating and other water-related activities, Lough Erne's magnificent 75-km-long waterway offers uncongested cruising opportunities with 154 islands, many coves and inlets to explore. It has an interesting mix of pagan and Christian relics and traditions which have withstood the centuries. The medieval town of Enniskillen is built on a bridge of land between Upper and Lower Lough Erne. The town's origins go back to prehistory, when it was on the main highway between Ulster and Connaught. The County Museum, housed in the Castle keep, displays the brilliant uniforms, colours and Napoleonic battle trophies of the famous Inniskillings Regiment, which fought at Waterloo.

Amongst the many islands to visit, Devenish is particularly interesting, with its perfect twelfth-century round tower, tiny church and remains of a fifteenth-century Augustinian abbey. In the cemetery of Boa, the largest island, are two ancient stone Janus idols, thought to date from the first century. Belleek is famous both for its fishing and its china, which comes mostly in the form of objets d'art. Two of Northern Ireland's most attractive Georgian houses are to be found in Fermanagh: the neo-classical mansion of Castle Coole, with its Palladian features, built in 1795 for the Earl of Belmore, and Florencecourt House, seat of the Earls of Enniskillen, famous for its rococo plasterwork.

## BELCOO

**Corralea Forest Lodge**
Belcoo, Co. Fermanagh BT93 5D2
Tel: 028 6638 6325

The Lodge stands in a superb location on 14 hectares of a forested nature reserve on the shores of Lough Macnean, with glorious views over the lough and to the hills beyond. When the Catteralls came here over 25 years ago, the farmhouse was derelict: they built a new house amidst this breathtaking scenery. The bedrooms, all on the ground floor, have patio doors, enabling guests to step outside and enjoy the view.

The property has its own private landing stage and boats are available for hire. Sika deer roam the estate and 37,000 trees were planted in 1970.

The lounge is large and the separate dining room is where breakfast and evening meals can be served, if booked in advance. The dining room is non-smoking. Guests may bring their own wine to dinner. This is the perfect place for bird watching, painting and walking.

Upper Lough Macnean has the reputation of being the most pollution-free lake in Northern Ireland and the best place for pike in western Europe.

OWNER Mrs Terry Catterall OPEN March 1–October 31
ROOMS 2 double, 2 twin; all en suite
TERMS double/twin £24, single £29;
child reduction; single supplement No credit cards

## COUNTY TYRONE

The least populated of the six counties in Northern Ireland, Tyrone is in the heart of Ulster and is bordered to the north by the Sperrin Mountains, bare hills with fertile green valleys. The main towns are county town Omagh, Cookstown and Dungannon, which has a textile industry and crystal factory.

The meaning of the Beaghmore stone circles, seven Bronze Age stone circles and cairns, is still unknown. The Ulster-American Folk Park at Camphill, Omagh, which recreates the America of pioneering days and the Ireland those pioneers left, grew up around the cottage where Thomas Mellon was born in 1813. Also in County Tyrone is the ancestral home of President Woodrow Wilson. The farm is still occupied by Wilsons, who will show callers around the house.

### BALLYGAWLEY

**The Grange**
15 Grange Road, Ballygawley, Co. Tyrone BT70 2HD
Tel: 028 8556 8053

Dating from 1720, the Grange had a thatched roof until recently. It now has the appearance of a more modern house, with white stucco and new windows. It stands in a lovely, walled garden of lawns surrounded by flower beds.

Mrs Lyttle is very friendly, and the house has a pleasant, lived-in feeling. The attractive lounge has a piano and TV. The dining room, from which stairs lead to the first floor, has lots of character and is full of knick-knacks. There are sideboards decorated with silver and china. Pets outside only, smoking allowed in TV lounge. There is one ground floor bedroom. The Grange is on the edge of Ballygawley a few metres from the roundabout.

OWNER Ella Lyttle OPEN April–December
ROOMS 2 double, 1 twin; all en suite
TERMS £17–18; child reduction

## Killycolp House

21 Killycolp Road, Cookstown, Co. Tyrone BT80 8UL
Tel: 028 8676 3577 Fax: 028 8676 3577

This attractive house built in 1736 is surrounded by farmland, which is now mostly leased out and overlooks Tullyhogue Fort, where the kings of Ulster were crowned.

The bedrooms are bright and attractively decorated, except for the twin which is on the small side, and most have nice views. There is a double room on the ground floor and the rooms have TV and tea- and coffee-making facilities.

Guests have use of a sitting room, and breakfast is served in the entrance hallway. Pets are welcome. Smoking is allowed in designated areas only.

Killycolp House is signposted off the A29 south of Cookstown.

OWNER Mrs Elizabeth McGucken OPEN All year except Christmas
ROOMS 1 family, 1 twin, 1 double; all en suite
TERMS £25

## Grange Lodge

7 Grange Road, Dungannon, Co. Tyrone BT71 7EJ
Tel: 028 8778 4212 Fax: 028 8778 4313
Email: grangelodge@nireland.com

This attractive spacious Georgian country house is set in 1.25 hectares of pleasant gardens. Well proportioned reception rooms include a large drawing room, a cosier, smaller study with TV and a panelled snooker room with piano.

The Browns, who also own a retail business in Dungannon, are superb hosts–friendly, welcoming and perfectionists in maintaining their very high standard of accommodation and food. The bedrooms are pretty and comfortable and all have TV, hair-dryer, telephone and tea- and coffee-making facilities.

A stay here would not be complete without sampling Norah Brown's cooking, which is superb both in the extremely high standard of the food itself and the way in which it is presented.

Grange Lodge

Dinner for house guests is served in the elegant dining room, at separate tables covered in white tablecloths and decorated with pretty flowers and candles. Non-residents are catered to in another dining room, completely self contained with its own entrance.

Dinner must be booked in advance. Norah has recently started offering cooking lessons in her kitchen for small groups. Pets outside only.

No smoking. Visa and Mastercard accepted. To reach Grange Lodge from the M1 junction 15 on the A29 Armagh road, turn left at sign for Grange, then right and house is first white walled entrance on right.

OWNER Norah & Ralph Brown OPEN February 1–December 20
ROOMS 3 double, 1 twin, 1 single; all en suite
TERMS £39; single supplement
MEALS dinner from £25

## MOY

### Charlemont House
4 The Square, Moy, Dungannon, Co. Tyrone BT71 7SG
Tel: 028 8778 4755 or 8778 4895 Fax: 028 8778 4895

Charlemont House, a lovely Georgian townhouse, occupies a corner site in the central square of the small town of Moy, which lies halfway between Armagh and Dungannon.

The McNeice family has been associated with inn-keeping in Moy for many generations, and also runs Tomney's Bar and Lounge and Moy Reproductions, located just a few doors down the square. The bar is completely authentic, with small, dark rooms and a great atmosphere.

The house has elegant proportions and is an amazing place, full of Victorian furnishings and furniture. The lounge has old floral wallpaper, pinkish chintzes, black and pink patterned carpeting, black furniture (including a piano), romantic pictures and all kinds of glass and china.

The breakfast room in the basement is less flamboyant, with an Aga cooker and pottery adorning the high shelf around the room.

The property stretches right down to the River Blackwater at the back, reached through a courtyard. Guests can sit here on fine days, surrounded by old coach houses, then go through an archway to a pretty, partly walled, compact garden with more tables and chairs. No pets, smoking in the lounge only. Visa accepted.

OWNER Mrs Margaret McNeice OPEN All year
ROOMS 3 twin, 2 double, 2 single, 2 family;
3 en suite, 3 public bathrooms
TERMS £22.50; child reduction

## Muleany House

86 Gorestown Road, Moy, Co. Tyrone BT71 7EX
Tel: 028 8778 4183

Muleany House was purpose-built some 15 years ago and is a substantial, porticoed whitewashed building. Mrs Mullen is a most friendly, chatty lady, who does her own baking and enjoys meeting her guests. The good-sized bedrooms have tiny shower rooms and additionally there are two public bathrooms with bathtubs. Two bedrooms are on the ground floor.

  Well suited for families, Muleany House offers a baby-sitting service, laundry facilities and a large games room with pool table, small organ and open fire. There is also a smaller lounge with TV, and a dining room where evening meals are served, if ordered in advance. There are two self-catering units in the grounds. Most major credit cards accepted. No pets, no smoking in the bedrooms or dining room. The house is about 1.6 km from Moy: take the B106 to Benburb, then the right fork towards Ballygawley.

OWNER Joanne Mullen OPEN All year except for Christmas
ROOMS 9 double/twin/family/single; all en suite
TERMS £19.50; single supplement £5; child reduction
MEALS dinner £10–15

## OMAGH

### Bankhead

9 Lissan Road, Omagh, Co. Tyrone BT78 1TX
Tel: 028 8224 5592

This small farmhouse is at the end of a long private road and has pleasant views over farmland with the Drumragh River just below. It was built by the Clements in 1970 and is part of an 11-hectare beef and sheep farm. The bedrooms are furnished simply, and are fresh and bright. They are all on the ground floor. There is a small, neatly kept TV lounge with an open fire, and the dining room has a TV and sitting area.

  The terrace is pleasant for sitting outside on fine days, and guests have use of the garden. Pets can be accommodated in a shed. Bankhead can be found off the A5 towards Omagh by crossing the Drumragh River and turning left immediately into Lissan Road.

OWNER Sadie Christina Clements OPEN All year
ROOMS 2 double, 1 single; 1 public bathroom
TERMS £17; child reduction
MEALS light supper

## Ballantine's B&B

38 Leckpatrick Road, Artigarvan, Strabane, Co. Tyrone BT82 0HB
Tel: 028 7188 2714 Fax: 028 7188 2714

This family home has a friendly atmosphere and stands in its own garden with lovely distant views of farmland and hills. It is a modern house with three small bedrooms, sharing two bathrooms. There is a TV lounge with an open fire, a conservatory and dining room has one table, where evening meals are served if arranged in advance. Guests are welcome to use the house bicycles. The Ulster American Folk Park is 24 km away. No smoking, pets outside only. The house is located by turning off B40 opposite Leckpatrick Dairy and it is the first on the right.

OWNER Jean Ballantine OPEN January–November
ROOMS 1 double, 1 twin, 1 single;
1 private bathroom, 2 public bathrooms
TERMS £16 pps; child reduction
MEALS dinner

## Erganagh House

21 Greenpark Road, Omagh, Co. Tyrone
Tel: 028 82252852 Fax: 028 82252852
Email: erganagh@;ineone.net

Erganagh is a clean, square looking late-18th century building approached by a driveway through parkland. Earlier in life it was a rectory and for the last few years has belonged to the Mayers family, who recently started a bed & breakfast buisness. The bedriooms are all large, with pleasant views and en suite bathrooms, and the house has a relaxed atmosphere. A self catering unit in an old farm building will be available. This is a good area for fishing, hill walking and cycling. Erganagh is on the B48 between Omagh and Gortin, and the entrance is on the right approximately one quarter mile after the Gateway Inn. No credit cards. Smoking permitted in some areas.

OWNER Tom & Collette Mayers OPEN closed for Christmas
ROOMS 3 double/twin en suite
TERMS £40–50;single supplement
MEALS dinner £28

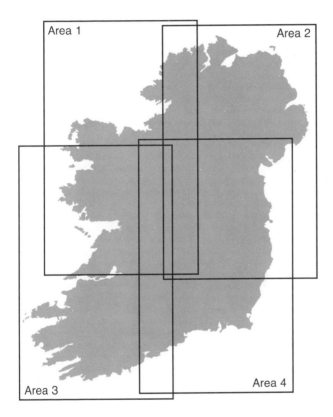

Area 1

Area 2

Area 3

Area 4

Area Maps

# Area I

Area 2

Area 3

Area 4

# Index